MW01042644

Technical Traders Guide to

COMPUTER ANALYSIS OF THE FUTURES MARKET

Technical Traders Guide to

COMPUTER ANALYSIS OF THE FUTURES MARKET

Charles LeBeau and
David W. Lucas

Editors of
Technical Traders Bulletin

BUSINESS ONE IRWIN
Homewood, Illinois 60430

This publication is designed to provide accurate and authoritative information in regard to the subject matter covered. It is sold with the understanding that neither the author nor the publisher is engaged in rendering legal, accounting, or other professional service. If legal advice or other expert assistance is required, the services of a competent professional person should be sought.

Warning and Disclaimer:
THE COMMODITY FUTURES TRADING COMMISSION AND THE NATIONAL FUTURES ASSOCIATION REQUIRE THAT WE STATE:

HYPOTHETICAL OR SIMULATED PERFORMANCE RESULTS HAVE CERTAIN INHERENT LIMITATIONS. UNLIKE AN ACTUAL PERFORMANCE RECORD, SIMULATED RESULTS DO NOT REPRESENT ACTUAL TRADING. ALSO, SINCE THE TRADES HAVE NOT ACTUALLY BEEN EXECUTED, THE RESULTS MAY HAVE UNDER OR OVER-COMPENSATED FOR THE IMPACT, IF ANY, OF CERTAIN MARKET FACTORS, SUCH AS LACK OF LIQUIDITY. SIMULATED TRADING PROGRAMS IN GENERAL ARE ALSO SUBJECT TO THE FACT THAT THEY ARE DESIGNED WITH THE BENEFIT OF HINDSIGHT. NO REPRESENTATION IS BEING MADE THAT ANY ACCOUNT WILL OR IS LIKELY TO ACHIEVE PROFITS OR LOSS SIMILAR TO THOSE SHOWN.

In commodity trading there can be no assurance of profit. Losses can and do occur. As with any investment, you should carefully consider your suitability to trade commodity futures and your ability to bear the financial risk of losing your entire investment. Do not assume that the theories, systems, methods or indicators presented herein will be profitable or that they will not result in losses.

The information contained herein has been obtained from sources believed to be reliable, but cannot be guaranteed as to accuracy or completeness, and is subject to change without notice. The risk of using any trading method rests with the user.

From a Declaration of Principles jointly adopted by a Committee of the American Bar Association and a Committee of Publishers.

Project editor: Rita McMullen
Production manager: Ann Cassady
Jacket Designer: Phil Kantz
Compositor: TCSystems, Inc.
Typeface: 11/13 Century Schoolbook
Printer: The Book Press, Inc.

Library of Congress Cataloging-in-Publication Data

LeBeau, Charles.
Technical traders guide to computer analysis of the futures market / by Charles LeBeau and David W. Lucas.
p. cm.
Includes index.
ISBN 1-55623-468-6
1. Commodity futures—Data processing. 2. Futures market—Data processing I. Lucas, David W. II. Title III. Title: Computer analysis of the futures market.
HG6046.L43 1992
332.64′5—dc20 91–28565

Printed in the United States of America

1 2 3 4 5 6 7 8 9 0 BP 8 7 6 5 4 3 2 1

Foreword

This book took a lot of work, and it shows. Most books I have read on the subject of technical analysis fail to lay a firm foundation for the techniques and trading methods that follow. In my home town, New Orleans, every cookbook listing a recipe for a good Creole dish starts with the instructions "first make a roux." The roux is the base, the foundation of the recipe, and great care must be spent on its development and implementation. The chef knows that the dish will fail unless the proper foundation has been prepared to support it.

This book by Mssrs. LeBeau and Lucas is rich in its "roux." The authors have carefully included the history and rationale for each of their concepts and detailed technical studies. I have not read another book of this type where the foundations were so carefully crafted and well laid. It was a pleasure to read.

Only the most useful and important computer-generated technical studies are covered. The fact that the studies chosen are those "of value" is well supported by their widespread popularity; these are the indicators that have repeatedly proven their usefulness over the test of time and thousands of users. It is a credit to the authors that they did not include those techniques that lie on the fringe of usefulness and whose applications are suspiciously tied to the quixotic interpretation of the user.

Though I have never seen Charles' and David's office, I imagine that on the wall or taped to their computer monitor there is a big "K.I.S.S." sign. That is just what they have done with their book. Without dodging any of the complex issues that bog down most technical writers, they have managed to keep their subjects simple and well organized. The reader is given all the rationale behind the various techniques and then shown how to employ each study. Chuck and David have also provided vital information that most writers fail to mention—how to avoid the ugly trades and false signals with their costly pitfalls and aberrations.

If you are an active futures trader using a computer or if you intend to become one, this book will prepare you for the real world of futures trading.

Tim Slater
President
CompuTrac Software, Inc.

Preface

Over the last 15 years, highly sophisticated software has been developed to assist futures traders in their technical analysis. The charts that traders previously plotted by hand are now automatically updated on a computer monitor, where they can be reconfigured in an instant. Fast and powerful personal computers are now easily affordable by anyone who has sufficient risk capital to trade futures. Inexpensive and readily available software packages allow the modern futures trader to quickly and easily calculate indicators such as stochastics, moving average convergence and divergence, parabolic stop and reverse points, and directional movement indicators, as well as a host of other informative technical studies that can be quickly displayed with only a keystroke or two.

Unfortunately, there is a substantial gap between the instructions that accompany the analytical software and what the user must actually know to trade effectively. Most software manuals are intended to take the customer only as far as obtaining the correct technical study on the screen and then, at best, offering a paragraph or two about the general purpose and application of the indicator. This book will attempt to bridge that gap and explain in detail the most popular and useful computer-generated technical indicators. Most important, we will offer practical advice on the correct application of these indicators to futures trading.

We are professional futures traders and registered commodity trading advisors. In addition to managing money in the futures markets, we publish a monthly educational newsletter, *Technical Traders Bulletin,* which is a means of sharing ideas and knowledge among professional traders. Many of the methods and strategies explained in the book are from that publication. We have been actively trading futures for more than 20 years and have been using computers for technical analysis since the first commercial programs became available. In the early days of computer analysis, the data and equipment to receive it cost more than $3,000 per month. Our computer terminal in Los Angeles had to be connected to a main frame on the East Coast by annoyingly undependable telephone lines, which, when they worked, allowed us to access a small handful of basic technical studies.

Since those early years we have upgraded our equipment and trading software many times, continuously adding to our knowledge and experience. A great deal of what we have learned has been through trial and error as a result of having used these technical studies to make thousands of trades in the futures markets. We have found that it is always easier to learn from our mistakes than our successes. A profitable trade is usually the result of doing many things correctly, whereas a losing trade can often be the result of doing only one thing poorly. Since the mistakes are easier to isolate, they can teach us valuable but expensive lessons. In this book we are offering our readers the opportunity to learn what we have learned without going through the expensive trial and error process that we have experienced.

This is very much a "how to" book. First we will provide a step-by-step explanation of how to design your own personalized trading system. Then we will give detailed instructions and examples of how the various computer-generated technical studies can be incorporated into your trading plan. We will also explain how to use your computer to test your trading system and evaluate its strengths and weaknesses. Finally we will provide some examples of typical day trading systems and strategies that have been employed by traders using computers. Along the way we will point out many costly errors and pitfalls that can be avoided. Many of these mistakes were painful and expensive lessons, and there is no reason our readers should have to repeat them.

We hope that you will benefit from the practical suggestions and valuable advice offered throughout the book. The numerous graphs and charts of actual markets should be especially helpful in learning how to analyze the indicators displayed on your monitor. Careful study and implementation of the material in the book will allow you to make the most effective use of the power of your computer and help you to become a better trader.

Charles LeBeau and David W. Lucas

Acknowledgments

It would be impossible to mention all of the people who have added, directly or indirectly, to our store of knowledge about trading the futures markets. It is safe to say that we have each been in contact with thousands of traders and learned something from nearly every one. A partial list of those who have helped us learn enough about futures trading to even consider writing a book includes (in no particular order) Richard Teweles, Grayson Whitehurst, John Gilmore, Fred Miller, Ed Mader, Perry Kaufman, Henry Herschaft, Pat Malloy, Carol Brookins, John Herrick, Richard Kapsch, Tom Madden, William Davis, Jim Nason, Walt Bressert, Steve Nison, Ralph Vince, Roy Reeves, Joe DiNapoli, Phil Zachary, John Bollinger, Newton Zinder, Dennis Draper, Hal Saunders, Charles Harlow, Frank Pusateri, Bob O'Connor, Harry Makoff, Don Powers, Arthur Sklarew, Dick Russian, Harold Sussman, George Lane, Larry Williams, Terry Young, Humphrey Chang, Gary Inouye, Steve Kane, Mike Halloren, Earl Hadady, David Winter, George Ragsdale, Steve Notis, Spencer Davis, Bruce Babcock, Neal Weintraub, John Lane, Jim Sibbett, Greg Garrott, and Bill Ohama.

Our newsletter, *Technical Traders Bulletin,* got its start with the kind help of the people at FutureSource. We continue to use their excellent data feed and software. We are also indebted to Tim Slater at Computrac Software, Chris Cooper at Technical Tools, Bill Cruz at Omega Research, Tom D'Angelo at Pro-Manage Software, and Tom Berry of Tom Berry Software.

Suzanne Charles and Robert LeBeau are responsible for the outstanding graphics and for minding the store while the authors were grinding out the manuscript oblivious to the world around them. They deserve special thanks for their hard work. The manuscript would never have been produced without them.

Special thanks go to Alan (Doc) Leonard for aid and moral support above and beyond the call of duty; to our hardware and software consultant Larry Grodin, who has bailed us out of innumerable computer glitches (but who now owes us at least two golf strokes for this plug); to Joe Ulloa, who first got David interested in the arcane world of technical analysis; and to David Johnston, who was Chuck's mentor more than 20 years ago and who taught us the importance of disciplined money management.

Special thanks also to the many subscribers of *Technical Traders Bulletin* for their support, suggestions, and trading ideas.

Most importantly, we would like to express our undying gratitude to our families for their loyalty and patience. This is as much their book as ours.

Contents

Introduction

"Far better it is to dare mighty things, to win glorious triumphs, even though checkered by failure, than to take rank with those poor spirits who neither enjoy much nor suffer much, because they live in the gray twilight that knows no victory nor defeat."

Theodore Roosevelt, 1899

Using Personal Computers

The goal of this book is to assist the reader in using a personal computer and analytical software to make trading decisions in the futures markets. It isn't necessary to have a computer to trade in futures, but it can be a big help, and most modern traders would consider the computer to be an indispensable tool. The transmission of data from the futures exchanges by FM signals and satellite is fast, accurate, and relatively inexpensive. The hardware and software are inexpensive and are getting cheaper, faster, and easier to use every year.

Computers are blessed time savers if used properly but can be distracting time wasters if used improperly. They allow us to quickly store and review almost infinite amounts of data and to look at that data from variable perspectives. We can study a chart representing many years of price history in any one of a hundred futures markets, and then, by touching the keyboard, we can zoom into a detailed look at the tick by tick transactions that have occurred in the last few seconds of real time trading.

The computer allows us to take any set of price data and manipulate it in infinite ways. We can smooth it, accelerate it, magnify it, compact it, color it, transport it, overlay it, store it, and erase it. Our possibilities are almost endless, and therein lies the problem as well as the opportunity. What exactly are we looking for and how will we know it when we find it? We hope that we can help you organize your thinking and allow you to use your personal computer to focus on the essentials.

Building Your Own System

In the first chapter of this book, "System Building," we will suggest the minimum framework for a complete trading system. It will be up to you to decide exactly what you want in your personal trading plan, but we will try to ensure that you don't leave out any essential components. Just like houses, trading plans are better if you design them to suit your personal preferences. Mistakes in the basic design of either houses or trading plans can be very costly to fix later.

Our overriding philosophy when publishing our newsletter, *Technical Traders Bulletin,* is that a speculator must have a carefully crafted plan for trading the markets—one that has been created to fit the trader's unique personality and level of risk tolerance. We can't emphasize this too strongly. The average purchaser of a trading system designed by someone else soon abandons the system he or she has spent good money on, even if it is trading successfully. The reason is that the system was designed and built by someone having no notion of the personality and preferences of the person who would be doing the actual trading.

The best trading systems are always created by the user. Before you start, be honest with yourself. Only you know what it will take to make you feel comfortable and productive. Ask yourself these questions:

Do I prefer to follow every short-term market fluctuation, or would I rather trade long-term?

How much time am I willing to spend each day to develop tomorrow's strategy?

How much of my stake can I afford to see disappear when I've made a bad trading decision?

Can I stand the stress of short-term trading, or would I be more comfortable stepping back and observing the markets from a distance?

If I want to trade short-term, does my other occupation allow me to take the time, or would the conflict be detrimental to my trading?

Trading Isn't Easy

Also crucial is to decide how much effort you are willing to devote to the pursuit of profit. Make no mistake, creating and trading a profitable system is hard work and can be emotionally stressful. Our observation is that many people who have spent a lifetime becoming successful in their chosen careers approach futures trading as being just an easy way to add to their incomes. Published statistics tell us that the vast majority of these people fail in the attempt. One piece of wisdom we want to impart is that it is indeed possible to make money, even substantial money, in futures—but don't expect it to be easy. Most successful traders have devoted a great deal of time and effort to the markets. Don't expect to succeed with less.

Finding the Right Tools

In the "Technical Studies" chapter of the book we describe the various indicators that can be created with most of the common software packages. We will advise you how and where each of the many indicators or technical tools should be used within the framework of a trading system. Obviously, if we were trying to build a house with a set of carpenter's tools, we would need to know the proper tools for each job. If we had no instruction or guidance and tried pounding nails with a saw, we would quickly conclude that the saw was a useless tool. Likewise, if we try to apply a stochastics oscillator as an entry or exit signal in a strongly trending market, we might also conclude that it is a worthless tool.

The technical studies chapter describes various tools of computer analysis and explains the types of markets in which each can be most effective. One caveat: We have tried to write comprehensively and explain a great many technical indicators in detail, but we have neither the space nor the expertise to cover all of the technical tools available.

Test before You Trade

The personal computer has also revolutionized the creation and testing of trading systems. As recently as the mid-1980s it was necessary to be an experienced programmer to test your cherished assumptions about your pet technical study or trading system. The only alternative to programming it yourself was to hire someone to do it for you, a time-consuming and expensive procedure. It is no longer necessary to be a programmer, although some traders still prefer to write their own software. The new, readily available software takes much of the work out of testing, allowing the average trader to test endless permutations of nearly any imaginable trading strategy. The "System Testing" chapter describes various testing procedures, tells you what testing can and can't do, and explains why testing is not always the panacea traders hope it will be.

Sharing Ideas on Day Trading

The last chapter, "Day Trading," is for the many traders who prefer the emotionally charged world of short-term trading. While the general principles that make a futures trader successful apply no matter what the time frame, day trading has generated a whole new group of strategies, and these often are substantially different from those used over the longer term. Most of the methods we describe in this chapter were submitted to *Technical Traders Bulletin* by our subscribers. Many day trading systems tend to be relatively subjective, leaving a lot of room for interpretation. We've tried to be as specific as possible in our descriptions. Because we have not actually traded with most of these systems, we make no claims about their effectiveness. However, we can say they have one aspect in common with longer-term strategies we've seen: There is a direct relationship between the experience level of the practitioner and the complexity of the trading system. Contrary to what you might expect, the more experienced the trader, the simpler the system.

We Don't Know It All

As we mentioned, this book is limited not only by space but by the limitations of the authors' expertise and experience. Our experience is limited for many obvious reasons and for a few that are not so obvious. Over many years of trading, we have operated on the basic premise that futures prices and the patterns of those prices are not neatly structured. We have been unable to observe any underlying framework that determines the orderliness of the markets. This philosophy about the general disorderliness of the markets has led us to confine our analysis to looking for trends or their absence and to the application of appropriate indicators and strategies that allow for the possibility a trend may begin or end at any moment. We do not believe that specific prices in the future can be accurately forecast, nor do we believe that specific turning points can be forecast by any method.

We do believe that substantial profits can be made by promptly recognizing trends in progress and by quickly taking advantage of turning points as they occur. Our technical analysis has been devoted to methods of finding and measuring the strength of trends, then closely monitoring those trends to observe, as quickly as possible, when the trend might be changing. Our goal in technical analysis has been, and still is, to be accurate observers of actual prices, rather than to be forecasters of any specific future prices.

Our philosophy about the nature of markets has prevented us from becoming experienced in cycles, waves, astrology, Fibonacci ratios, Gann angles, and many other methods that presuppose an inherent order to the markets. We have seen many examples of traders who have made money by using assumptions of an inherent market orderliness. We have no quarrel with them and will not dispute the fact that many of these traders have been very successful. But we are inclined to attribute their success to good money management techniques and to disciplined risk control, rather than to the validity of their timing theories or forecasting methods.

One of the disadvantages of computer power is that it allows such a thorough analysis of past data that almost any number of repetitive patterns and observations can be found. The computer gives us the capability to do such an exhaustive analysis over any set of numbers that we now can find patterns, cycles, waves, and other supposedly recurring relationships not only in futures prices but in sets of random numbers. We have never seen it demonstrated that these are anything but the occasional coincidences inevitably occurring when a sufficient number of variables are applied to massive amounts of data. These do not prove the existence of any true cause and effect relationships.

If there were indeed any detailed underlying pattern or structure of prices, the discovery and implementation of that knowledge would quickly destroy the futures marketplace. After all, if the market is somehow orderly and prices are preordained by some unknown controlling force, the trader who breaks this code or determines this orderliness should never experience a losing trade. If anyone "knew" what was going to happen in the future, no one else would trade with this trader.

We would propose that there is some amount of randomness and that there are some trends. There are also some periods of serial correlation. We aren't trying to add our opinion to the ongoing debate on this controversial topic, but we want to explain the absence of many very popular and perhaps valid technical theories in our coverage of computerized trading methods. With the exception of the day-trading strategies, we have elected to confine our writing to those technical tools we have actually used and to relate the first-hand experiences and observations gained while trading with the indicators we've selected.

In actual application, our technical approach does not differ a great deal from methods that presuppose an inherent orderliness to the market. The major difference lies in our focus on measuring and analyzing what *is* happening, rather than forecasting what *should* happen. We have often observed that successful traders, those who have been able to profit from waves, cycles, astrology, and other assumptions of inherent order, have been experienced and disciplined enough to wait until actual price action confirmed that their assumptions were correct. If their success was solely dependent on their preliminary assumption or forecast, waiting for the market to confirm that forecast would not be necessary and would, in fact, be quite costly. We have also observed that the entries and exits of these forecasters are often surprisingly similar to our own. The main difference lies in giving credit to a dominant cycle or to a Gann angle that allowed these traders to know something in advance, while our analysis resulted from accurate observations of price activity with no forecasting involved.

As for the occasional accuracy of astrology and other outright forecasts, anyone who makes enough forecasts is destined to be right once in a while. An occasional accurate forecast should not be allowed to validate this methodology, and it proves nothing. Indeed, the publicized records of these forecasters are sometimes impressive, but somehow they never include a record of all the predictions that failed to materialize. If their underlying assumptions were correct, they should never be wrong. We have seen claims of planetary influence on futures traders, but how could the influence of the planets control the futures markets when we know there must always be an equal number of buyers and sellers? Does the planet Mars selectively decide that trader A and not trader B is going to be influenced by its position? Shouldn't the alignment of the planets influence all of the traders so we have all buyers and no sellers?

The Real Objective Is to Make Money

Trading futures is often described as a game, but don't forget that winning this game is measured only in dollars and cents. The trader who identifies and correctly numbers the waves of an Elliott wave pattern or correctly measures the existence of past cycles hasn't won the game. He or she hasn't won anything. Chances are that such "success" at putting numbers on past waves won't even produce a profit.

Obviously, there is no right or wrong approach to the business of trading futures. Fortunately for us as traders, being right is not the objective. Very little is ever actually known in this business and even less can ever be proven. Therein lies the challenge and the opportunity. We would be the first to admit that what we have stated here—plus most of what follows—consists of personal opinions and conclusions, rather than facts.

This book is about finding the best ways to analyze what happened in the past and how to correctly observe what is happening in the present. We think of technical analysis as being primarily concerned with a careful and detailed inspection of the present that will allow us to profit in the future. If you are looking for a method of actually knowing the future, you are not going to find it here or anywhere else.

Please don't be deceived by the appeal of the technical studies we describe. Although they are essential tools, they themselves are not the critical elements of success. They can't predict. They can only help you get on the correct side of the market often enough to make a profit now and then. It is the system or the trading plan you carefully assemble with the correct combination of indicators that will determine your success. We have tried to impart specific ideas and knowledge about trading systems, technical studies, system testing, and day trading. We hope you will find each of them helpful.

Not a Book for Beginners

For those of you to whom this is a new subject, here are a few guidelines to philosophy and nomenclature. We try not to slip into jargon, but inevitably some creeps in and we want to be sure that everyone fully understands what he or she is reading.

However, this book is not intended to be a primer for beginning traders. Many good books currently available are better for traders who are not experienced. We are not going to stop and explain basic terminology like *long, short, spread, whipsaw, trend,* and the like. We are writing this book for more experienced traders, and we don't want to waste their valuable time on definitions of basic trading vocabulary.

Also, to conserve time and space in the book, we tend to give examples that relate only to the buy side of the market. We don't always stop to explain that the sell side is just the reverse. Unless we specifically indicate to the contrary, it is safe for our readers to assume that the sell signals are just the opposite of buy signals.

Readers Beware

We have tried to be as accurate as possible, but there will always be an error or two that slips in now and then. We are not just referring to typographical errors but to errors in techniques, procedures, and even logic. Trading futures is not a science and never will be. Many of the things we thought we knew a few years ago could not stand up under rigorous computer testing, so we had to change our opinions and strategies. Much of what we relate in the book has been rigorously tested, but much of it has not. We continue to learn, and we reserve the right to change our minds and our opinions in the future. You will find that good traders learn that being wrong now and then is O.K.

This book is our best effort, and we haven't written anything intended just to sell books or win popularity contests. In fact, we have probably offended a few friends by challenging their trading methods and beliefs. Differences of opinion are what make the markets. What we have written is what we believe, and it is sincerely intended to help traders improve their methods and results.

Chapter

1 System Building

Introduction

Why Build a System?

Futures trading systems can only succeed if they are followed religiously, and to do that you must be comfortable with your system and have confidence in it. Without confidence, the trades will not be implemented uniformly and there will be a tendency to second guess many of the signals. The process of building and carefully testing your own trading system will help instill this necessary level of confidence prior to the first actual trade.

Creating your own trading system not only helps to develop the critical element of confidence but allows for customizing the system to suit your personal preferences. For best results, each system has to be designed to fit the temperament and preferences of the trader who must implement it. The trader who designs his or her own trading method will have an intimate familiarity with the tempo of the trading, as well as with the nature of the risks inherent in the procedures that must be followed. The trader then will be much more likely to follow the system at critical junctures. If two traders are using the same system and it is the type of system that encounters frequent losses, one trader may be able to accept those losses and keep on trading, while the other might lose confidence and decide to quit. One trader will be a winner, and the other will be a loser. One trader will claim that it was a great system, and the other will claim that it was a dismal failure—and both traders will be correct in their assessments.

As we can see, because futures trading is so highly personal, the best system for one trader may be totally unacceptable to another. There are any number of elements of a trading system where individual preferences can come into play. For example, some traders are not comfortable buying on strength or selling after an extended decline. These traders can opt to design a system that buys only after a decline and sells only after a rally. Many traders who hate the whipsaws that can occur with close stops will prefer to develop a system that has very wide stops. Some traders will require frequent activity from their system, because they crave the constant action of being in the markets, while others will prefer to be very patient, cautiously entering the markets only when the opportunity seems nearly perfect.

Professional trading advisors are faced with an even more difficult task, because they must design systems that not only satisfy their personal preferences but must satisfy the anticipated preferences of their clients. The trend in professional systems has been toward conservative systems that have modest profitability with minimal drawdowns. The institutional and public investors are probably best served by these systems, because they are generally nervous skeptics who are likely to withdraw their funds or switch advisors at the first signs of adversity. Individual traders who have the benefit of designing their own trading system may well want to forsake the cautious approach and seek to make as much money as fast as possible, with little concern for the psychological and financial impact of severe drawdowns. By personally designing and testing their own system, they will be better prepared to endure the inevitable losing periods that would cause less-confident traders to abandon such an aggressive approach. If you happen to be one of these aggressive traders, just make sure the system you design accurately reflects your tolerance for losses as well as your appetite for gains.

Paying for Benefits

Building a trading system is a continuous series of interrelated decisions, with each choice offering both a benefit and a cost. The system designer must prudently evaluate many alternative solutions and carefully weigh each benefit versus its cost. The secret to ultimate success will depend on your ability to precisely select procedures that will provide the desired results at the least cost while conforming to your personal preferences in system characteristics. For example, avoiding whipsaws can easily be accomplished by widening your stops. However, the price paid will be the disadvantage of suffering larger losses. The astute system designer will attempt to solve this problem by coming up with the solution that avoids the most whipsaws with the least increase in the size of losses. There never seem to be any "free lunches" when it comes to designing trading systems. Assume there is a cost or disadvantage to every benefit and do the analysis to determine exactly what that cost is, and then decide if the benefit is worth the price.

Define the Problem, Then Solve It

To succeed as system builders, we need to become accustomed to thinking in terms of precisely identifying the problems at each step and then selecting the most appropriate solution from the many solutions that are available. Since there are numerous solutions for each problem, we must select the most suitable answer in terms of personal preferences, system goals, and costs. There are seldom any actual right or wrong answers. There are merely workable solutions at acceptable costs. As we pointed out, the first task is to identify problems.

Here is our list of the major problems that a trading system must address and some suggestions of possible solutions. We hope our simplified step-by-step approach will guide the system builder down the path toward developing a profitable and workable trading system that can be followed with confidence.

Problem 1: Identifying the Tradeable Markets

Well over a hundred different futures contracts are listed on just the U.S. commodity exchanges, with new contracts appearing almost every month. In our opinion, we now have far too many markets to follow all of them properly and to trade them efficiently. Even with the aid of our computers, an extraordinary amount of time and trading capital is required just to deal in 30 or 40 markets, so attempting to analyze 100 or more markets is obviously out of the question.

The first step in building a practical trading system must be to distill our universe of futures contracts down to a manageable number. Before we even start to worry about trends, entry methods, or the many other elements in our trading system, we must first set some minimum standards of tradability so we can isolate the markets we want to follow. We do not want to waste our valuable time and resources analyzing markets we would not trade even if we had a signal from our best indicators.

Liquidity is the Key

The primary factor to consider in selecting markets has to be liquidity. Can we get in and out of the market quickly and efficiently? We don't want to subject ourselves to costly fills on orders or see prices gyrating wildly on light volume, especially if that volume is our orders being filled. We want to make sure we are dealing in markets where the spread between the bid and ask prices is reasonable for the amount of contracts we intend to trade. We want to avoid markets where the price sequences are irregular and where large gaps are the rule, rather than the exception.

The best measures of liquidity are volume and open interest. We would suggest establishing minimum standards, such as 5,000 contracts of daily volume, in the contract month we wish to trade, plus 20,000 total open interest (all contract months combined). If you are a large-volume trader or a professional advisor, you will undoubtedly want to make the minimums even higher. We suggest using volume as well as open interest, because often there can be large amounts of open interest that are the result of long-term spreading and hedging. Because of its inactivity, this open interest does little to contribute to day to day liquidity (see Exhibit 1–1). Computer data shown in this exhibit makes it easy to monitor volume and open interest.

In addition to liquidity, we also need to consider other important contract features, such as historical volatility and the availability of accurate fundamental and technical data. Markets with a history of wide-swinging trends would be preferred over quiet narrow markets

EXHIBIT 1–1

Contr	Open1	High	Low	Last	Volume	OpnInt
YXU1	21040	21090	20955	21040s	4219E	4545A
USU1	9323	9324	9321	9324^	144910A	247620A
SX1	5430	5500	5410	5490s	94820A	217910A
CZ1	2330	2394	2330	2392s	128640A	510600A
GCQ1	3695	3700	3690	3698s	15311E	49155A
DMU1	5552	5554	5522	5531s	28500E	64163A
SFU1	6412	6413	6372	6381s	17312E	36424A
CLU1	2155	2172	2145	2151s	32576A	60387A
CTZ1	6860	6948	6842	6940s	3955E	17872A

where there is seldom the opportunity for substantial profits, even if our timing was accurate. Ready access to prompt and accurate fundamental and technical data is required, even if we do not use the data in our own analysis. The fact that such data is available will serve to attract other traders and enhance market liquidity.

Avoid New Markets

We would also caution traders not to get involved in new markets. In spite of any volume and open interest criteria, be sure and wait until any new futures market has gone through at least two or three delivery cycles before you add a new commodity to your possible portfolio. You will never actually know what you are trading, or its true value, until you know precisely what can be delivered against the futures contracts. Some of you might remember that there was once a diamond futures contract on the long-since-failed West Coast Commodity Exchange. Significant delivery problems having to do with the quality of diamonds being delivered put the diamond futures traders out of business and contributed to the failure of the exchange itself.

There are lots of markets to trade without being a pioneer or a guinea pig for the new contracts that are routinely introduced with great fanfare only to quietly fade away after a few months. Let the members and the hedgers do the groundwork and get the contract going. They have a vested interest in the success of these contracts and the necessary experience and capital to trade them in their incubation stages. The 5,000 daily volume and 20,000 open interest liquidity standards should help you avoid almost all of these questionable markets.

Liquidity Must Be Monitored

Applying these minimum volume and open interest standards allows us to filter the markets down from over 100 to about 20, which becomes a manageable number to follow on a daily basis. Keep in mind that, as fundamental and technical situations change, the prices, volume, and open interest will adjust. Volume will tend to flow into rising markets, while flat and downward markets will tend to lose volume. Don't worry about missing any big price moves. Price action attracts volume quickly, so you should be participating quite early if there is a big trend developing. This means that volume and open interest need to be checked on a regular basis, and we suggest you review the liquidity of all the markets at least once a month. You will find that your selection of markets will change from time to time as volume and open interest expand or contract across your minimum standards. In the meantime, these volume and open interest guidelines will save you money by keeping you out of many quiet, trendless markets and allow you to concentrate your technical skills on the markets with genuine potential for major profits.

As you routinely monitor volume and open interest, you will find that expiring contracts and other seasonal factors may cause dramatic changes in the open interest. Normally, these factors should not cause a commodity to cross back and forth over your open interest threshold. Daily volume is more likely to traverse back and forth across your threshold number, so it is best to average the volume over a period of 10 days or more before making any decisions about adding or dropping a particular market from your portfolio.

Now that you have a manageable number of markets to follow, you can proceed to the next problem—identifying the trends in those markets. In the meantime, you might want to make sure your software program is set up to track volume and open interest. Or, if you are not receiving daily volume and open interest via your computer, you can check it periodically in many financial publications.

Problem 2: Identifying the Trend

Whenever the word *trend* is used, it should be defined relative to a time period. In this instance, we are looking for trends that are expected to last for three to four months or longer, so the various technical studies we use can be based on daily, weekly, or even monthly time periods. Keep in mind that, at this point, we are not using these studies for market timing but only for market direction. Once we have established the direction of the markets, we will work on the appropriate timing of our entry.

For now, we are concerned only with the very simple but critical question: Are the markets we follow trending up, down, or sideways? (Yes, we consider sideways to be a trend direction.) There are many simple technical indicators and even some fundamentals, like basic supply/demand analysis, that can be used to help us identify the direction of trends. However, fundamental analysis, like many other topics, is beyond the scope of this book.

Trend-Finding Tools

Let us look at some of the common technical studies that can be used to solve the problem of establishing the direction of markets. We have always had good results with various applications of simple moving averages. Particularly, we like using a 3-day moving average in combination with a 12-day moving average or a 9-day moving average combined with an 18-day moving average. For example, if the 3-day moving average is above the 12-day moving average, we would say the market is trending up. Conversely, if the 3-day moving average is below the 12-day moving average, we would conclude that the market is trending down. As you can see, there is only up or down and no possibility of identifying a sideways market when using only one or two moving averages. (See Exhibit 1–2.)

It is possible, however, to construct a sideways reading if we use more than two moving averages. For example, using the popular combination of the 4-, 9-, and 18-day moving averages: if the 9 is above the 18 but the 4 has gone below the 9, we could conclude that the market was

EXHIBIT 1–2

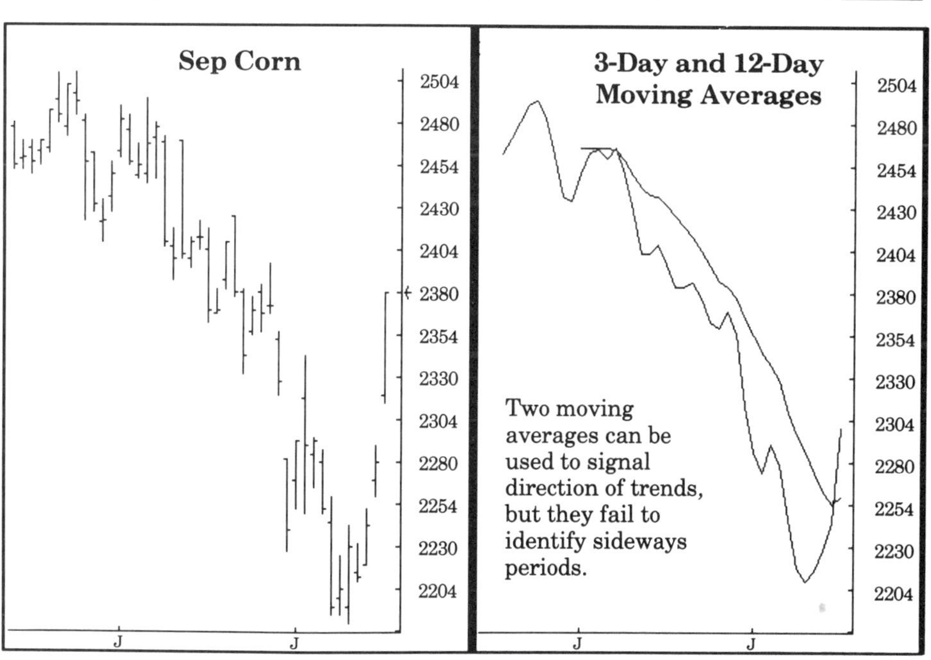

sideways. Conversely, if the 9-day moving average was below the 18-day moving average, but the 4-day moving average has moved above the 9-day moving average, we could conclude that the trend was also sideways. An uptrend would be identified only when the 4 was above the 9 and the 9 was above the 18. A downtrend would be identified when the 4 was below the 9 and the 9 was below the 18. (See Exhibit 1–3.)

In addition to moving averages of all kinds, some classic and very acceptable direction indicators are: trendlines, linear regressions, parabolics, point-and-figure studies, and directional movement indices. Much like the moving averages, most of these indicators do not identify a sideways market, and it would take a combination of these indicators to do so. One of the most effective means to identify sideways markets requires the use of multiple indicators, so, when the indicators disagree, the market is considered to be trendless or sideways. We could get a sideways reading anytime we used two indicators that failed to agree or confirm by indicating the same direction. (See Exhibit 1–4.)

Keep It Simple

Some traders have developed specific trend indicators for each market they trade, trying to develop the perfect system on a commodity by commodity basis. For example, they might select a separate combination of moving averages for each market. In our opinion, the selection of a trend-identifying technical study boils down to a matter of simplicity and convenience. At this point in our system, the study selected should be easy to read without any subjectivity or confusion regarding interpretation. Rather than attempt to design one very complex technical indicator that does everything in our system, we have opted to break our system building into functional elements; then we select a simple but

EXHIBIT 1–3

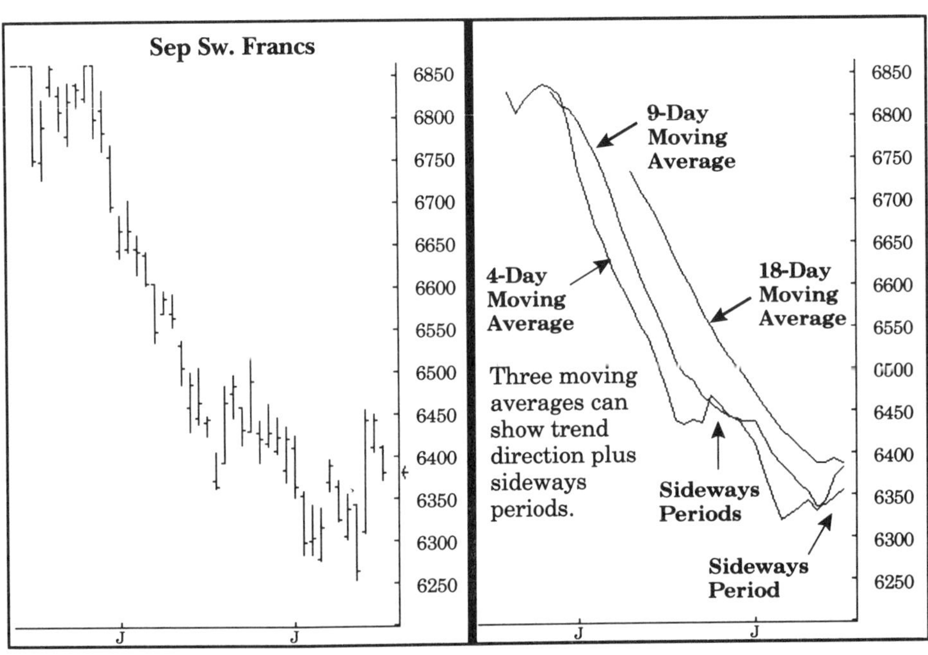

EXHIBIT 1–4

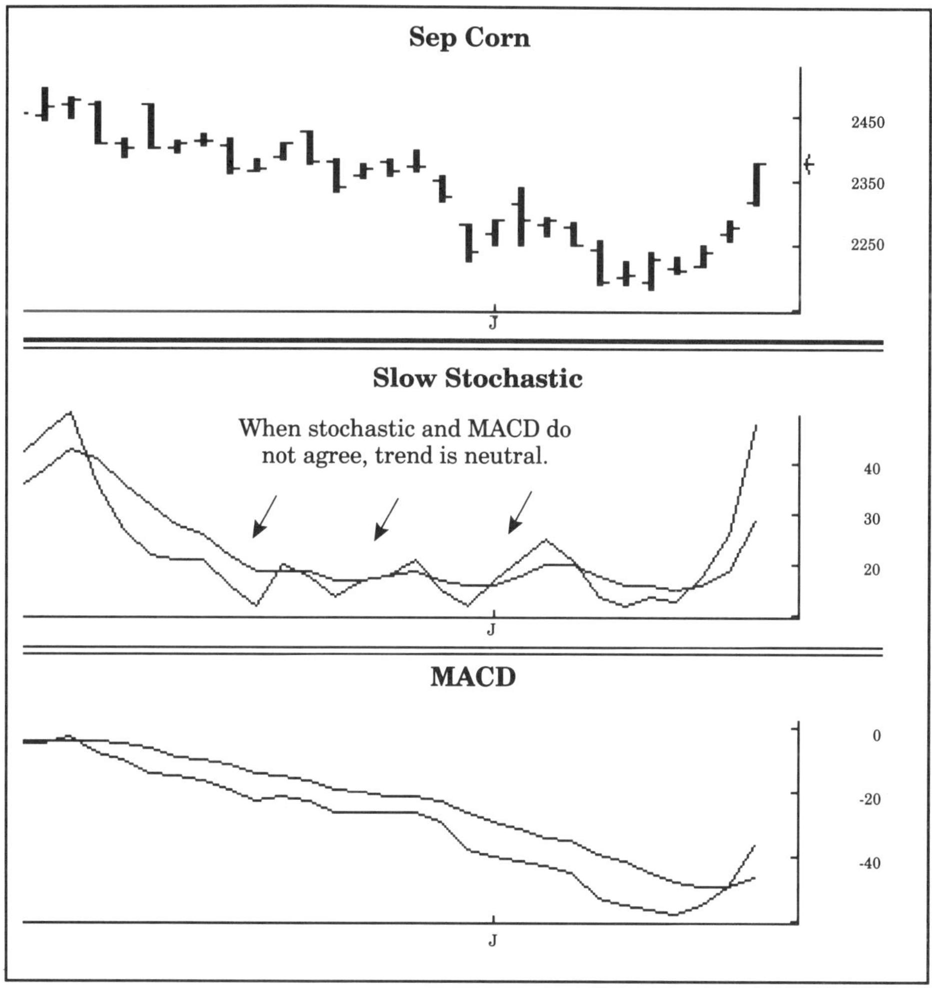

effective technical tool for each function. For now, let us assume that we are using two trend indicators and, when they agree on a direction, then there is a trend in that direction. When they fail to agree, we will say that the trend direction is sideways.

Once we have established the direction of each market, our trend-following system calls for respecting the direction of each trend. If the direction is upward, we want to employ a buy-only strategy until the trend changes. If the trend is downward, we will use a sell-only strategy. In sideways markets, we cannot employ trend-following strategies. We have a choice of staying out of the sideways market or using a countertrend strategy that buys dips and sells rallies.

We do not recommend reversal strategies, which fail to identify sideways markets and are always in the market going from long to short and vice versa. These reversal systems tend to be continuously whipsawed in sideways markets and have no hope of success unless the markets trend for sustained periods.

Now that we have sorted our 20 markets by direction, we are ready to proceed to the next step—timing the entry points.

Problem 3: Timing the Entry

Most traders fail to acknowledge the complexity of system building and simply attempt to find one Holy Grail indicator that will do everything. These traders are ready to believe that one ideal indicator will identify all the trends, will time their entry, and will even signal exits and reversals. Wouldn't it be nice if the markets were really that easy? The popular practice of relying on one indicator to perform a series of functions is inevitably doomed to failure, because, when the nature of any one of the elements of the system changes, the whole system will fail. In our opinion, it makes more sense to isolate and examine each of the problems and then carefully select appropriate indicators to deal with each problem. By employing a multiple problem/solution approach, we hope to design a flexible and dynamic system that will survive in the real world of ever changing market conditions.

Ready, Aim, Fire

Skillful entry into a commodity position might be compared to firing a pistol at a target. First we must aim (find the direction). Then we cock the hammer (get ready), and finally we carefully squeeze the trigger (enter the market). At any time, the markets consist of at least three trends. The first is the long-term trend (weeks and months), which we used to determine the direction of the markets. The second is the intermediate-term trend (the last few days), which we must now identify using more-sensitive indicators. The final trend is the very-short-term price action (yesterday and today), which we will use to trigger the precise entry.

In solving the problem of identifying the trend, we suggested a few of the many possible indicators to determine direction: various moving averages, point-and-figure charts, long-term linear regressions, trendlines, and combinations of indicators. Once the long-term direction of the market has been decided, our next task is to find an intermediate-term indicator that will give a series of signals within the long-term trend. We need a series of signals, because the first intermediate signal will have occurred before our long-term indicator allows us to trade in that direction. Remember the obvious sequence: short-term signals will occur first, then the intermediate, and finally the long-term signals. By the time we identify a long-term trend, the first intermediate and short-term signals will have already occurred. Therefore, we want to use intermediate and short-term signals that will repeat several times within the longer-term trend.

Pick an Indicator

A list of useful intermediate indicators might include DMI crossovers, channel breakouts, moving averages, parabolic signals, trendline violations, point-and-figure studies, and any number of pattern recognition methods. Every trader has a favorite indicator and one is probably just as good as the next. It is important to keep in mind that we are building a system around a combination of indicators, so the importance of a single indicator tends to be diminished within the total system. All you need to do is to find an indicator you trust and one that will give a series of shorter-term signals within the time period of the long-term trend.

Actual entry is now triggered by the market activity following the intermediate signal. Again there is a choice of trigger mechanisms. For example: place an entry stop at a new high or low for the move, or pick a stop point beyond today's high or low. Perhaps you will want to be very cautious and wait to enter only after a series of highs or lows. If you are less patient, you might elect to enter on the first close in the right direction. The important point to remember here is that you want the price action to confirm your other indicators and to let the market itself trigger your entry. Most good trades start out being immediately profitable. Our goal is to be in sync with all three of the market trends right from the start.

Patience Is Rewarding

Testing conducted by the System Trading and Development Research Team (a System Writer Plus user group) showed that the results of a dual moving average crossover system could be improved dramatically by waiting for a breakout above the high of the day on which the moving averages cross. By waiting for the breakout to enter, the cumulative return on the theoretical account for the five and a half year test period was increased by 177 percent (from 22 percent to 61 percent). The profit per trade jumped by 235 percent! The researchers tested 56 combinations of moving averages in 10 different commodities over the period of January 1984 through June 1989. The research team concluded that waiting for the market to put them into the trades increased the profit per trade, reduced the necessary capitalization, reduced the number of trades, and significantly increased net profits.

Now we still have another problem to solve before we enter. We need to protect ourselves from major losses by setting a stop loss.

Problem 4: Setting the Stop Loss

Any experienced trader will acknowledge that stop-loss orders are essential to avoid catastrophic losses. Traders who venture into the markets without stop losses are doomed to failure—the only variable being the amount of time it will take for them to be wiped out. Stop losses are like premiums on an insurance policy and should be considered as an unavoidable cost of doing business.

Too Close versus Too Far Away

Stop losses, in general, seem to fall into two categories: those that are too close and those that are too far away. The ideal stop would be one that is far enough away to be just barely outside the range of random or technically meaningless price movements yet close enough to comfortably control the risk on the trade. We have found these ideal parameters to be mutually exclusive, which forces us to choose between stops that are either too close or too far away. Let's examine the pros and cons of both choices.

Close stops offer the obvious advantages of small losses on each position and modest total risk on a portfolio of open trades. However, this procedure leads to the financially debilitating and psychologically irritating experience of being stopped out of many trades that would have been very profitable had the original position been allowed to run its course. We propose that traders can overcome this problem by simply figuring out a suitable re-entry method that puts them back into the market, in the original direction, in time to capture most of the remaining potential profit. However, as always, there is a trade-off. This logical step of just getting back into the market must inevitably lead to increased activity, which adds substantially to transaction costs and slippage.

A system that employs close stops will encounter the disadvantage of a higher percentage of losing trades to gain the advantage of smaller average losses. A system that employs wider stops will tend to have a higher percentage of winning trades than the close stop system. The distant stop avoids the re-entry problem and keeps slippage and transaction fees under control. This is accomplished at the expense of a substantially increased average loss per trade and a much greater total risk to the portfolio. We seem to be faced with trying to decide the lesser of the two evils or with arriving at some more palatable compromise between these equally objectionable alternatives.

The Ideal Stop

An acceptable stop-loss procedure might be developed by attempting to set the stops at points just slightly outside the range of random price swings. In case one of these stops is hit while the trend is still intact, we need a re-entry method that will put us back into the trade once the short-term trend resumes the direction of the longer-term trend. This procedure seems to be a workable compromise between the too close or too far away conundrum. Setting the stops outside the range of randomness would avoid most of the annoyance and expense of frequent whipsaws. A re-entry method would then avoid the frustration of missing any subsequent major moves. This sounds simple enough, but defining randomness gets down to the basic essence of trading futures; and if we could do that accurately enough, we wouldn't even need stops—all our trades would be winners. We can design a less than perfect but still acceptable procedure that incorporates the basic principle of setting stops that will allow us to avoid most of the short-term randomness.

One possible approach would be to calculate the standard deviation from a moving average of prices and then set the stops in increments of standard deviations away from the moving average. Not all software systems offer these standard deviation bands (now more commonly called "Bollinger bands" after the technical analyst on FNN, who popularized the bands as a technical tool). (See Exhibit 1–5.)

As a practical (and probably just as effective) alternative to the complicated standard deviation approach, we can use an average daily price range as the minimum stop-setting distance to avoid most of the small, whipsaw-producing price gyrations. We can easily set up a 5- or 10-day moving average of highs and lows and then place our original stops at a minimum distance that is equal to the range between the moving averages. As the market moves in our favor, the stop can also be trailed by the amount of this difference. This technique will avoid what we might call "intra-day randomness," because it keeps the stop far enough away to avoid average daily fluctuations. To stop us out would require an abnormal one-day fluctuation or a series of adverse daily price changes. This method may not produce the ideal stop but could be very useful as a means of finding a minimum distance for a stop that would avoid unnecessary whipsaws.

Other acceptable stop-setting methods you might want to investigate are chart points, such as support and resistance levels, recent daily highs or lows, parabolic stops and assorted envelopes, or trendlines. Since there are no "perfect" stops, there is no need to get carried away with overly complex techniques to solve the problem of where to place

EXHIBIT 1–5

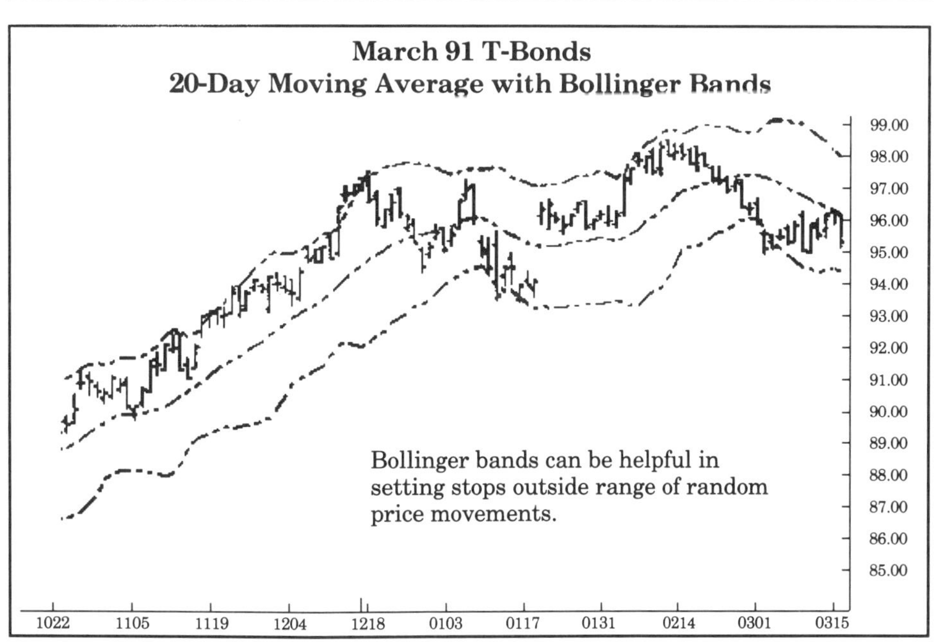

them. In fact, we have tested many methods of setting initial stops and have found that a simple dollar amount works just as well as any of the more complicated procedures.

Be Consistent with Stops

Whatever method you select, it is important to be consistent and well disciplined. For example, consider the results of a trader who starts out with a $500 stop and after five consecutive whipsaws has lost $2,500 and missed five potentially profitable moves. He then decides to use wider stops and proceeds to lose $1,500 on the next trade. He has now experienced the worst of both methods, having lost too much money on the last trade without the benefit of having made the potential profits on the first trades. Either the $500 stop or the $1,500 stop applied uniformly over the period of our example would have produced a much better result than the disaster produced by the inconsistent approach. You cannot have wide stops sometimes and close stops at other times without good reason. And, with the exception of allowing for variances in market volatility, there probably aren't any good reasons for wide variations in stops!

Hindsight can sometimes be a useful tool in determining stop points. John Sweeney, the former editor of *Technical Analysis of Stocks and Commodities* magazine, has suggested measuring the maximum adverse price excursions of past winning trades to determine how wide a stop point would have been necessary to remain in all of the winning trades while eliminating the losers. This method has some merit if you carefully compare the bottom-line results, which must include an analysis of the effect of wider stops on all of the losing trades. You might be better off by having closer stops and missing some of the profitable trades. Also keep in mind that this method is pure hindsight, which makes no allowance for changes in volatility that are likely to occur in future time periods. Also, it is important to keep your stops outside the range of future randomness, not past randomness. However, if you believe the future is likely to closely resemble the past, Sweeney's approach makes some sense and is probably better than most stop-setting methods we have observed.

Problem 5: Timing the Exits

It has been our observation that traders spend entirely too much money and effort searching for methods of timing entries into the markets. Somehow, a very mistaken belief has developed, that success depends on entry timing and that, if the entry is done precisely, everything else will follow. As far as futures traders are concerned, the search for the perfect entry system has become much like the search for the Holy Grail. Unfortunately, the truth is that the entry is probably one of the least important ingredients in a complete and well-designed trading system. We assert that the real key to profits is knowing how to exit. We have seen many traders who make money in spite of their absurd entry methods, not ever realizing that their most prized entry strategies have very little if anything to do with the outcome of their trades.

Messages from Outer Space

We once knew a trader who claimed he received entry signals from mysterious beings in outer space. He claimed to receive these messages via his "interplanetary cellular phone" constructed from a Coca-Cola bottle with a broken piece of radio antenna sticking out of the top. This fortunate (or unfortunate) trader actually made money because he had a knack for exiting his trades correctly. He couldn't bear to lose money and endure the taunts of the other traders sitting around the boardroom, so he was very quick to close out a losing trade. He would blame the loss on static or some sort of cosmic interference that had garbled his secret message. When he stumbled into a winning trade, he would prolong the experience as long as possible, so he could brag to his cronies about the validity of his messages from outer space and poke fun at their seemingly futile efforts to make money studying fundamentals and charts. He was brutal in his criticism of conventional trading methods and gloated at his own success. He was absolutely unbearable when he was on the right side of a market. This fortunate trader was in the habit of cutting his losses and letting his profits run, so he made money. His success was the amazement of the boardroom, who joked about the talking Coke bottle and the crazy trader who talked back to it. As crazy as he was, this trader was unconsciously following an excellent exit strategy that allowed him to make money. However, if you asked him, he would swear his success was due entirely to the entry signals he received from the Coke bottle.

Not surprisingly, many popular entry systems today are based on theories even less valid than the Coke bottle messages. If you stop and think, what is the difference between receiving perceived messages from a computer hooked to a satellite dish or receiving imagined messages from a Coke bottle? If you believe in what you are doing and act on the messages, you are starting out nearly equal, and the trader who is best at exits will make the most money. In spite of what anyone might claim, those who succeed in futures trading all share the common denominator of good exit strategies.

A Brief Review

Let's review where we are now. The first thing we did was to screen the various futures markets to find what qualified as "tradeable." Then we went about defining the direction of each of our selected markets. Next, we discussed entry timing and related it to firing a pistol at a target. Then we dealt with finding a logical point for the stop loss.

So here we are, with an open position and a stop loss. We either are going to make some money or get stopped out. The loss is going to take care of itself, if our stop gets hit, so our primary concern at this point must be to find ways to maximize the profit.

As the trade proceeds in our anticipated direction, we are faced with trying to decide between taking a quick but certain profit or staying with the trade hoping for a larger gain. In general, beginning traders tend to lose money by having a good percentage of profitable trades with a few very big losers, while more experienced traders lose money by piling up lots of small losses. (We have to admit we haven't gone out of our way to study strategies of losing traders, but it's hard to avoid stumbling across them on a regular basis.)

Systems that take small profits must have a very high percentage of winning trades to succeed, yet we are tempted daily by the old adage: A bird in the hand is worth two in the bush. Nailing down the small profits, rather than allowing them to slip away and turn into losses, helps improve the batting average substantially. On the other hand, we have been cautioned many times to let our profits run. What is a trader to do in the face of such conflicting advice?

We think a trader needs to have a minimum acceptable profit level that is directly related to the amount of money being risked, if the stop loss is hit. Most of the profitable traders we have studied have average gains that are clearly larger than their average losses, often in the range of two to one. Allowing for commissions and slippage that must be factored into the results, you might need to set out for a profit ratio of nearly three to one to wind up with a ratio of two to one on a net basis. Long-term trend followers, as you might expect, tend to have large profit to loss ratios at the expense of having a low percentage of winning trades. But even then, their profit ratios are not as high as one might imagine, with about four to one being at the very high end of the range.

Popular Exit Strategies

Let's discuss some of the more popular exit strategies. The enter and hold for big profits method works over the very long haul if you don't mind huge drawdowns and painful losing periods that will be very discouraging and very costly over the short run. These methods are suitable only for trading your own capital in large amounts and with tremendous confidence, experience, and discipline. Unfortunately, these are attributes that most of us lack. The major risk inherent in this "go for the big profit" method is that the trader will almost inevitably wind up quitting in the midst of a severe losing period. Look carefully at the disclosure documents of any professional advisor who follows long-term trading strategies and you will find hundreds of closed out accounts. These are the accounts of clients who quit while the overall track record of the advisor was quite profitable and impressive. The vast majority of traders cannot stand to see large profits given back, and they cannot psychologically withstand the inevitable drawdowns, no matter how carefully they have been warned or educated. Be very careful about adopting this strategy for yourself, because you will be in for a painful test of your confidence and commitment, which could prove disastrous.

A less popular exit strategy worth examining is the targeted exit method, where trades are closed out at predetermined price objectives. As we stated previously, every strategy seems to have its trade-offs. We see some major problems with the concept of being able to forecast specific targets with any degree of accuracy. Everyone can spot some obvious support and resistance levels that might cause a trend to hesitate; but beyond such obvious analysis, we doubt if more accurate targeting is actually a realistic possibility. No one knows where a market is going.

The trader using targeted exits gains an advantage, in that he or she will be spared the problem of watching large unrealized gains being lost. On the other hand, he or she will surely suffer a share of disappointment when many of the prices don't quite reach the forecast objectives. The trader will also have to learn to endure the frustration of seeing a modest profit taken, when a much larger profit might have been made with a little more patience.

We consider targeting as a workable exit method for trading, if you feel you have a knack for picking targets and then not looking back at what might have been. You must also be careful to avoid a natural tendency to gradually begin reducing the profit objectives to obtain a higher batting average. This is a tempting adjustment that could cause serious problems, if the average profit to average loss ratio is allowed to drop too far.

The Compromise Exit Strategy

One of the best profit-taking strategies we know is a compromise that offers the advantages of taking quick profits while still allowing the potential for big profits. You simply operate a two-unit trading account and take the profit on one position at a conservative targeted price and let the second position run in hopes of catching a big winner. This method requires more capital than a one-unit account, but we think it has obvious advantages. The quick profit on one contract will often give you a free ride on the second contract, so you can afford to be very patient. With one profit in the bank, you can afford to give the second position enough slack to avoid getting stopped out prematurely.

As we have learned, whenever we speak about the benefits of a strategy we must also look closely for its negative aspects. In this case, we do not have to look far. The obvious drawback of the two-unit strategy is that, if you get started in the wrong direction, you will suffer losses on two positions instead of one. If you have a very good entry method and have observed that most of your trades start out in the right direction, the two-unit strategy could be an excellent choice of exit strategies. But, before you adopt this strategy, be sure to check your past results to see if you could have withstood twice the losses in the periods when your entry timing was off.

For the one-unit trader, we would advise an exit method that gives the market some room (wide stops) until it becomes overbought or has had an unusually big run in your favor. Then tighten up the profit-taking stop, so you protect the majority of the gain but still have the opportunity for more profits if the market keeps going in the right direction.

We sometimes use a six-bar relative strength indicator (RSI) to tell us when the market is overbought and the stops should be raised. For example, when the relative strength indicator gets above 75 and then drops by 10 points or more, we like to raise our stops to the low of the last three trading days and trail them as the market moves up. Often this

EXHIBIT 1–6

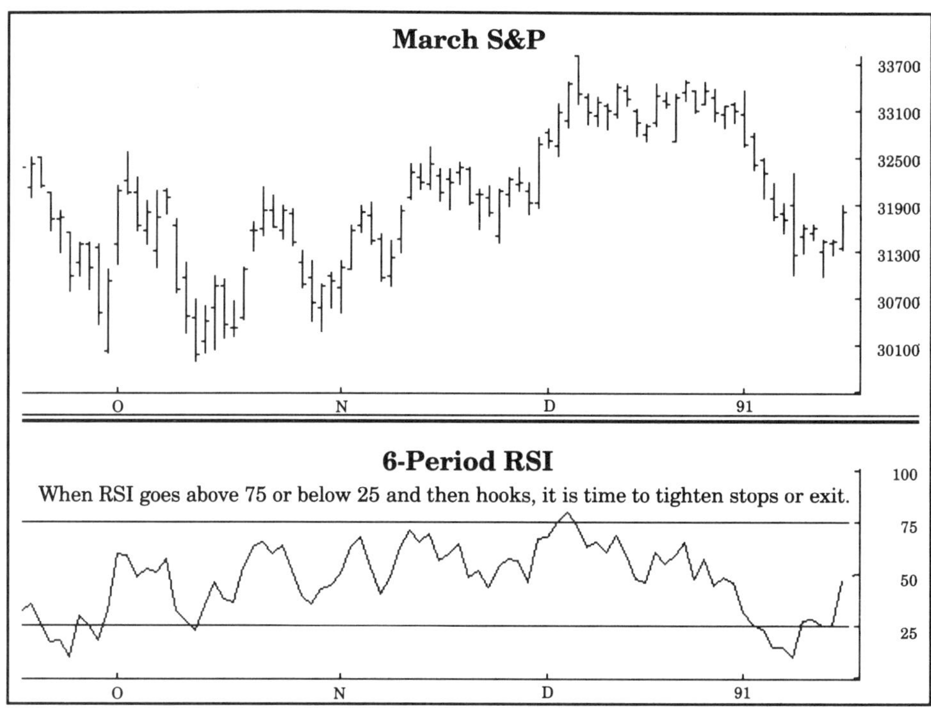

procedure allows us to stay in a strong market and gets us out very near the top. (See Exhibit 1–6.)

Another simple but very effective method is to just use a trailing stop at all times and stay in the trade until the stop is hit. Using this method, you will be aware of exactly how much profit you are likely to give back at any time. As simple as this exit method might seem, it stands up well under historical testing, and it is difficult to find a better exit. The trailing stop can be combined with the overbought/oversold method (using RSI) described previously to provide the opportunity to exit closer to the top now and then.

Profits from Random Entries

How good is your present exit strategy? A good way to test your exit proficiency is to enter a series of hypothetical trades at random, with no concern for direction or timing. Then, place your exit stops and implement your profit-taking strategy. After running through 30 or more of these hypothetical trades, if your results (in terms of gross profits) are not better than break-even, your exits need to be improved.

Problem 6: Timing the Re-Entry

In the previous section, we discussed the importance of proper exit timing. A good exit can make the difference between winning and losing on a trade, and it is probably the single most important element of any system. Unfortunately, in our efforts to get out of the markets before giving back too much of our hard-earned profit, we may frequently exit before the trend has actually ended. In those cases where the trend continues, we need to have a method to re-enter the market. Major trends are much too rare and valuable to be missed, so we need to make sure we can get back into markets where our previous exit proves to have been premature.

The nature of our re-entry may have to be entirely different from our original entry, because the market is now in the midst of a strong well-defined trend where the volatility of the price swings is much greater than at the beginning of a trend. We are at a point where we are confident about the direction of the market, and what we need here is a quick re-entry so we don't miss the balance of the move.

The "Fail-Safe" Re-Entry

One fairly obvious strategy that is certain to put us back into the market, if the trend continues, is to buy any new high (or sell any new low, if our previous trade was a short sale) under the general assumption that the market's ability to overcome one of these classic resistance points is a sign the trend is resuming. In recent years, as technical analysis has grown more sophisticated, the breaking of a high or low on a chart rarely brings in the expected surge of new buying or selling like it used to do in the "good old days" when hand-plotted charts were the tools of the trade. Making new highs or lows used to trigger lots of stop losses and bring more traders into the market, and the trend would continue for another "wave." It doesn't necessarily work that way anymore.

Now the markets are more likely to react to indicators like stochastics divergences and MACD crossovers that may not be visible to the uncomputerized eye. Although buying new highs is bound to insure that you will never miss a big move, the disadvantage of this approach is that buying the highest price in sight is seldom the best way to enter a market. If the market does not follow through as we hope, we could be in for a very big loss. Rather than waiting for a new high before re-entering, we would be better off if we re-entered as soon as the adverse price movement that prompted us to exit in the first place has run its course.

A Place to Use Oscillators

Oscillators that can identify overbought and oversold areas can work very well for re-entries. Working with an example within an uptrending market, let's assume that we got stopped out of a profitable long position, on a correction that was more severe than we were prepared to accept. We could now be watching the relative strength (RSI) or stochastics for a signal that the current decline is over. One technique that we favor is waiting for the stochastics oscillator to go below a specific level and then turn back up. A stochastics decline anywhere below 40 followed by a rally should produce a workable re-entry. Normally, a stochastics buy trade is signaled by a decline below 20 or 30 and then turning up. However, since we are in a well-defined uptrend, the stochastics indicator is less likely to reach a very low reading. The stronger the trend, the higher the level at which the stochastics is likely to turn. (If the stochastics only goes down to about 50 or 60 and then turns up, we probably won't even be stopped out of our original position, so we won't have to worry about re-entering.) Once the new buy trade is under way, we can put our new stop loss under the low of the correction and then raise it to our break-even point if a new high is actually reached. Real trends die hard, so the probability of our re-entry being a successful trade is quite good, especially when we can enter after a decline, instead of waiting for new highs to be made.

Why Not Stay In?

At this point, you are probably wondering about the advisability of getting out of the original position if we are so fond of the current trend. The advantage is going to become quickly apparent when our "correction" turns out to be not a temporary correction but a complete change in the major trend. We will be out of the market with a big profit and will not have re-entered. This is about as close to the perfect exit as is possible in the real world of trend following. The secret to success with the re-entry is to wait for the end of the temporary correction and to buy quickly as soon as we begin to resume the direction of the major trend. Waiting for the market to make a new high is waiting much too long, yet we need to see enough strength to indicate that the correction is really over. We are talking about a very fine line here, one that requires some careful thought as well as a sensitive and reliable indicator.

As an example of how sensitive the re-entry indicator might be, one recommended method is to use a very short-term oscillator such as a three-day relative strength index (RSI) as the timing signal. (See Exhibit 1–7.)

Normally, a three-day RSI whips back and forth so frequently that it has very little value as an indicator. Since this is a very sensitive indicator, any correction that is large enough to stop us out of our original position will have brought the three-day relative strength down to a very low level. When the RSI hooks back up above the 50 midpoint, we can assume the correction is over. We then buy the next day as the market takes out the high of the day that generated the +50 RSI reading.

The RSI technique gives us two signs the trend is resuming (the +50 reading and the confirmation), yet it is quick enough to get us back in the market well before a new high is made. Other countertrend indicators, like stochastics, Percent R, and the Commodity Channel Index, might also be used in a similar fashion. Percent R is a sensitive indicator that will perform very much like the three-day RSI. The idea is to use one of these indicators to signal when the correction is over. The indicator has to be set up to be more sensitive than usual, because what we want to measure here is the short-term correction, not the trend itself.

EXHIBIT 1–7

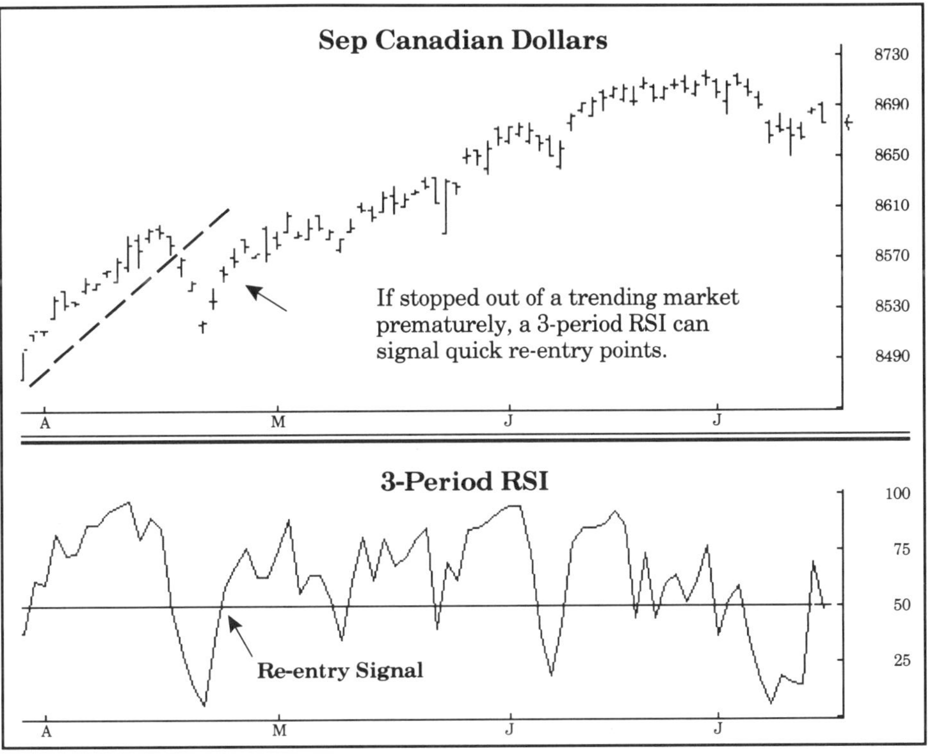

Coordinate Exits and Re-Entries

Another helpful point on re-entries is that we can expect better results if the indicators for re-entry are synchronized with our exit strategy, so the price action triggering our exit will automatically cock the re-entry indicator we intend to use. For example, when we are stopped out of a long position, the stochastics reading should fall below 40, the Percent R should drop to −90 (−100 is at the bottom of the Percent R scale and 0 is at the top) and the RSI should drop to below 50, depending on which indicator we plan to use for our re-entry. They will then be cocked to give us a re-entry signal when they hook back up from these lower levels. If our indicators are cocked properly, we will not risk missing any subsequent resumption of the trend. If the trend continues before our indicators cock, we risk missing the move. Remember, the exit strategy is the more important strategy, so use the best possible exit strategy and then adjust the sensitiveness of the re-entry indicators to cock after the exits.

Because of our preference for sensitive re-entry signals, we are going to be subjected to some whipsaws and losses now and then. (There is always a trade-off whenever we are gaining some advantage or benefit.) It is hoped that, after only one or two consecutive re-entry losses, we will either be back in the trend or our major trend indicator will have reversed direction or started going sideways. In either case, we won't have had to endure a long series of re-entry whipsaws.

Maybe it's a personal quirk of ours, but we have always hated to see much of our unrealized profits given back. We think our goal of locking in the profits rather quickly is the appropriate strategy for most traders. But be forewarned: This technique of being quick to take profits will prove to be very frustrating, unless it is coordinated with a well-planned re-entry so that you don't miss the important big moves.

Next we will give some important advice on how to properly monitor your system, so you can tell when it needs fixing and when to leave it alone. Gains and losses are not the only way or even the best way to measure how well your system is actually doing. Many failures can be detected before any serious losses occur.

Problem 7: Monitoring the System

Do all systems eventually fail? We wish we knew! We do know that markets and market conditions will change; but perhaps human nature and human reactions, such as fear, hope, and greed, do not change. We could argue either side of the "Do all systems fail?" controversy. We think the most prudent approach is to always assume and prepare for the worst. Therefore, let's assume that, in spite of our hard work and expertise, the best possible system we can assemble might eventually fail. (We define failure as losing so much of either our equity or our confidence that we can no longer follow the system.) With the assumption of possible failure lurking in the background, our best defense is to recognize predefined symptoms of failure well before we run out of money or patience. We need to develop a well thought out early warning system, so we can either change the system or abandon it for good reason.

The Bottom Line

The natural tendency for most system followers is to focus simply on the bottom-line performance. Are we making money or are we losing money? The problem with this logical bottom-line approach is that all systems lose money periodically, so only an obviously abnormal losing period gets our full attention. By then it may be too late. What we need to develop is an informative and objective set of predetermined non-bottom-line criteria that can warn us of possible problems well before any major losses occur.

Imagine a typical situation where a system has shown a modest profit over the most recent month of trading. So far so good, as they say. A closer inspection might reveal that there were 14 trades made during the month, and only 2 of those trades were successful. Fortunately for us, the profits from the 2 good trades were enough to offset the 12 losing trades. Here is a good example of how the bottom-line analysis might easily deceive us. After all, this was a profitable period, so why worry? Should we be concerned about the fact that there were only two winners out of the last 14 trades? Maybe. Maybe not.

What should we expect in terms of winners versus losers? Are two winners out of 14 trades something that we can expect from time to time, or is it a warning that our system might be coming apart at the seams? We need to be aware of the current situation, and more important, we must also be able to put it into a meaningful perspective. What about the activity over the last month? Were 14 trades more than we might have expected? Is this normal or abnormal? What is the likelihood of this activity rate continuing?

As you can see, there is a great deal more to monitoring a system than just a casual look at the bottom line. We need to give the whole evaluation process some careful thought and then attempt to compile some standards of anticipated performance, so we have something to compare with our current performance.

Historical Benchmarks

The best way to develop guideposts by which to judge our current performance would be to carefully compile significant performance data while we are still in the process of testing our system over historical data. The data obtained by testing is then available for comparison with current data as we trade real time.

As an integral part of the monitoring process, it is important to be able to identify the source of the problem once we are forewarned that a problem might exist. Maintaining current and historical performance data on a commodity by commodity basis should be helpful in isolating the specific problem areas. Going back to our 14 trades in a month example, it might be very helpful to know that 9 of the 12 losing trades were in currencies and to further observe that we encountered three consecutive losses with combined positions in yen, Swiss francs, and D marks. Closer investigation might reveal that perhaps there was some central bank intervention or some other unanticipated factor that produced the total of nine losses in our various currency positions.

Now it becomes particularly meaningful to know that past experience and testing showed that we might expect as many as five consecutive losses in currencies and that three losses in a row was not an unusual occurrence. This knowledge might lead us to conclude there was nothing substantially wrong with the system's entries and exits. We might also decide that it may not be prudent to have multiple currency positions on the same side of the market. If our historical data showed that we could expect to have as many as 5 losses in a row trading one currency, we must be prepared to have 15 losses in a row if we trade three currencies in the same direction. The problem turns out to be more related to portfolio selection and diversification than to market timing.

The following statistics need to be developed from historical data and then used to monitor current performance on a commodity by commodity basis. You might find it helpful to compile an average or normal expectation for each statistic and to note the range of the extremes, so you can quickly put the numbers into perspective.

For example, our historical data on T-bonds might look something like this:

- Frequency of trades per period = 1.5 trades per month average, with 0 trades and 5 trades in a month as extremes (worst cases in tests plus real time).
- Percent winners versus losers = 32 percent winners on average, with worst period being only 1 winner out of 8 trades and best period being 6 winners in 7 trades.
- Longest string of consecutive losses = 7. Consecutive winners = 5.
- Average gain per winning trade = $1,420; biggest winner = $5,330.
- Average losing trade = $490; biggest loser = $2,700.
- Largest drawdown in equity from T-bond trading = $7,880.
- Time required to recover from largest drawdown = 11 months.
- Longest period of time to make new high in equity from trading T-Bonds = once went 21 months without making new peak to peak high in equity.

This is only a small sample of the many kinds of data that could prove helpful in monitoring a system. You could improve and expand on the list with your own thoughts about what you would like to know. Compiling and maintaining all of this data looks like a lot of work, and it is. But the operation of the trading system itself should be almost entirely mechanical, so your free time can be spent on monitoring the system objectively, instead of just watching the trades in progress.

Watching a system without predetermined guidelines causes traders to find excuses to override the system or perhaps change it unnecessarily. Most traders tend to err on the side of making too many unjustified changes in their system after a series of losses. The losses may well have been within the range of normal expectations or have been caused by a factor that is not the fault of the system. Most traders never bother to define normal or abnormal performance (other than bottom-line results), so panic often sets in when it shouldn't.

Let's go back and take another look at that month where we made a little money but had only two winners out of 14 trades. Assume our careful analysis showed the following: Out of the 12 losers, 6 of them were consecutive losses in T-bonds, while the other 6 losses were spread among five different commodities. The obvious problem appears to be the cumulative losses on the losing T-bond trades, which totaled $2,400 ($400 per trade average, with the largest loss being $850).

A careful look at the data tells us that the number of trades in T-bonds in a month (six) was abnormal and, in fact, set a new extreme by exceeding the previous extreme of five trades in a month. That does look like a problem. However, the total loss ($2,400) as well as the average loss ($400) was low, compared to our previously collected data. The largest loss in the string ($850) was not extreme. The six consecutive losses were not an extreme but close. Conclusion: We went through a very erratic period in bond trading that bears close watching, but we would not alter our trading system at this point. We have added to our range of expectations in trading T-bonds and now have six trades in a month as a new extreme in terms of activity. The activity level should be monitored closely (do not wait until the end of next month or we might be looking at 12 consecutive losses). If the unusually high activity level persists, we should try to learn if there is a fundamental cause that would lead us to believe the choppiness was only a temporary factor that would disappear of its own accord. If the problem appears to be within the system itself, we might want to use slower indicators or to add a confirmation element to the T-bond trading to try and cut down on the activity and whipsaws.

In Summary

Monitoring the system is the final element in our disciplined approach to system building. At the very least, we hope our insights have helped our readers identify the various issues that need to be addressed. There are many solutions to each of the seven problems we have presented, and we have only suggested a few possible alternatives. Even then, the solutions we offered serve mostly to illustrate our thought process and approach. The methods we described may not be the best solutions for you, and they may not be the best for us. We will be continually seeking new and better ways to resolve each of these problems—and so should you. But before you can begin to find answers, you must understand the nature of the problems and appreciate the necessity and benefits of solving them.

As you can see, system building is not as simple as just finding a "super" indicator that we like. If it were, we would all be much richer. Remember, every benefit offered has its cost. Make sure you identify all of the hidden costs before you decide that a particular solution is the best. When faced with apparently equal ways to solve a problem, select the simple one over the complex one. Try to be logical and objective at all times, and do not let your emotions and eternal optimism or pessimism get in the way. When making your plans, always assume and prepare for the worst—and then be grateful for your good fortune when the worst doesn't happen. When the worst does happen, be grateful for your foresight and preparedness; you will survive and prosper.

Suggested Readings

Sweeney, John. "Using Maximum Adverse Excursions for Stops." *Technical Analysis of Stocks and Commodities, Trading Strategies* 5, pp. 149–50.

Wright, Charles. "The Magic of Setup and Entry." *System Trading and Development Newsletter* 1, no. 1 (October 1989), pp. 2–5.

Chapter

2 Technical Studies

Introduction

Types of Indicators

Any successful trading system must have some objective, repeatable method of entering and exiting the markets. These methods can be divided into several types. There is the classic Edwards and Magee chart analysis, which has the advantage of being both simple and comprehensive but has the disadvantage of being extremely subjective. Then there are very complex and mathematically based methods, such as autoregressive integrated moving average (ARIMA) or Fourier spectral analysis. We have seen no evidence that mathematically complex timing models are superior to any other types of analysis.

There are surprisingly large numbers of traders who wishfully assume some structure underlies the market that, once uncovered, will lead to riches. These traders embrace some very popular methods, such as Elliott wave, Gann analysis, and even astrology. These strategies are staunchly defended by a small but vocal group of trader/fanatics who operate mostly on faith and can offer little evidence or logic to support their beliefs. They work long and hard while quietly suffering their losses, believing their failures are caused only by their personal lack of expertise in finding the exact parameters of the truth they know to be hidden in the markets. Occasional gains give them sustenance, while the losses become their penance for not working hard enough or spending enough money to uncover the carefully guarded secrets that control the marketplace. Unfortunately for them, these mysterious secrets were revealed only partially at the expensive seminars and private consultations with the current guru (who as a generous friend to mankind, is willing to share revelations for only a few hundred dollars). We believe that, if any underlying structure really is controlling the markets, it has obviously not been discovered yet. But most of all, we believe that whoever does find the ultimate secret to riches is unlikely to share it with us at any price.

Finally, in our listing of indicator types, we come to those that are the subject of this chapter. This group of computer-generated technical studies are relatively simple indicators usually derived from prices. Far from being the secret to riches, they are common plain-brown-wrapper methods that may never reveal any ultimate truths about the market. These relatively well-known indicators have been designed to give us easily understood signals that will help us to enter and exit the markets.

A great deal has already been written about most of the indicators. But we feel that much of the literature in this area has been too academically inclined, with little in the way of practical application and guidance. We have no quarrel with academic analysis and we are, in fact, indebted for what it has taught us. However, we feel that most traders are not aware of the many less than obvious but extremely practical uses and limitations of each indicator. Nor are they aware of the many ways in which these techniques can be woven into a trading system.

Learning to Use the Indicators

Novice traders often tell us that they have no idea what most of the squiggly lines on their computer screens are telling them. Even experienced traders can find the squiggles a little daunting. We will try our best to plug some of the information gap with opinions and advice that is based on our experience and on the experience that other traders have shared with us over the years.

You will find a few common threads that run through the various analyses. Each has its place and serves some useful function in a well-designed trading system. Some technical indicators are most effective in trending markets and some perform best in nontrending markets. Although all of these indicators are based on price, each is calculated differently. For us, there is no best or worst or even favorite technical study. We will tell you what we believe to be the proper and most efficient uses of each indicator, being as specific as possible. There will be many choices with no right or wrong answers, so in the final evaluation it is up to you to decide which if any of them you wish to use, and how.

We will cover technical studies that relate best to the futures markets, not to the stock market. Stock market studies are a subject unto themselves. With the exception of the direct study of volume and open interest that we will cover, the remainder of the studies are calculated solely from prices. Essentially all of them are available on easily obtainable commercial technical analysis software.

Keeping the Math to a Minimum

In most cases, the mathematical derivation of each study is relatively simple. We will try not to be too mathematical; but, in some cases, it is important that a user understand how and why the calculations produce a specific result. This is critical for two reasons. First, there should be no misunderstandings about exactly what an indicator does and does not do. Second, you will find that many of the analytical software packages on the market differ in their calculations of what should be the same technical study.

A simple RSI oscillator from one program can look substantially different from the supposedly identical study displayed by another, even when derived from the same data base. The cause can be either faulty programming, an incorrect understanding of the formula that produces the indicator, or a personal bias on the part of the software designer. In most cases the differences are minor, but we urge you to be aware of potential anomalies. Unless the programming is ridiculously bad, these variations do not in any way invalidate the technical studies that are produced. You will find that consistency is much more important than scrupulously accurate calculations.

This is not intended to be a comprehensive book where we try to say a little something about everything. Several of those have been written. If we have left out your favorite technical indicator, it is because we hesitate to speak authoritatively about a study we have not actually used and feel comfortable with. There are gaps in our knowledge; probably some important ones. Our failure to discuss a method or indicator in no way implies that the method or strategy is inferior. We're certain that we've barely scratched the surface here, but we have no intention of attempting to write about something outside of our expertise.

Exchanging Ideas

We don't want to mislead anyone into thinking that we invented or originated all of the analyses and techniques in this chapter. We do have extensive experience in actual trading, research, and testing; but many of the best strategies have been brought to our attention by traders and subscribers to our newsletter, *Technical Traders Bulletin*. One of the primary purposes of the newsletter is to serve as a medium for the exchange of trading ideas. As the editors of a technical publication, we regularly hear ideas from traders throughout the world. Essentially, all of our subscribers are active in the futures markets, with a small sprinkling of stock traders who are getting ready to venture into futures. The majority are commodity trading advisors, brokers, bankers, foreign exchange dealers, in-house technical analysts, and the like. The remainder are private investors who have a computer and some analytical software.

We are grateful to everyone who has ever called us and passed on information, opinions, experiences, and ideas, even if they thought the offering was insignificant at the time. We've tried to carefully separate the wheat from the chaff as much as possible and see for ourselves what works and what doesn't. As you will see, we don't hesitate to venture an opinion or two that may not be provable one way or another. However, we intend to sprinkle in enough facts and logic to give weight to our opinions and conclusions.

Directional Movement Indicator (DMI) and Average Directional Movement Index (ADX)

The vast majority of profitable trading systems incorporate some form of trend following, yet most of the time the markets are not trending strongly enough to generate worthwhile profits. Because successful traders employ a policy of taking small losses and letting profits run, the nontrending markets seem to move only far enough to produce the small losses. As a result, trend followers are typically losing money most of the time in most of the markets. Their best hope of success depends on finding an occasional market that has a trend strong enough to produce big profits. The common method of "finding" big markets is to diversify into many different markets in hopes of stumbling into one of the profitable markets by chance. Unfortunately, diversifying in this fashion only adds more losing markets than winners. This common procedure of diversifying to find the best markets results in a vicious cycle of having to endure a broad range of bad markets to be assured of getting into only a few good markets.

Fortunately, there is a very practical solution to the problem of identifying and measuring the trendiness of markets. The proper interpretation of the average directional movement index (ADX) allows traders to significantly improve their odds of finding good markets and avoiding bad ones. We have probably done more work and more research with ADX than with any other indicator, because we have found the ADX to be a surprisingly valuable technical tool with many practical applications.

To provide our readers with a thorough understanding of ADX, we must begin with a basic explanation of the directional movement indicator (DMI), which is used to produce the ADX.

The DMI Concept

Directional movement is a concept that J. Welles Wilder, Jr., first described in his 1978 book, *New Concepts in Technical Trading Systems,* a classic work on technical analysis which we heartily recommend. (See "Suggested Readings," at the end of the chapter.) The directional movement indicator (DMI) is a useful and versatile technical study that has two significant functions. First, the DMI itself is an excellent indicator of market direction. Second, one of the DMI's derivatives is the important average directional movement index (ADX), which not only allows us to identify markets with trends but also gives us a means to quantify the strength of the trends.

The directional movement calculation (DI) is based on the assumption that, when the trend is up, today's high price should be above yesterday's high. Conversely, when the trend is down, today's low price should be lower than yesterday's low. The difference between today's high and yesterday's high is the "up" directional movement, or +DI. The difference between today's low and yesterday's low is the "down" directional movement, or −DI. Inside days, when today's high or low does not exceed yesterday's, are essentially ignored. The +DI and −DI are each averaged for a period of days and then divided by the average "true range." The results are normalized (multiplied by 100) and displayed as oscillators. For the mathematically inclined, we have included the details of the calculations. Fortunately, we can now produce the necessary indicators with only three or four keystrokes on a computer.

Calculating Directional Movement (DM)

1. Directional movement is the largest part of today's range that is outside yesterday's range.

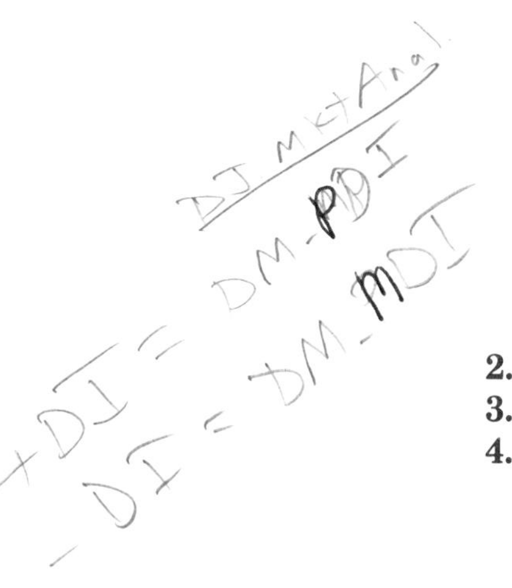

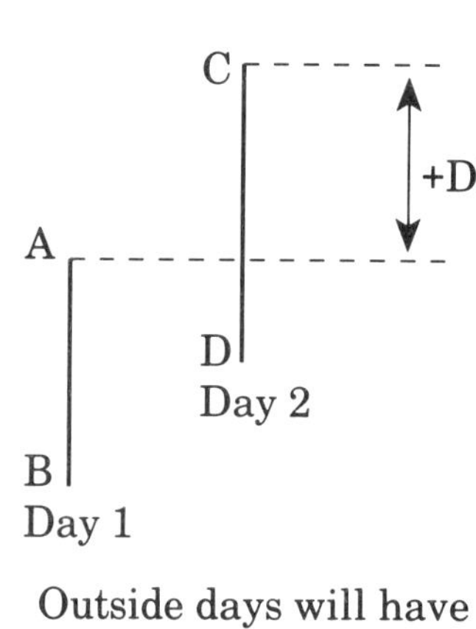

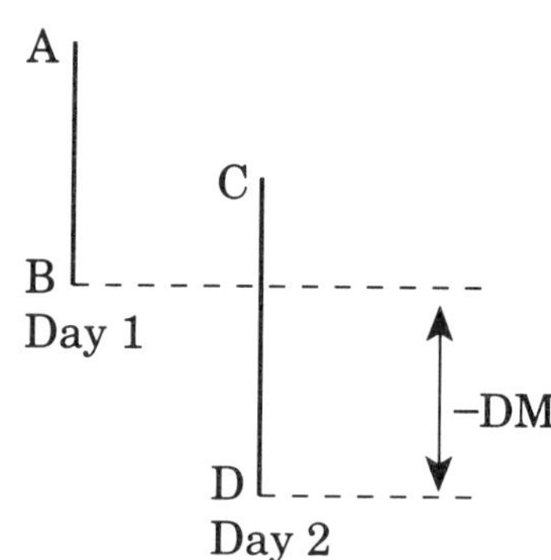

2. Outside days will have both a +DM and a −DM. Use the larger.
3. Inside days have zero DM.
4. Limit days will have a DM measured as in the diagrams above. For example, for a limit up day (first diagram) +DM would be the difference between A and the upward limit reached the next day, C.

Calculating ADX

1. Measure directional movement (DM).
2. Measure the true range (TR), which is defined as the *largest* of:
   a. The distance between today's high and today's low.
   b. The distance between today's high and yesterday's close.
   c. The distance between today's low and yesterday's close.
3. Divide the DM by the TR to give the directional indicator (DI).

$$DI = DM / TR$$

The result can be either positive or negative. If positive, it is the percentage of the true range that is up for the day. If negative, it is the percentage of the true range that is down for the day. +DI and −DI are normally averaged over a time period. Wilder suggests 14 days. The calculation then becomes:

$$+DI_{14} = +DM_{14} / TR_{14} \quad \text{or} \quad -DI_{14} = -DM_{14} / TR_{14}$$

+DI and −DI are two of the three values normally displayed as the DMI.

The third is the ADX, which is derived as follows:

4. Compute the difference between +DI and −DI.

$$DI_{diff} = \mid [(+DI) - (-DI)] \mid$$

5. Compute the sum of +DI and −DI.

$$DI_{sum} = [(+DI) + (-DI)]$$

6. Calculate the DX or directional movement index.

$$DX = (DI_{diff} / DI_{sum}) * 100$$

The 100 normalizes the DX value, so it falls between 0 and 100. The DX by itself is very volatile and is not usually displayed.

7. Compute a moving average of the DX to create the average directional movement index (ADX). Normally, the smoothing is by the same number of days used to calculate +DI and −DI.
8. A further smoothing can be created by calculating a momentum-type derivative of ADX called the average directional movement index rating (ADXR).

$$ADXR = (ADX_t + ADX_{t-n}) / 2$$

where t = today and t − n = the number of days ago used to calculate ADX.

When plotted as oscillators on the computer screen, if the +DI is above the −DI, the directional movement is up. If the +DI is below the −DI, the directional movement is down. As the two lines diverge, the directional movement increases. The greater the difference between +DI and −DI, the more directional or trending is the market. Wilder used 14 days as his basis of calculation, because 14 was his idea of an important half-cycle. As you'll see, we think there are other, more optimal time periods to be used, depending on what you plan to be doing with the DMI and ADX.

The DMI studies usually appear together as three lines on the computer screen: +DI, −DI, and ADX. (Some programs conveniently allow the ADX to be displayed separately.) As we mentioned, the results of the DMI calculations are normalized (multiplied by 100), so the lines will oscillate within a range from 0 to 100. The important ADX is derived directly from +DI and −DI, and it measures the extent to which a market is trending. The higher the ADX, the more directional the market movement has been. The lower the ADX, the less directional the market movement has been. Note that, when we say "directional," we could mean either up or down. The ADX does not distinguish between a rising or falling market. It is important to clearly understand that the ADX measures the amount of trend—not its direction. It is perfectly normal for the ADX to be rising sharply as prices fall, because by rising it is indicating the increasing strength of the downtrend.

It is the other oscillators, +DI and −DI, that show direction. When +DI crosses above −DI, the direction of the trend is up. When −DI crosses below +DI, the direction of the trend is down. The farther apart the two lines separate, the stronger the trend. (See Exhibit 2–1.)

In his book, Wilder also mentions the calculation of the average directional movement index rating, or ADXR. This is simply the sum of

EXHIBIT 2–1

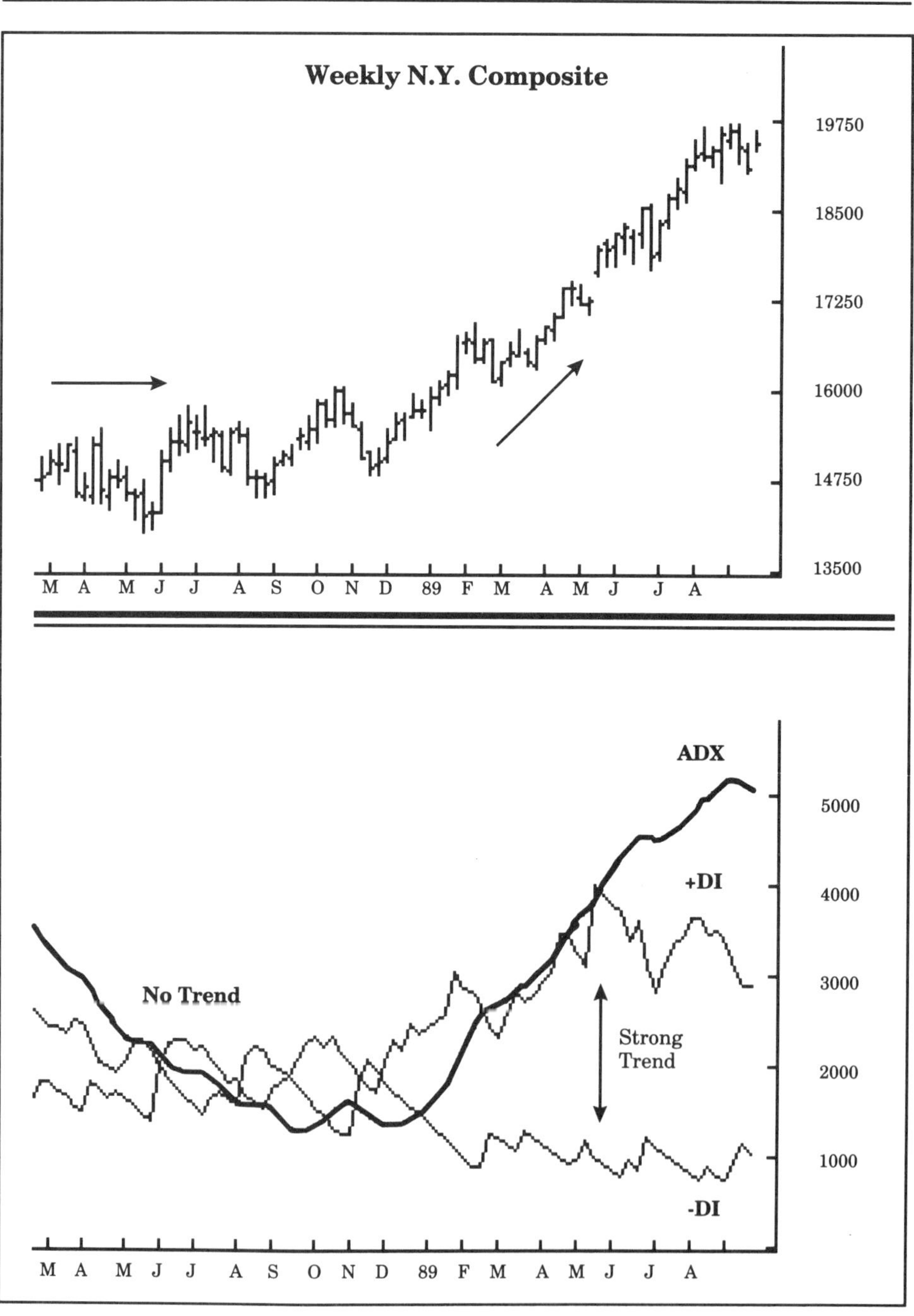

the ADX at the beginning of the period (say 14 days ago) plus today's ADX, divided by two. This additional smoothing of the ADX was done by Wilder to so dampen the fluctuations that the ADXR could be used in calculating a method of comparing markets called the Commodity Selection Index. In our opinion, the ADX has been smoothed sufficiently in its original form and additional smoothing is unnecessary. In fact, for our purposes, the smoothing that is done to obtain ADXR actually reduces the effectiveness of the indicator.

Testing DMI Performance

Quite a few tests of DMI and ADX have been published. The results have generally been more favorable than for most indicators. Here are just a few samples.

Bruce Babcock tested DMI and described the results in his book *The Dow Jones-Irwin Guide to Trading Systems* (see "Suggested Readings" at chapter's end). The DMI method that Babcock tested goes long on the close, when net directional movement is positive. When net directional movement is negative, the system reverses to go short. The results of Babcock's testing showed that, over a five-year period, the 28-day DMI was profitable in a wide range of markets. However, interim losses were substantial because no stops were employed. The system Babcock tested was the most simple possible use of the indicator, and many of Wilder's basic rules were violated. Importantly, Wilder's suggested entry technique of waiting for a penetration of the high or low of the DI crossover day was ignored (we've found Wilder's advice on entries significantly reduces whipsaws). In Babcock's testing, profit taking was strictly on crossovers, with no attempt to take earlier profits. Under these conditions, for the DMI to show consistent profits is remarkable! Although we don't recommend trading DMI this way, Babcock's testing does show that a fairly long-term DMI might be a useful timing indicator.

A more realistic test/optimization was done by Frank Hochheimer at Merrill Lynch Commodities. Hochheimer tested two cases: Case 1, which followed Wilder's basic trading rules, and Case 2, which simply traded on crossovers. In most markets, 11 years of data were used. Since this test was also an optimization, he tested +DI and −DI by varying the number of days used for each independently (something we don't recommend). Not surprisingly, Case 1, which followed Wilder's suggestion of entering on a buy or sell stop at the previous day's high or low, was more profitable. The optimization of the DI periods showed that the best time intervals were in a range of 14 to 20 days. Our independent testing of ADX over a different set of data confirms the profitability of this 14 to 20 range, with the best over-all results at an interval of 18 days.

In *The Encyclopedia of Technical Market Indicators,* Colby and Meyers did a very interesting test of DMI incorporating the ADX. They entered on +DI and −DI crossovers only when the ADX was rising. They exited when the ADX ticked down or when a reverse crossover occurred. They tested only the New York Composite, on a weekly basis and using time intervals of 1 to 50. The best profits were achieved over time intervals of 11 to 20 weeks. They noted that, of the many indicators they tested, the DMI method had the lowest drawdown and was worthy of further study.

At first glance, it might seem that Colby and Meyers were following the trend by trading only when the ADX was rising. However, since they implemented trades based on the +DI and −DI crossovers after the ADX was rising, the system was more of a countertrend method, because the rising ADX was the result of the trend in existence prior to the current crossover. When the +DI and −DI cross after the ADX is rising, it would signal a trade in the opposite direction from the trend being measured by the rising ADX.

We have found DMI to be only moderately useful as a timing indicator, in spite of some of the favorable test/optimization results previously quoted. The DMI is a trend-following indicator and subject to exactly the same weaknesses that plague any form of trend following. When the markets are not trending, the +DI and −DI cross back and forth repeatedly, producing one painful "whipsaw" loss after another. They are sensitive indicators that produce good results in trending markets, but it is exactly this sensitivity that causes all the whipsaws when the markets are in a trading range. However, we are very enthusiastic about using ADX, the derivative of DMI, as a filter to help select the "most likely to succeed" trading method for each market at any given time.

Using ADX

We suspect that ADX has often been overlooked or discarded as an indicator, because of its apparent lack of correlation to price movements. Someone casually observing the ADX rising as the prices declined might conclude that the indicator was giving misleading indications about market direction. It is extremely important to understand right from the start that the ADX alone does not tell us market direction. The ADX may fall when prices rise and it may rise when prices fall. The function of the ADX is to measure the strength of the trend, not the direction of the trend. You must use an additional indicator, such as DMI, for market direction. (See Exhibit 2–2.)

Some technicians attribute a great deal of importance to the level of the ADX as an indication of trend strength, and they would argue that a reading of 28 indicates a stronger trend than a reading of 20. We've found that the direction of the ADX is much more significant than its absolute value. An upward change, for example from 18 to 20, indicates a stronger trend than a negative change from 30 to 28. A good rule of thumb is that, as long as the ADX is rising, any level of the ADX above 15 indicates a trend. We recommend that you become familiar with ADX and use it in conjunction with your favorite technical indicators. You will soon discover certain levels for a rising ADX that produce outstanding results with your pet indicator. One indicator may work well when the ADX is rising through 15, and another indicator may not work well until the ADX rises above 25. When the ADX is declining at any level, it is an indication that the market is moving sideways and forming a trading range. We will examine the implications of the ADX rising and

EXHIBIT 2–2

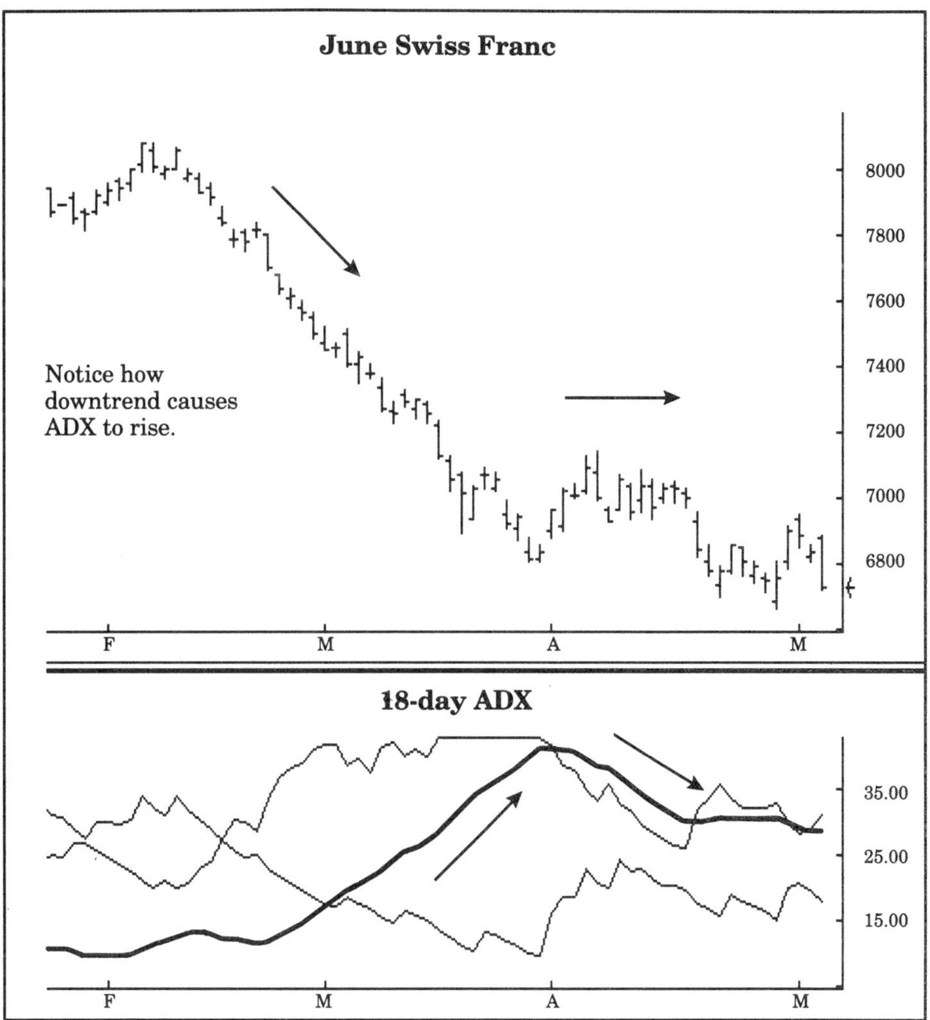
June Swiss Franc
8000
7800
7600
7400
7200
7000
6800
Notice how downtrend causes ADX to rise.
F
M
A
M
18-day ADX
35.00
25.00
15.00
F
M
A
M

falling in more detail and suggest appropriate trading strategies. (See Exhibit 2–3.)

Rising ADX. A rising ADX indicates a strong trend is underway and suggests that trend-following trading strategies are in order. Technical indicators that depend on strong trends to produce big profits, such as moving average crossovers and breakout methods, should work very well. Almost any method of following the existing trend should produce excellent results in the favorable environment being forecast by the upward sloping ADX. (See Exhibit 2–4.)

Keep in mind that the rising ADX is also providing valuable information about what trading techniques are likely to fail. Knowing what not to do can be almost as important as knowing what to do. For exam-

EXHIBIT 2–3

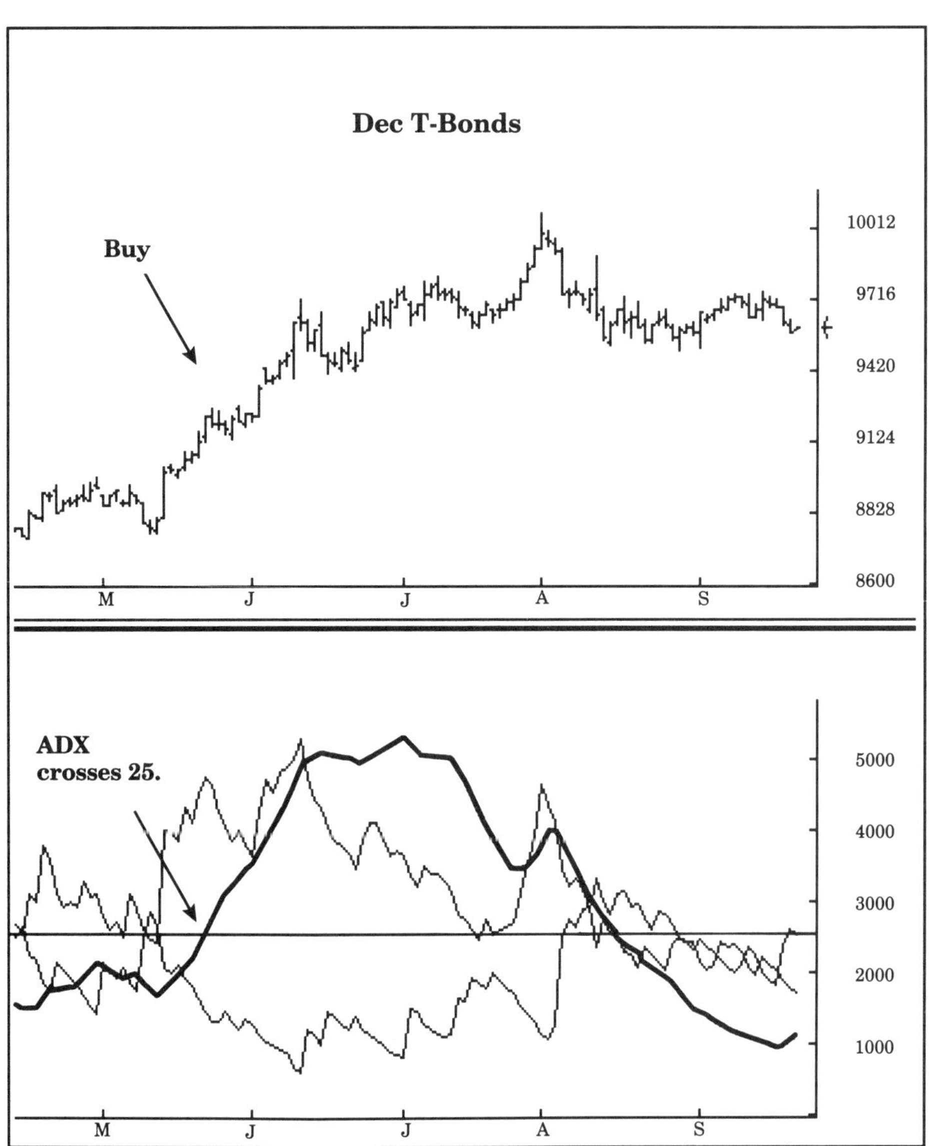

EXHIBIT 2–4

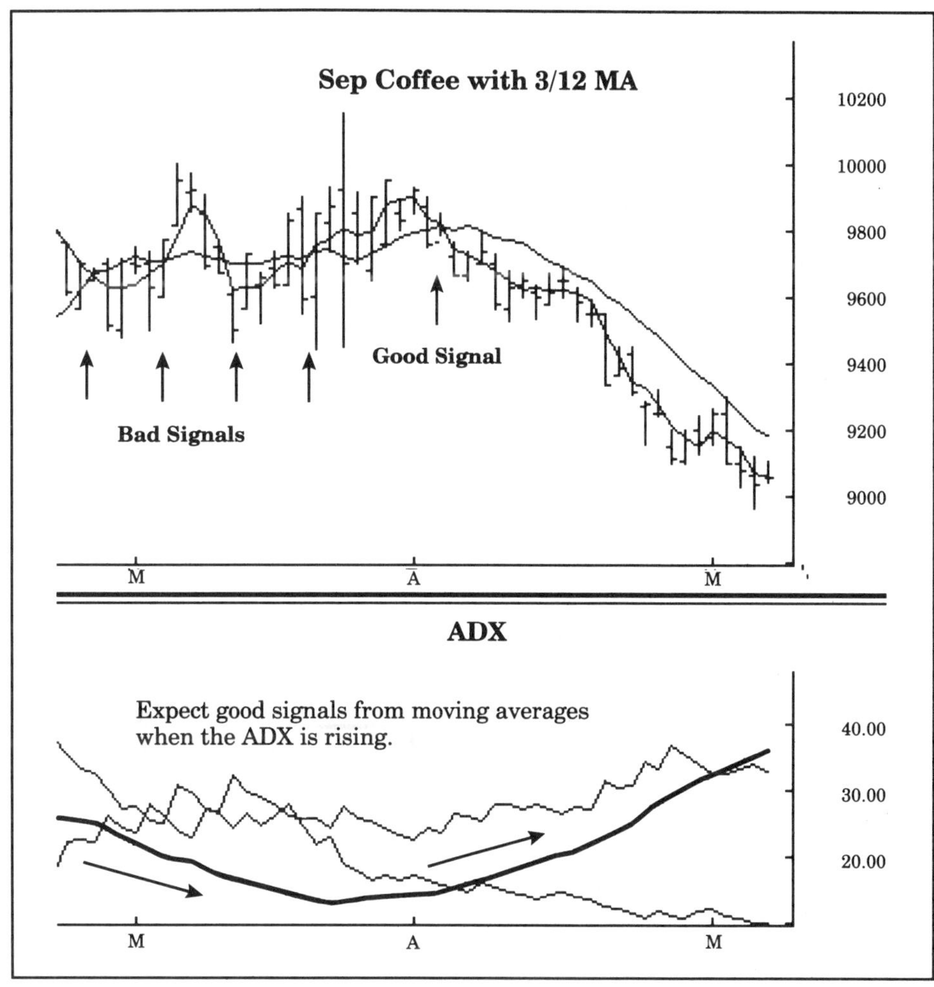
Sep Coffee with 3/12 MA
10200
10000
9800
9600
9400
9200
9000
Good Signal
Bad Signals
M
A
M
ADX
Expect good signals from moving averages when the ADX is rising.
40.00
30.00
20.00
M
A
M

EXHIBIT 2–5

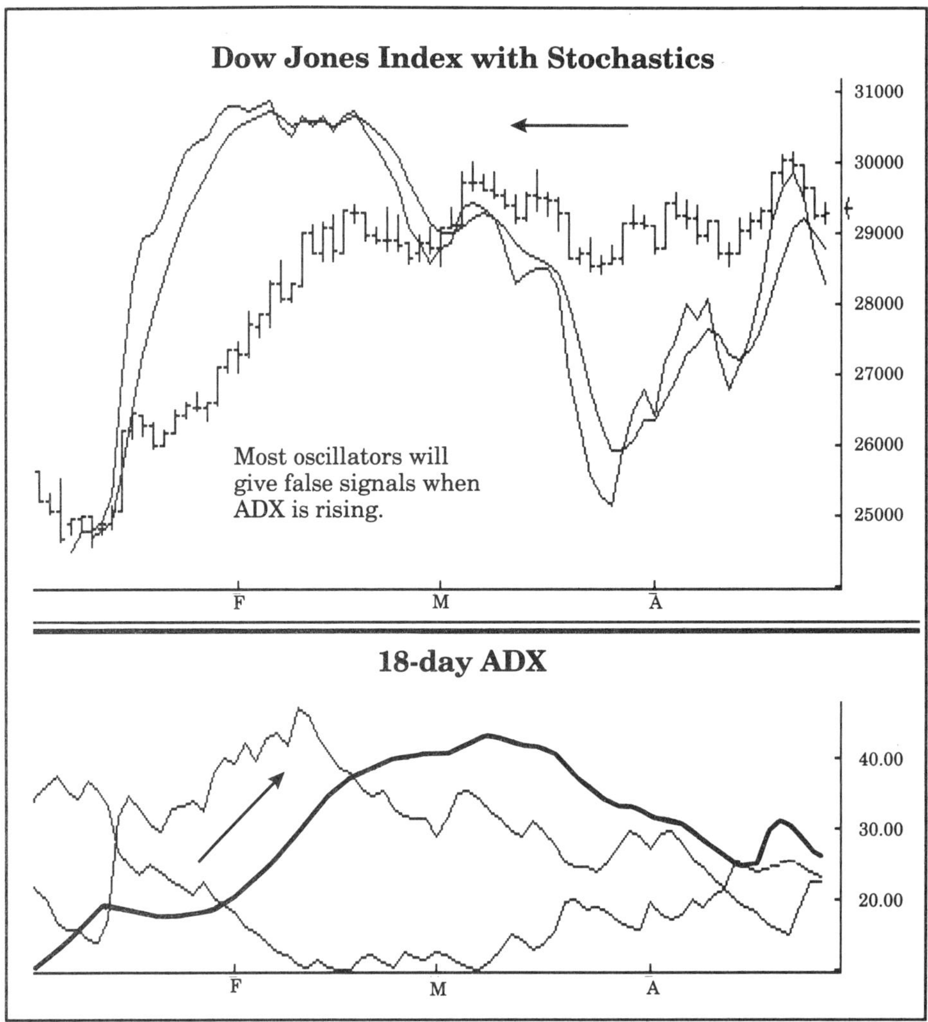

ple, a popular trading technique is to employ overbought/oversold oscillators, such as RSI or stochastics, and to look for sell signals when a market is trading at an overbought level. However, if the ADX is rising strongly, it would serve warning that a strong uptrend was underway and that sell signals on oscillators should be ignored. When the ADX is rising, overbought/oversold indicators tend to get to one extreme or another and stay there, giving repeated signals to trade against the trend. If the oscillator signals were to be followed, the losses could become very substantial. The fact that the ADX is rising doesn't necessarily mean that we can't use our favorite oscillators. It simply means that we want to take only the signals going in the direction of the trend. (See Exhibits 2–5 and 2–6.)

Falling ADX. A falling ADX indicates a trendless market, where countertrend strategies should be used instead of trend-following methods. Overbought and oversold oscillators that buy on dips and sell on rallies are the preferred strategies while the market is in this trading-range environment. Indicators like stochastics and RSI should

EXHIBIT 2–6

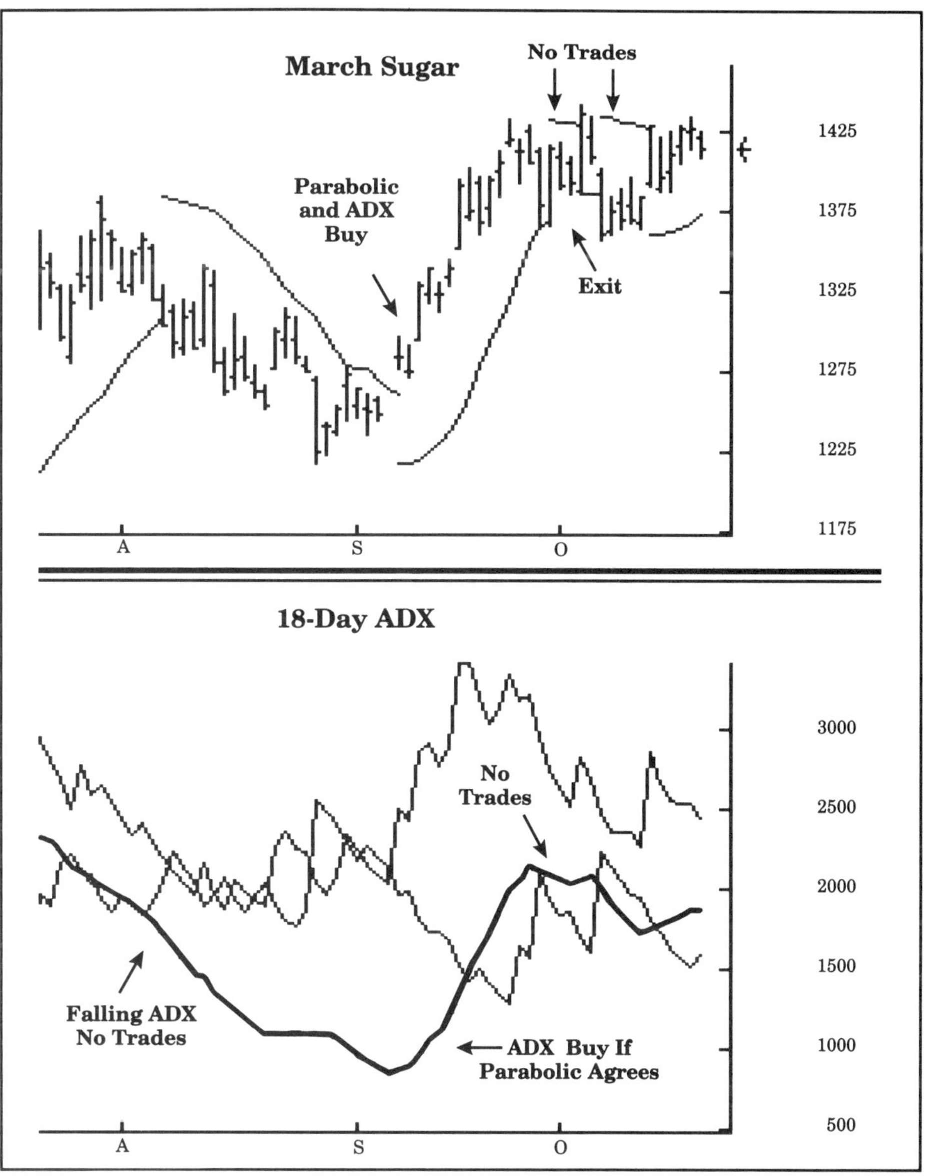
March Sugar
No Trades
Parabolic
and ADX
Buy
Exit
1425
1375
1325
1275
1225
1175
A
S
O
18-Day ADX
No
Trades
Falling ADX
No Trades
ADX Buy If
Parabolic Agrees
3000
2500
2000
1500
1000
500
A
S
O

EXHIBIT 2–7

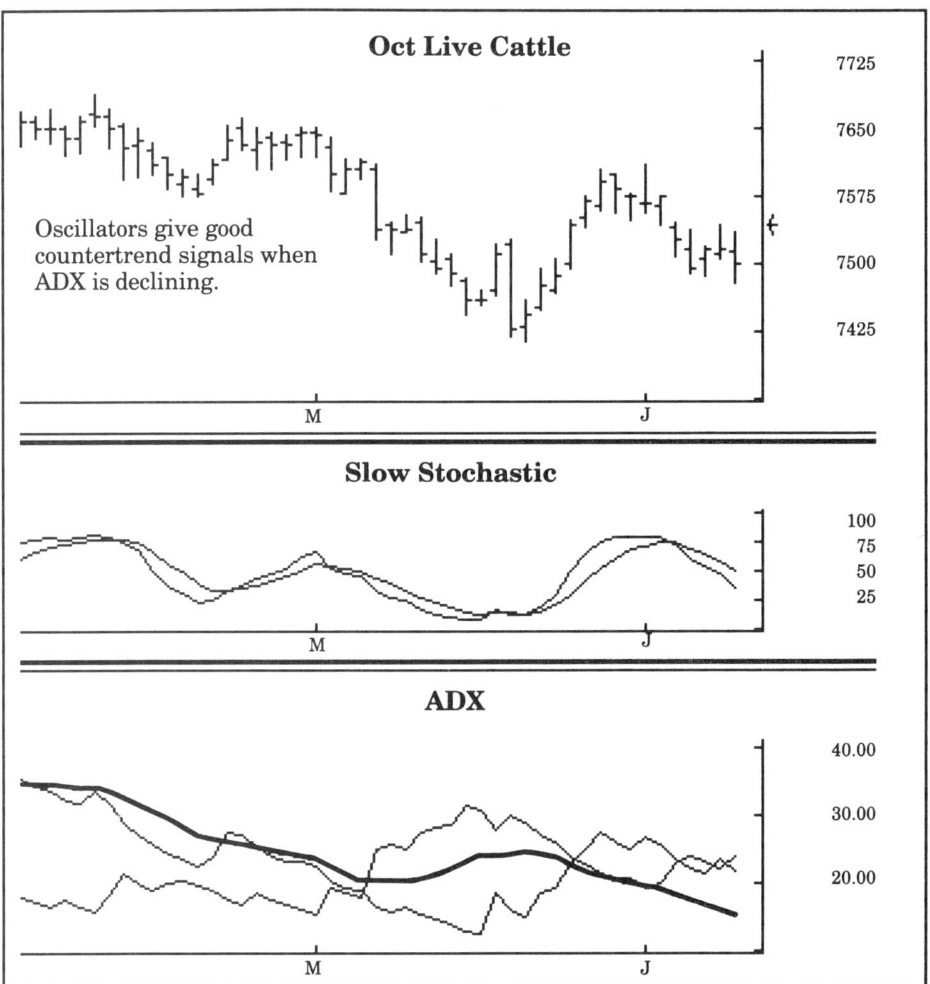

give valid signals as the market trades back and forth within the boundaries of its trading range.

Because buying dips and selling rallies in a trading range will produce only modest profits at best, many traders prefer to trade only in the direction of major trends. In that case, it would be best to simply not implement any of the trend-following signals when the ADX is declining. Of course, the ideal plan would be to have a profitable countertrend strategy in addition to a trend-following strategy and to implement whichever method is called for by the direction of the ADX. (See Exhibit 2–7.)

Problems with ADX: The Spike. We would be doing a disservice if we implied that the ADX would solve all of the problems that a trader might encounter. The ADX has its share of shortcomings. One of the problems we have observed is the longer-term time periods (we prefer 18 days, as we mentioned earlier) that work best in most markets will have a problem adjusting to a sudden change in direction taking the form of a spike. Spikes normally occur at market tops, when the prices suddenly go from a strong uptrend directly into a strong downtrend. The source of

EXHIBIT 2–8

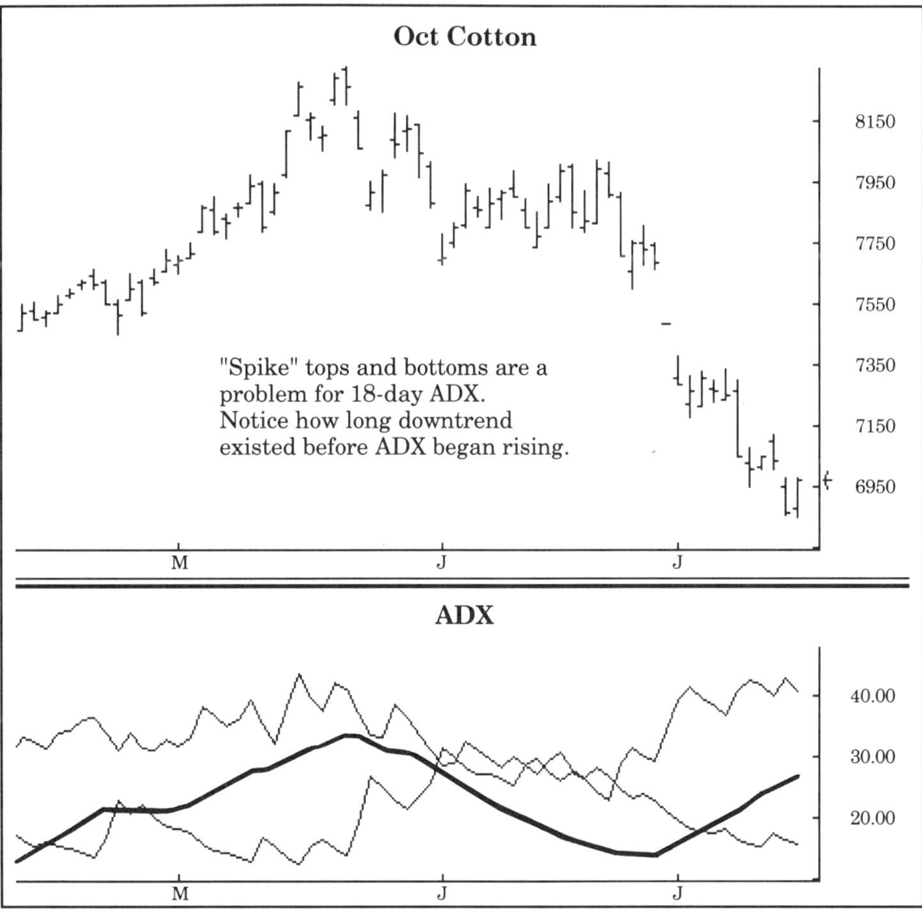

the problem with the ADX is the new downtrend which the ADX will fail to recognize promptly. The ADX will still be including the historical period of strong positive directional movement in its calculations, while inputting the new period of strong negative directional movement. As a result of the conflicting input, the ADX will begin to decline for a time until the old positive directional movement drops out of the data and the ADX begins to rise again because of the new downtrend. In a market that has made a spike top, the ADX may not indicate a trending market in sufficient time to catch much of the rapid downward move. (See Exhibit 2–8.)

We are in the process of trying to find a solution to this problem. One possibility might be to switch to a shorter period ADX when a market is at a level where a spike top might be expected. We have observed that some markets tend to make spike tops routinely (metals and grains, for example), while others tend to make broad-basing tops (bonds and stocks). The ADX copes with the broad tops very nicely without the problem associated with spike tops. We would prefer to avoid any subjective categorization of markets if at all possible, so we are continuing our research into more objective solutions. Fortunately, market bottoms are rarely spikes, so the ADX does a very timely job of identifying uptrends as they develop.

Problems with ADX: The Lag. A characteristic of ADX that might appear to be a problem is that it tends to be a bit slower than many technical studies. When the ADX begins to rise, many trend-following indicators would have already given a signal to enter. For example, the +DI and the −DI will cross before the ADX begins to rise. More than likely, at the time of this early entry signal, the ADX was declining, so the entry should have been ignored. In practice, what happens in this situation is that the rise in the ADX becomes the timing signal to enter the market in the direction of the trend. The faster technical study winds up being used only for direction and the ADX is used for the entry timing. Once the trend is underway, the faster indicator may well give additional entry signals which, if the ADX continues to rise, should be followed. You will find that it takes some thought and planning to coordinate the ADX with other technical tools.

We view the lag as a small price to pay to avoid the costly whipsaws that might occur if trades were entered while the ADX was declining. However, the amount of delay can be adjusted to suit individual markets and personal preferences. A few markets seem more likely to trend than others. For example, the currency markets have trended well over recent years. In markets that have shown good trending characteristics, the time period of the ADX can be shortened to provide faster signals. If being late on entries bothers you, shorten the period of the ADX. If whipsaws bother you, keep the time period near the 18-day range.

Delay does not seem to be a problem when using countertrend methods while the ADX is declining.

Day Trading with ADX. Perhaps because of the distortions caused by large gaps between yesterday's close and today's opening prices, the ADX does not perform as well when applied to chart periods of less than a day. By using five-minute charts and a 12-period ADX, the gaps from opening to close can be eliminated after an hour of trading, and the ADX will give its usual indications about the strength of the trend during the first hour. However, many day traders prefer to use 30-minute or 15-minute charts, in which case the possible distortions of the DMI and ADX caused by close to opening gaps is hard to avoid.

Most of the time, the standard 18-day ADX can provide valuable longer-term information that will assist in day trading. The day trader should respect the existence of any trends indicated by a rising ADX and enter short-term trades only when they are in the same direction as the trend. When the ADX is falling, short-term trades can be taken in either direction. Almost any day-trading method can be improved by first consulting the ADX to determine if there is a trend. (See Exhibit 2–9.)

In summary, we have found the ADX to be one of the most useful of all technical studies. When we are trading in our managed programs, the ADX is usually the first indicator we consider before proceeding with further analysis. We have found that the measure of trendiness discerned from the ADX is an invaluable guide in selecting the best strategy for each market. The simple but critical information provided by the ADX allows us to increase our percentage of winning trades by a considerable margin. Our many tests of the results of following trends

EXHIBIT 2–9

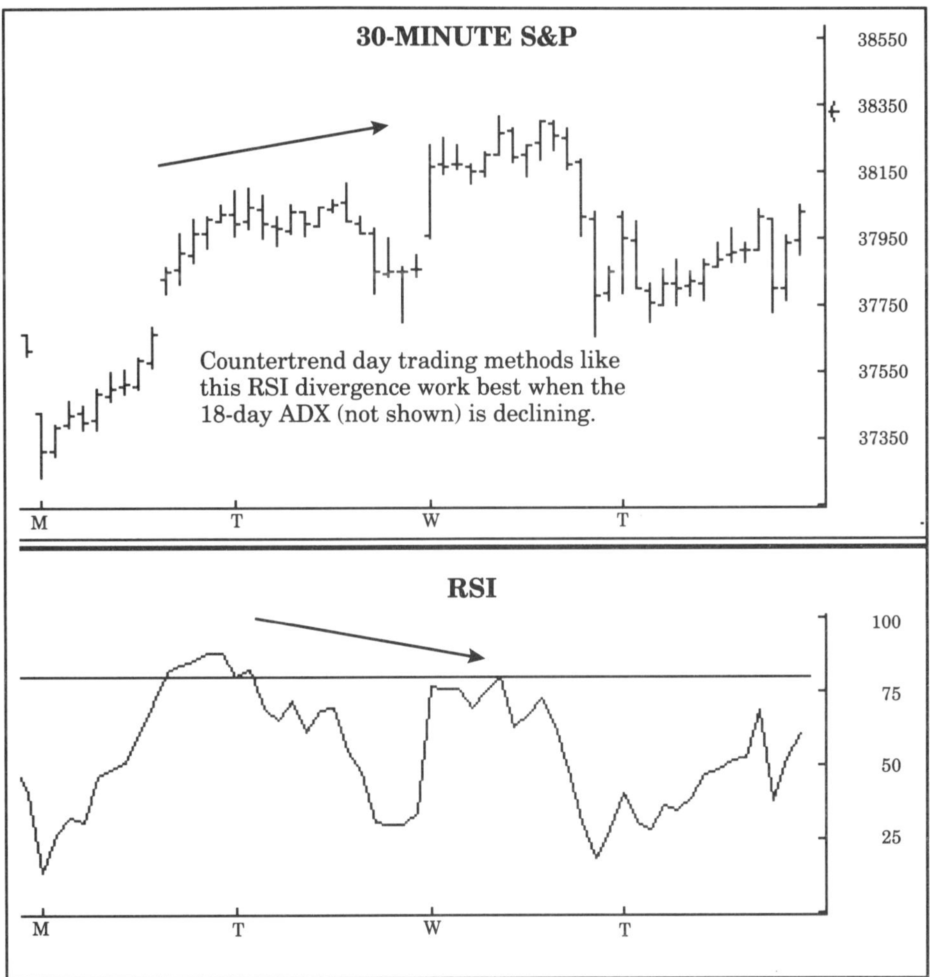

only when the ADX is rising have conclusively demonstrated its value in this regard. Waiting for a rising ADX often means being later than we would like on entering; but the level of confidence in the ultimate success of the trade, plus the obvious benefits of decreasing the number of losing trades, is more than ample reward.

In addition to its usefulness on entries, the ADX can be extremely helpful in determining exits on trades. A significant pattern pointed out by Wilder is the potential short-term top or bottom signaled by an interaction of the +DI, −DI, and ADX lines. A market turning point often occurs with the first downturn of the ADX line after the ADX has crossed above both the +DI and −DI lines. We agree with Wilder's conclusion that this downturn can be a good time to take trend-following profits, or at least to close out the majority of contracts that are part of a profitable multiple-contract position. (See Exhibit 2–10.)

The ADX can be very useful for exiting in another way. When the ADX is declining, it indicates that small profits should be taken, rather than attempting to let profits run. When the ADX is rising, it indicates that larger profits are possible and that we should avoid exiting prematurely. Having an accurate indication of when to take small profits

EXHIBIT 2–10

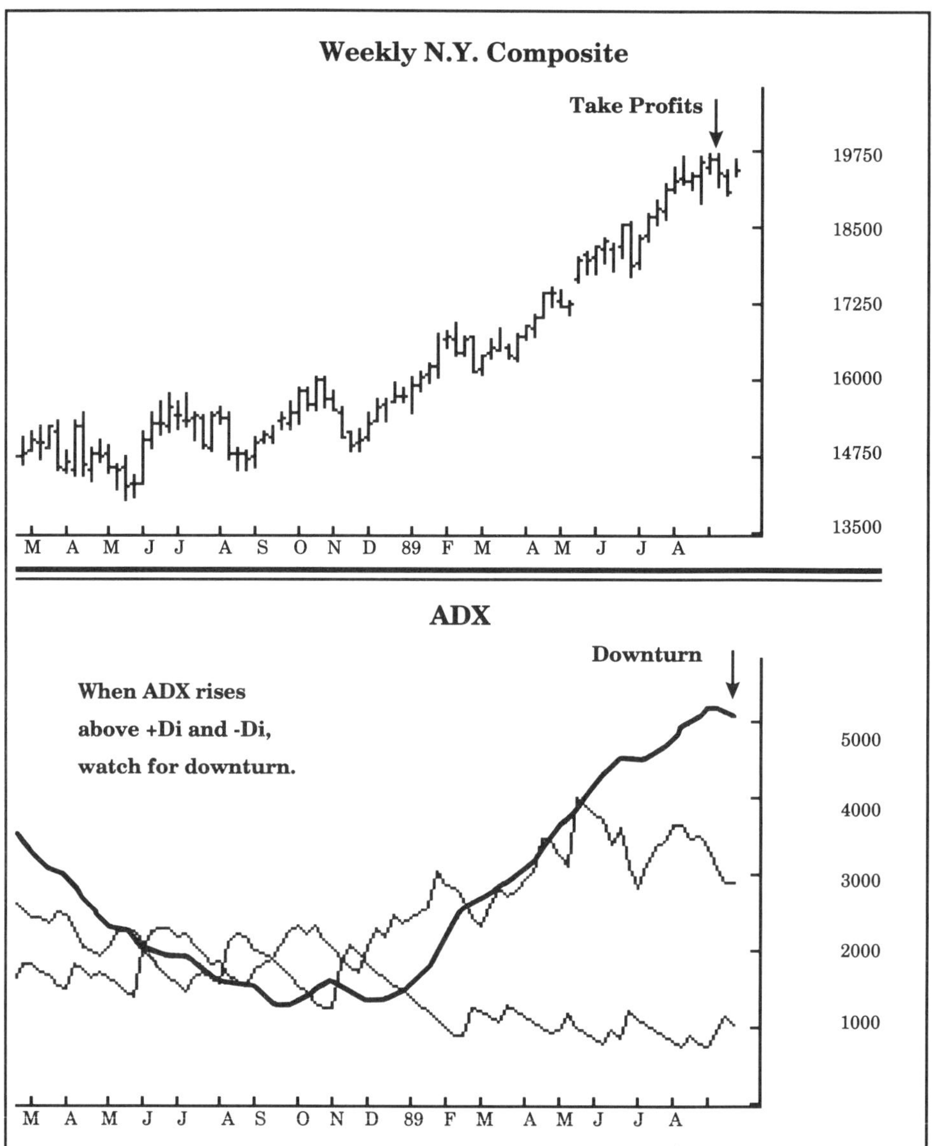

and when to wait for bigger gains can be a tremendous advantage to any trader. This seldom discussed application of ADX might be just as important as its use in selecting entry techniques.

Bands, Envelopes, and Channels

Trading with an envelope formed by bands around a moving average (or around some similar indicator) is a well-known and effective method of smoothing out the short-term whipsaws common to most trend-following systems. Most technical traders have used them at one time or another. Essentially all present-day software packages provide the ability to display various forms of envelopes surrounding a moving average.

A variety of interesting channels and envelopes can be used as the foundation of a profitable trading system. We will organize our discussion into two sections. The first section will deal with envelopes that are formed by placing bands around a moving average. The second section will deal with channel breakout systems.

Section One: Trading with Envelopes

Envelopes can be as simple or as sophisticated as you want to make them. The simplest is a single moving average, with a band on either side calculated as a percentage of the moving average value for the current interval. For example, a 10-day moving average, with a band 5 percent away from the average. The area within the two bands theoretically acts as a buffer zone that will tend to contain prices, especially when the underlying market is in a trading range. The beginnings of a trend will normally be indicated when prices break outside of the bands. Trend corrections or the end of the trend will see prices move back inside the bands toward the moving average. (See Exhibit 2–11.)

Another simple type of envelope is one that uses an absolute point value on either side of a moving average. For example, a 10-day moving average in U.S. T-bonds might be surrounded by bands that represent 1 and $^{16}/_{32}$ points, or $1,500. Normally this fixed dollar envelope will be used for placing stops to control risk, rather than as a method to enter new trades.

EXHIBIT 2–11

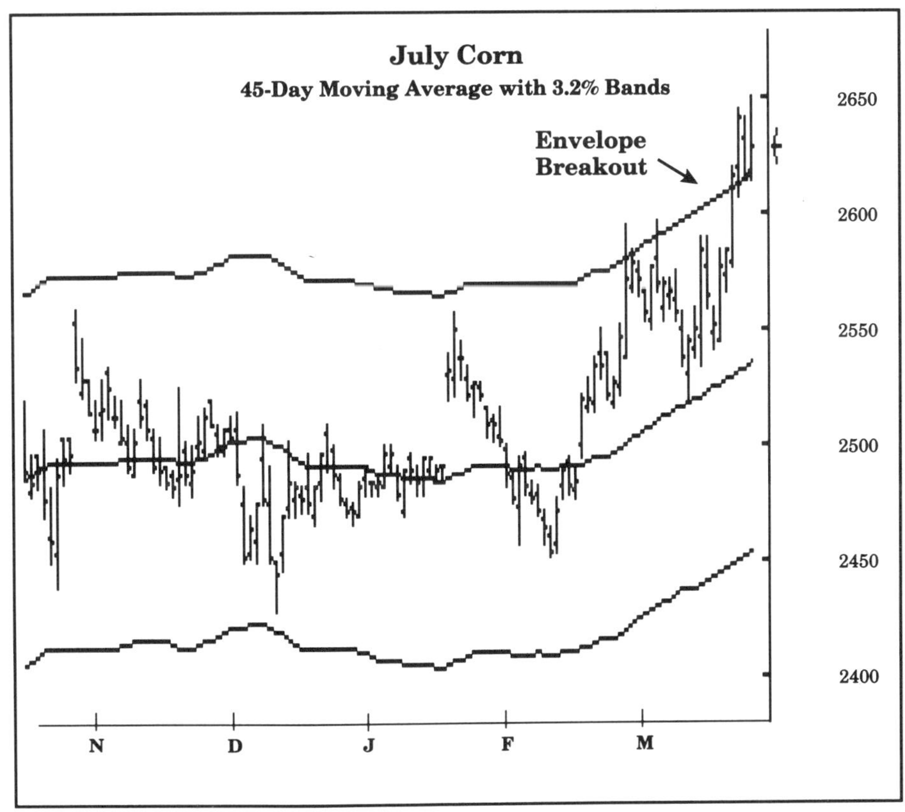

The variations of the two types of envelopes described above are almost infinite. For example, the moving average can be exponentially or otherwise smoothed. The percentage of prices that will be contained by the bands can be varied for the long side versus the short side, biasing the study in favor of increased volatility in the direction of a trend. For example, in a rising market the band could be placed 5 percent above the moving average and 10 percent below it. Another possibility is using a moving average of highs or lows as the bands on either side of the moving average of closes. Bands are intended to contain and define the price action within a trading range. Any breakout beyond either of the bands should signal the beginning of a trend, because the prices are no longer wandering within the envelope.

Bollinger Bands

A fairly recent and popular addition to the ranks of channel studies are alpha-beta bands, now more often called Bollinger bands (after John Bollinger, market analyst for CNBC/Financial News Network). Alpha-beta bands and Bollinger bands are statistically defined bands around a short-term moving average. The computer software first calculates a simple moving average and then calculates a moving standard deviation from the average. (See Exhibit 2–12.)

Bollinger generally uses a band having two standard deviations on either side of the moving average. He explains that two standard deviations will theoretically contain the vast majority of subsequent data. He also points out that the standard deviation calculation involves the

EXHIBIT 2–12

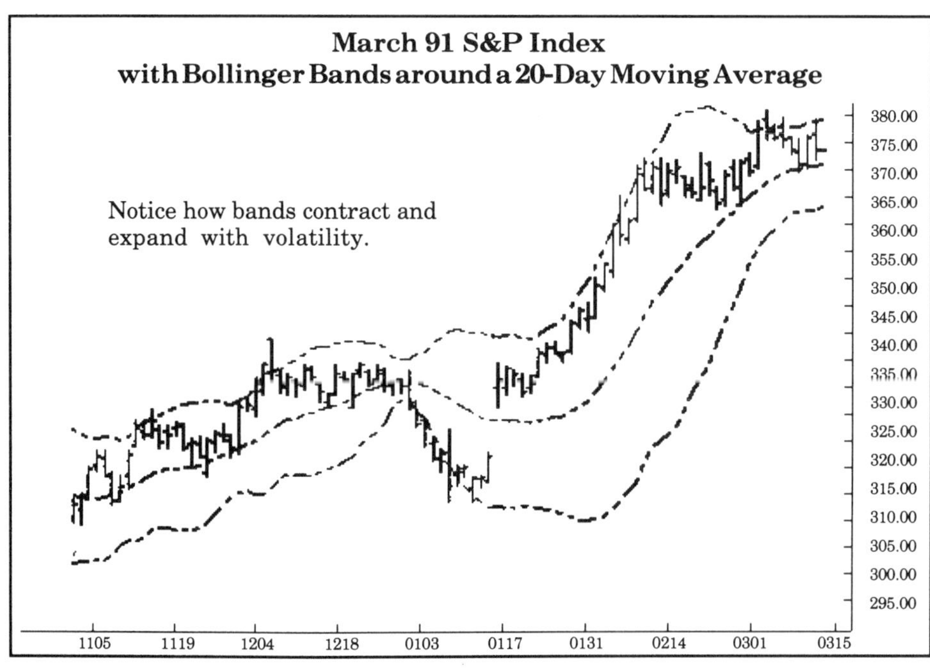

Source: Courtesy of the Knight-Ridder Trade Center.

squaring of the deviations from the average price, making the calculation very responsive to short-term price changes. The bands rapidly expand and contract with market volatility, making them sensitive to recent market action. The recommended setting is 20 days, with a two standard deviation envelope. Both values often vary, depending on the market being studied and the way in which the bands are being used.

Bollinger bands are normally used with other technical studies to detect trend reversals in the stock market. If prices are close to the lower band, and another study confirms the reversal, it should be safe to buy. For example, an RSI divergence might be used to confirm a bottom in the lower portion of the envelope. (See Exhibit 2–13.)

EXHIBIT 2–13

Source: Courtesy of Knight-Ridder Trade Center.

Instead of being two standard deviations away from the moving average, which is probably only suitable for stock trading, the alpha-beta bands can be set at any increment of standard deviations from the moving average. The usual futures market setting for the alpha-beta bands is only one standard deviation on either side of the moving average. The basic concept behind the statistically derived envelope widths is that the current volatility of the particular market being studied is what determines the placement of the bands. Using these self-adjusting bands means that volatile markets will automatically have wide envelopes and less-volatile markets will have narrower envelopes.

One caveat about statistically derived bands: sampling theory states that 30 data points are the minimum necessary to derive a statistically significant result. Bollinger bands normally use 20 or less days. The bands may be said to contain some portion of the subsequent data, but don't infer that any of the normal statistical assumptions apply. Bollinger firmly cautions against making any statistical assumptions beyond the simple observation that the bands will usually contain most of the recent price action.

Envelope Trading Rules

There are almost as many possible trading rules for envelopes as there are rules for constructing them. The rules are (or should be) based on the idea that the envelope contains a significant amount of the price movement of a market, and that a move to or beyond one of the bands is aberrant price behavior and should be acted upon.

EXHIBIT 2–14

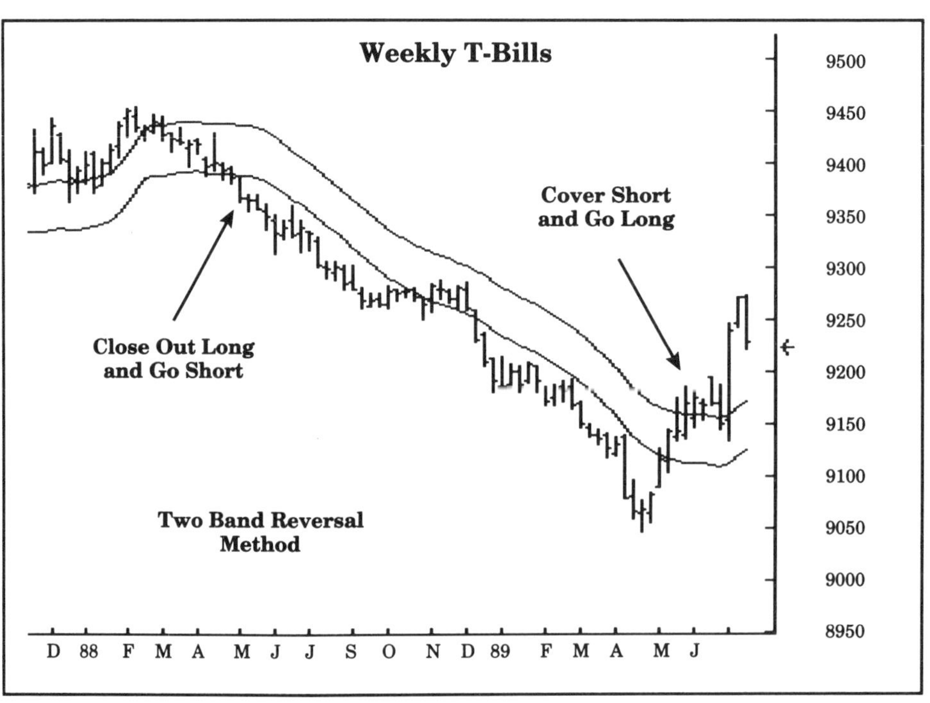

Here are the traditional trading rules for envelopes:

1. Enter the market in the direction of the breakout when a band is penetrated. This signals that a trend may be beginning.
2. Exit and reverse the position when the opposite band is penetrated. (See Exhibit 2–14.)

We suggest using penetrations based only on closes outside the bands to avoid some of the whipsaws. The prices will often poke through the bands during the day, only to close back inside.

Or, alternatively :

1. Enter the market when a band is penetrated the same as above.
2. Exit the market when the moving average between the bands is reached but do not reverse. (See Exhibit 2–15.)

Both sets of rules ensure that a major trend will not be missed. The first set of rules is basic and results in a pure reversal system. We have an inherent skepticism about reversal systems and prefer the second set of trading rules. In the second set, the bands are also used for entry, but the moving average is used for exit. If prices are within the bands after a trade is closed out, the market is in a neutral zone and there will be no new trades until there is a new breakout. Another reason we prefer the second set of rules is because the theoretical risk on any one trade is reduced to the distance between the band and the moving average, instead of the total distance from band to band.

EXHIBIT 2–15

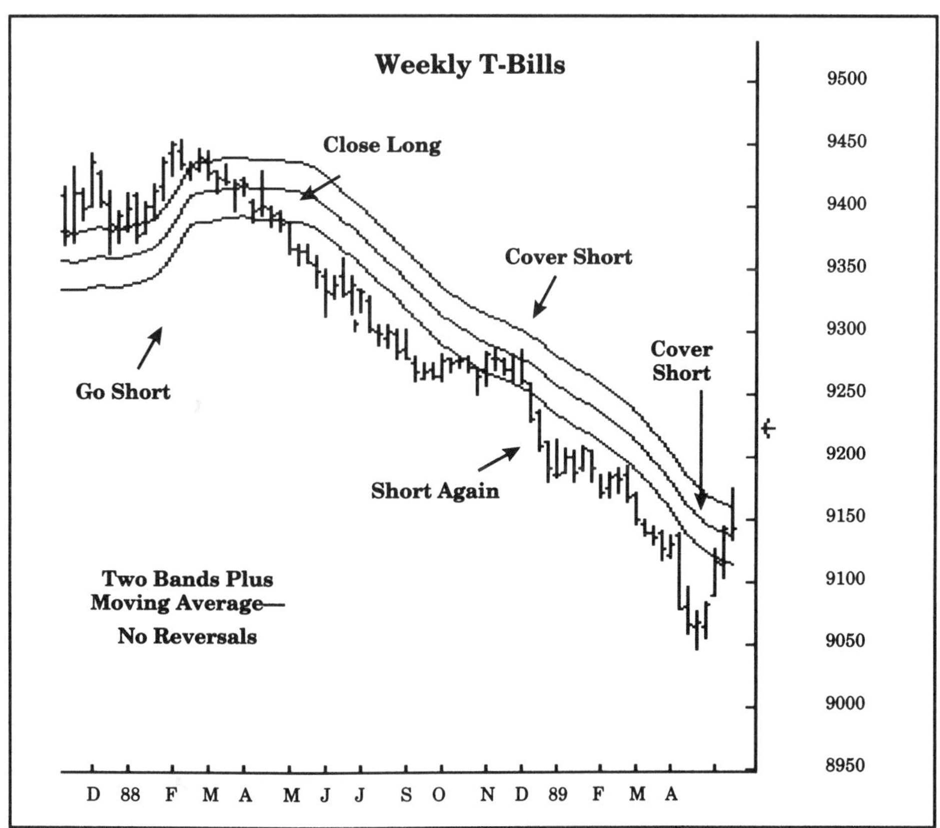

"Optimum" Percentage for the Bands

The "correct" values for the moving average and the surrounding envelope are elusive. The most extensive testing we've seen covers the period from 1960 to 1978. It appears in an article by Irwin and Uhrig in the December 1983 issue of *Review of Research in Futures Markets* (see "Suggested Readings"). The authors used a breakout of the bands for entries and exited when the moving average in the middle of the envelope was crossed. (They used the second set of rules mentioned above.) They then optimized for the best combinations. Here are the numbers they found to be most profitable:

Commodity	Moving Average	Percent Band
Corn	45 days	3.2 %
Soybeans	20	4.0
Wheat	39	4.2
Sugar	36	4.8
Copper	39	1.0
Cocoa	43	6.2
Live cattle	15	1.8
Live hogs	10	2.1

Even a casual look at today's markets shows that these values are no longer optimal, and they only serve to illustrate the futility of optimization (some important caveats about optimizing are discussed in the system testing section of this book, Chapter 3). Similar to moving averages, envelopes work well in trending markets and not so well in choppy markets, and the "best" envelope will change over time. Frequent optimizing to find the correct values is useless. We recommend that you trade in the direction of the trend when outside the envelope and use countertrend methods within the envelope.

Trading within the Envelope

A logical and effective technique we rarely see discussed involves the use of the bands as overbought/oversold indicators, so the trading takes place within the bands, instead of outside. We have used this method with great success when a market is in a trading range. The trading rules are relatively obvious and simple. Buy just as the price touches the lower band. If the trade goes against you, as indicated by a close below the lower band, exit quickly and take the small loss. If the trade moves immediately in your favor, as it often will, hold onto the profitable position and reverse the trade at the upper band, applying the same rules in reverse. This method seems to work, because it combines the discipline of taking small losses and big profits with the trading strategy of buying dips and selling rallies. The real secret is to make sure you are in a trading range.

How do you know when the market is in a trading range and when it's trending? An objective method is to use the ADX as we describe in the section on DMI/ADX. If the ADX is falling, trading within the envelope can be very rewarding. If the ADX is rising, the market is trending and you're better off using the trend-following envelope method. (See Exhibit 2–16.)

Section Two: Trading Channel Breakouts

In addition to envelopes that are defined by distance from a moving average, there are channels defined by high and low points over a specified time period. The simplest of these channel methods is a pure reversal system, which is always in the market. An upper band is formed by the high of the past 10 days, for example. A lower band is formed by the low of the same number of days, with the two bands forming a channel. The channel will change in width as old highs or lows are dropped and as new highs or lows are made. The system is long when the highest price is penetrated, and it stays long until the lowest price is penetrated. Since this is a reversal system, when the long is closed out a short position is assumed.

Many tests have been conducted showing that channels are one of the most effective trading tools available. Perhaps the most well-known

EXHIBIT 2–16

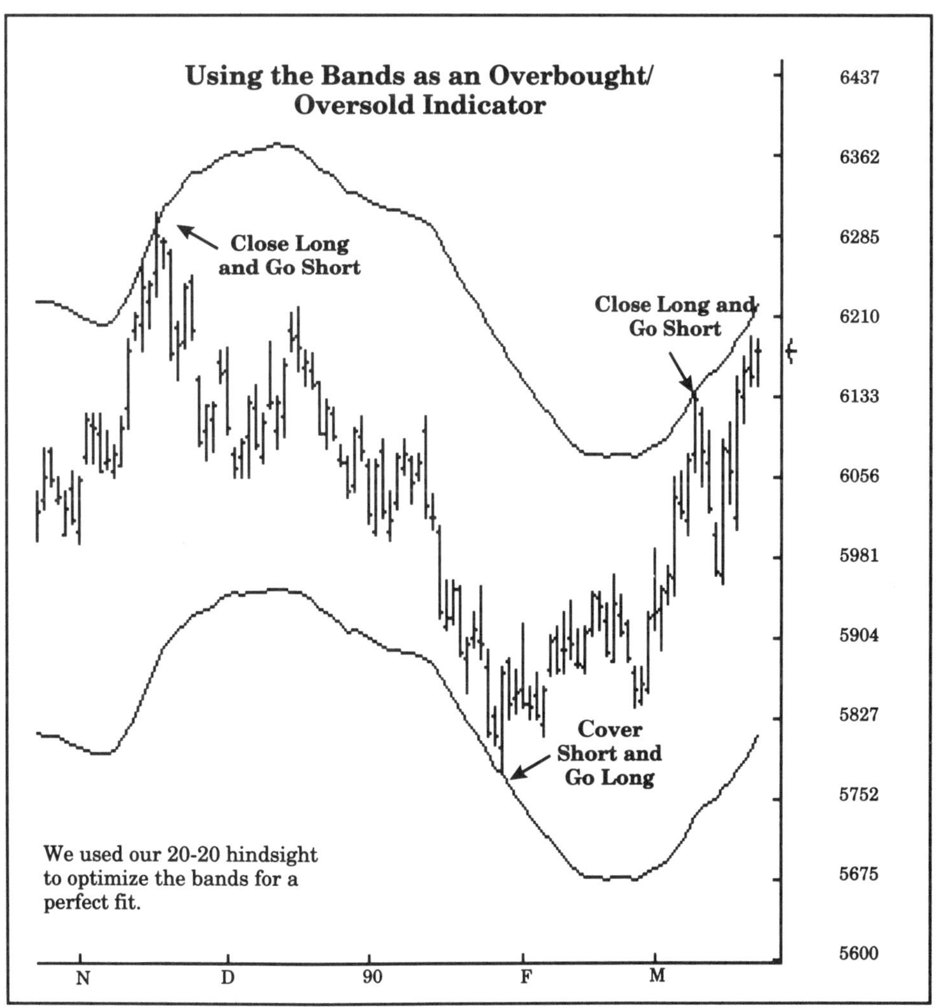

of these was a channel breakout study done by Frank Hochheimer of Merrill Lynch about 10 years ago. In addition to Hochheimer, many other respected traders have observed the merits of channel trading. For example, although best known for his work with moving averages, Richard Donchian is also known for his channel trading, using his four-week rule. (See Exhibit 2–17.)

This system was popularized by Donchian in the 1960s as the *Weekly Rule*. He used a four-week time frame, buying when prices exceeded the four-week high and selling when prices dropped below the four-week low. Testing shows the system to be reasonably profitable over time, although the extremely large drawdowns can be very breathtaking. As you might imagine, the risk at any given time can be almost unlimited, depending on the size of the four-week range. Because the system does not employ risk-control stops, in a diversified account the total portfolio risk would be tremendous. (See Exhibit 2–18.)

A very popular and expensive system marketed in the 80s, was basically the same as Donchian's or Hochheimer's method, except that the time frames were periodically reoptimized for each commodity. After many years of very profitable trading, the drawdowns in 1988 were so severe that many users of the formula were forced to stop trading it. In fairness to the system, 1988 was a disaster for many trend-following methods.

EXHIBIT 2–17

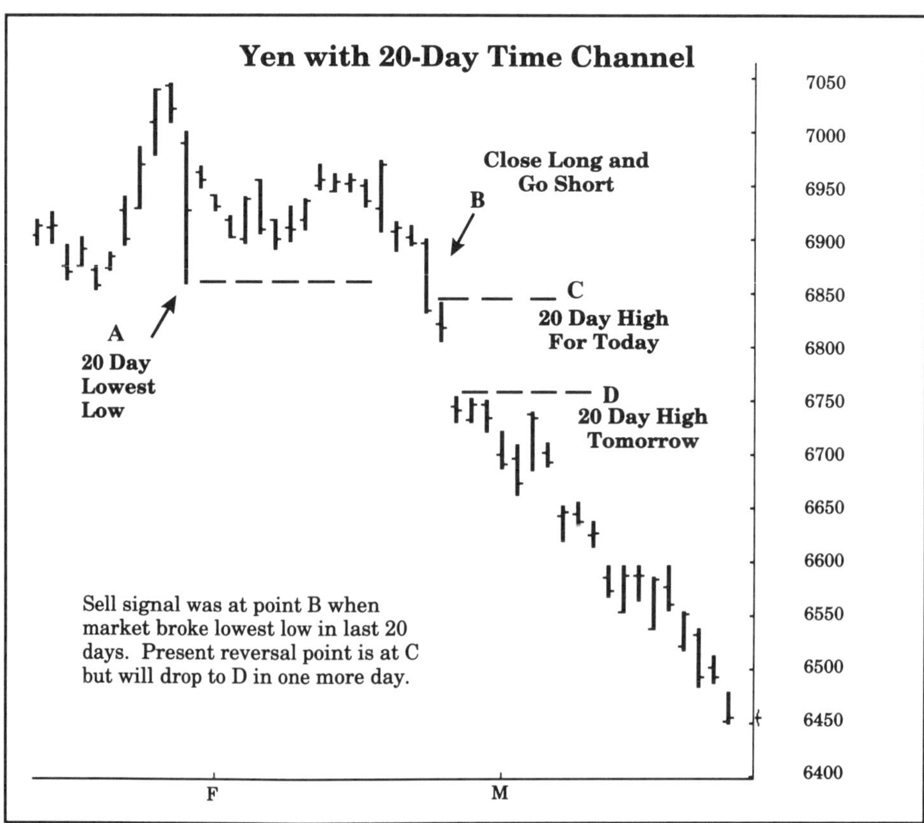

EXHIBIT 2–18

Sample Results of 4 Week (20 Day) Channel Breakout System
Jan 86 through Dec 90

	Soybeans	D.Marks	Gold	Bonds	Cr. Oil
Net Profit*	(850)	17,737	6,040	13,062	47,970
Maximum Drawdown**	(7,325)	(7,212)	(7,490)	(12,062)	(9,040)

*No Deductions For Slippage or Commissions.
**Largest Drawdown on Total Portfolio was $24,050.

Selecting the Time Values

What is the optimum number of days to use in constructing a channel breakout system? Hochheimer's Merrill Lynch study produced the following optimized number of days for a channel breakout system:

Commodity	Number of Days	Commodity	Number of Days
Cocoa	18	Soybean meal	57
Corn	38	Wheat	22
Sugar	40	Pork bellies	38
Cotton	70	Soybean oil	42
Silver	4	Plywood	48
Copper	29	Hogs	8
Soybeans	51	Cattle	13

As you might expect with an optimized study, these channels proved extremely profitable over the six-year period of the test (1970–76). However, even with the benefit of optimization, only 42 percent of the trades were profitable. It should also be noted that the drawdowns were very substantial and that the four-day channel in silver produced 1,866 trades (more than one trade per business day).

It is easily possible to create a channel breakout system with values optimized for each market, but in our experience these systems break down fairly quickly. As Bruce Babcock has shown in his test of Donchian's method, a single number can work and be profitable for a diversified portfolio (see Babcock's *The Dow Jones-Irwin Guide to Trading Systems)*. In fact, the system's profits were excellent if the S&P 500 were excluded.

William Gallacher, in his wonderfully witty book, *Winner Takes All: A Privateer's Guide to Commodity Trading,* tested a 10-day breakout system on 10 different commodities over a period of 130 weeks. The results showed that this simple 10-day channel produced profits at a respectable rate of 24 percent annually. (By the way, we don't know if Gallacher's book is still in print, but if you ever see it, buy it. It's one of our all-time favorites.)

Lukac, Brorsen, and Irwin tested 12 different trading strategies across 12 actively traded markets for the period from 1975 through 1984. Three of the trading systems they tested were channel systems. The basic channel system they tested produced profits every year and had the highest net return (33.4 percent annually) of any of the systems in their study. The directional Parabolic system was a close second, and one of the modified channel systems was third. It is interesting to note they published optimized time periods for the channels that were substantially different than those produced by the Hochheimer study.

Our testing and experience with channel breakouts, which is fairly extensive, shows 18 days to be a good number that works well in many commodities over long periods. Frankly, we're of the opinion that almost anything in the range of 10 to 30 days will be profitable over time. The drawdowns will be of different sizes and will occur at different times as the numbers are changed.

Reducing the Risk with a Neutral Zone

A creative way to lessen the drawdowns inherent in channel breakout systems without giving up too much of the profit potential was developed by a money manager of our acquaintance in southern California. His system used different time periods for entries and exits. The exit bands for his method were shortened to one half the time period of the entry bands. For example, if the signal to buy soybeans is a penetration of the high of the last 20 days, the inner channel and exit point would be the low of the last 10 days. This addition to the Donchian system has the advantage of drastically reducing overall portfolio risk. It also takes away the pure reversal nature of the system by creating a neutral zone in which there is no trading. This should have the effect of reducing whipsaws in choppy markets, as well as preserving more of the profits because of quicker exits.

Unfortunately for this money manager and his clients, his innovations managed to solve most of the drawdown problem but not all of it. After several years of outstanding performance, one of the large drawdowns, which are the inherent disadvantage of channel systems, took its toll and he is no longer in business.

Channel Breakouts as Confirmation

We've found in our testing that some types of trend-following entries can be considerably improved if a recent channel breakout is used as a confirmation. Contrary to popular opinion, new highs and lows are not always bad places to enter a market. After all, if gold goes from $300 to $800 it's making new highs all the way. A breakout is another way of reaffirming that the trend is a powerful one. These seem especially effective if the breakout comes as a reversal from a prior breakout in the opposite direction, not just as a new recent high or low.

Commodity Channel Index

The Commodity Channel Index was first described by Donald Lambert in the October 1980 issue of *Commodities* (now *Futures*) magazine. Despite CCI's 11-year history and its inclusion in nearly every futures-oriented software package, we know of very few traders who actually use it. We're not sure why, but we suspect part of the reason might be the scarcity of available literature on the indicator, as well as Lambert's insistence on tying CCI to cycle theories. In spite of the cycle theory references, Lambert's original article is still probably the most comprehensive explanation of how to use CCI.

Like most technical studies, CCI requires some understanding of its derivation before it can be used effectively. The mathematical and statistical concepts behind CCI are a bit difficult to understand at first glance, because the formula is more complex than that of RSI, MACD, and stochastics, which can be more or less intuitively understood. CCI's formula is partly statistical, which makes it difficult to visualize the relationships between the changing price patterns and the resulting indicator patterns.

The CCI formula creates a conveniently used number that statistically expresses how far recent prices have departed from a moving average. If prices have moved far enough, a trend is assumed to have been established, and a trading signal is generated. We tend to group technical studies into two groups: those that are best employed as countertrend indicators, such as RSI and percent R, and those that are good trend followers, such as moving averages. The CCI is a trend follower.

Reviewing Lambert's Basic Theories

The CCI formula calculates a simple moving average of average daily prices [(high + low + close) / 3], and then calculates the mean deviation. The mean deviation is the sum of the differences between each period's average price and its simple moving average. The mean deviation is then multiplied by a constant (0.015, supplied by Lambert) and divided into the difference between the simple moving average and today's average price. The result is expressed as a single number that may be either positive or negative. The trader can vary the number of periods used to calculate the simple moving average. As you might expect, shortening the time span makes the index faster and more responsive to small market movements, while lengthening the time span slows down the index and smooths out market volatility.

On a computer screen, the CCI is usually displayed as an oscillator or histogram that ranges above or below a null or zero line. Since the index measures how far prices have diverged from a moving average, the CCI allows us to measure the strength of the trend. The theory is that the higher the CCI value the stronger the trend and the more profitable a trade in the direction of the trend is likely to be. (See Exhibit 2–19.)

EXHIBIT 2–19

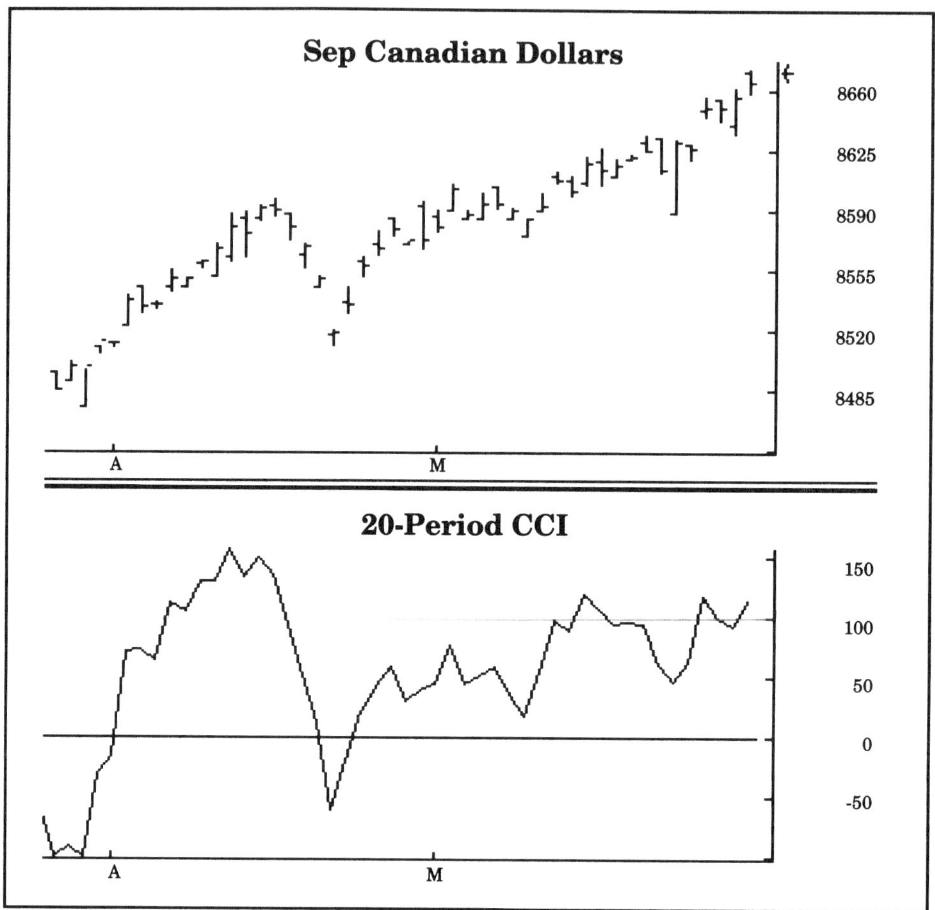

Lambert originally designed the CCI to find the beginnings and ends of assumed seasonal or cyclical commodity price patterns. He felt the necessity to have an indicator that would define where the cycles start and where they stop. This seems to be an apparent contradiction of cycle theory, because, if you know there is a cycle, you must know where it begins or ends, otherwise there is no cycle. The obvious need for an indicator like CCI indicates the assumed cycles must have been very questionable or nonrepetitive in the first place.

Lambert made the moving average portion of the formula variable, so the user could somehow fit the CCI to the assumed cycle length of the commodity under study. His research indicated that, for best results, the length of the moving average used in the CCI should be less than one third the length of the assumed cycle. However, the tables of test results in the article indicated that a moving average of five worked best, despite the cycle length (more evidence of the weakness in Lambert's cycle assumptions.)

Regardless of its reason for existence, the CCI uses a simple moving average, rather than an exponential, so the prices in the distant past would drop out and not affect the results. The somewhat arbitrary 0.015 constant used in the CCI formula was added to scale the index, so

70 percent to 80 percent of the values would fall within a channel between +100 percent and −100 percent. Lambert's original premise was that fluctuations within the boundaries of the channel are considered to be random and not worth trading. He suggested that long positions be established only when the CCI exceeds +100. A subsequent drop below +100 becomes a signal to close out the long positions. The rules on the short side are the same: sell below −100, buy back above −100. (See Exhibit 2–20.)

As we mentioned previously, Lambert did some studies that indicated that the period length of the CCI should be set at less than one third of the cycle length of the commodity under study. He tested a number of different period lengths, ending up with 20 as a standard, but suggested that this number be tailored to fit each commodity. (We don't agree that the period lengths should be adjusted to fit past data.) Twenty is the CCI default value used in most software.

EXHIBIT 2–20

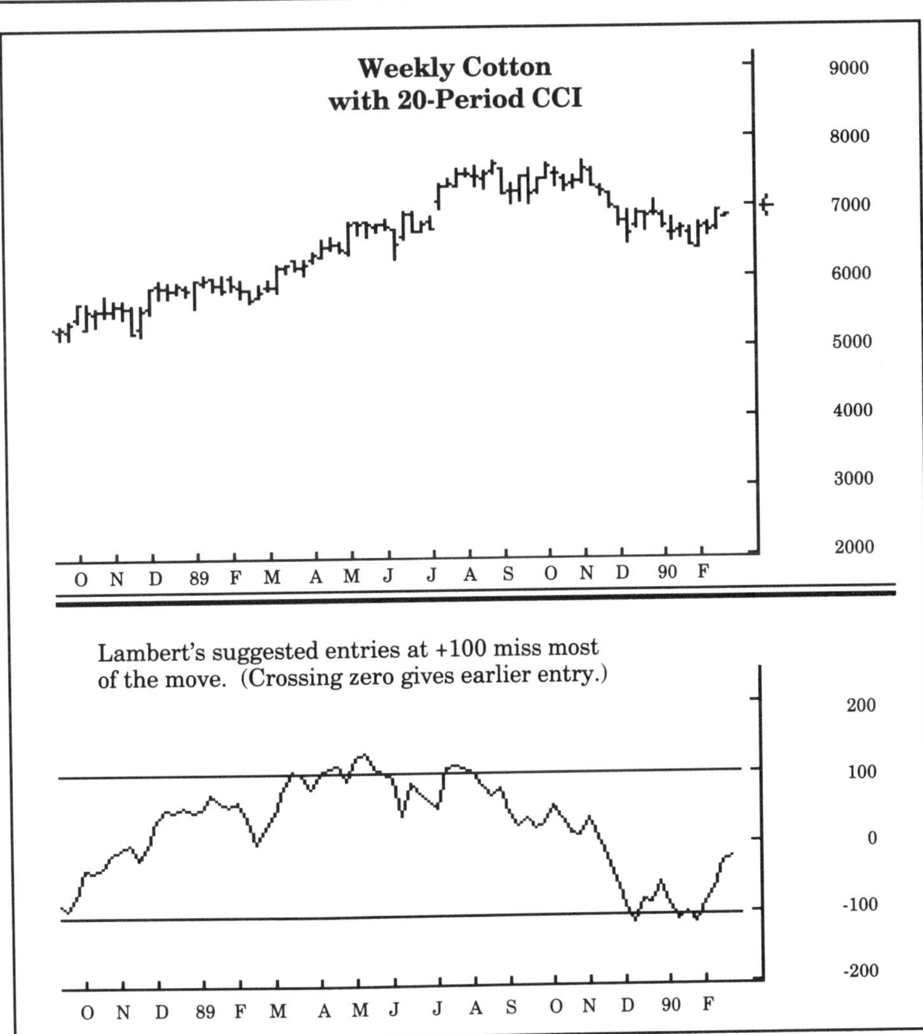

Some Positive Testing Results

Colby and Meyers, in their book, *The Encyclopedia of Technical Market Indicators,* tested the CCI against weekly New York Composite prices, using the original trading rules. They attempted to find the optimal time period, a process that strikes us as curve-fitting, but their results are interesting. The most profitable time period tested was a very lengthy 90 weeks. Anything within a range of 40 to 100 weeks was close, however, and may easily be as profitable today as the 90-week period. Our caveats about optimization can be found in chapter three.

Colby and Meyers did notice one critical aspect of the 90-week CCI that should be no surprise. The 90-period CCI almost always misses the early phases of a new trend. In today's volatile stock market, missing the early days of a trend often means missing most of the profit potential. Lambert's original studies showed the shorter-period CCI to be a leading or coincident indicator rather than a lagging indicator, but he was using time periods of 5 to 20 days. To adjust for the time lag created by the 90-week CCI, Colby and Meyers decided to ignore the +/−100 extremes and use crossings of the null or zero line to get earlier entry and exit signals. They called this indicator the "zero" CCI, and found it to be much more profitable than the original +/−100 signals. As an aside, it is worth noting that Colby and Meyers' testing of the weekly NYSE Composite using the zero CCI concept produced much better results than the popular 39- or 40-week moving average systems currently advocated by many stock market traders.

Using CCI as a Long-Term Trend Indicator

A monthly based CCI can be very effective at showing long-term market trends. Take a look at the following monthly charts, with a 20-period CCI using signals at the zero line instead of at the +/−100 mark.

The first chart (Exhibit 2–21) is Japanese yen. In addition to the consistency of the trading signals, two other points are worthy of notice on this chart. First, the faster the acceleration of the CCI from 0 to 100, the more strong and definite the ensuing trend. Second, a rapid falloff of the CCI after a run outside 100 generally means the trend is diminishing in strength and profits should be protected by the use of trailing stops at this point. On the T-bond chart (Exhibit 2–22), note the use of CCI trendlines for early exits.

We suggest trying the 20-period monthly CCI for long-term direction, while using a shorter-term indicator for timing entries and exits in the direction of the monthly trend. This strategy should be especially effective during the periods when the CCI is rapidly accelerating from 0 to 100. After the monthly CCI peaks, it might be wise to consider suspending trading this market until it begins to accelerate again.

The same phenomena that are apparent in the monthly CCI are also visible in the weekly charts. Rapid acceleration from 0 to 100 seems to mean that a trend is definitely established. Try using the weekly CCI for timing trades in the direction of the monthly charts, when the CCI is in an acceleration period. Exit when the weekly CCI peaks or when an-

EXHIBIT 2–21

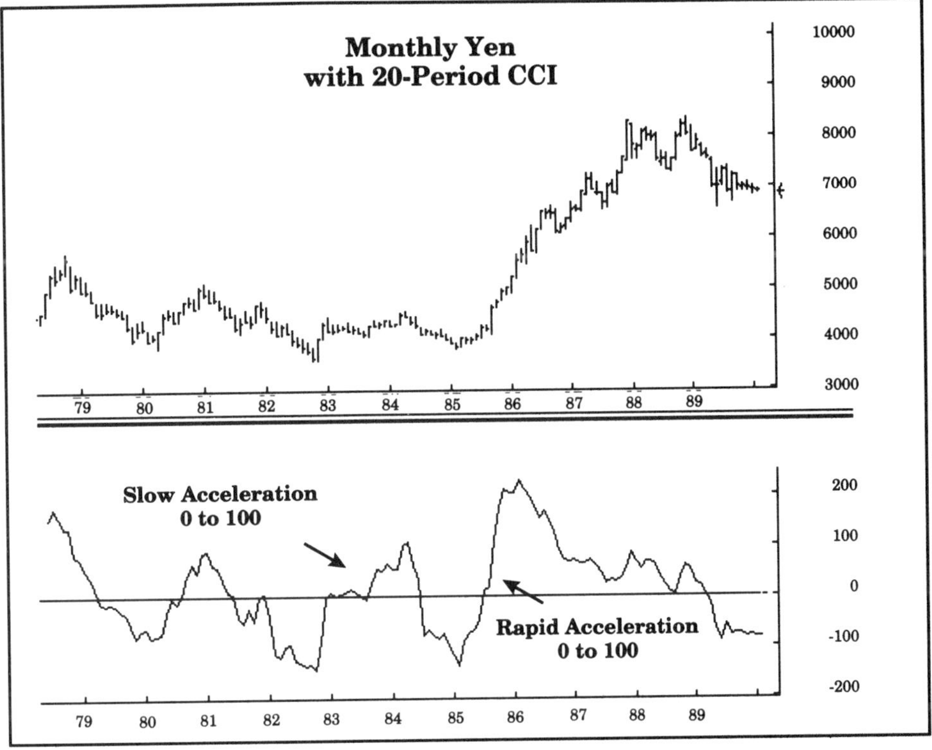

EXHIBIT 2–22

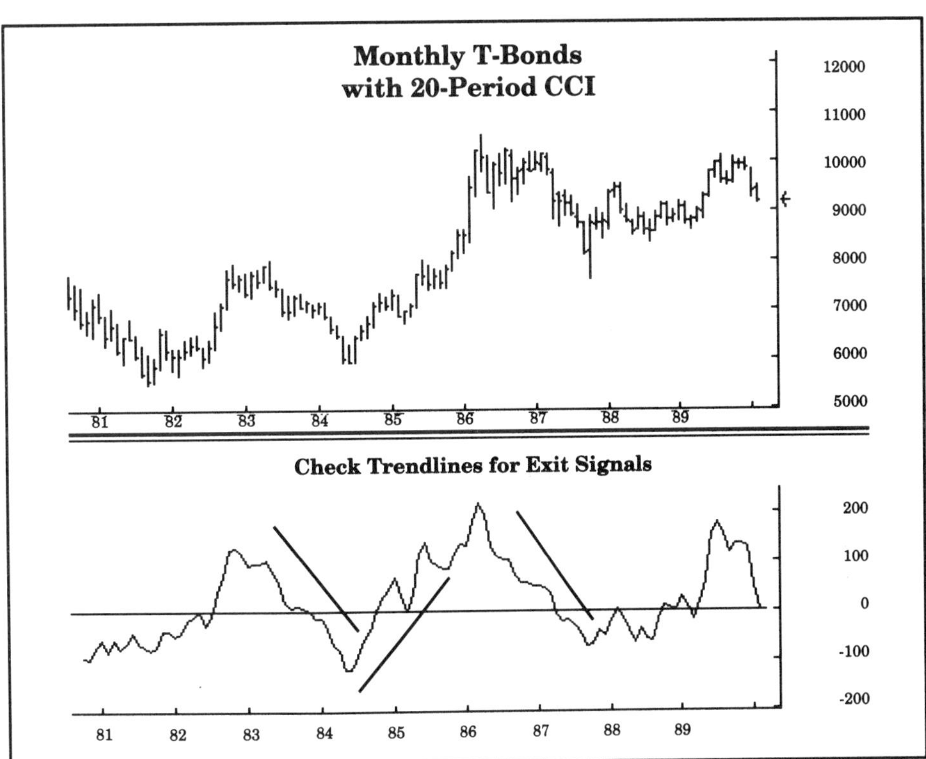

other indicator warns you the intermediate-term trend is losing strength. An alternative strategy might be to start a trade with small lots, when the zero line is first crossed, and then add positions as the CCI accelerates and the trend strengthens. Start dumping positions as the CCI stalls out and indicates the market is running out of steam.

Trading multiple positions based on weekly charts would obviously work best in the slower-moving markets, where the risk is controllable and where a large long-term position might be desirable (See the Eurodollar chart, Exhibit 2–23.)

Using the Daily CCI

Our research showed that the 20-day CCI, used by itself, did not work very well in most markets. Its main bugaboo, missing the beginnings of strong trends, can be a real negative in fast-moving volatile markets. This slowness can be overcome by using a 10-day (or even shorter) CCI or by entering at the zero line. But the faster methods become extremely vulnerable to frequent whipsaws. We could always adjust the period of the CCI to fit each market, but we feel strongly that this is simply curve-fitting and advise against it.

We recommend that, for interday trading, the CCI should be combined with another indicator. Since one of the CCI's problems is its tendency to mistake volatility for a trending market, it seems logical to

EXHIBIT 2–23

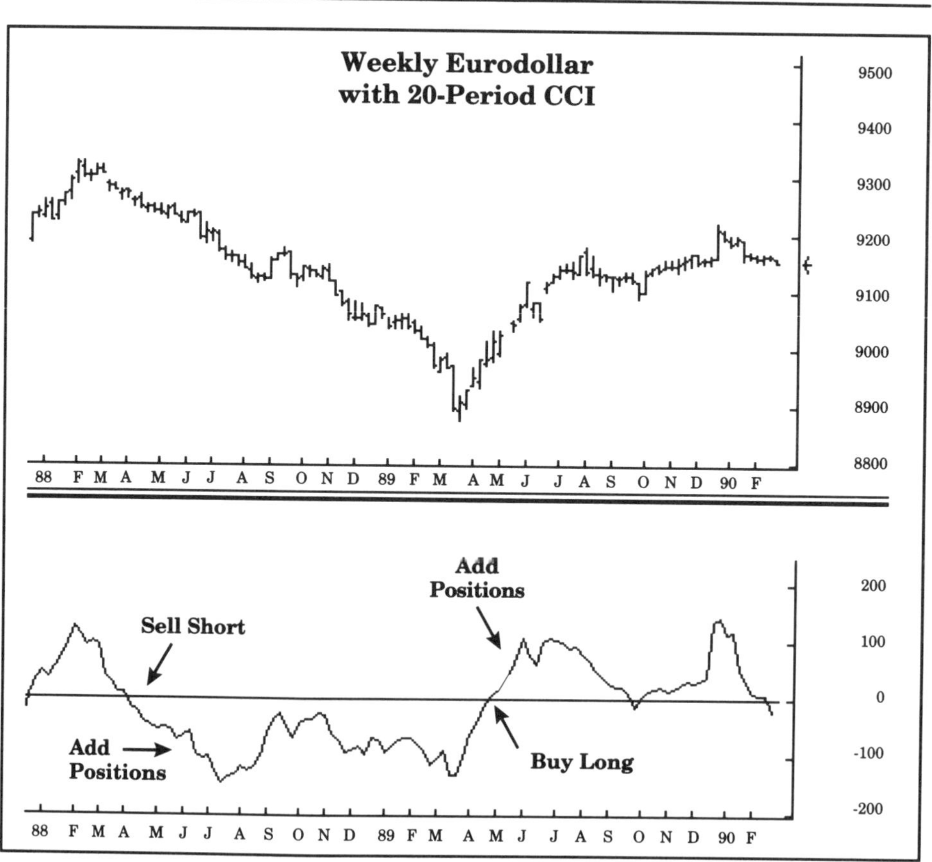

turn to the DMI/ADX as a backup trend identifier. If the ADX is rising, the market is trending and can be traded on the CCI signals. If the ADX is falling, the market is choppy and should not be traded—at least not with a trend-following indicator like the CCI. Exit after the CCI has peaked and begun to move back toward the zero line. An alternative exit strategy might be to use trailing stops at recent lows or highs after the CCI begins to correct. Our testing shows either of these basic approaches to be useful.

A Few Observations

Our research has shown us that, in a general sense, the CCI is a tool, much like ADX, that can help give a valuable measurement of the overall trendiness of a market. As we pointed out earlier, the faster the CCI is accelerating, the more strongly the market is trending. While it is perhaps mathematically possible for the CCI to move upward while the market does not, this is unlikely to happen. Keep in mind that the CCI can provide important information to a trader even when it is not giving entry signals. If a market stays inside the +/−100 range most of the time, it's demonstrating the absence of a trend, so avoid that market or use a countertrend trading strategy.

We found that often the best markets to trade are the markets where the CCI has recently spiked beyond 100 several times in the same direction. We also observed that the first move counter to an established CCI trend is usually a big loser. If a market has been trending and has shown a series of CCI moves to one side of the 100 range, as we just described, don't reverse directions on the first CCI move that breaks 100 in the opposite direction. The brief excursion to the opposite side of the range is probably an opportunity to add another position, rather than a reversal of trend.

Avoiding the Whipsaws

We also observed that our often recommended technique of waiting for confirmation after a trading signal is an excellent method of eliminating most of the whipsaws with the faster CCI periods. We found that, when the CCI spikes past the +/−100 threshold, it is almost always best to require confirmation of the signal prior to taking any action. When the CCI gets above 100, for example, wait until the market makes a subsequent higher close before buying. It has been our observation that a great many of the 100-level penetrations turned out to be only one- or two-day affairs, particularly with the shorter time periods. The confirmation entry method avoided most of the whipsaws and still caught all of the big moves. The confirmation technique also allows us to switch to the faster CCI we need to overcome the lag problem without getting whipsawed as we would expect. For example, a 10-day CCI with a confirmation requirement would give much faster signals and probably produce fewer whipsaws than a 20-day CCI employed in the conventional fashion. (See Exhibit 2–24.)

EXHIBIT 2–24

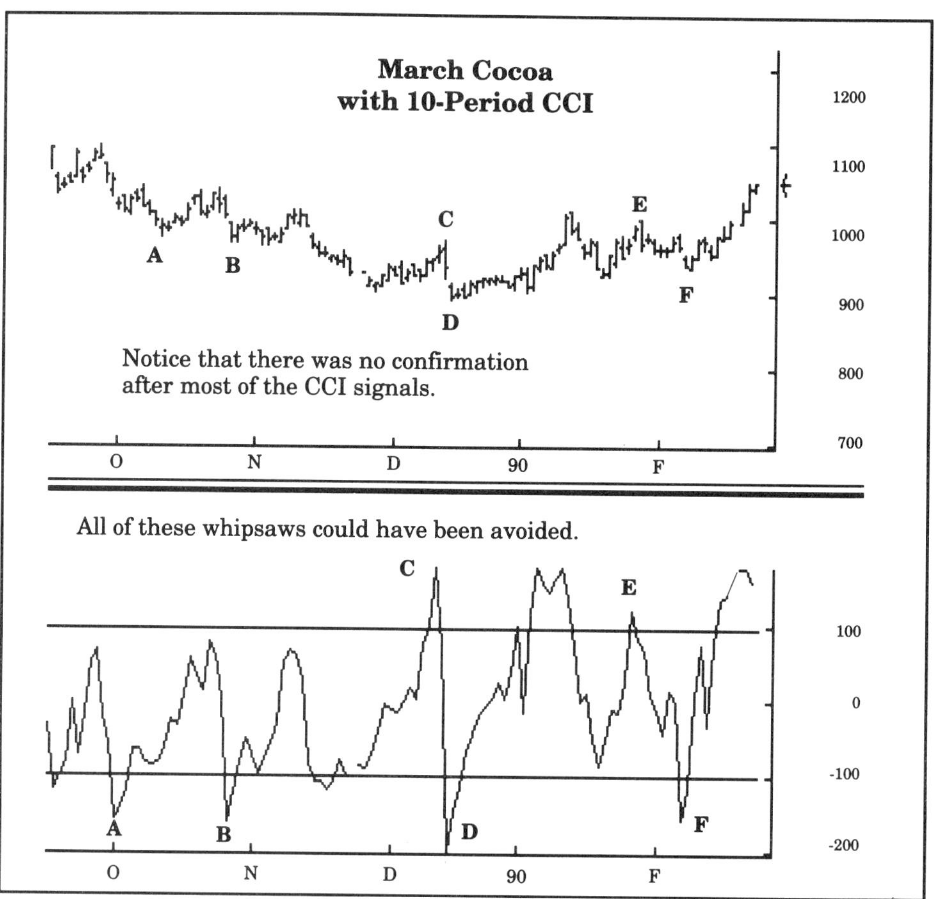

Divergence

Divergence isn't a separate technical study like the others in this chapter, but we mention divergence so often that we thought a detailed explanation of it would prove valuable.

The study of divergence has a long history, going back at least as far as the 1890s, when Charles Dow first formulated what later came to be known as the Dow theory. The Dow theory relies on confirmations between various Dow indices to give signals that reveal stock market trends. Before the advent of derivative technical studies, intermarket relationships and volume and open interest studies were essentially the only vehicles available for the study of divergence. These are still very popular and the basis for a great deal of interesting and valid work (for instance, Bill Ohama's Titanic and 3-D patterns in the stock market). Nowadays, most futures traders are much more interested in divergences between technical studies and the underlying markets than in the more classic Dow theory divergences.

It is difficult to find a detailed discussion of divergence. The probable reason for this is that divergences tend to be a relatively subjective sort of trading signal. Similar to classic Edwards and Magee chart patterns, it is easy to see divergences in hindsight, but it is often difficult to see them as they are unfolding. It is also very difficult to effectively computer test trading models based on divergences.

Divergences between Technical Studies and Markets

Divergences normally are best spotted using some sort of oscillator, such as stochastics, RSI, or MACD. Put simply, when a market makes a new high or low, and a technical study based on that market fails to also make a new high or low, we have divergence. By definition, this means that both the study and the underlying market will show spike highs or lows that should be readily identifiable. (See Exhibit 2–25.)

In practice, it isn't always that easy. Often a large divergence formation that correctly called a market turn will contain several minor divergences that appear insignificant in retrospect but looked important at the time. Several smaller false signals often appear for every major valid signal. The problem, of course, is recognizing which divergence is meaningful and which is not at the time it happens. Most technicians use some other means of chart analysis for confirmation, such as classic

EXHIBIT 2–25

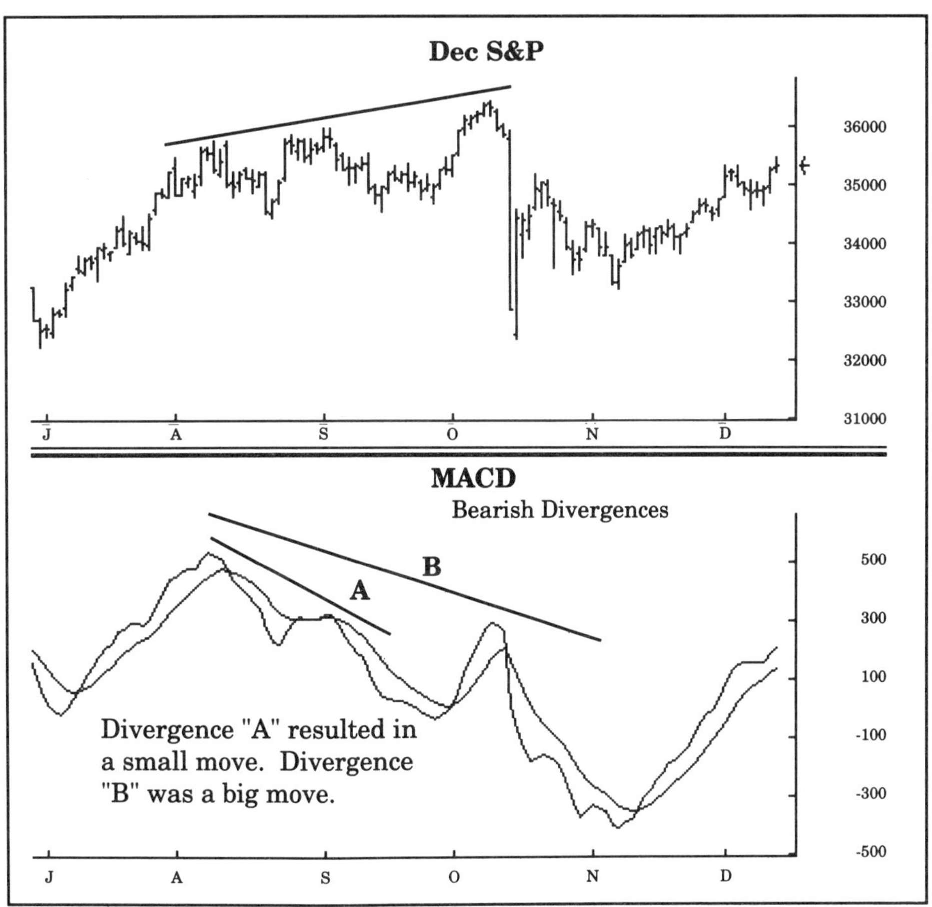

chart patterns, or they rely on multiple divergences, comparing several different technical studies and believing that there is safety in numbers. We're not sure there is any advantage to waiting for divergences in multiple indicators. Because oscillators tend to be generally similar in their action, multiple divergences will appear almost as frequently as single divergences.

It is possible to see divergences in trend-following indicators, such as DMI and even in moving averages, but our feeling is that they are not as valid as those that appear using oscillators. (See Exhibit 2–26.)

Trending versus Nontrending Markets

One way to winnow potentially false divergences is to decide whether you're in a trending or nontrending market and treat the signals accordingly. There are a number of indicators that can help measure trendiness—for example, Wilder's ADX, linear regression, or even basic chart watching.

The major difference between the two types of markets is that, in a nontrending market, divergence trades can be taken in either direction, while in a trending market divergence signals against the trend should generally be ignored (with the possible exception of trying to catch the major tops and bottoms). Trend direction, assuming there is a trend, can be decided by using simple indicators, like a relatively long-term moving average.

EXHIBIT 2–26

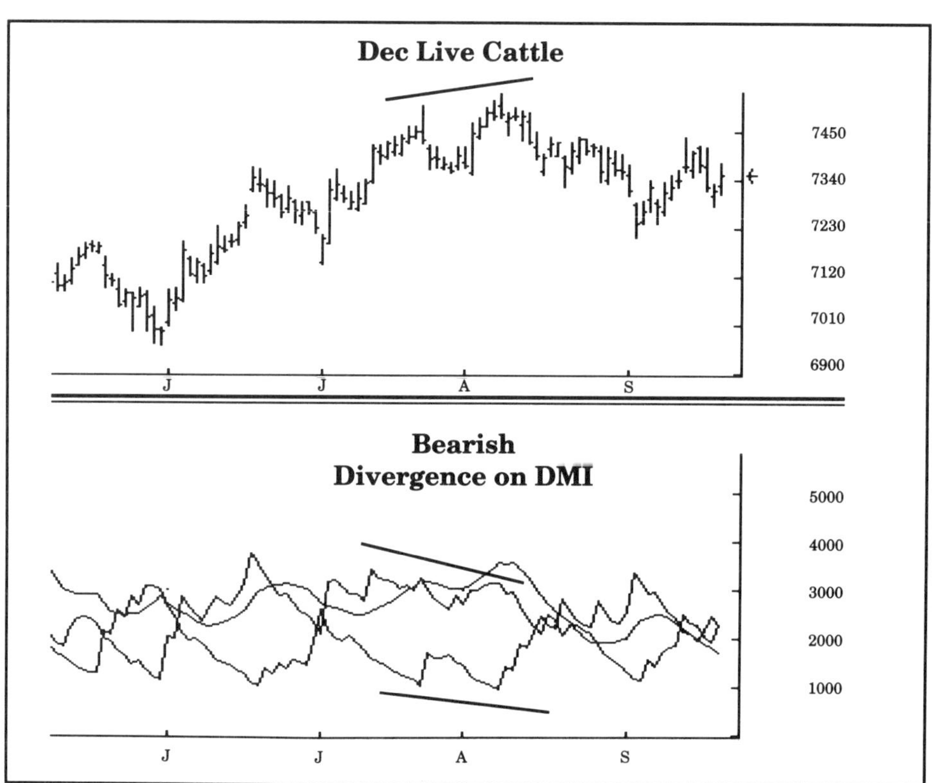

Basic Trading Rules

Divergences are particularly dangerous signals, because you're normally trying to pick a top or bottom of some sort. The most important thing to remember about trading divergences is to wait until the divergence is confirmed by a close or series of closes in the direction of the new trend. Don't anticipate. Most charts are littered with the remains of potential divergences that turned out to be trend continuations. If you anticipate your entry, you run the risk of being on the wrong side of a significant market move, especially if, as is usually the case, the divergence is at a market top or bottom and the potential divergence puts you on the wrong side of a breakout. (See Exhibit 2–27.)

The best exits for divergence trades, assuming you've entered correctly, depend on the type of market you're in. In a trending market, if you've managed to get in on the correct side of the trend, your entry was no different (except for being earlier) from a normal trend-following entry. Adjust your exits accordingly by using a relatively loose exit technique that will keep you in the trend but not give up too much profit—for example, Wilder's Parabolic or a relatively large trailing stop, or both. If you've picked a short-term top or bottom in a choppy market, use very tight trailing stops or a profit target, or both.

Serial Divergences

Divergences often occur in a closely spaced series in a single market. Obviously, only the last divergence in the series is any good, but the

EXHIBIT 2–27

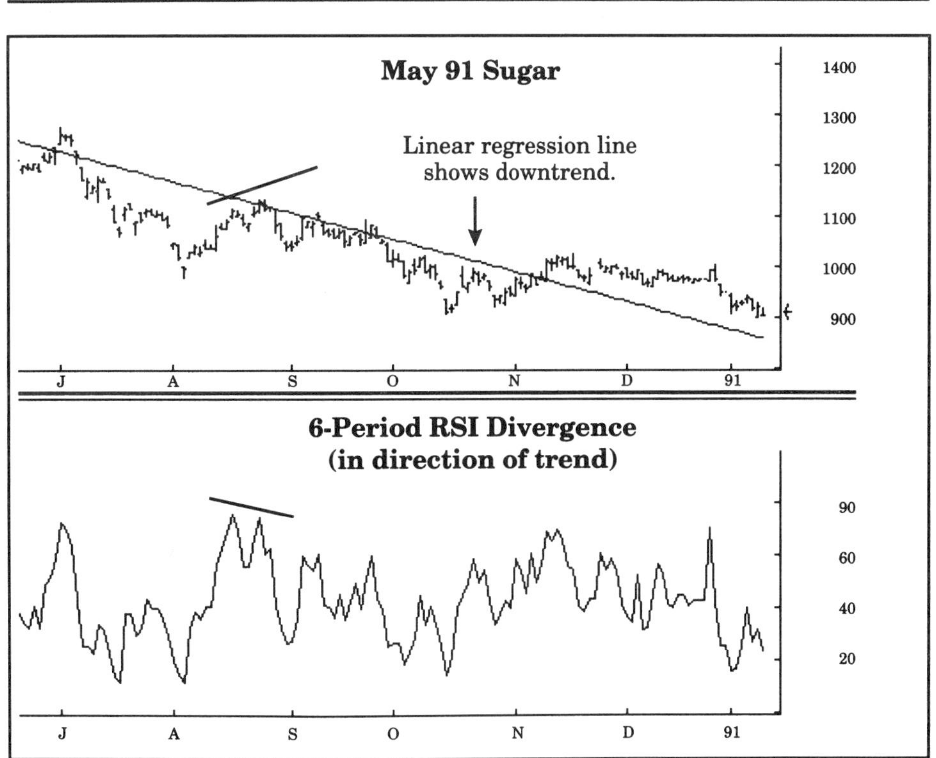

longer the series the stronger the signal. One observation is that divergences seem to cluster in threes, thus so-called A-B-C divergences and George Lane's "three drives to a top." Our observation is that double and triple divergences occur in trending markets, while perfectly valid single divergences occur in nontrending markets. The action in the stock indices (March–April 1991) is an example of multiple oscillator divergence in a trending market. (See Exhibit 2–28.)

It is difficult, if not impossible, to know when to take the first divergence as a signal and when to wait. Many large market reversals in recent years were signaled well in advance by single divergences. Just as many were preceded by multiple divergences (see S&P/RSI weekly chart in Exhibit 2–29). There is often more art than science to this, as you can see. It would seem that we have to take the first divergence and simply put up with the losses when there are multiple signals.

Related Market Divergences

It is important to be aware that divergences between related markets, or between a cash market and its related futures market, are every bit as valid as the divergences between a technical study and its underlying market. As we stated earlier, the Dow theory is based on related market divergences.

These related market divergences offer excellent entry signals and should not be ignored. The stock indices, in particular, often show divergence at or near new market highs (see the chart Dow/S&P futures divergence, in Exhibit 2–30). As is often the case, the relatively narrow-based Dow Jones Industrials pushed to new market highs in early

EXHIBIT 2–28

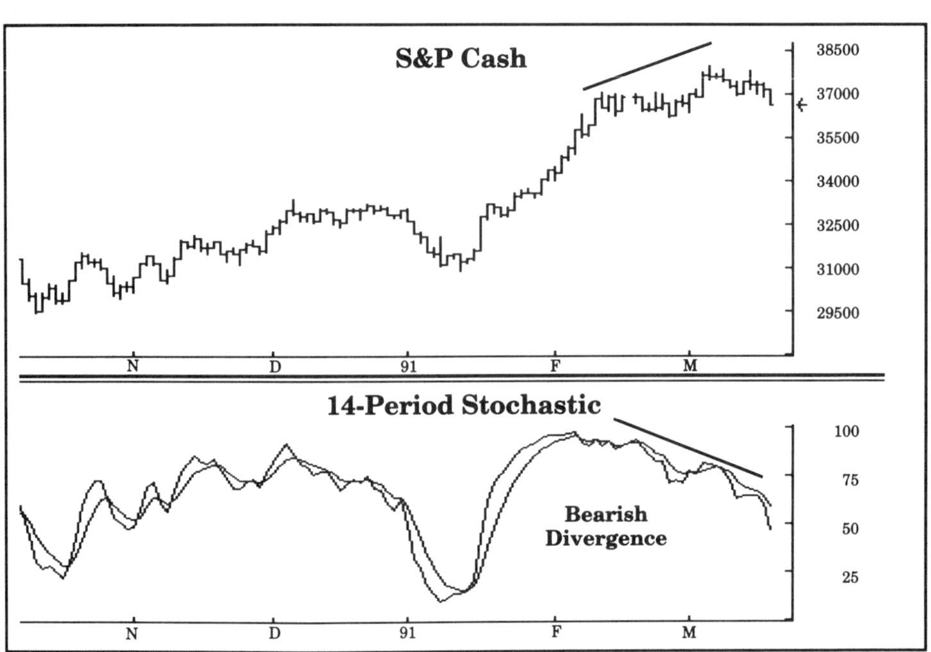

EXHIBIT 2–29

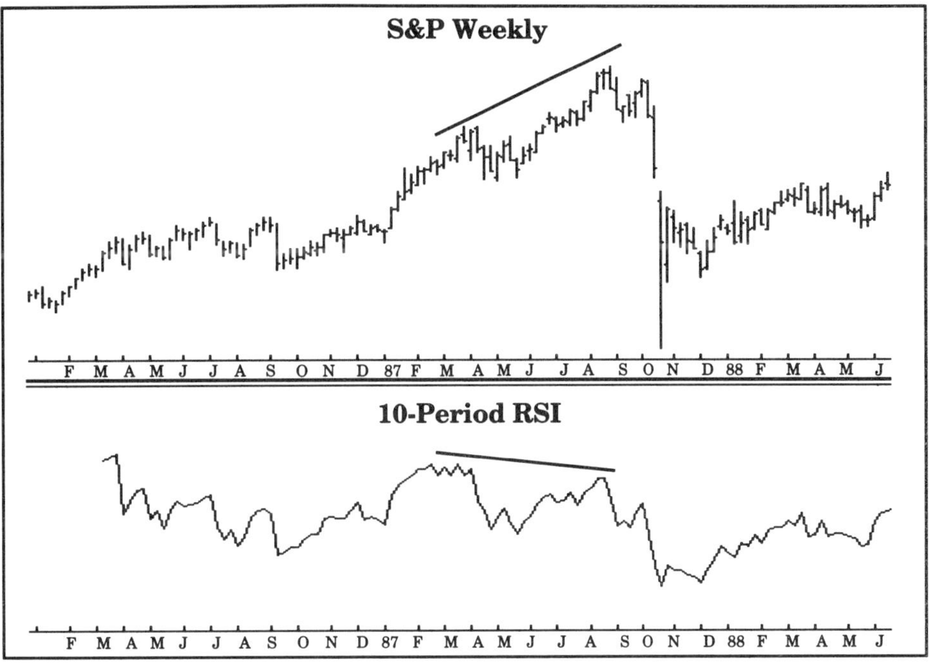

EXHIBIT 2–30

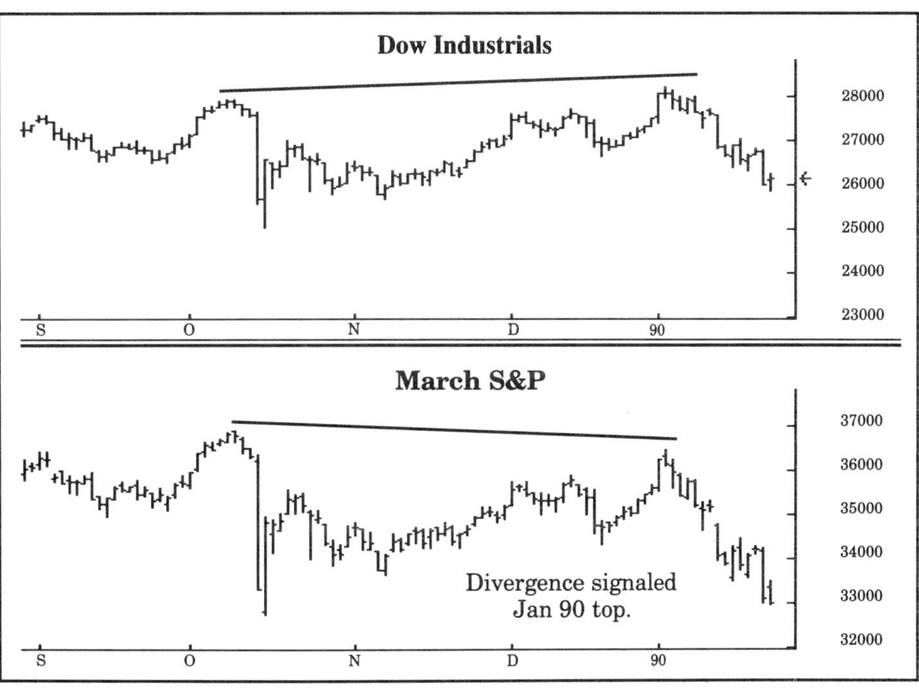

January 1990, while the S&P futures did not confirm the new market high (neither did many other stock indices).

The speculation is that this is normally due to increased hedging in the futures markets, which depresses prices enough to show a nonconfirmation. For whatever reason, they are common at stock market tops and are a good reason to believe the market is due for a correction. The same phenomenon occurred in August 1990, as the Dow reached new all-time highs. (See Exhibit 2–31.)

Just to show that this is not necessarily confined to the stock market, there are interday and intraday divergences in the petroleum complex. (See Exhibits 2–32 and 2–33.)

EXHIBIT 2–31

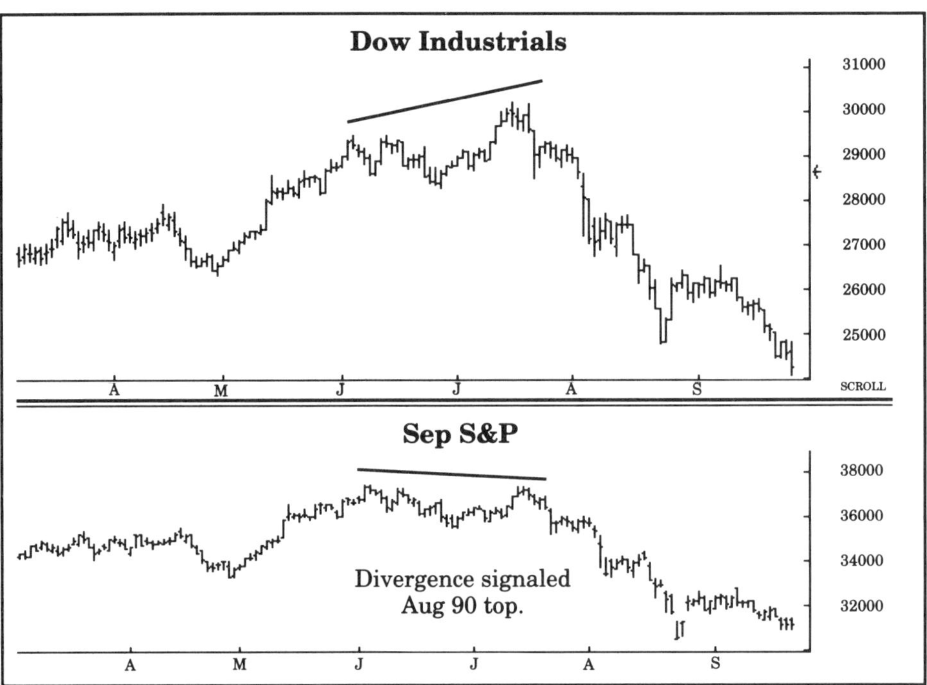

EXHIBIT 2–32

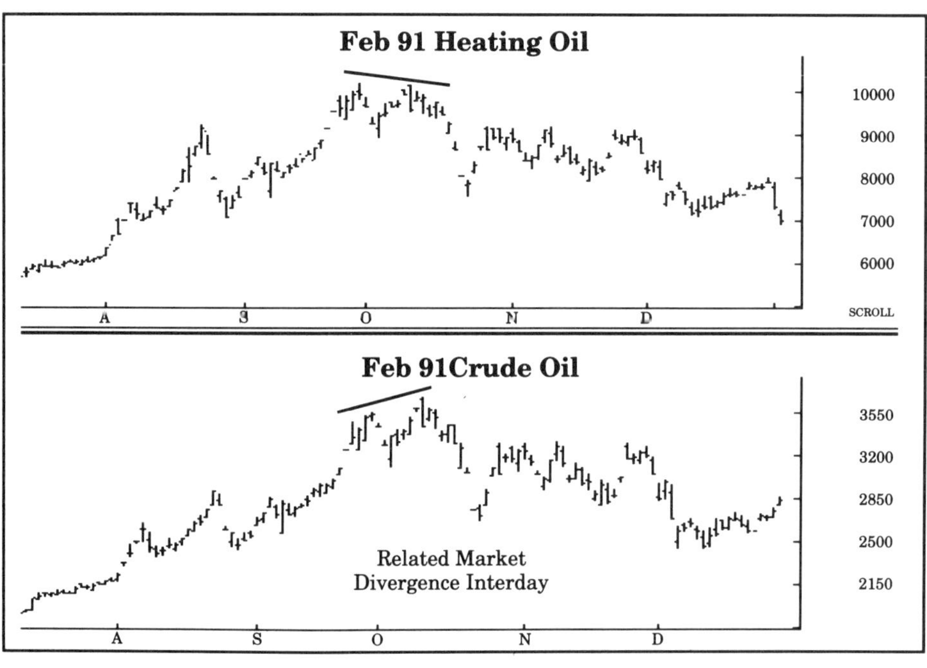

EXHIBIT 2–33

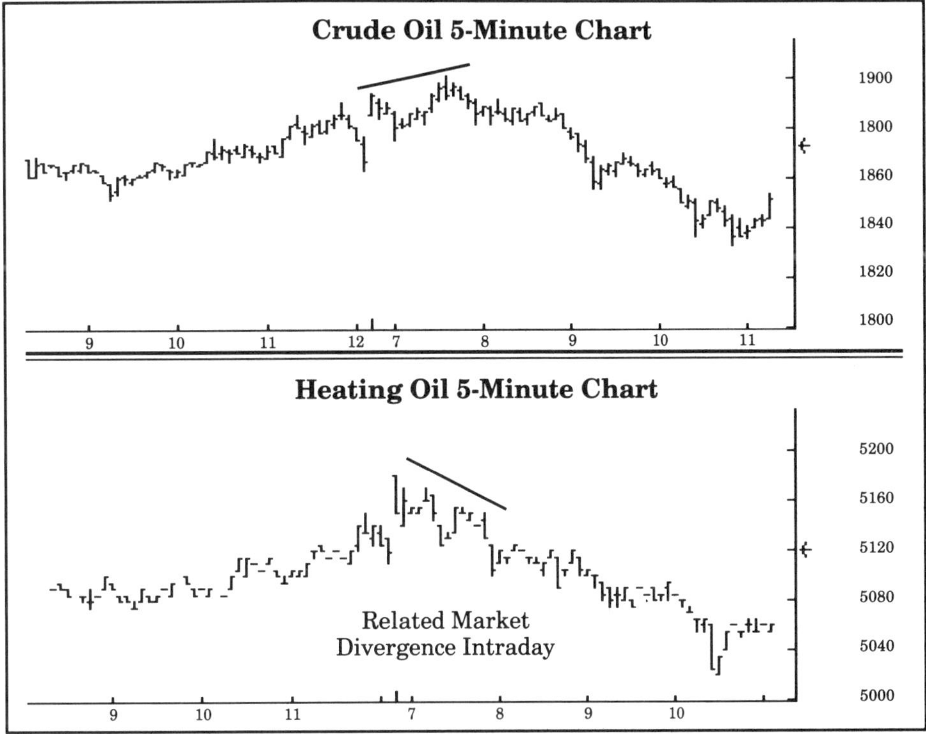

Other divergences to watch for are T-bonds versus T-notes (we have seen this combination used successfully for day trading), soybeans versus bean oil or meal, and divergences among currencies. The basic principle to apply is that you want to trade in the direction of the market that fails to confirm. For example, if soybean meal makes a new low and bean oil doesn't, you would want to buy bean oil. Or to put it another way, buy the strong one on buy signals and sell the weak one on sell signals. The possible exception to this rule is when one contract does not have sufficient liquidity. Then you might want to trade in the contract with the most volume.

The Set-Up Pattern

George Lane points out a form of divergence he calls "bull and bear set-ups." (See "Suggested Readings at chapter's end.) These patterns are formed when the oscillator makes a new high or low and the prices fail to confirm. George concludes that, when a bear set-up occurs after an uptrend, the next rally may be an important top. (See Exhibit 2–34.) Use the reverse logic for bull set-ups after downtrends.

One of our newsletter subscribers took this pattern and reached a seemingly opposite conclusion. He observed that the bear set-up is often followed by an explosive breakout to the upside. We see an element of

EXHIBIT 2–34

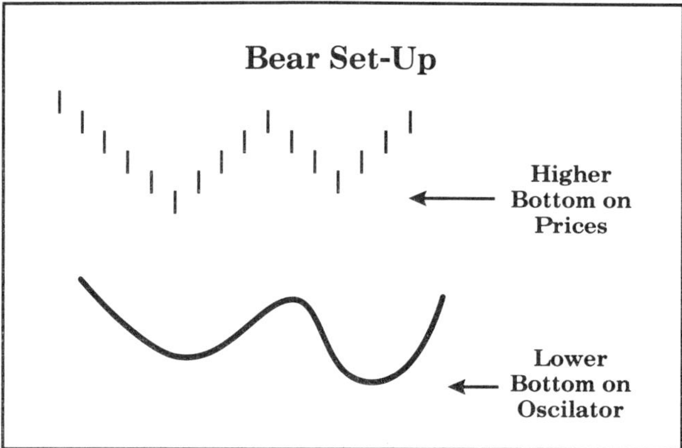

truth in both observations, which can lead to an exciting combination of unusually profitable trades. If you buy the next rally after a bear set-up, as our subscriber advocated, you could get a very explosive trade on the long side. This big trade to the upside would then be followed by the top that George Lane is looking for—and you can expect a nice trade to the downside.

Momentum and Rate of Change

In our regular talks with other traders, we have found that more of them use momentum than almost any other tool, except perhaps moving averages. Momentum isn't always used as their primary study, but the traders monitor it closely and use it with other technical studies to arrive at more timely trading decisions. Among the many reasons for the popularity of momentum are its simplicity, its versatility, and the fact that it is considered to be a rare "lead indicator." Rather than merely reacting to the direction of prices, momentum can change directions before prices change direction. Very few technical studies can provide a trader with this valuable lead factor.

Because of the versatility we mentioned, momentum is difficult to classify as either a trend-following or a countertrend indicator. It can be used to show the direction of a trend, and it can also provide very good overbought/oversold warnings, making it useful as a countertrend trading tool. This seemingly simple indicator actually contains a great deal more information than is immediately apparent, and the wealth of information inherent in the calculations leads to momentum's multiplicity of possible uses. A thorough understanding of what the calculation is measuring should help us to use momentum to its fullest potential.

The momentum indicator provides an accurate measure of a market's velocity and, to some degree, a measure of the extent to which a trend is still intact. The calculation is simple: Subtract the closing price *n* days ago from the closing price today. The result will be a positive or negative number that is plotted around a null point or zero line. The formula is:

$$M = P_t - P_{t-n}$$

where M is momentum, P_t is today's closing price, and P_{t-n} is the closing price *n* periods (usually days) before P_t. The *n* value is the only part of the formula that can be varied by the trader, with the most commonly used value being 10. Some software packages allow the user to select the period's open, high, low, close, or some other value for price. We see no reason to use anything other than closes in the calculation.

The result of the calculation is a technical study that moves back and forth across a zero line (which makes it an oscillator). If the market is moving upward, momentum will cross above the zero line and generally slope upward. If the market is moving downward, the momentum oscillator will cross below the zero line and generally slope downward.

So far this may seem like pretty simple stuff, but the momentum oscillator possesses other, more complex properties. For example, the farther apart P_t and P_{t-n} are in price, the greater the distance between momentum values. As the market moves rapidly upward (we're assuming a bull market), so will momentum. But as the market nears its peak and the closing prices become closer together, momentum will slow drastically and the slope of the momentum line will flatten or turn downward even though the prices may continue to advance. As the market peaks and negative values of $P_t - P_{t-n}$ appear the momentum line will begin to dip down toward the zero line. The momentum is signaling clearly that the market velocity has slowed. The momentum calculation has measured not only the speed or velocity of the advance but the rate at which the advance has slowed. It is describing both the market's velocity and the rate of change of that velocity as the market nears and passes its peak. As the market declines further and negative momentum values predominate, the momentum line will approach and eventually cross the zero line, signaling a change in trend direction from bullish to bearish. (See Exhibit 2–35.)

What causes momentum to react this way? For momentum to increase in value and for the line to slope upward, recent price gains must be greater than older price gains. If recent price gains are the same as older price gains, the momentum line will be flat, even though the market is still going up. If recent price gains are less than those of before, even if prices are still rising, the rate of change will have slowed further and the momentum line will actually drop. The flattening and subsequent decline of the momentum line is clearly signaling, in advance, something a simple price chart might not show us. Momentum gives us an early indication that the market's velocity has slowed and that the rate of price increase is now decelerating. (See Exhibit 2–36.)

EXHIBIT 2–35

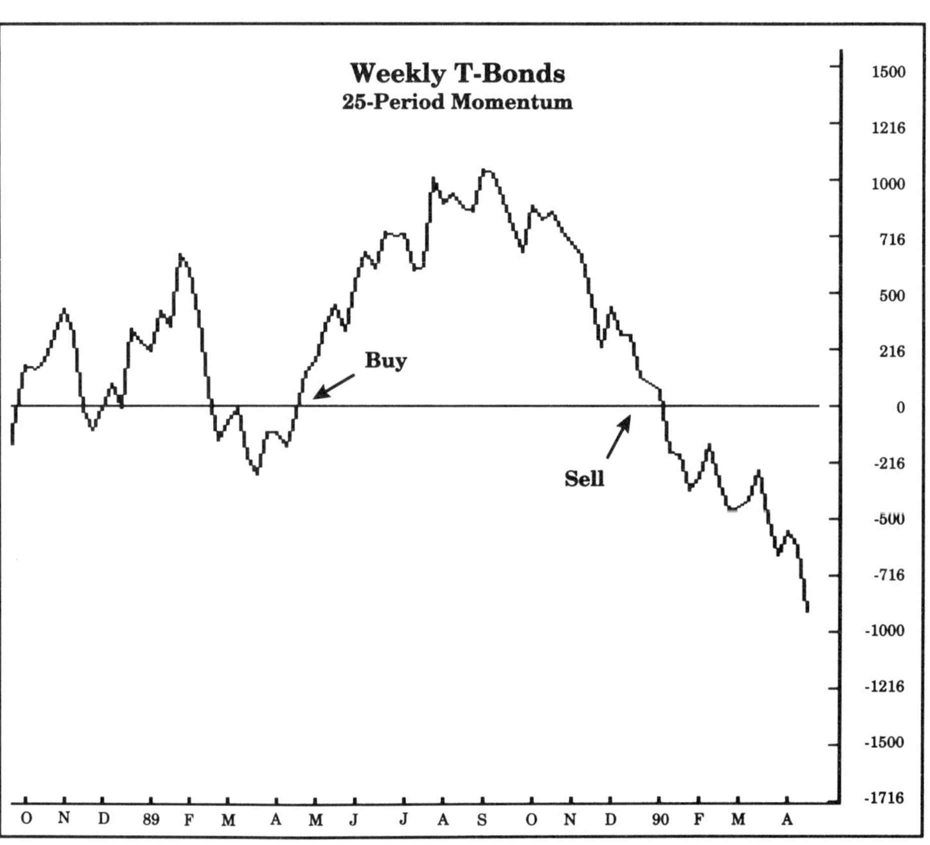

EXHIBIT 2–36

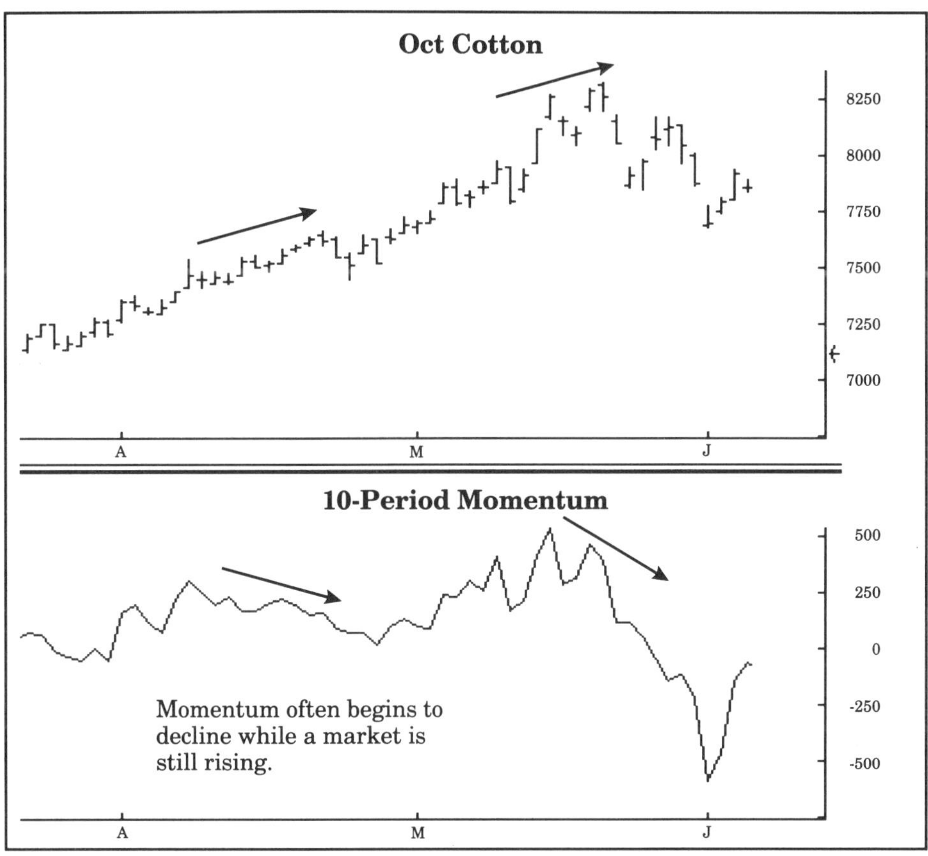

Rate of Change

We will very briefly mention rate of change here, because most of today's software packages provide this indicator in addition to momentum, even though they are essentially identical. The rate of change formula is:

$$ROC = 100\ (P_t/P_{t-n})$$

The 100 level is equivalent to the zero or null line on the momentum graph. The only possible difference or advantage we can imagine is that, when using ROC instead of momentum, there are no negative numbers to deal with. The trading rules and practical applications are the same for both indicators.

Basic Momentum Signals—Trend Following

When used as a trend-following indicator, the most important momentum signals come when the zero line is crossed. When the line is crossed in an upward direction, momentum is bullish. When the line is crossed in a downward direction, momentum is bearish. We would not advise taking a position against the direction of the momentum.

The number of times the momentum crosses the zero line will vary in frequency according to the time period used in the momentum calculation. Just like most other indicators, shorter time values will usually make momentum faster and more responsive in crossing the zero line. Longer values will normally slow momentum signals down by reducing the frequency of the crossovers. The smoothing effect of the longer periods is obviously not the result of averaging more data because the formula does not average the closing prices. It is simply logical that it would take longer, if there is a trend, to return to a price established 40 days ago than to return to a price established only 10 days ago. We have seen traders successfully use a wide range of momentum periods of anywhere between 10 and 40 days. Many traders who work with cycles like to fit the period of the momentum to the cycle length of the market they are trading.

Since lengthening the momentum period will make the oscillator less responsive, and shortening it can cause whipsaws, some traders have found it helpful to use a relatively short and highly responsive momentum value and then put boundaries above and below the zero line. Then they use a crossing of the boundary lines, instead of the zero line, to signal new trades. When the momentum oscillates within the boundaries, it doesn't signal new trades. This has the effect of making the market "prove" itself before entering a position and eliminates many whipsaws generated by frequent crosses of the zero line. (See Exhibit 2–37.)

EXHIBIT 2–37

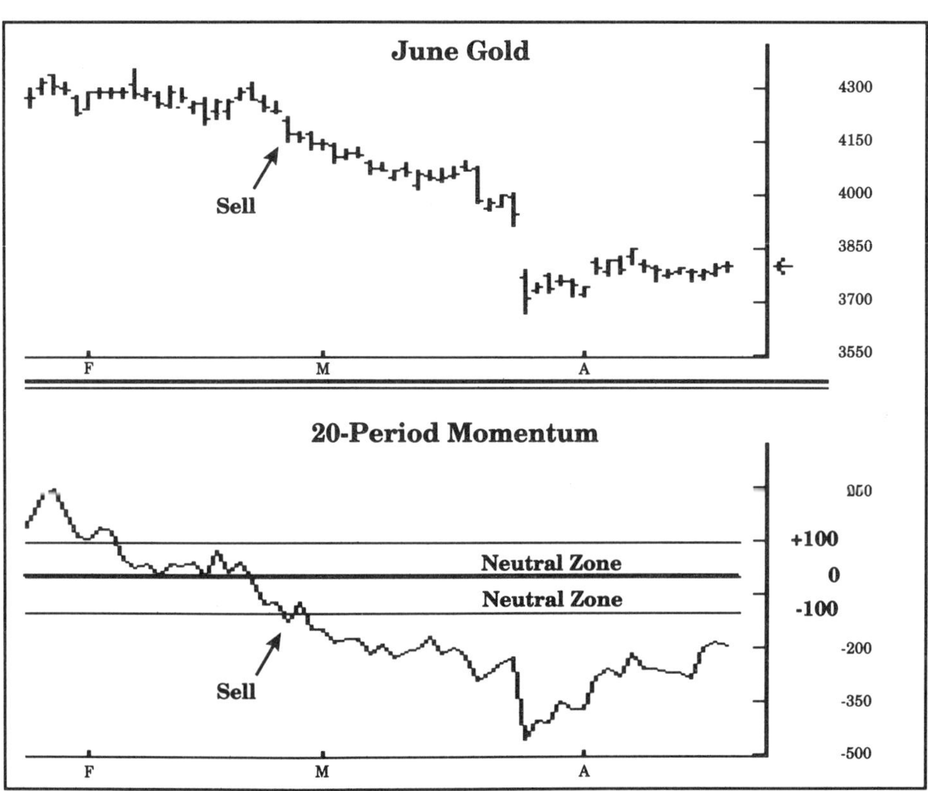

Be aware that the most significant profits are made when both momentum and prices are accelerating. As we described, the slope of the momentum line will decrease as the rate of price gains lessens. An obvious and effective application of momentum would be to refrain from implementing new trades, unless the momentum line is sloping in the direction of the trend. When the momentum is moving back towards the zero line, by definition the trend is weakening or nonexistent, so trading in this area may prove to be futile. (See Exhibit 2–38.)

Basic Momentum Signals—Countertrend

Because momentum measures the acceleration or deceleration of a market, it becomes very useful as an overbought/oversold indicator. When the market reaches a top, momentum will level off or begin to decline, often well before the actual market peak. A similar divergence in directions will occur at a market bottom. Assuming no major changes in market volatility, lines drawn on a long-term chart connecting momentum tops and bottoms will be parallel to and on either side of the zero line and will represent overbought/oversold zones. The basic trad-

EXHIBIT 2–38

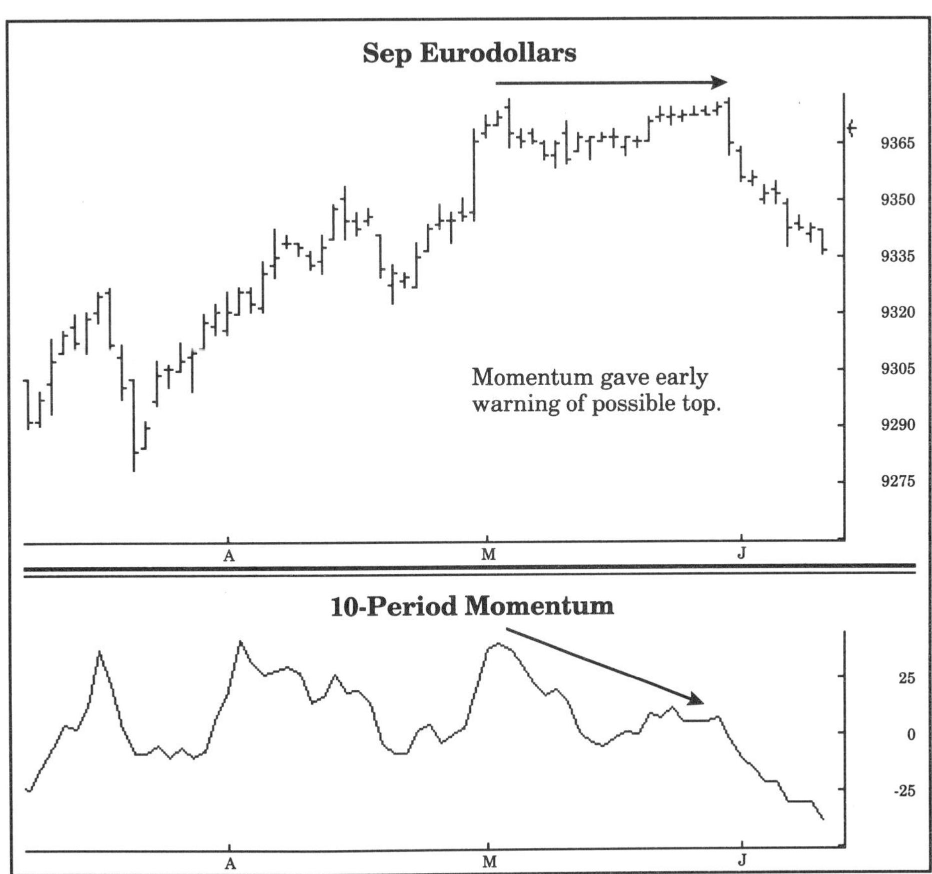

ing strategy here is to sell just when the upper zone is penetrated, placing a protective stop above recent highs, and to buy just when the lower zone is penetrated, placing a stop below recent lows. Profits can be taken when the opposite zone is reached. (See Exhibit 2–39.)

This countertrend strategy will be productive when recent market action is in a trading range, but if the market breaks out by any significant amount, it will obviously fail. We have seen formulations that attempt to deal with this problem by so normalizing the momentum line that it always falls within a range of +1 or −1, or +100 or −100. This is done by dividing the momentum values by some constant divisor. We see little value in this approach. Normalizing an oscillator's values won't stop a market from breaking out if it wants to do so. Normalized momentum would act much like RSI or some similar indicator in a trending market. The values would cluster at the top or bottom of the scale and give continual buy or sell signals. Standard, nonnormalized momentum will continue to rise or fall to theoretically infinite levels, confirming trend continuation and telling the trader not to use countertrend trading strategies.

EXHIBIT 2–39

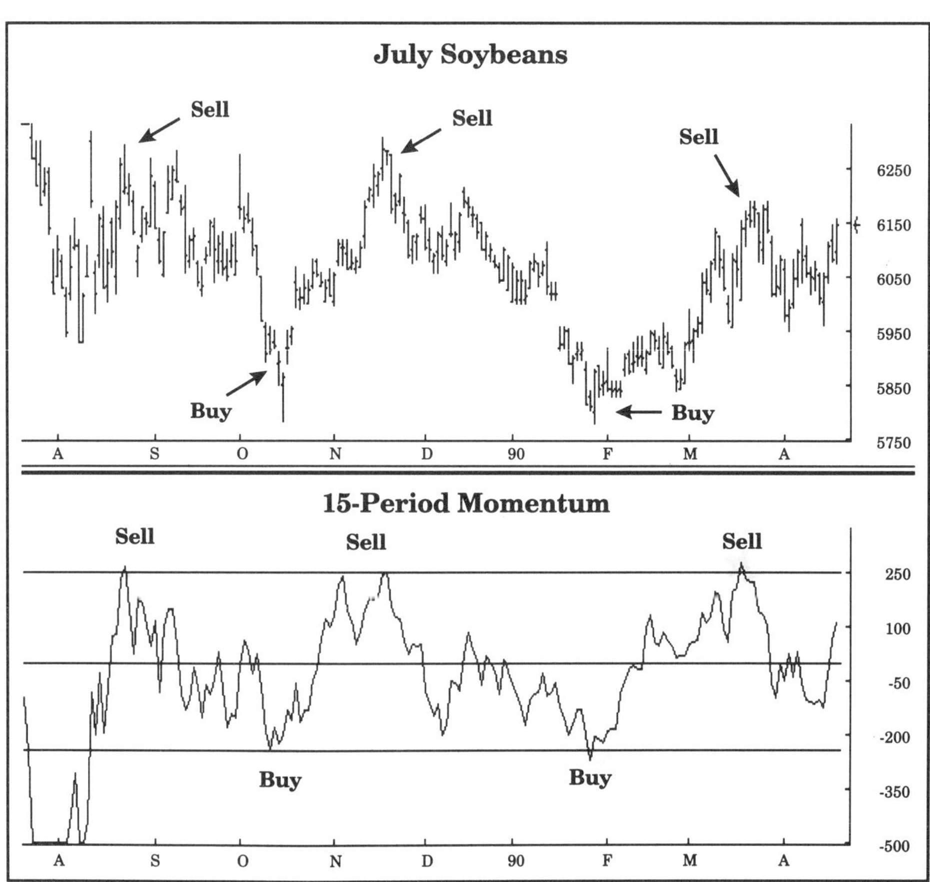

Trading Long-Term with Momentum

One of the most productive uses of momentum is to define a long-term trend and, once the trend is defined, trades should be taken only in that direction. This discipline should significantly improve profitability by weeding out potential losing trades that fight against the tide. Momentum not only tells you the trend direction but gives a good idea of its strength; this is valuable information that can keep you out of trouble. (See Exhibit 2–40.)

Our research shows us that, in most markets, a 25-period momentum based on weekly charts is a surprisingly dependable long-term trend indicator. Trend trading is especially rewarding when the momentum line is moving rapidly away from the zero line. However, be very cautious about trend following when momentum is beginning to peak and when the momentum line slopes back toward the zero line.

A logical combination of technical studies here would be to use the long-term momentum to find the trend, use the intermediate-term moving averages to enter trades while the momentum is strong, and then use a shorter-term countertrend indicator, such as stochastics or RSI, for profit taking when the momentum weakens.

In one of the few tests of momentum in recent literature, Colby and Meyers in their book, *The Encyclopedia of Technical Market Indicators* (see "Suggested Readings"), optimized rate of change over nearly 20

EXHIBIT 2–40

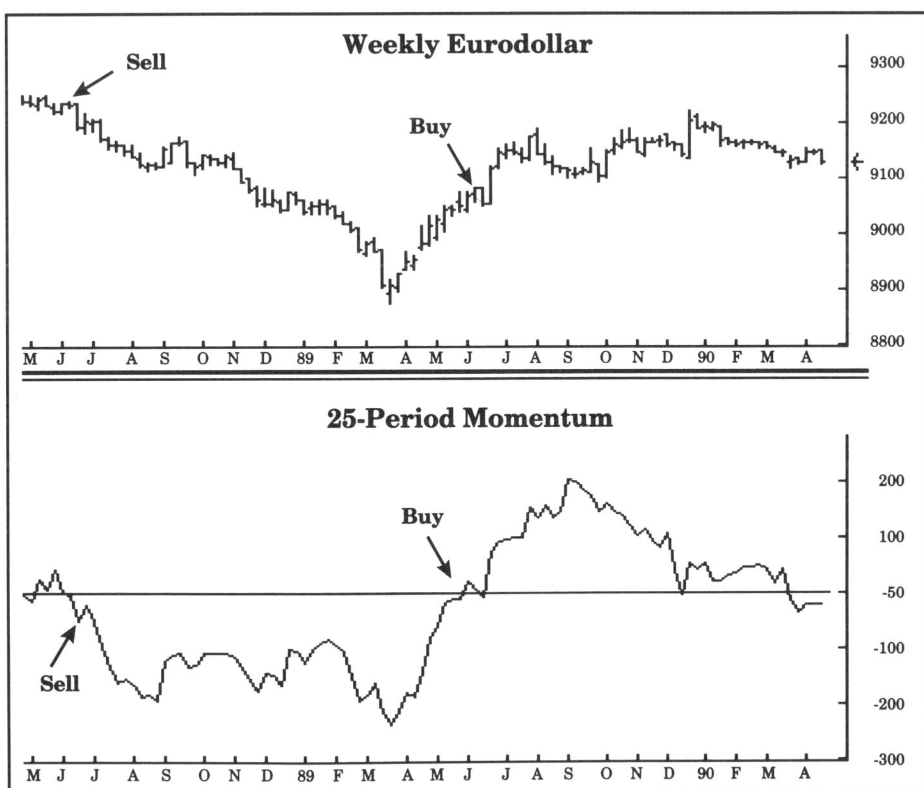

years of NYSE data. (Rate of change is essentially an identical indicator to momentum.) Their trading rules were simple: Buy as the indicator crosses above the zero line, sell as it crosses below the zero line. Holding a position from a first crossing through a peak and closing out after an opposite crossing may be academically interesting, but we think it shows an ignorance of the basic properties of the momentum (or ROC) study. Trading momentum as a reversal method ignores the fact that a slowing of momentum is a signal to exit the market, or at least to trade it differently than you would if the line is still sloping upward. Not surprisingly, overall profit results were disappointing and drawdowns were quite severe.

Some very simple testing of momentum was also done by Bruce Babcock and described in his book, *The Dow Jones-Irwin Guide to Trading Systems*. He tested a 10-day and 28-day momentum using a simple crossover reversal method, with no stops. The results were break-even, which is encouraging, considering that neither momentum nor any other oscillator should be traded this way. See the system testing section, Chapter 3, for some similar results found in our own testing of momentum.

Trading Momentum Divergence

We have often observed that divergence between a technical study and the underlying market, or divergence between related markets, frequently gives effective trading signals. Divergence between an oscillator like momentum and an underlying market would occur when the market and momentum make a spike high, both retreat, and then the market makes a new high that is not confirmed by a new high in the momentum oscillator. The theory, essentially, is that the divergence indicates that the market has weak underpinnings and will fail to continue its upward direction after making the new high.

Price and momentum divergences are plentiful and powerful. A 10-period momentum based on daily charts will reveal many divergences and many significant trading opportunities, especially if the longer-term 25-week momentum is in its declining phase. Our standard caveat about trading divergences applies: Wait until the divergence is fully confirmed before entering the market. A premature entry will likely leave you on the wrong side of a trending market, with no reason and no excuse for being there. (See Exhibit 2–41.)

Momentum of Other Indicators

Many of the technical studies we mention in this book measure, in one way or another, the strength of a market. This is normally revealed by the slope of the line created by the study's calculation. For example, a steeply trending moving average usually means that the underlying market is trending strongly. The steeper the slope, the stronger the trend. Determining the exact degree of steepness can be very subjective, if we only look at the technical study; but if we calculate a momentum or rate of change of the indicator, we can very objectively quantify the

EXHIBIT 2–41

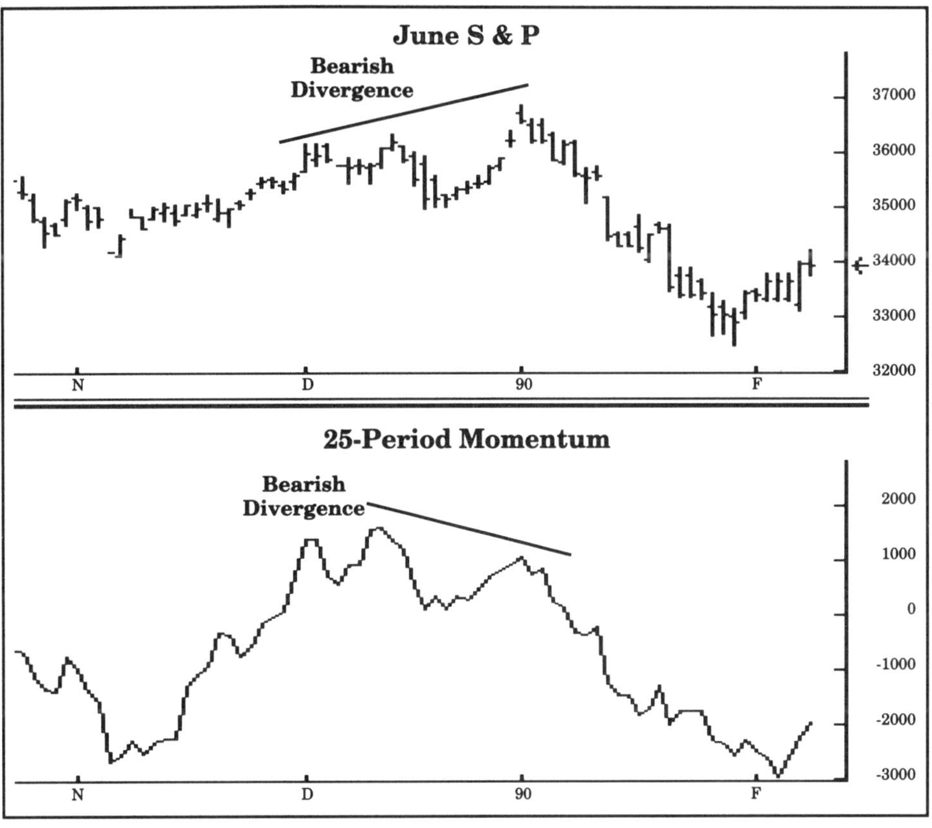

degree of slope. This opens up all sorts of possibilities. We can filter out weakly trending markets and concentrate our trend-following efforts on markets with unusually strong trends. Or, if a market is not trending, we can buy dips and sell rallies.

We believe that momentum has many worthwhile applications and ranks as one of the most useful technical studies available to the futures trader. An imaginative and resourceful technician should find many interesting uses for this indicator, which leads prices instead of following them.

Moving Averages

Probably more actual money is being traded today using moving averages than with all other technical indicators combined. Because they can be used for everything from finding very long-term monthly trends to setting stops for day trading, and for anything in between, moving averages have been the subject of more discussion in the technical literature and elsewhere than any other study. One of the reasons they enjoy such popularity is that, when the markets trend, these simple little lines work as well as or better than indicators that require a Ph.D. to calculate and interpret.

Moving averages smooth out market fluctuations and short-term volatility and give the trader some idea of which way the market is going. Just as important is what they don't do. Unless you plot them as an oscillator, they provide no overbought/oversold information at all. They are trend-following indicators in the purest sense. They always show the direction of a trend, yet they don't measure how strong or weak the trend is. Their function is to identify the direction of the trend and then smooth or dampen its volatility. Moving averages do these important tasks very simply and very well.

There are so many possible types and combinations of moving averages that it is pointless to attempt to list them all. Most of the more esoteric varieties were created in the 1970s, when moving averages were considered to be very sophisticated and advanced technical analysis tools. A lot of talented and creative technicians spent most of their time figuring out new ways to improve and employ moving averages. This interest in moving averages was well rewarded: The 70s were a time of endlessly trending markets when moving averages worked extremely well. Most of the more inventive types have since fallen into disuse (like Maxwell's "modified accumulative" or "average-modified"). Three major categories have survived the test of time: simple, weighted, and exponential.

Simple Moving Averages

The *simple* moving average is calculated by adding and then averaging a set of numbers representing market action over some specified time. The calculation usually involves closing prices, but may also be calculated from highs, lows, or an average of all three. The oldest data point is dropped as a new one appears; thus, the average "moves" and follows the market. A line connecting the daily averages will have the effect of smoothing recent market volatility.

A large data set representing a large amount of past data will create a smooth line. For example, the chart shows a 50-day moving average, based on daily closes. (See Exhibit 2–42.) As you can see, most of the time prices are on one side or the other of the moving average. Also, as trends develop, the moving average will slope in the direction of the trend, giving us the trend direction and some indication of its strength based on the steepness of the slope.

Longer-term moving averages will smooth out all the minor fluctuations and show only longer-term trends; shorter-term moving averages will show shorter term trends at the expense of the long term. A smaller data set representing only more recent data will create a more responsive line. The chart shows a 5-day moving average overlaying the same chart as did the 50-day. The 5-day hugs the data much more closely, following each little price change. Short-term trends are easily seen, but the trends that were so apparent with the 50-day average have become more difficult to define. (See Exhibit 2–43.)

Long-term and short-term moving averages each have their uses—and their drawbacks. Notice that, although it stays with the trend, the 50-day moving average is often far from the actual prices, and it changes direction much later than the prices. In practice, a trade based on a

EXHIBIT 2–42

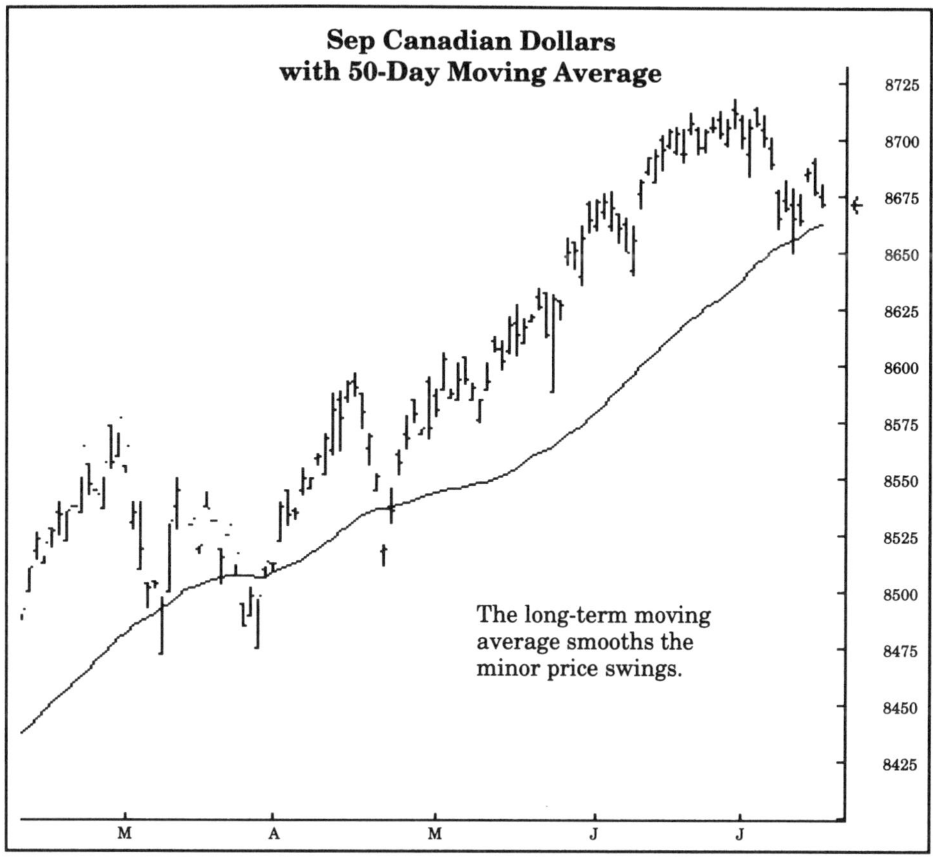
Sep Canadian Dollars
with 50-Day Moving Average
8725
8700
8675
8650
8625
8600
8575
8550
8525
8500
8475
8450
8425
The long-term moving
average smooths the
minor price swings.
M
A
M
J
J

EXHIBIT 2–43

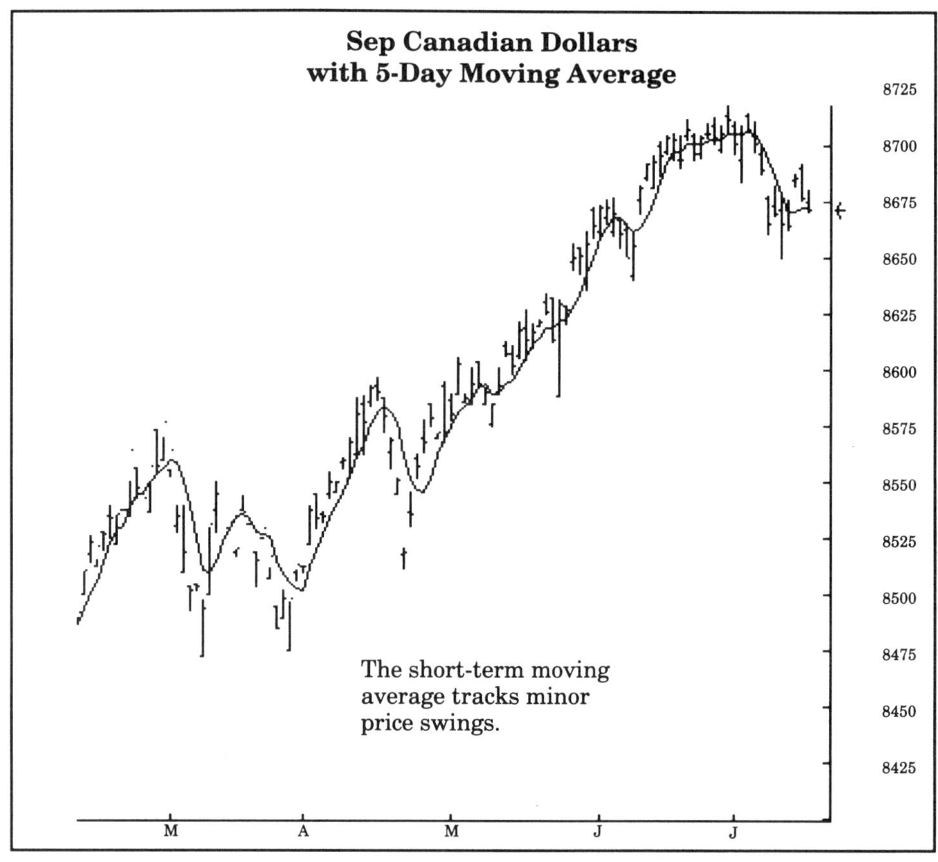

moving average of this length would be slow to enter the market and slow to exit. The slow entry gives up a substantial portion of the early part of the trend, and the slow exit gives up much of the profit. On the other hand, the 5-day moving average is quick to enter and exit, but it is not in harmony with the major trend and is on the wrong side of the market as often as not.

Another interesting property of simple moving averages (and many other technical studies, for that matter) is that they are as much affected by old prices that drop out of the average as they are by new prices. A sudden turn in a moving average can mean that recent prices have turned. It can also mean that recent prices are relatively neutral and that significant prices have been dropped from the other end of the data. This isn't necessarily bad. After all, the intent of a moving average is to smooth the data. But it is something to be aware of. This phenomenon can sometimes account for what seems to be an inexplicable change in a moving average or other indicator.

Weighted Moving Averages

The simple moving average gives equal weight to each price it uses in the data series. Some traders, in the belief that recent prices are more important than older prices (and perhaps to partially overcome the data problem described above), like to create moving averages that react quickly to recent data and slowly to older data. The *weighted* moving average assigns greater importance to more recent data by weighting each day's data differently. This is usually done by multiplying the most recent data point by a given number (for example, the number of data points used in the moving average), adding the result to the overall calculation, then multiplying the next most recent point by a lesser number, and so on. The resulting line will be more responsive to recent market activity than the simple moving average.

Exponential Moving Averages

The simple and weighted moving averages are only capable of reflecting the data in the number of data points chosen for the calculation. The *exponential* moving average assigns greater importance to more recent market action, much like the weighted moving average. However, the exponential moving average continues to take into account all of the data points, dropping nothing out. A 5-day exponential moving average normally includes more than 5 days of data and might include data from the entire life of a futures contract. In fact, these moving averages might be better identified by their actual "smoothing constants," since the number of days of data in the calculation is the same for a so-called 5-day average as for a 10-day average. The exponential calculation can have the undesirable quality of arriving at different moving average values depending on your starting point. Trader A's 5-day exponential moving average might be different than trader B's if they started their calculations on different dates. For practical purposes, the two values will probably be close enough that they would both cross over a 20-day moving average on the same day; but there is no certainty that they would. Since our task is to describe the practical application of indicators, rather than their calculation, we will skip the boring formulas. The details of the exponential calculation are rather lengthy and are well explained in previous works we have referenced. (However, see Exhibit 2–44.)

Despite the seeming sophistication of weighted and exponential moving averages, nearly every test we've seen or done ourselves has shown the simple moving average to be superior to the others in terms of trading results. Our own research indicates that weighting the data to emphasize recent events makes the indicator overly sensitive, thereby negating the original purpose of the moving average: to smooth market action. Weighted and exponential moving averages tend to generate more trades in tight, trading-range markets than simple moving averages. The result is usually costly whipsaws. This tends to confirm a theory we have long held: Any entry method that is the result of an abstruse calculation is probably more trouble than it's worth. Futures trading is more art than science, and mathematical accuracy does not insure profitability.

Although these calculations are simply key strokes on the computer keyboard, we recommend using simple moving averages only. Save your system complexity for more scientific applications, like money management and risk control.

EXHIBIT 2–44

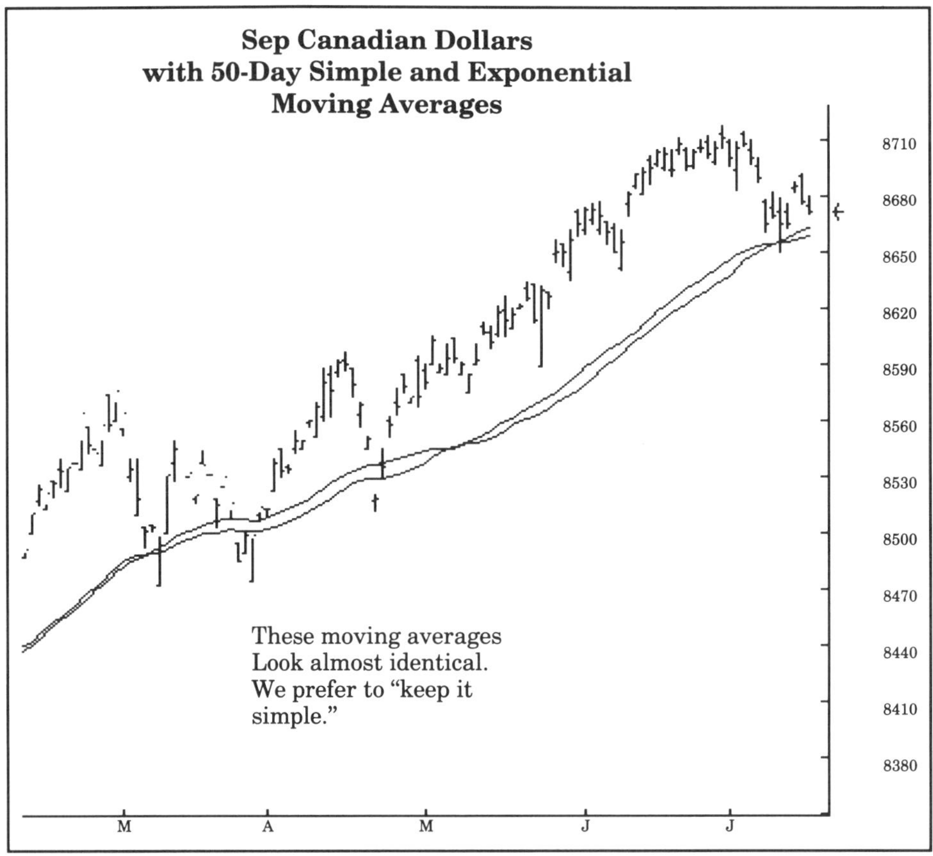

Moving average trading systems can use either a single moving average or any number of moving averages in various combinations. We've used single, dual, triple, and even quadruple moving average systems. We suppose that any multiple is possible; but the variations with only three or four can easily become overly complex and, as you have probably observed by now, we see no advantage in using anything more complicated than necessary.

Single Moving Average Systems

The simplest and often the most effective moving average is the single moving average. It is most useful as a long-term trend indicator, rather than as a daily trading device. For example, Colby and Meyers, in *The Encyclopedia of Technical Market Indicators,* optimized for a single moving average over 75 years of monthly NYSE data, using a simple reversal system. They found 12 months to be the optimum number, beating a buy-and-hold strategy by a large margin. In our experience, this simple 12-month moving average is a stock market timing device that's hard to beat. (See Exhibit 2–45.)

The basic rules for trading with a single moving average are simple: Buy when prices (normally closes) rise above the average, sell when prices drop below the average. This results in a simple reversal system that is always in the market. We do not recommend this system of

EXHIBIT 2–45

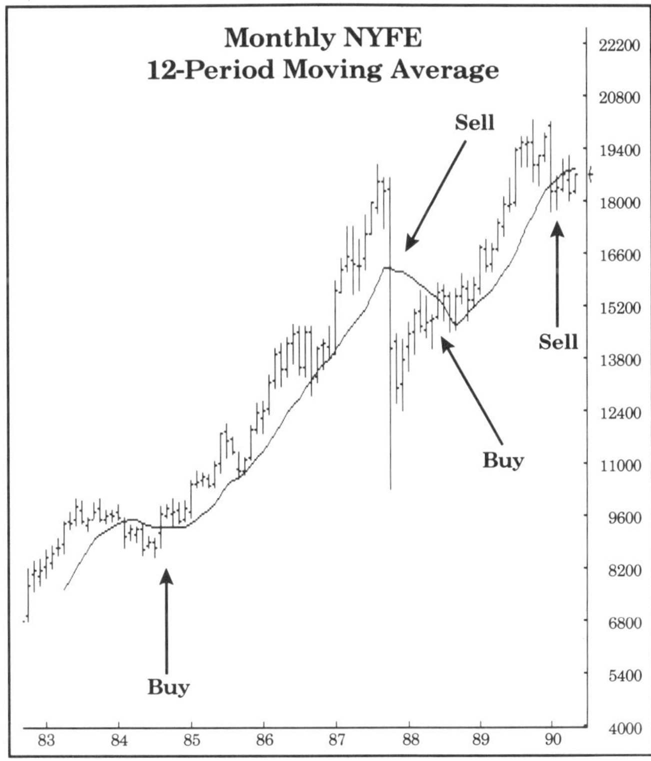

trading. No matter what moving average you choose, in the long run there will be periods of profit and periods of loss, the overall result being more or less zero sum minus transaction costs. Probably the best use of a single simple moving average is as a trend filter. If prices are above the average, trade only on the long side of the market, using some other, more responsive methods for entry and exit. If prices are below the average, trade only on the short side. (See Exhibit 2–46.)

Dual Moving Averages

The most popular moving average systems use two moving averages. These generally consist of a longer-term average that serves to define the trend and of a shorter-term average that gives trading signals as it crosses the longer-term average. The best known of these is Richard Donchian's 5-day/20-day system, which, by the way, is not a simple reversal system but uses an elaborate set of filters. (See Exhibit 2–47.)

The basic signal with two moving averages is the crossover. Buy when the shorter average crosses over the longer and sell when the opposite occurs. It is also possible to use the crossovers as trend turning points and trade only in the direction of the indicated trend, using some other shorter-term methods for entry and exit.

Most research we've seen and done shows that dual moving average systems tend to be more profitable than other combinations of moving averages. The research also shows that all moving average systems

EXHIBIT 2–46

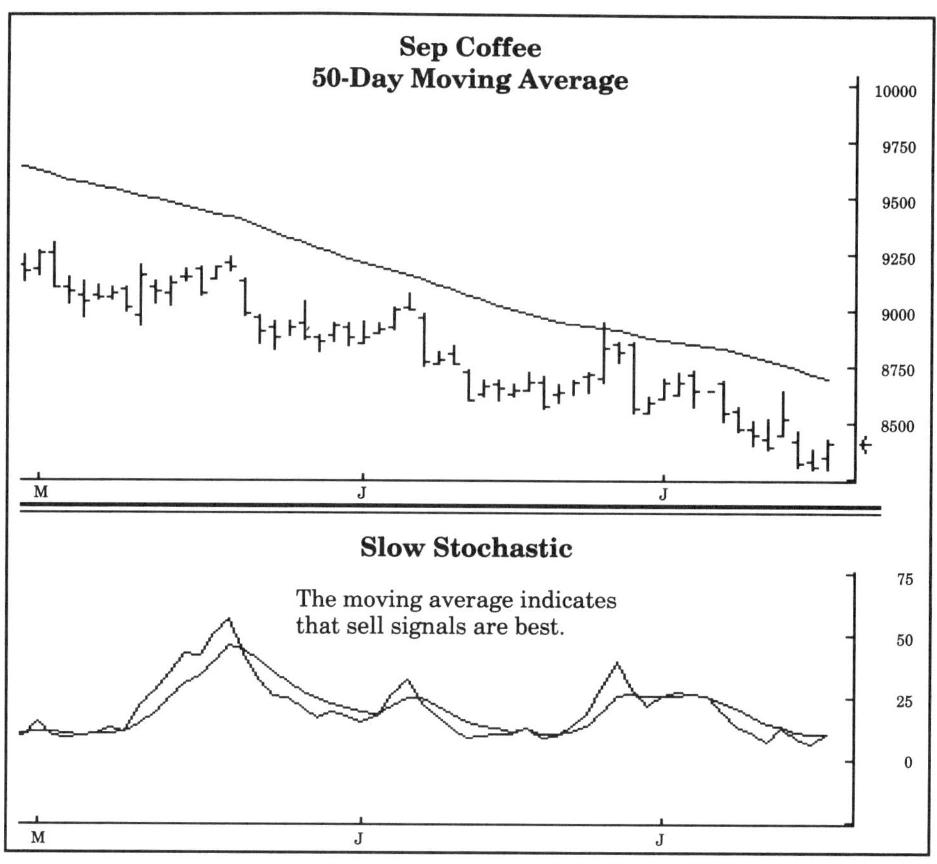

EXHIBIT 2–47

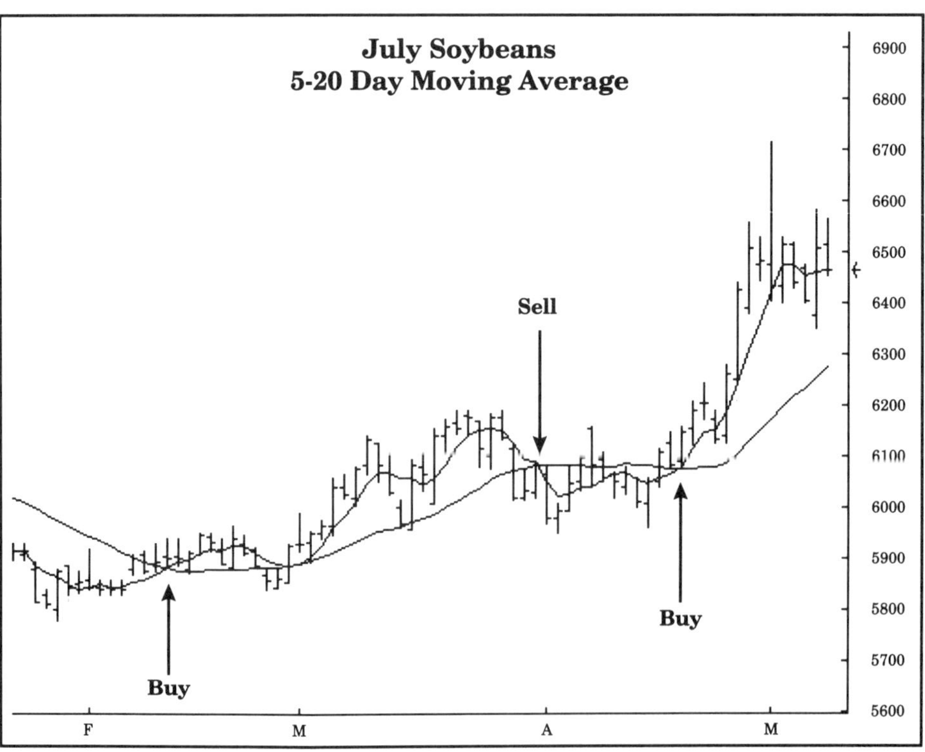

have sustained periods of gains and losses depending on the trendiness of the markets. Moving average systems, in general, are notorious for giving back too much of their hard-earned profits. Anyone who traded Donchian's system during the trending 1970s made regular and substantial profits, because of the big trends that prevailed during that period. The same system lost heavily during the middle and late 1980s.

Three Moving Averages

The most popular triple moving average is the widely followed 4-9-18-day method popularized by R. C. Allen in the early 1970s. The third moving average opens up a huge number of potential trading possibilities. Generally, when a market has bottomed, the major indication of a trend change is the 4-day crossing the 18-day. The confirming signal is the 9-day crossing the 18-day. As prices peak, the preliminary indication of a possible trend change will be the four-day crossing the nine-day. Taking profits at this point would help to overcome the profit give-back characteristic inherent in moving average systems. The trend reversal will be completed only when the 4-day and the 9-day cross the 18-day.

We like the triple moving average systems, because they offer the advantage of a neutral zone, as opposed to the continuous reversal trading called for by the single or double moving average methods. For example, in the 4-9-18 system, when the 4 crosses the 9 we exit our position and we don't take a new position in the market until the 9 crosses the 18; we also like the triple system because the 4 crossing the 9 is a quick profit-taking mechanism that overcomes some of the problem of giving back too much profit that we mentioned before. We believe that exits should always be quicker than entries in a successful trading system. Entries should be slow and selective, perhaps requiring an uncommon event to provoke a trade. Exits should be slow enough to patiently allow profits to run, yet quick enough to eventually capture the major portion of the potential gain. (See Exhibit 2–48.)

Four Moving Averages

Using four moving averages is neither as strange nor as difficult as it sounds. Used properly, the four moving averages approach addresses some of the problems inherent in moving averages while losing none of the advantages. The method uses the four moving averages in sets of two. The two longest moving averages are used strictly as trend identifiers and are most easily utilized when set up as an oscillator. The two shorter moving averages are more sensitive and are used for timing the entries and exits (usually on a crossover basis) while trading only in the direction signaled by the longer-term oscillator. Trades against the trend are, by definition, filtered out. If an uptrend exists (as defined by the longer-term oscillator) only long trades will be taken as signaled by the shorter-term crossovers. Conversely, only short trades will be taken

EXHIBIT 2–48

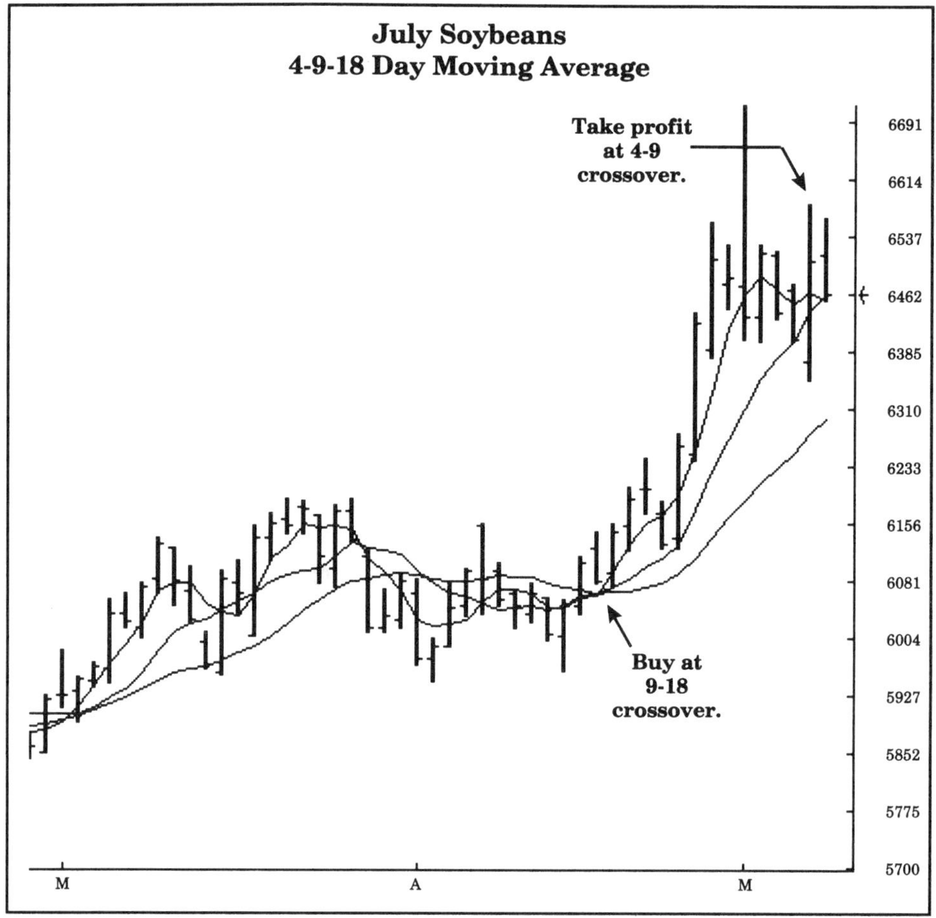

in a downtrend. There will be neutral periods during trend corrections and sideways markets when the short-term and long-term moving averages fail to confirm a direction. Whipsaws will not be entirely eliminated, but they will be significantly decreased. (See Exhibit 2–49.)

Displaced Moving Averages

One of the problems inherent in moving averages, or any other trend-following study, for that matter, is their inability to hug closely to a trend while still having the desired smoothing effect. As we've mentioned, slow moving averages smooth well but are often far from the action, while fast moving averages are overly responsive. Displaced moving averages attempt to remedy this defect. They are created by calculating a simple moving average in the normal way, and then projecting it into the future by displacing it a given number of days. As you can see from the accompanying chart (see Exhibit 2–50), the effect is that of moving the moving average forward in time. Just to see how they look, if your software won't do it (DMAs have been around a long time,

EXHIBIT 2–49

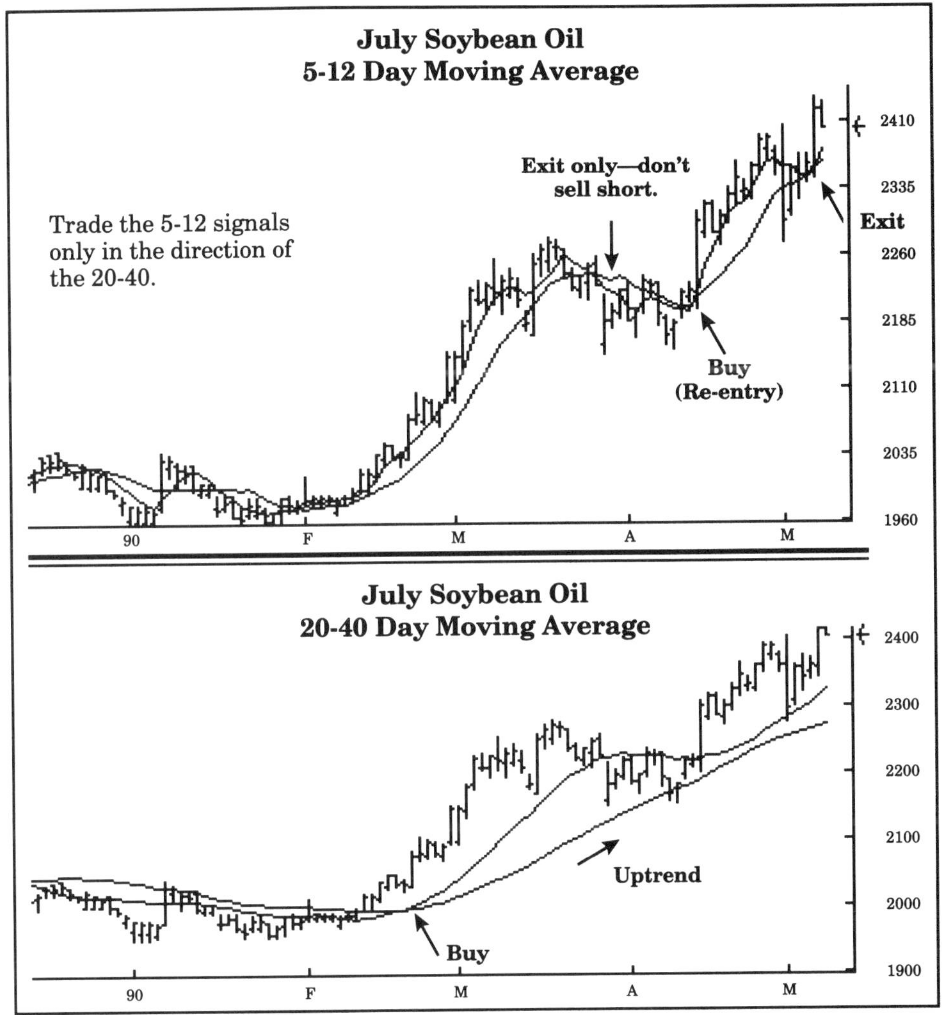

EXHIBIT 2–50

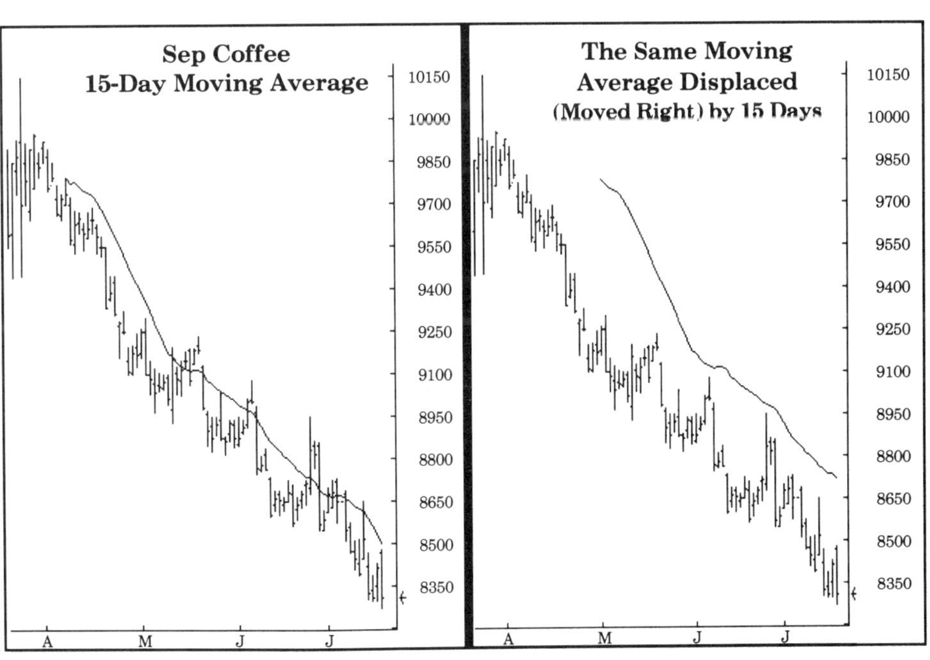

but are a recent phenomena in terms of popularity) create two charts, one with the prices and the other with a simple moving average, then place one on top of the other and hold them up to a strong light. Slide the moving averages to the right. You will see the result of displacing the moving average forward in time.

In most popular usage, the DMA is moved forward by the same number of periods used in its calculation. A 3 × 3 DMA is a three-period moving average moved forward three days. (See Exhibit 2–51.) Some traders prefer to shorten the displacement time period in relation to the moving average. A 10 × 5 DMA is a 10-day moving average displaced 5 days. (See Exhibit 2–52.)

The most common application of DMAs that we've run across is to use them as a short-term trend indicator. Joe DiNapoli, for instance, trades retracements within a trend defined by a DMA. (See Exhibit 2–53.) Other day traders prefer to use them to decide which side of the market to take intraday. For example, S&P futures trades may be entered only in the direction of a DMA calculated on 30- or 60-minute bars, using some other and more sensitive method to actually enter and exit the market. (See Exhibit 2–54.)

EXHIBIT 2–51

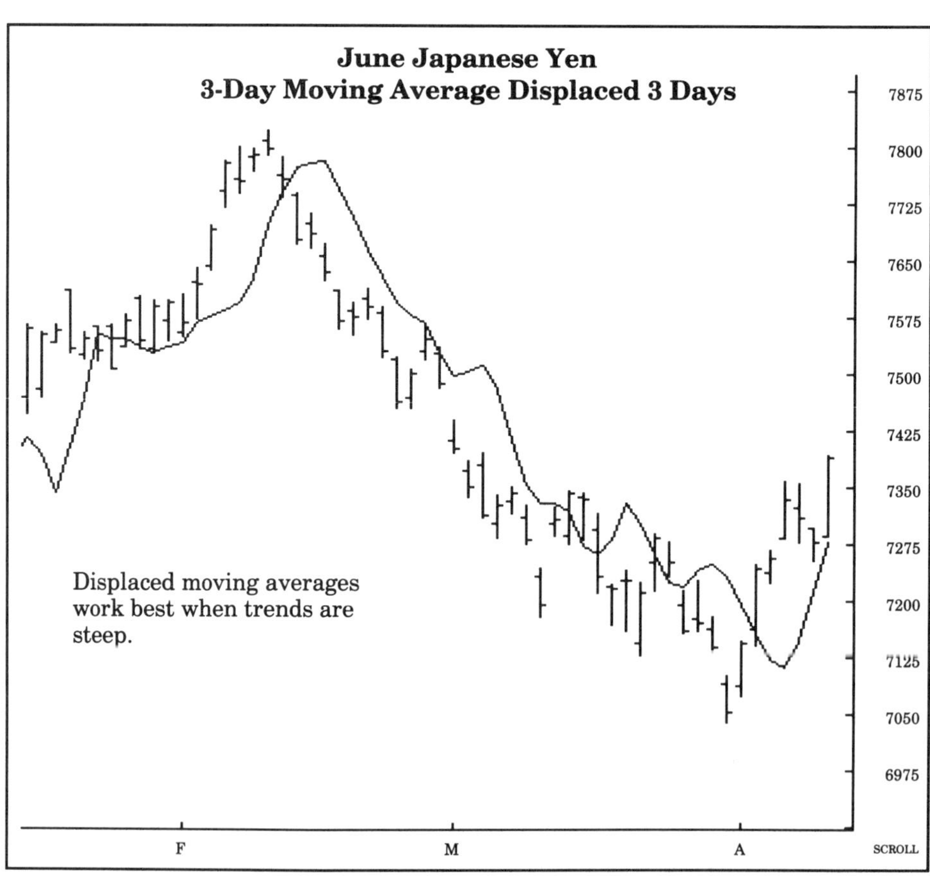

EXHIBIT 2–52

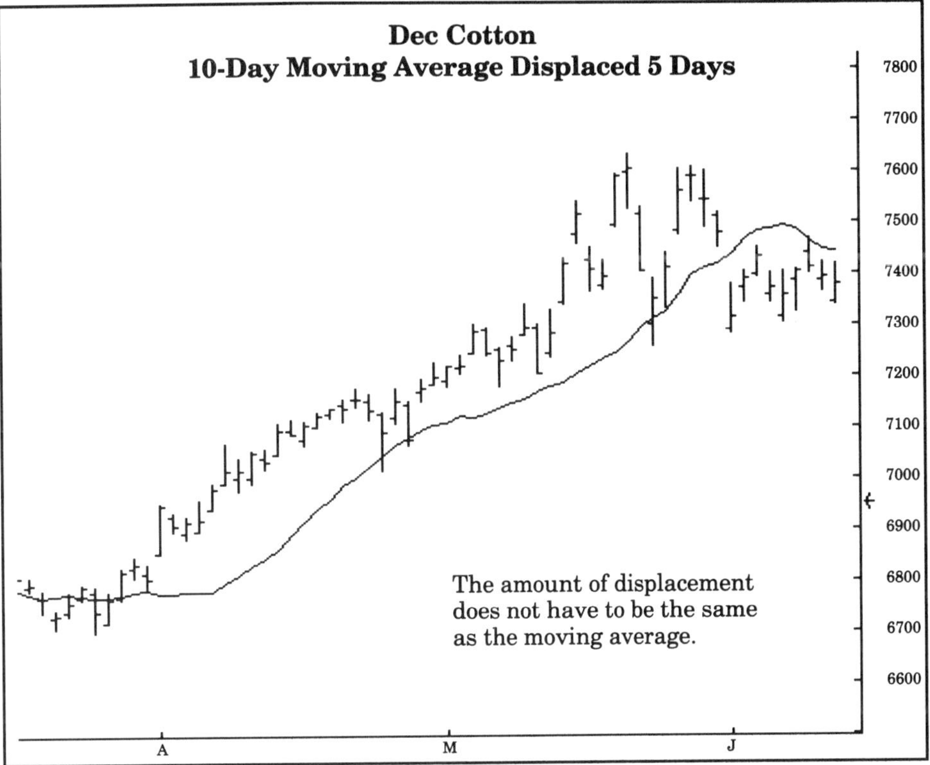
Dec Cotton
10-Day Moving Average Displaced 5 Days
7800
7700
7600
7500
7400
7300
7200
7100
7000
6900
6800
6700
6600
The amount of displacement does not have to be the same as the moving average.
A
M
J

EXHIBIT 2–53

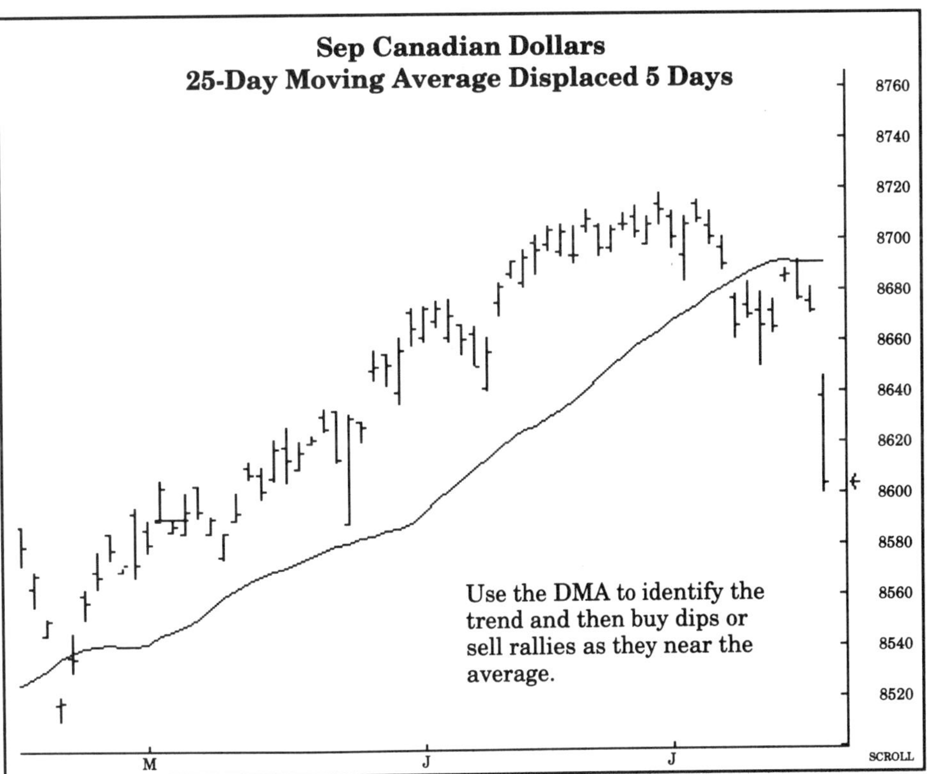
Sep Canadian Dollars
25-Day Moving Average Displaced 5 Days
8760
8740
8720
8700
8680
8660
8640
8620
8600
8580
8560
8540
8520
Use the DMA to identify the trend and then buy dips or sell rallies as they near the average.
M
J
J
SCROLL

EXHIBIT 2–54

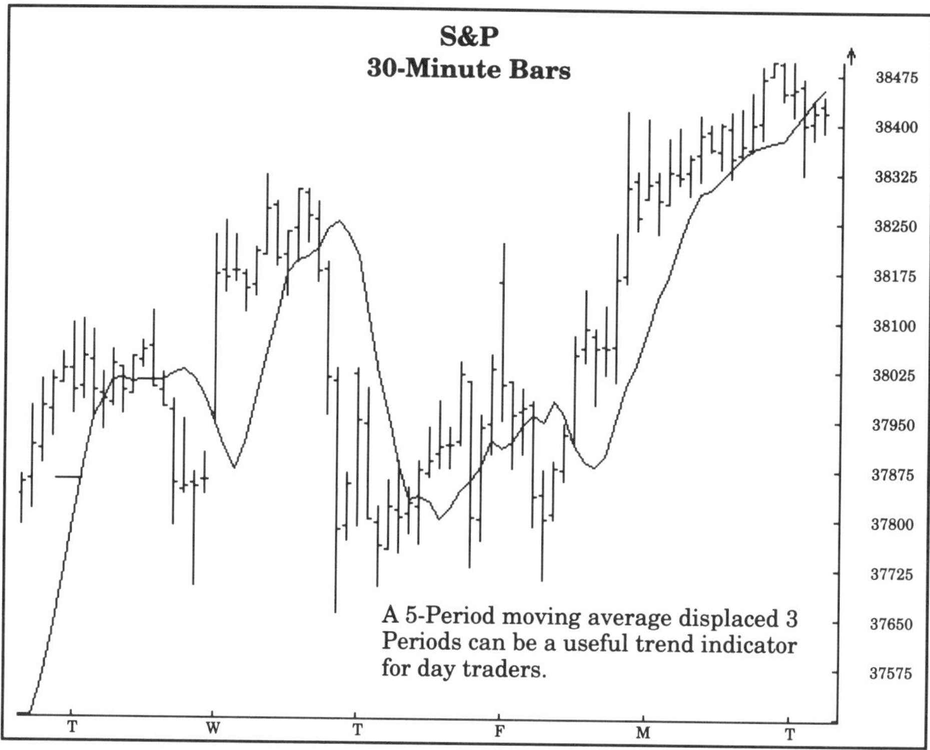

Finding a Filter

Rather than blindly following all crossovers, many traders use a variety of filters to decide if the initial signal is valid. Filters come in two categories: price filters and time filters.

1. Filtering signals by price normally means waiting for the price to meet some additional criteria before entering the trade. This might be determined by measuring the amount the price has penetrated the moving average or by measuring the distance that one moving average has crossed over another. The trader in this instance is looking for confirmation that the moving average crossing was not a random price event but is indeed a trend change. The new trade is not taken until the price has exceeded the moving average by a minimum amount. Another variation of this filter would be waiting for prices to move by a given percentage after a crossover. A further possibility (one that we've found is common) is waiting a given period after the crossover until the market has made a new high or low over the past *n* days—that is, a channel breakout. (See Exhibit 2–55.) One of our favorite filters or confirmation methods is simple: Wait until you get a close in the new trend direction.

2. Time filters involve waiting a number of time periods after the crossover before trading in the new direction. Many moving average traders have observed that most of the whipsaws are very immediate, and a slight delay in entry can avoid most of them. The waiting period would typically be from one to five days. If the price stays on the new side of the moving average for the minimum time period, it is assumed that

EXHIBIT 2–55

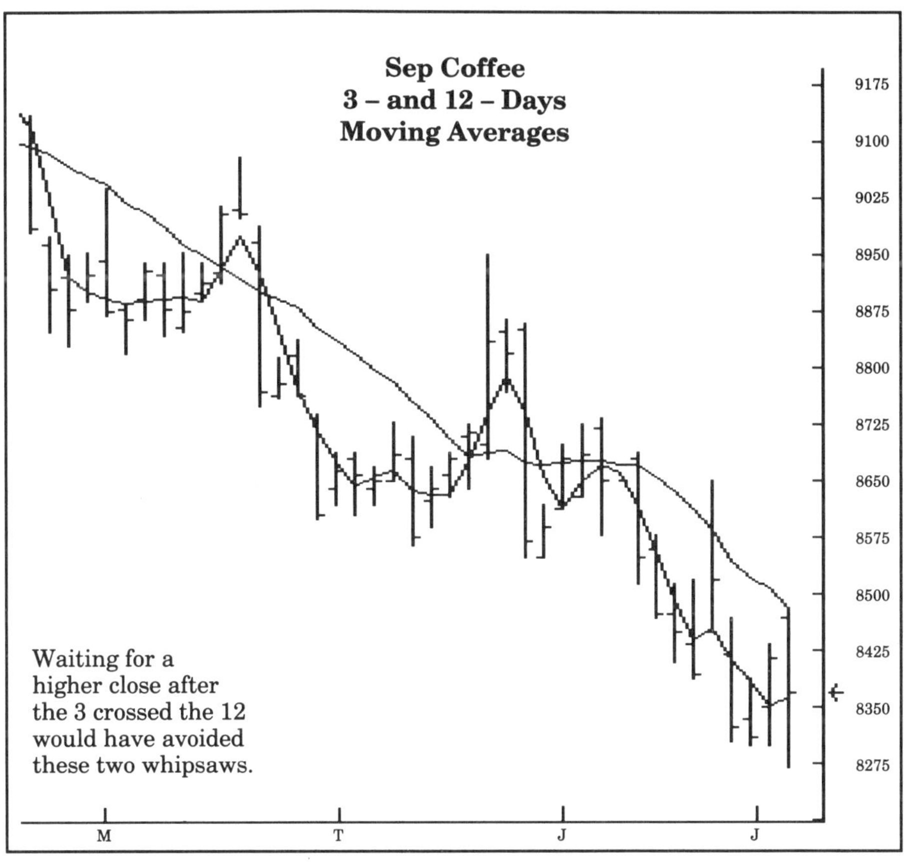

the signal was valid. Obviously, the waiting period will tend to reduce whipsaws, but it may also give such a late entry that a major portion of a move may be missed. (See Exhibit 2–56.)

Which Averages to Use?

There is no real answer to the question of what combination of moving averages works best. We once saw a massive computer-generated matrix that contained the year by year results of every moving average crossover between 1 and 100 going back for 15 years. The conclusion of this study over a portfolio of commodities was that moving averages only worked consistently if you knew in advance what particular combination to use in each commodity each year. The largest published test results that we're aware of were done by Frank Hochheimer in the early 1980s at Merrill Lynch.

We have done considerable work in this area ourselves and have tested hundreds of thousands of possible moving average combinations. We believe there is no magic answer. In practically every case, moving average values that worked well over past data didn't fare well in real-time trading. The testing method made no difference. In our testing, however, and in that of others where actual trade listings were

EXHIBIT 2–56

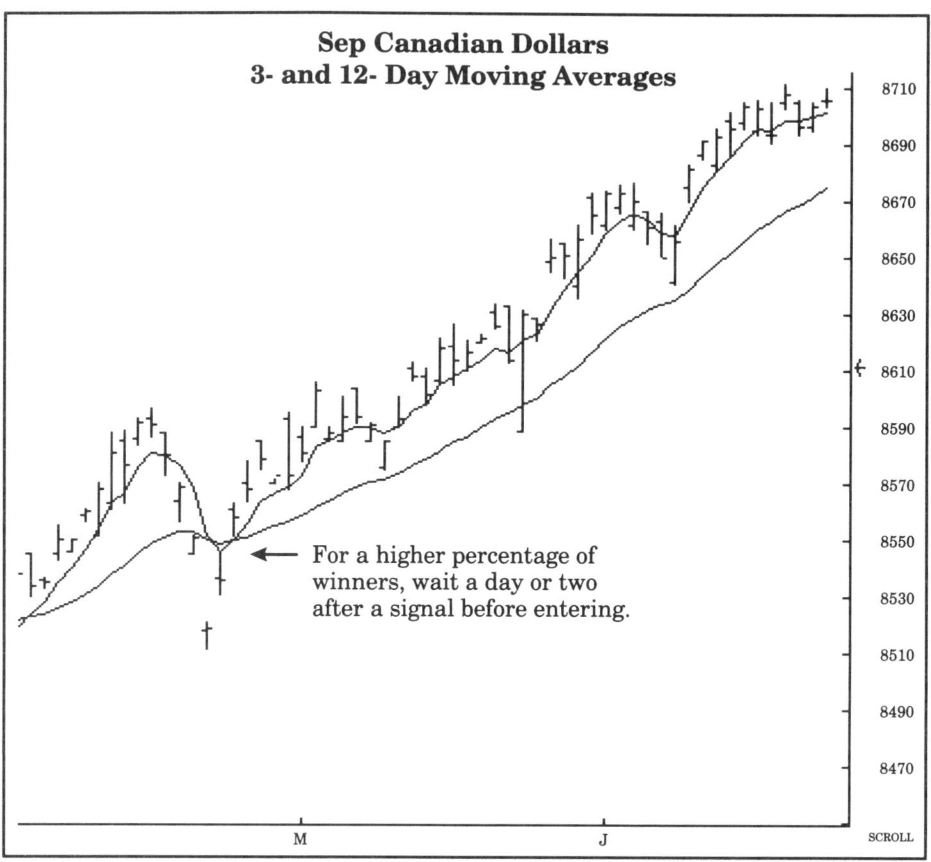

available, one phenomenon kept reappearing. As obvious as it sounds, almost any moving average combination is profitable if a market is trending, and almost no combination will produce profits if a market is not trending. The answer, therefore, is not in the search for the perfect moving average combinations. The answer lies in finding a reliable system that will isolate the markets in which moving averages, in general, will be profitable. Then we want to trade those markets in a manner calculated to capture the most profit with the least drawdown. Nontrending markets, we emphasize, should be avoided or traded using a countertrend type of indicator.

Making a Moving Average System Work

Moving averages are the simplest and most elegant trend-following study available. Within their limits they can be very effective, but their limitations can be severe. Most markets spend more time moving sideways than they do trending. A nontrending market can ruin the most carefully chosen moving average system. Here are some of our thoughts and conclusions on how to help a moving average system survive.

1. Try to confine your trading to only the trending markets. Diversification helps, but don't trade all markets indiscriminately. At any one time, usually less than 50 percent of all markets can be defined as trending. Most of the time the actual number is considerably less than that. Find a way to objectively define a market as trending, and only then apply moving averages. We recommend Wilder's DMI/ADX as a reliable study, one that indicates the extent to which a market is directional or trendless. A simple explanation is that, when the ADX is rising, the market is trending, and when it is falling, the market is directionless. The channel breakout filter mentioned earlier can also be effective.

2. Longer-term moving averages, in general, react too slowly for them to be useful for exits. Use an alternative exit strategy. We think the most common mistake made with moving averages is using the same set of moving averages for both entries and exits. If you use slow averages, you will be too slow to exit and give back most of the profits. If you use faster moving averages, you will have better exits but find yourself getting whipsawed on the entries. Even something as simple as a dollar trailing stop is normally better than allowing a moving average exit to give back profits.

The Moving Average Convergence-Divergence Trading Method

The moving average convergence-divergence trading method (usually abbreviated to MACD) was originally developed in 1979 by Gerald Appel as a stock market timing device. Although many traders still use MACD to trade exclusively in stock index futures and options, this doesn't mean that it can't be applied successfully to other contracts. As you will see, there are some excellent examples of MACD working effectively in various nonfinancial markets as well. After all, price action is price action, no matter what the market.

We like to place technical studies into either of two categories: those that are effective in trending markets and those that work best in choppy or nontrending markets. MACD is best used as a trend-following study. It works extremely well in orderly long-term markets, where you want to stay with the major trend while ignoring the minor price activity. One of the best applications of MACD is to use it on weekly or monthly charts as the indicator of long-term market direction. Normal use of MACD in nontrending markets will not be successful. Look for divergences when markets are not trending.

Briefly Looking at the Basics

MACD is a combination of three exponentially smoothed moving averages that are expressed as two lines. The first line represents the difference between a 12-period exponential moving average and a 26-period exponential moving average. The second line (called the *signal line*) is the approximate exponential equivalent of a 9-period moving average of the first line. The exponential values are 0.15, 0.075, and 0.20. The MACD can usually be displayed as either a line oscillator or a histogram.

Most software allows the user to change the values when calculating MACD. Some systems require entering the exponential values, while others use the actual number of periods for the three moving averages. We don't believe you should attempt to change the original values of MACD to curve-fit the data. However, it is important to note that Appel recommends two different sets of values: one for the buy side of the market and one for the sell side. Both use the 9-period (0.20) signal line, but the 0.15, 0.075 combination is for the sell side only. The buy side values are 8-period (0.22) and 17-period (0.11). (See Exhibit 2–57.)

Using a buy formula and a sell formula may require a whole new mode of thinking for casual users of MACD. It's always good to be original, but you should be aware of the developer's thinking when you use any technical study. If your software defaults to the sell side parameters, as is common, or if it does not allow you to change these values, you may not be using MACD as its originator intended. Ideally, your computer screen should be set up to display a chart of the futures price data and two additional charts, one showing the MACD buy side formula and the other the sell side formula. You will find the buy formula to be slightly quicker and a bit more prone to whipsaw. The sell formula is slower. It seems the intent was to buy quickly and try to hold and let the profits run. We think there might be a buy side design in these two

EXHIBIT 2–57

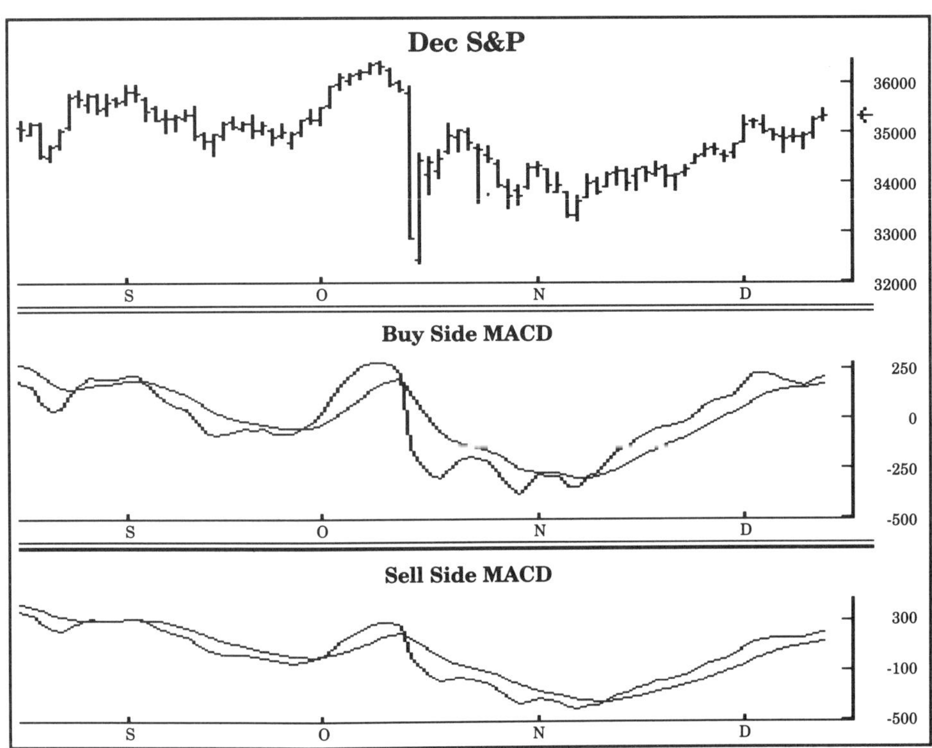

formulas, which is understandable considering their original purpose. For markets other than the stock market, you might consider just sticking with the standard sell formula, unless you have a reason to want a quicker and less reliable signal.

Trading with MACD Crossovers

The basic MACD signal is the crossover. Buy signals are generated when the faster line crosses the slower line from below, and sell signals are just the opposite. We want to caution you immediately that, in most markets, mechanically trading every MACD crossover will result in frequent whipsaws and substantial drawdowns. You would quickly find that narrow trading ranges play havoc with the indicator, giving many false signals and piling up losses. Thankfully, there are additional interpretations of MACD that can help a trader avoid the whipsaw problems and other pitfalls. (See Exhibit 2–58.)

Using Overbought/Oversold Levels

MACD can be used to signal points at which the market is becoming overbought or oversold and is vulnerable to a retracement. Looking at the faster moving of the two MACD lines, Appel sets the overbought/oversold areas for the S&P Index as +/−2.50 on the MACD scale. For the NYSE index, he recommends +/−1.20. Once the differential line

EXHIBIT 2–58

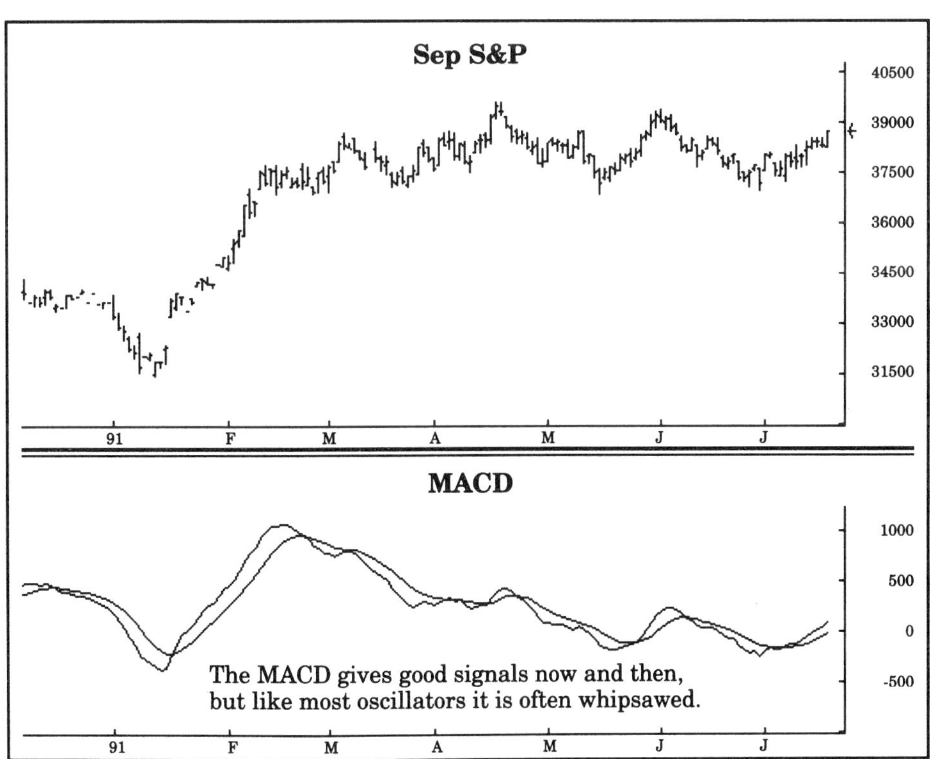

has reached these critical areas, any crossover generates a buy or sell signal. Crossovers that occur without reaching an extreme level can be ignored, so many of the whipsaws can be eliminated. With a little research, similar thresholds can be observed for any market that is in a broad trading range with wide price swings. Remember, MACD is best used as a longer-term trend-following tool and not a short-term trading timer. Signals that occur in the mid-range of the MACD chart should be taken only if another trusted indicator verifies that the trade will be in the direction of the trend. (See Exhibit 2–59.)

MACD Trendlines

One very interesting way of using MACD is to get a jump on a crossover signal by drawing a trendline on the MACD itself and then trading when the trendline is broken, rather than waiting for the crossover. A break in an MACD trendline can precede an important break in the market, and it serves as an early warning signal that a market is turning. MACD crossovers that are preceded by or in conjunction with a trendline break tend to have much more technical importance than MACD crossovers alone. Aggressive traders might consider entering the market immediately upon a trendline break in anticipation of a MACD crossover, while more cautious traders might prefer to wait for the actual crossover as a confirmation. Remember, if you trade based solely on a break in the trendline without waiting for the crossover, the trade will have little justification if the crossover fails to occur in the near future. You might find yourself in the unfortunate situation of using a MACD system but winding up in a non-MACD trade and looking for some other method to get you out. (See Exhibit 2–60.)

EXHIBIT 2–59

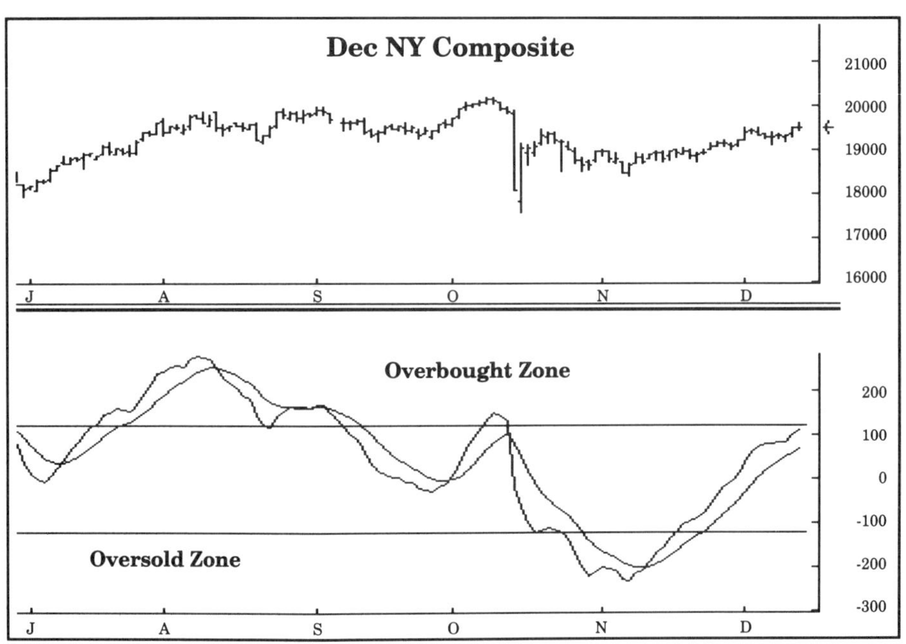

EXHIBIT 2–60

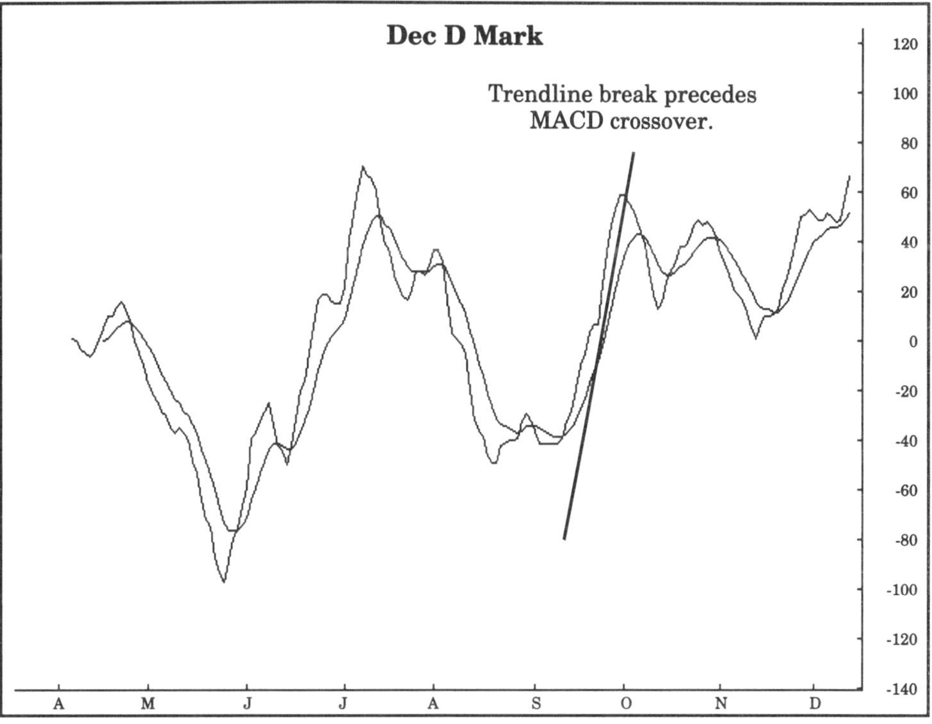

Look for Divergence

In our opinion, the most valuable and significant MACD patterns are divergences, especially in nontrending markets. These are two-step patterns that occur when the market makes a high or low and then a subsequent new high or low that the MACD fails to confirm (see Exhibit 2–60). Divergences are very effective patterns with most technical studies, and MACD is no exception. With MACD, divergences are most helpful for showing the resumption of a trend after a correction, rather than as trend reversal signals.

As with all divergences, it is best not to anticipate but to wait for the divergence to fully establish itself before entering the market. Nothing will make you feel more foolish than making a trade in anticipation of a divergence that never comes. You will be squarely on the wrong side of a strong trend. (See Exhibit 2–61.)

Combining Signals

As you might imagine, a divergence that occurs in conjunction with a MACD trendline break and a crossover is a powerful signal indeed. In general, the trendline break comes first as the market begins running out of momentum. The divergence pattern is next, generally coinciding with a double top or bottom in the market. Finally, the crossover at the market turn signals the entry.

EXHIBIT 2–61

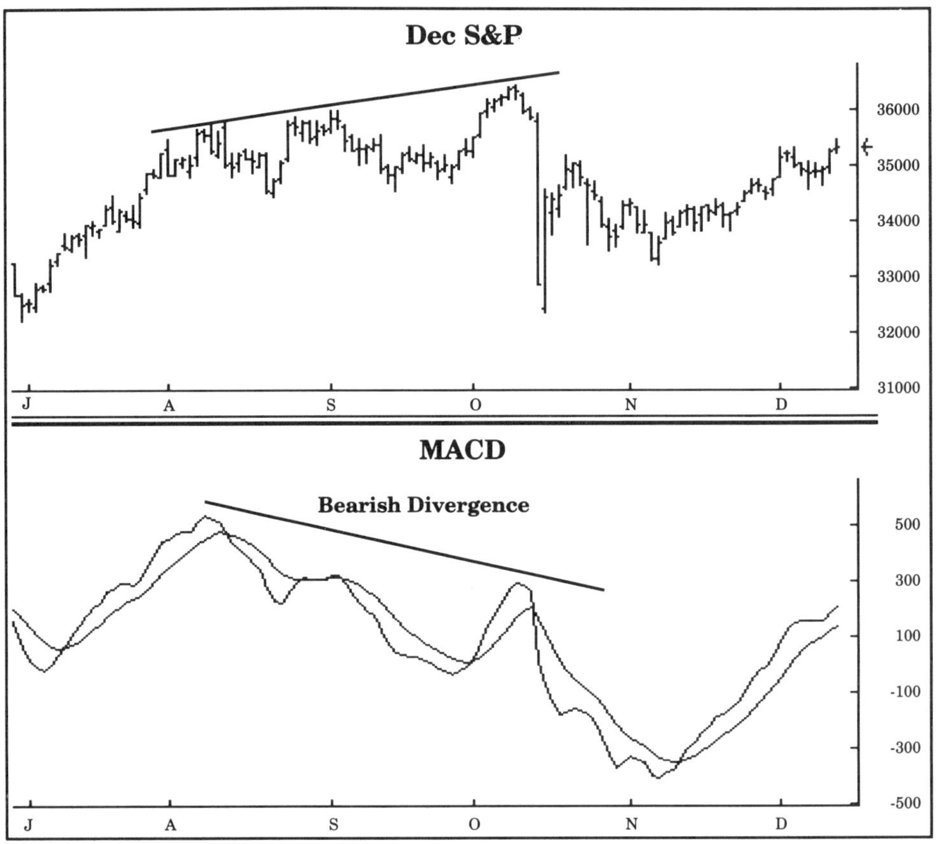

Remember, MACD crossovers alone are generally not significant unless accompanied by one or two of the patterns we have described. As we cautioned earlier, do not mechanically trade the crossovers and expect to make any money. Our testing shows that, when MACD is traded this way, it is a break-even system, less transaction costs. These results are similar to test results when other technical studies are traded this way and should be taken with a grain of salt, despite what you may have read. (See Exhibit 2–62.)

Trading with the Trend

Major trends can be identified by using a longer-term MACD to confirm the shorter-term MACD. Use a monthly MACD to confirm weekly patterns. Use a weekly MACD to confirm daily MACD patterns. Use a daily MACD to confirm intraday patterns. Trade the shorter-term signals only in the direction indicated by the longer-term MACD and you will avoid at least half of the potential whipsaws.

Another method would be to use a different technical study, such as a medium-term single simple moving average, or a dual simple moving average, to find the intermediate-term trend. Then take MACD signals only in the direction of the trend. (See Exhibit 2–63.)

EXHIBIT 2–62

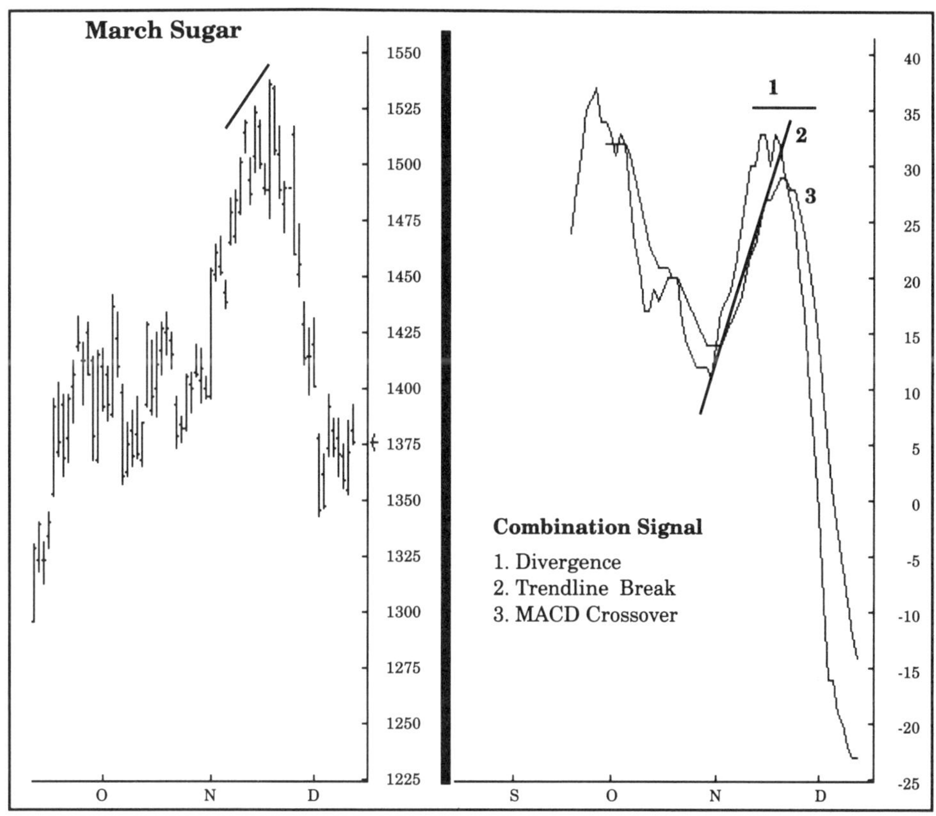

March Sugar
1550
1525
1500
1475
1450
1425
1400
1375
1350
1325
1300
1275
1250
1225
O
N
D
1
2
3
40
35
30
25
20
15
10
5
0
-5
-10
-15
-20
-25
Combination Signal
1. Divergence
2. Trendline Break
3. MACD Crossover
S
O
N
D

EXHIBIT 2–63

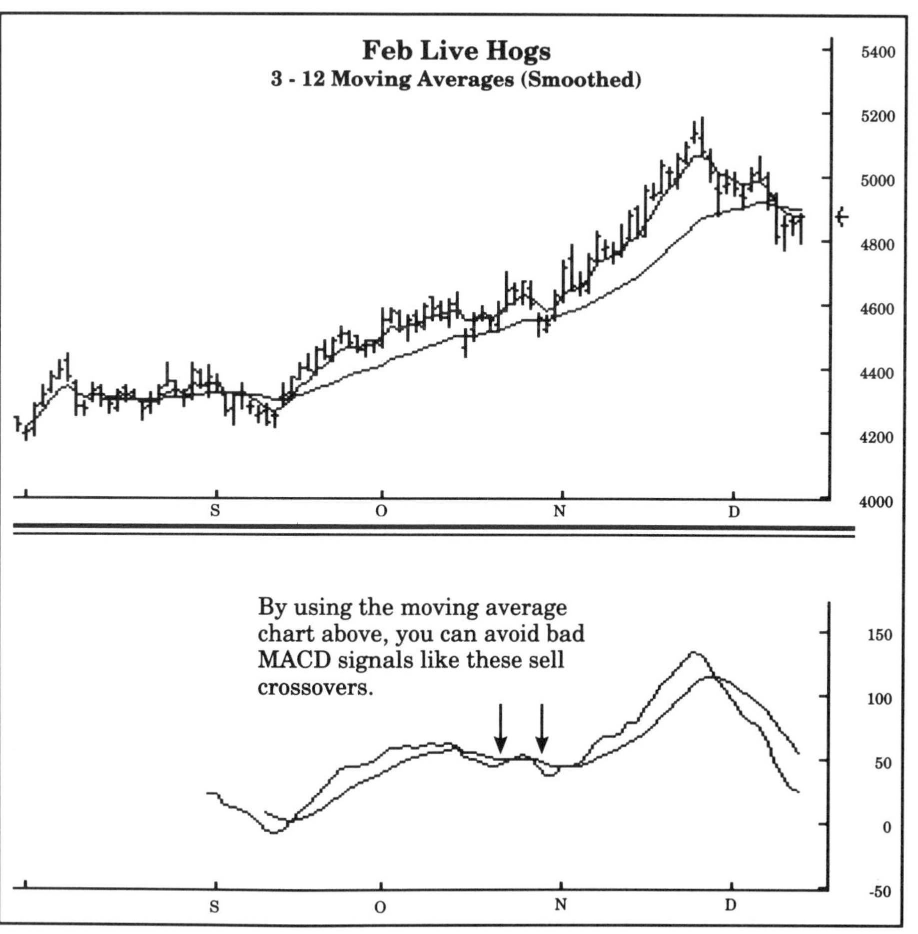

Feb Live Hogs
3 - 12 Moving Averages (Smoothed)
5400
5200
5000
4800
4600
4400
4200
4000
S
O
N
D
By using the moving average chart above, you can avoid bad MACD signals like these sell crossovers.
150
100
50
0
-50
S
O
N
D

EXHIBIT 2–64

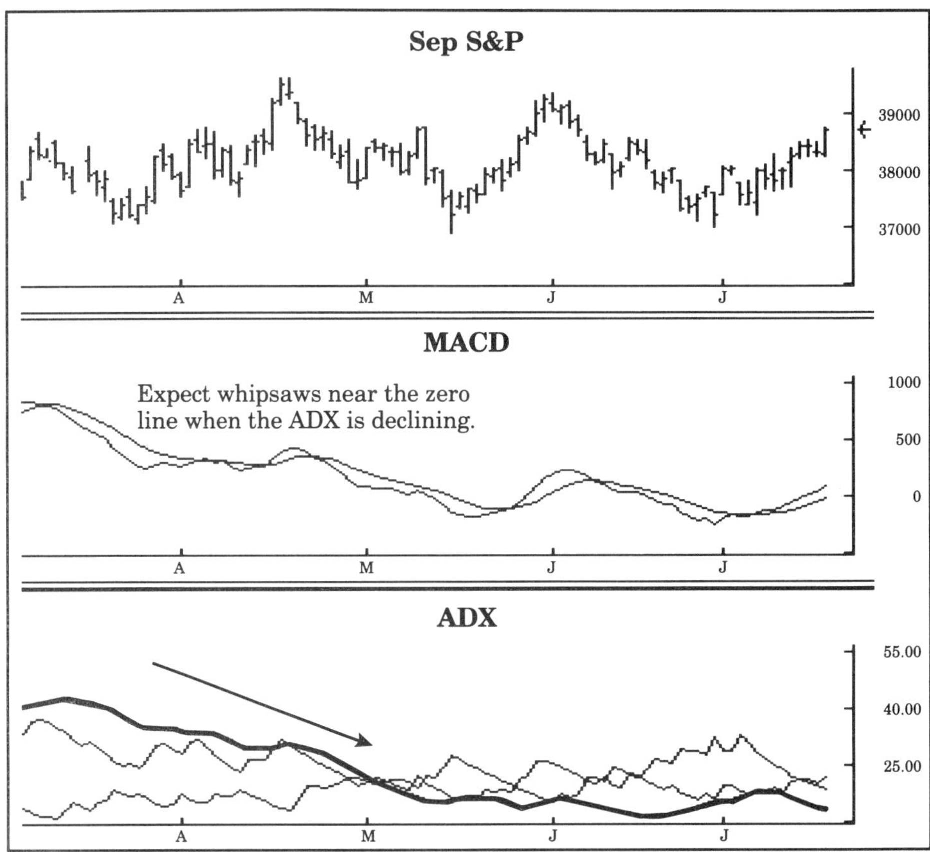

Whatever trend identifying method you select, it would be beneficial to be able to determine not only the direction of the trend but to measure its strength. The absence or presence of trends in a market can be measured by using Wilder's ADX. Use an 18-day ADX and, if the ADX is rising, the trend has strength and the MACD signals should do well overall. If the ADX is falling, the trend lacks momentum, normal MACD trades are likely to fail, and you should be looking for divergences. This should help filter out many of the non-trending markets that are responsible for losses when trading the MACD. (See Exhibit 2–64.)

Parabolic

The Parabolic time/price system is a trend-following technical study that attempts to address two problems inherent in most trend-following systems: giving back profits, because of lagging exit signals, and failing to include time as a factor, when calculating stop points. The Parabolic formula solves the price lag problem by tightening stops at an accelerating rate whenever a new high or low is reached. The Parabolic formula also factors time into its calculations, allowing the stop to remain distant for a brief period and then relentlessly moving it closer, regardless of the price action. The result of this time function is that prices must continue to move in the direction of the trend or the trade will be stopped out.

We consider the Parabolic to be an excellent technical tool when used for exits only. We don't recommend using it for entries or as a reversal system, as intended by its originator.

Parabolic's Origins

The Parabolic formula was first described by Welles Wilder in his 1978 book, *New Concepts in Technical Trading Systems* (see "Suggested Readings"). Wilder was looking for a system that could capture most of the gains in a trending market, without relying on some external method to retain profits. The Parabolic calculation results in a series of trailing stops that, if hit, indicate a trend reversal. The stops are recalculated every day (or for every time period you're using) and get tighter as the trend progresses. If the trend fails to continue, the moving stop will reverse the position and a new time period begins.

Used alone, the Parabolic is a reversal system that is always in the market pursuing a trend. We don't regard the Parabolic as one of the best stand-alone trend-following technical studies. However, in combination with other indicators it can be extremely effective. We believe Parabolic's greatest value is as a method of setting stops.

It is helpful to explain the nature of the various elements that make up the Parabolic in order to use it most effectively. As we mentioned, the Parabolic was intended by Wilder to be a reversal system. Wilder called the point at which the system reverses the "stop and reverse" (SAR). As you can see from Exhibit 2–65, the series of SAR points form a line similar to a trend line but curving in the shape of a parabola or French Curve, so that the stop points remain close to the market.

To calculate the first SAR, you must assume some starting point. Wilder recommended going back several weeks on a chart and finding a significant high or low to start the calculations. Most computer studies merely start at the left side of the screen; if the first few days are up, the formula will assume an uptrend. If the first few days are down, the formula will assume a downtrend. For practical purposes, it doesn't really matter in which direction the Parabolic starts, because it will eventually wind up on the side of the trend. We advise software users with variable window widths to make sure that the Parabolic window contains at least 100 data points. Without this minimal data, the first SARs may temporarily assume incorrect trends.

Once the original entry point and the first SAR are set, the formula for subsequent SARs is as follows: SAR (tomorrow) = SAR (today) + AF × EP − SAR (today). AF is the acceleration factor and EP is the extreme high or low point for the prior trade. Note that the previous extreme price and the acceleration factor combine to keep the SARs close to the trend.

EXHIBIT 2–65

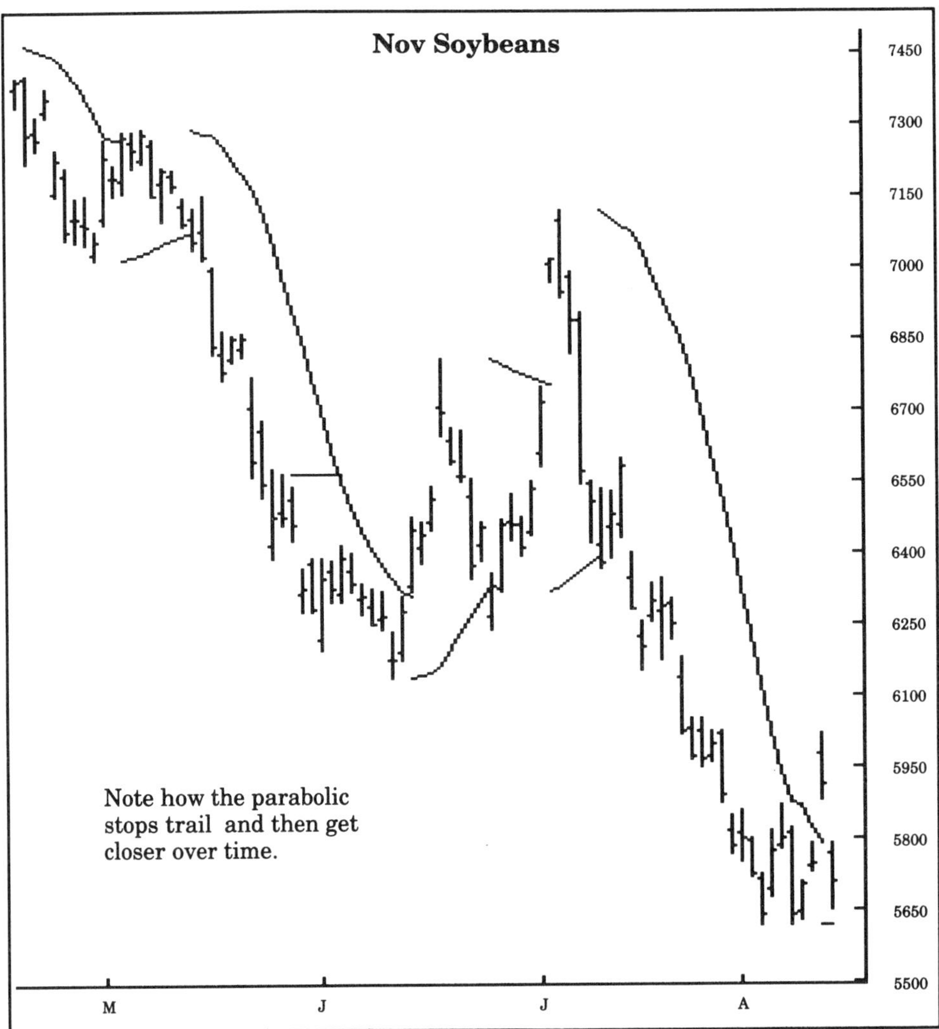

The previous extreme price, EP, is easily understandable. The AF, however, is what makes the Parabolic unique. The AF is a weighting factor. Wilder used an initial AF value of 0.02. The AF is then increased by 0.02 every time a new extreme price is made, causing the accelerating points on the chart. The AF does not increase unless a new EP is made, and it never increases past a value of 0.20. The acceleration factor's range, therefore, is 0.02 to 0.20, in increments of 0.02. These are default values for most packaged software, but they sometimes can be adjusted by the user.

Changing the Acceleration

Changing the AF values will have the effect of tightening or loosening the SAR stops, thus making the system more or less sensitive to market moves. If the AF is increased, the stops get closer and the system is more sensitive. If the AF is decreased, the stops get farther away and the system slows down. The following charts allow us to compare an AF value of 0.01 using 0.01 increments, and an AF value of 0.03 using 0.03 increments. As you can see in the chart below (Exhibit 2–66), the differences can be dramatic.

It is almost always possible to find a set of initial and incremental values for the Parabolic (or any study) that shows profits when tested against historical data. We recommend using the standard default values. Try to avoid curve-fitting the indicator to the data.

For those who are interested, Colby and Meyers in *The Encyclopedia of Technical Market Indicators* tested the Parabolic against 18 years of weekly New York Composite data, using it strictly as a reversal system. They showed it to be mildly profitable with the standard AF values and, of course, very profitable when optimized. They obtained best results by raising the AF from 0.02 up to 0.20. We would rather trust the test results that used the standard values; we are skeptical about this type of optimization. For example, if Colby and Meyers had used 15 years of data instead of 18, it's practically certain that their optimal AF would have been different. If they had tested each year of their data separately, in sequence, the AF for each succeeding year would be different from the last. Do you change the value every year? Every month? We believe it is far better to find values that perform reasonably well over time without change, rather than chasing the impossible dream of the perfect value for tomorrow.

EXHIBIT 2–66

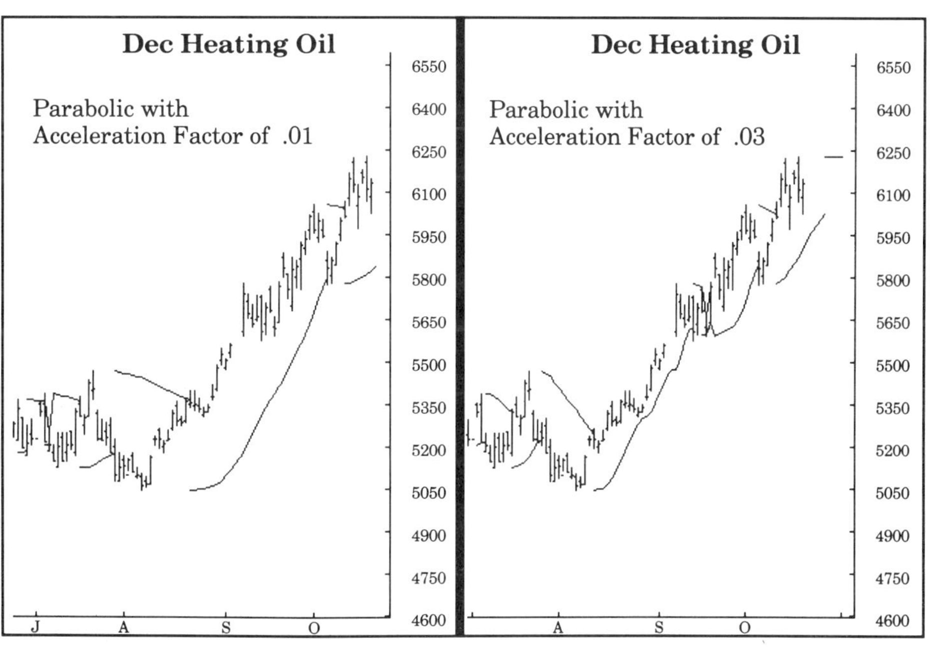

Wilder on AF Values

Wilder in his book (see "Suggested Readings") made the following important observation:

> I have tried many different acceleration factors and have found that a consistent increase of 0.02 works best overall; however, *if you desire to individualize this system in order to vary the stop points from what others may be using,* the range for the incremental increase is between 0.018 and 0.021. Any constant increase within this range will work well. [Emphasis added.]

Wilder seemed to be concerned about too many stops at one point in the market, and we share that concern. Some modification of the acceleration may be in order, not for the sake of optimization but to keep your stops different from the crowd. Remember, the Parabolic is a very well known and popular study, probably much more popular than Wilder imagined when he suggested individualizing his formula.

Trading with the Parabolic

Although the Parabolic solves one of the major deficiencies of most trend-following indicators by trailing stops closer to the market, it still suffers when a market turns choppy. Since nontrending markets are more common than trending markets, this makes the Parabolic a losing system under most market conditions. What's needed is a filter that reduces the exposure to choppy markets, and an entry timer that allows the Parabolic to do what it does best: trail stops in a trending market.

Wilder recognized the Parabolic's limitations and recommended using it in conjunction with his directional movement index (DMI) or the commodity selection index (CSI), although he didn't give specific guidelines or rules.

Kaufman's Directional Parabolic System

A good example of how to go about combining the Parabolic and the directional movement index is given by Perry Kaufman in his book, *The New Commodity Trading Systems and Methods.* He merges the two methods into a system he calls the "Directional Parabolic." Here is a summary of his rules:

1. Use a 14-day DMI.
2. If the DMI indicates upward movement, take only long Parabolic trades. If the DMI is down, take only short trades.
3. Enter a trade only if the systems agree. If they conflict, there is no trade.
4. Use the Parabolic stop as an exit only, not as a reversal.
5. Exit the trade if the ADX rises above the +DI or −DI and then reverses. This action indicates a weakening of the trend. (See Exhibit 2–67.)

EXHIBIT 2–67

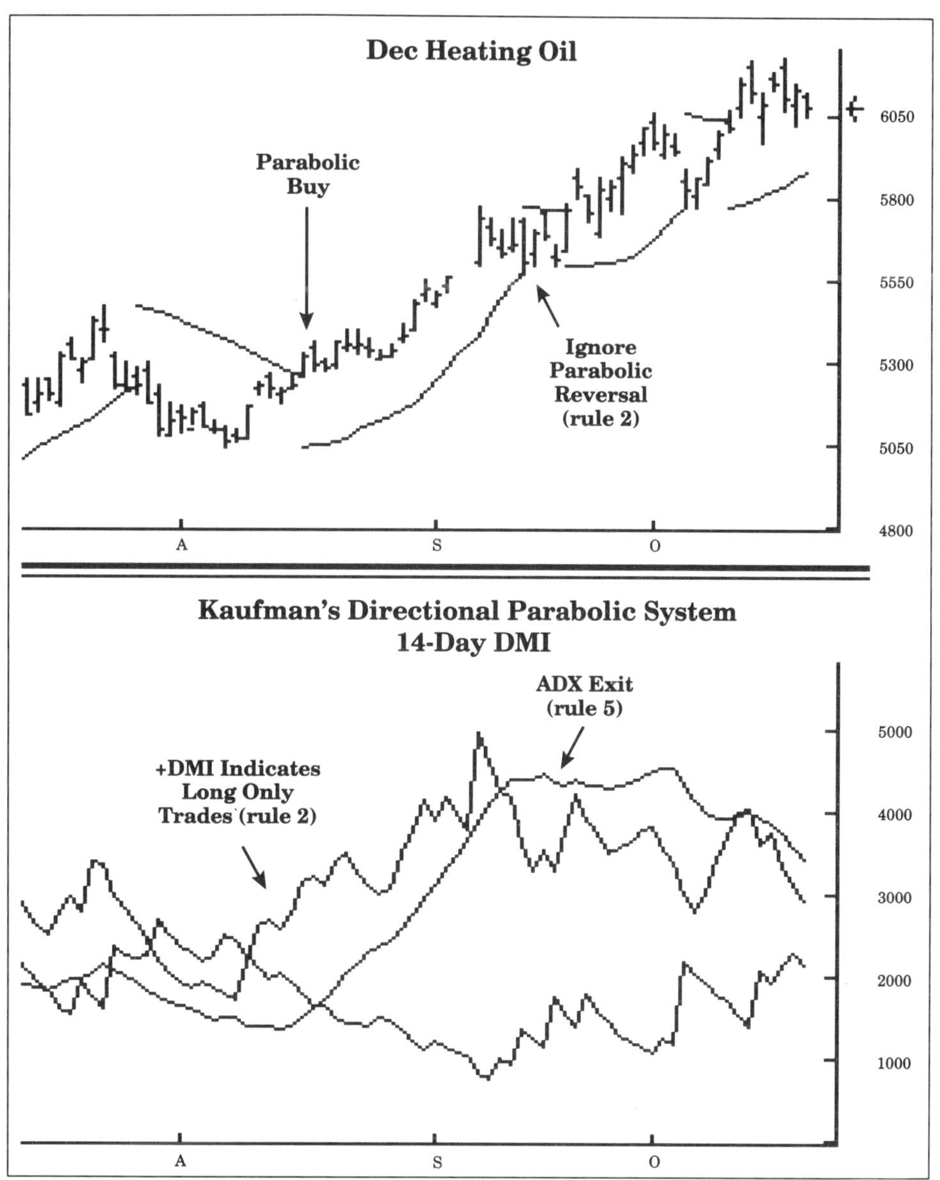

Another Parabolic Trading System

Here is an example of a simple method of trading with the Parabolic that incorporates the ADX and helps to eliminate many of the whipsaws. The method is much the same as Kaufman's, but it is simpler and relies on the Parabolic's tight stops for exits. It reflects three of the most important rules that should be adhered to when trading: Trade with the trend, control your risk, let your profits run.

Here are the rules:

1. Use an 18-day ADX and DMI. Do not initiate any trades when the direction of the ADX is downward.

2. When the ADX begins moving upward, enter in the direction of the DMI only if the Parabolic direction agrees. If the Parabolic does not agree, wait and enter when it reverses.
3. Once a trade is entered, use the Parabolic stops to exit.
4. After an exit re-enter when the prices cross back above the Parabolic, assuming the ADX is still rising and the DMI shows the trend is still intact. This time the Parabolic is used for the entry timing. (See Exhibit 2–68.)

The method is simple and logical, because the ADX changing to an upward direction indicates the beginning of directional movement. The DMI tells you whether the movement is up or down. The Parabolic provides confirmation of the direction and tight accelerating stops that control risk while capturing the maximum amount of profit.

EXHIBIT 2–68

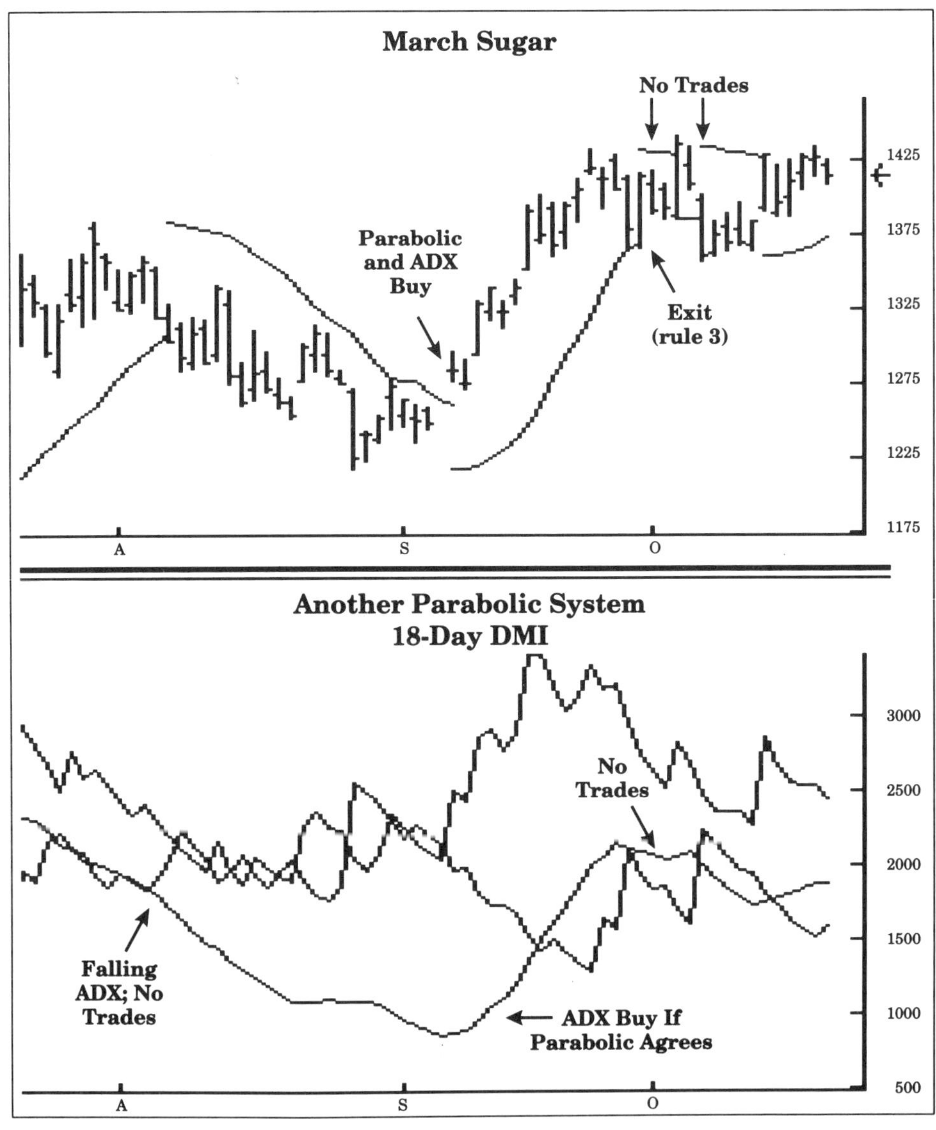

Percent R

Percent R—often shortened to plain %R—fits in the family of oscillators that includes stochastics and the Relative Strength Index (RSI). Percent R, like the others, is designed to identify overbought and oversold areas in a nontrending market.

Larry Williams' %R ?

Larry Williams is generally associated with Percent R because of his introduction of the indicator in his book, *How I Made One Million Dollars Last Year Trading Commodities*. We are told that George Lane of stochastics fame was the actual originator of Percent R, because it is really a stochastic, which uses the high price, rather than the low price in the numerator. The study is commonly referred to as Williams' Percent R, due to his extensive work in interpreting and publicizing the indicator. Because it is a stochastic, we'll keep our remarks brief and refer you to the stochastics section for a fuller discussion of its derivation and uses.

Common Trading Rules

Percent R is expressed as a value between minus 0 and minus 100. The value tells you where each time period's close fits, on a percentage basis, within the range of highest highs and lowest lows. The R in the indicator's name stands for range. When the closing price is in the upper portion of the range, the market is considered to be overbought. When the close is in the lower portion of the range, the market is considered to be oversold.

The normal time interval is 10. We suggest you use 10 or more as the time interval and −10 and −90 as the overbought and oversold levels.

There are three basic trading rules for using Percent R. These are the rules for the buy side. The sell side is the opposite. You buy when:

1. Percent R has reached 100.
2. Five trading days have elapsed since the last 100 was hit.
3. Percent R subsequently falls below 95. (To graphically see this, see Exhibit 2–69.)

Williams recommended using a 10-week moving average or momentum, or both, to establish a market direction, then trading only with the trend. Despite the original trading methods he described, we do not recommend it as a trend-following device. Many other studies work better for trading a trending market. This doesn't mean Percent R isn't worthwhile (see Exhibit 2–69), but, if the trend is strong, the values can stay at one end of the scale for days or weeks, while giving many false signals against the trend and few or no signals with the trend. Searching for the few worthwhile trades that Percent R gives you in trending markets can be a fruitless and expensive exercise. (See Exhibit 2–70.)

EXHIBIT 2–69

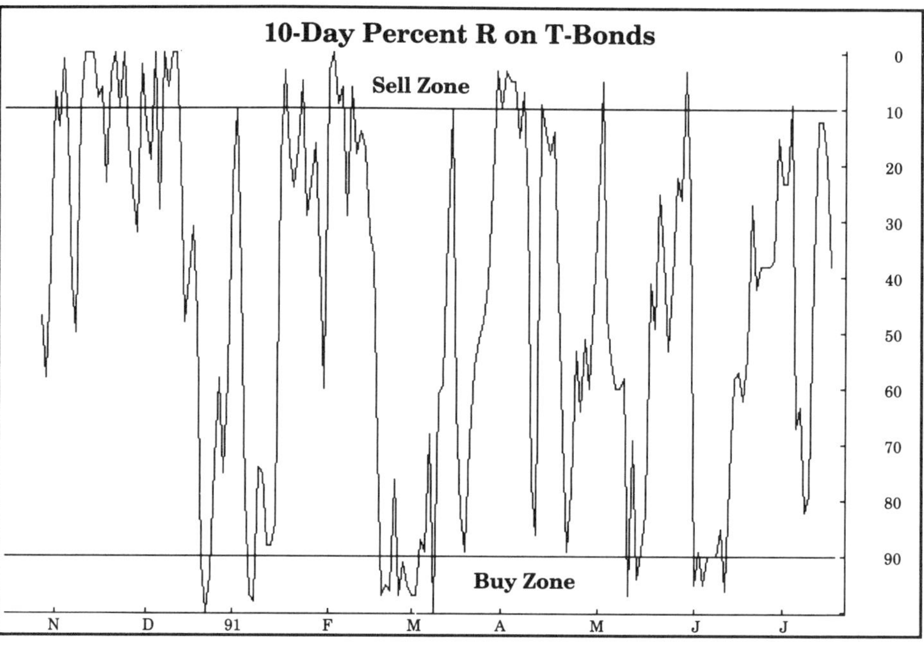

EXHIBIT 2–70

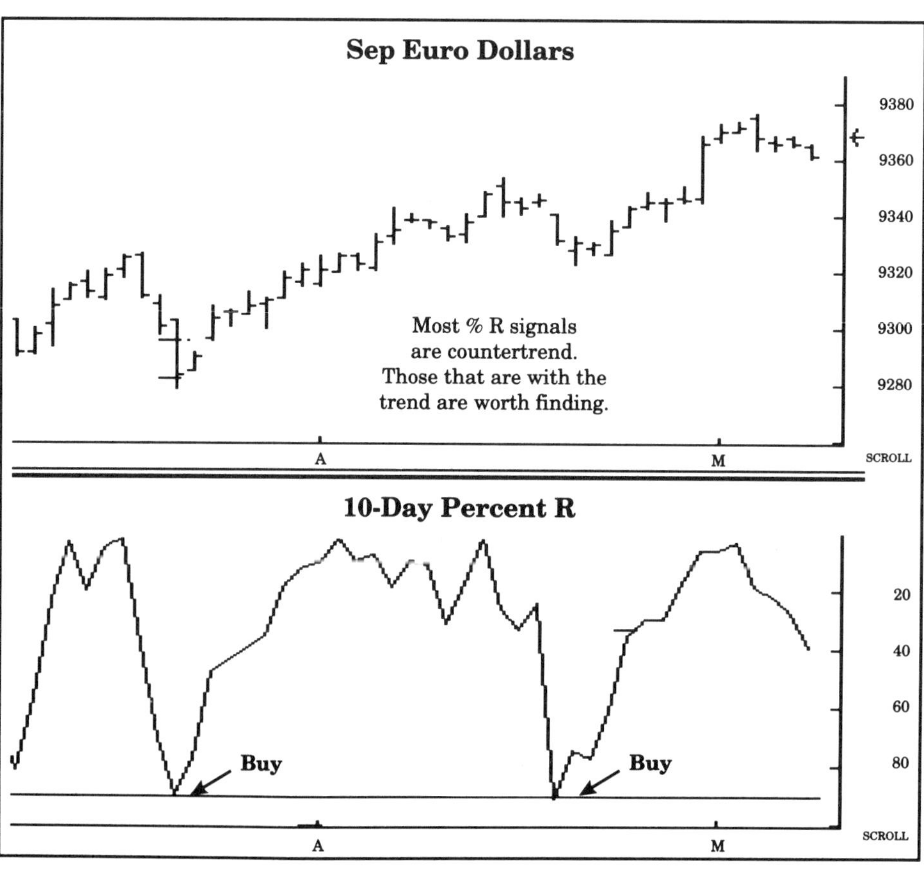

Profit Taking

Despite our negative comments about using Percent R in a trending market, it can be useful as an exit tool. If you've entered using moving averages, or some other trend-following method, waiting for the same indicator for exiting will often result in lost profits. Because it is very quick, Percent R can be useful in protecting profits.

Some tips on profit taking with Percent R:

1. If you're long, use the Percent R oversold zone (−90) to define the bottom of a correction within a trend. Exit or trail stops below the bottom of the correction.
2. Or, wait for Percent R to become overbought (−10). Then, when it hooks downward by 10 or more points, take profits, or trail tight stops. (See Exhibit 2–71.)

Divergence

Percent R, like any oscillator, can be very effective when divergence patterns are noted. When a commodity makes a new high or low, but Percent R fails to confirm by also making a new high or low, we have a divergence. These signals work best when both spikes in Percent R are overbought or oversold. As with most divergences in oscillators, the signals generated can be very powerful, particularly in a sideways market. Despite Percent R's quickness, you'll find surprisingly few divergences. Keep an eye out for these patterns. They're worth waiting for. (See Exhibit 2–72.)

Point and Figure

Point-and-figure charts have successfully withstood the test of time, having been used for at least 100 years longer than the software currently used to plot them. They can be a very complex subject, about which a great many books have been written. What we intend to do here is to examine some modern point-and-figure charting methods that relate to the computer user.

Point-and-figure charts can be valuable tools for the technician, because of their basic simplicity. Much like moving averages, they allow the chartist to filter out minor unwanted or insignificant price gyrations. The ability to eliminate spurious price data produces an easy to interpret chart of only those price movements that the user determines to be relevant. By filtering out distracting price static and by eliminating the time scale, point-and-figure charts represent the ultimate in simplicity: pure price movement.

The absence of a time scale and the absence of complete price data would probably be considered a disadvantage by most technicians. But for those who wish to focus on price only, or for those who use them in conjunction with other indicators, point-and-figure charts offer some unique advantages over conventional charting methods.

EXHIBIT 2–71

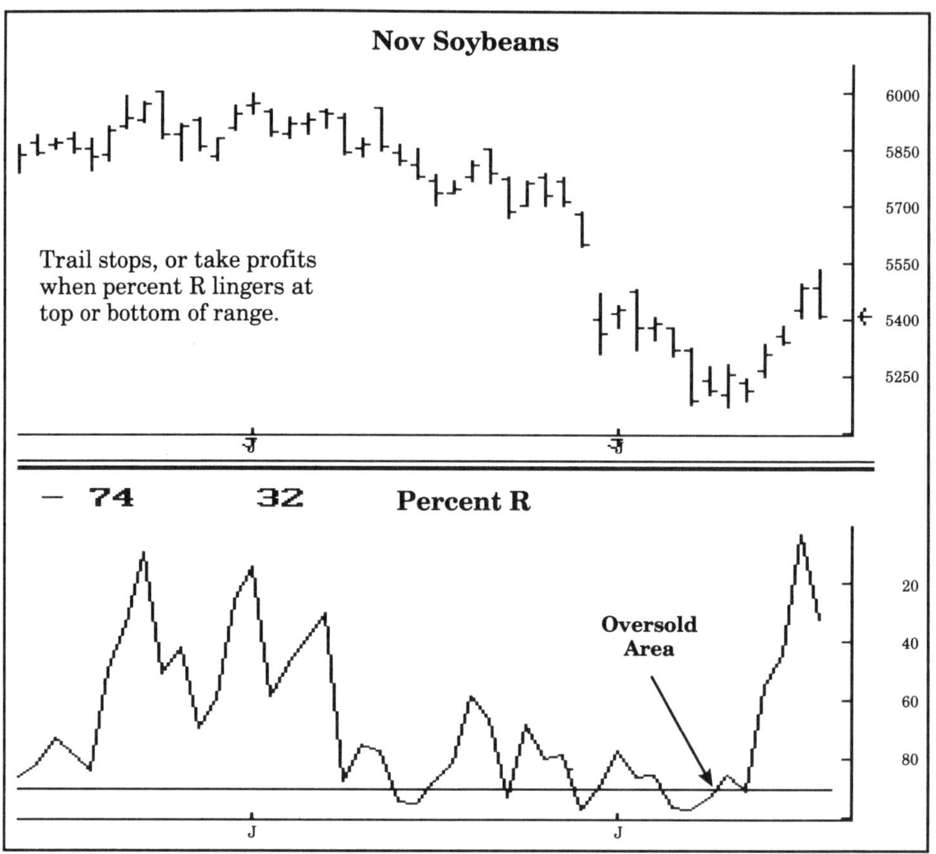
Nov Soybeans
6000
5850
5700
5550
5400
5250
Trail stops, or take profits when percent R lingers at top or bottom of range.
J
J
— 74
32
Percent R
20
40
60
80
Oversold Area
J
J

EXHIBIT 2–72

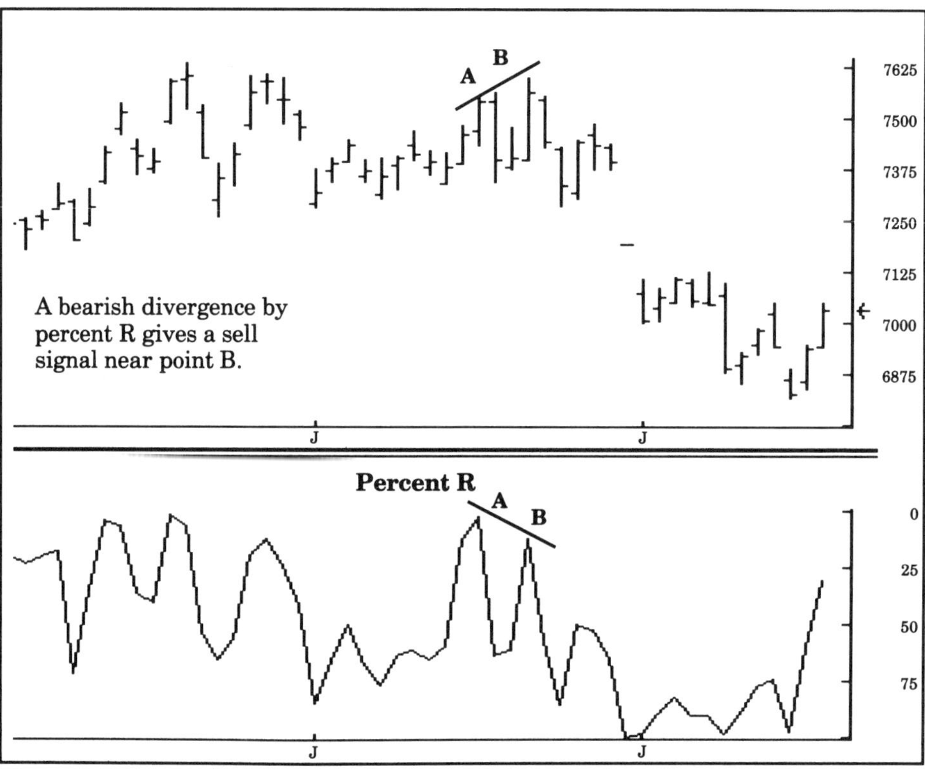
A
B
7625
7500
7375
7250
7125
7000
6875
A bearish divergence by percent R gives a sell signal near point B.
J
J
Percent R
A
B
0
25
50
75
J
J

A Brief Look at the Basics

Point-and-figure charts in this age of computers usually consist of Xs and Os plotted in columns. Early point-and-figure chartists, such as Charles Dow and R. D. Wyckoff, merely used dots (points), rather than Xs and Os, while other chartists elected to put prices (figures) in the boxes; hence the name "point and figure." A column of Xs represents a series of advancing prices, while a column of Os represents a series of declining prices. There is no time scale on the horizontal axis as there would be on a conventional bar chart. Each column might represent any length of time.

Two critical variables are to be determined when setting up a point-and-figure chart: box size and reversal units. Box size refers to the number of price units represented by each box. One box could represent 1 point or 100 points or more (anything from one tick to infinity). The reversal units refer to the number of boxes used to determine when a column of Xs reverses to a column of Os or vice versa. A one-box reversal means that a change in price direction in the amount of the value of one box would result in a new column of Xs or Os being plotted to the right of the previous column. The charts are most often set up with a three-box reversal.

On a point-and-figure chart, only price changes in the amount of one box or more are recorded. For example, if the value of one box is 10 points and the last plot in a column of Xs was at 110, a move to 115 would not be plotted. The market would have to move to 120 or higher before another X was placed in the column. If we were using the standard three-box reversal, prices would have to decline to 80 before we would begin a column of Os. As long as prices remained between 81 and 119 there would be no new plots on the chart. (See Exhibit 2–73.)

EXHIBIT 2–73

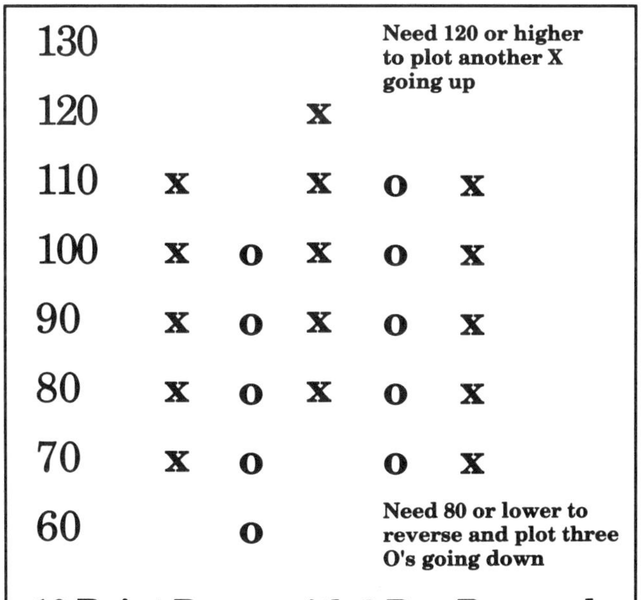

130						**Need 120 or higher to plot another X going up**
120			X			
110	X		X	O	X	
100	X	O	X	O	X	
90	X	O	X	O	X	
80	X	O	X	O	X	
70	X	O		O	X	
60		O				**Need 80 or lower to reverse and plot three O's going down**

10 Point Boxes with 3 Box Reversal

Determining Box Sizes and Reversals

The box sizes and reversals determine the sensitivity of the chart and the number of columns and patterns it will produce. Now that we have computers constructing the charts in seconds, we can be very flexible in our selection of box sizes and reversals. Trial and error has become a practical approach to finding the best increments for each commodity. It was a difficult and time-consuming task, but point-and-figure charts were being optimized long before computers were in use. When searching for the desired increments, some important guidelines should be kept in mind. We need to consider both risk and volatility.

For example, if it is our plan to limit losses using stops of $300, we wouldn't want to use box sizes of $300 and a three-box reversal, because we could be stopped out without ever making an entry on the chart. Therefore, risk must be a consideration in setting up the chart. Small box units allow for tighter risk control when using the charts to select stop points. Many point-and-figure chartists use a three-box reversal as their stop point after a profit run. Smaller units are also preferred, because they allow the chartist to record small price movements in the direction of the trend. The extension of the column with more Xs or Os should result in capturing more of the price move, because the reversals will be measured from a more profitable level.

We suggest that our readers use the following method to find the initial box values and then modify them if they need. First we set up a pair of 10-day moving averages, with one moving average based on the highs and the other based on the lows. Take the current difference between the two moving averages and use one half of that difference as the value of a box. Sometimes a little rounding is necessary and some chartists (not us) like to round to a nearby Fibonacci number. After finding the box size, we recommend using the standard three-box reversal. With this shortcut you will find that you can usually produce a surprisingly workable point-and-figure chart on your first attempt. (See Exhibit 2–74.)

Some authors have suggested setting the initial box size at about 3 percent of the market price. Any percentage of price method is very crude and makes no allowance for market volatility. We like our average hi-lo method much better, because it adjusts for volatility and will produce good results with charts of different time increments. For example, the hi-lo method will give bigger box values for weekly data, whereas the percentage method would produce the same box size for both daily and weekly data.

Reading between the Trendlines

The simplest way to use a point-and-figure chart is to buy whenever you start a new column of Xs and to reverse and go short whenever you start a new column of Os. Box sizes and reversal units can be adjusted to filter out whipsaws. Point-and-figure-charts also form patterns very similar to ordinary bar charts. We don't have space to go into all of the pennants,

EXHIBIT 2–74

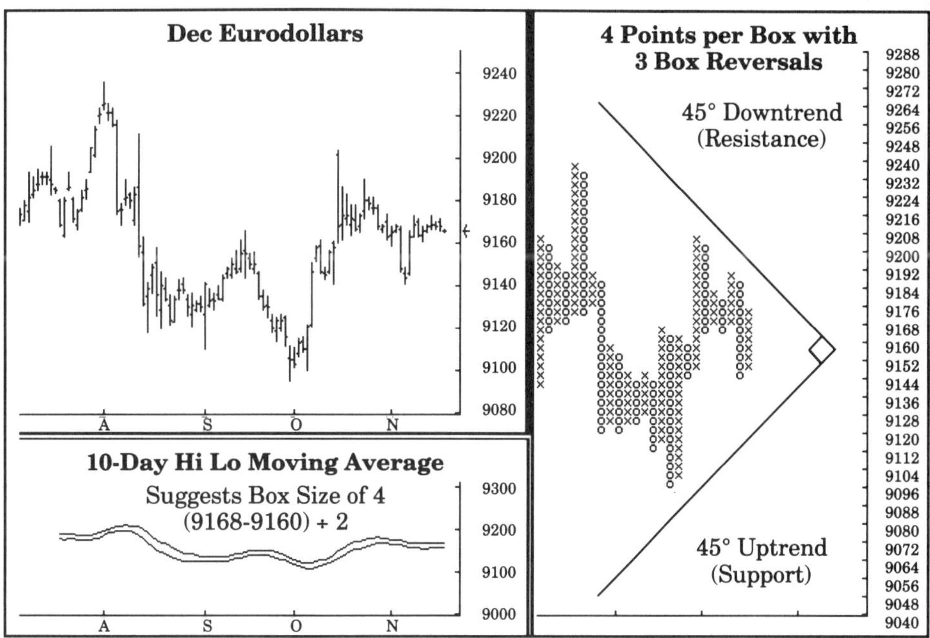

wedges, head-and-shoulders, and the like. There are, however, two trendlines that are particularly important and worth mentioning.

The 45 degree trendline has been consistently used by point-and-figure chartists to identify potential support and resistance areas. The up-trendline is drawn at a 45 degree angle upward and to the right from the lowest point at the bottom of the lowest column of Os. The down-trendline is drawn downward and to the right at a 45 degree angle from the top of the highest column of Xs.

Parallel channel lines drawn across a series of tops or bottoms are also very useful when trading with point-and-figure charts. They, too, are used for support and resistance, much like the 45 degree lines. Many experienced point-and-figure traders consider the breaking of a parallel channel line to be much more significant than making a new high or low on the chart. (See Exhibit 2–75.)

"Counting" Your Profits

Some point-and-figure chartists contend that price objectives can be forecast by either of two popular counting methods. They are appropriately referred to as the *horizontal count* and the *vertical count.* The horizontal count is based on the same principle as the old bar charting method—of measuring the width of a consolidation and then projecting the same distance up or down to obtain a price target.

To use the horizontal count, we determine the width of the consolidation pattern and then count the number of columns within it. Next, we count an equivalent number of boxes upward from the bottom of the consolidation to obtain our first objective. For a second objective, we would start the upward projection from the top of the consolidation.

EXHIBIT 2–75

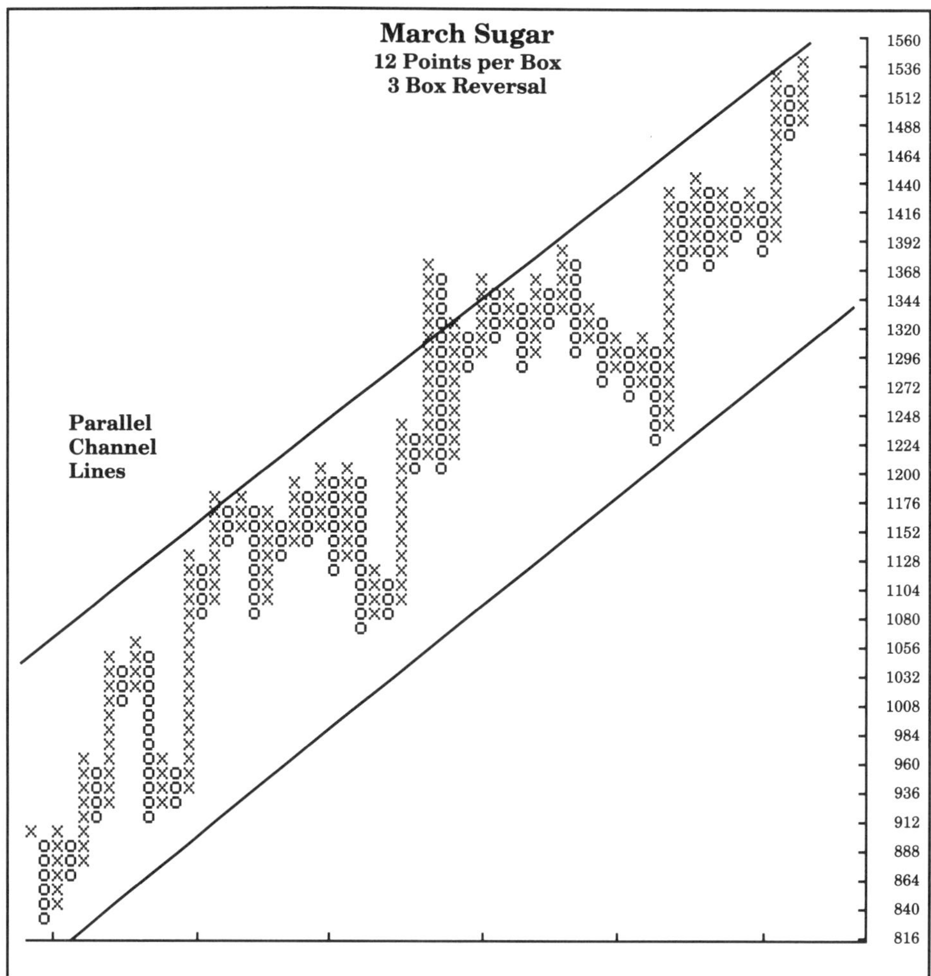

The vertical count is very similar. For a target on a long position, we would count the number of Xs in the first column after a bottom has been identified and multiply the number of Xs by the reversal units (usually three). Then we would count upward from the bottom of the first column of Xs to establish our most conservative target price. A more optimistic objective can be determined by counting upward from a breakout point or from the top of the consolidation. A great deal of subjectivity can creep into the counting, and we are always suspect of methods that attempt to forecast specific prices. We found an example of a market where the counts worked very well, but in all honesty we had to do some hunting to find it. We could have shown many more examples where the counts weren't even close. (See Exhibit 2–76.)

Fading the False Breakouts

One of the most successful and unusual point-and-figure techniques we have come across is based on an idea given to us by a subscriber, who is a very experienced point-and-figure trader. He has observed that, if a point-and-figure chart breaks through a double or triple top and fails to

EXHIBIT 2–76

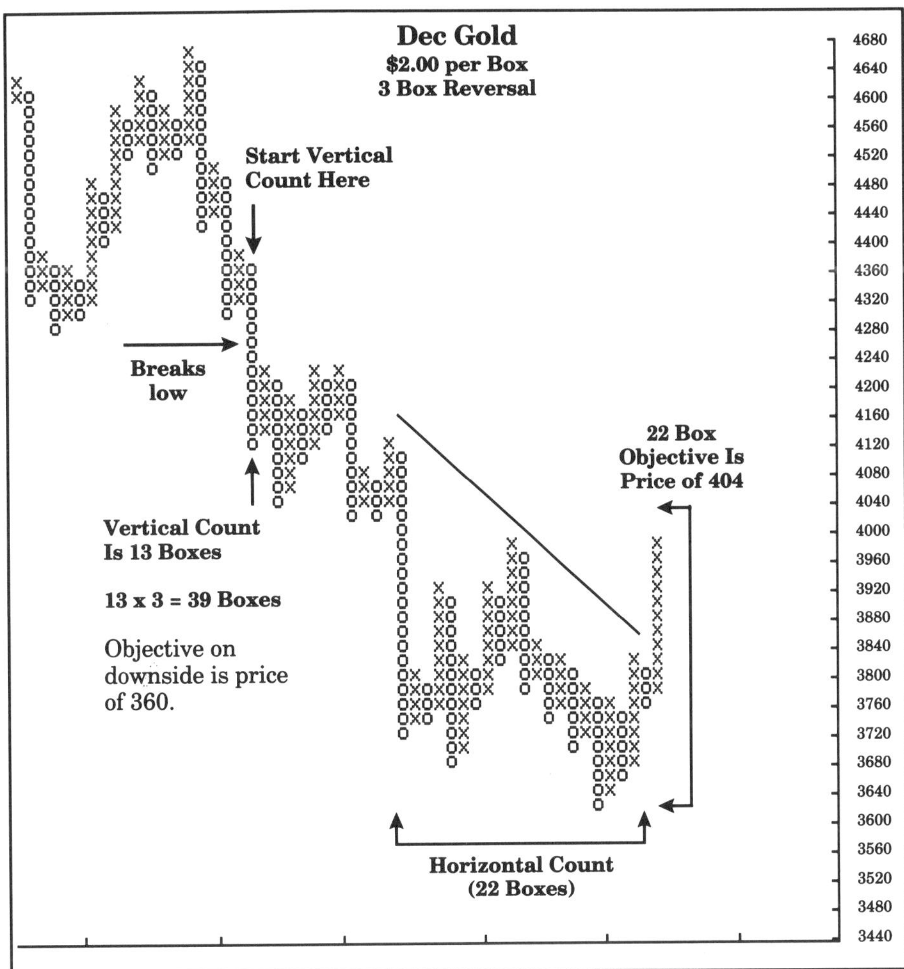

follow through by three boxes or more, there is often a quick profit to be made by following the next reversal in the opposite direction. (See Exhibit 2–77.)

Summary

The point-and-figure technique can give an entirely different and often revealing perspective to a commodity chart. Such charts seem to work well enough to be the basis of many profitable stand-alone trading systems. The charts are still popular on the exchange floors and are still used by some professional trading advisors. Most modern day technicians prefer to use them along with other technical indicators, such as stochastics and relative strength. Several traders have commented that point-and-figure charts can be particularly helpful in Elliott wave analysis, where the charts can be set up to filter out many of the unwanted or extraneous waves. (Since we don't use wave analysis, we can't comment.)

Point-and-figure charts used to be considered easy to maintain but very difficult to set up. Now that the computers can do the work and the

EXHIBIT 2–77

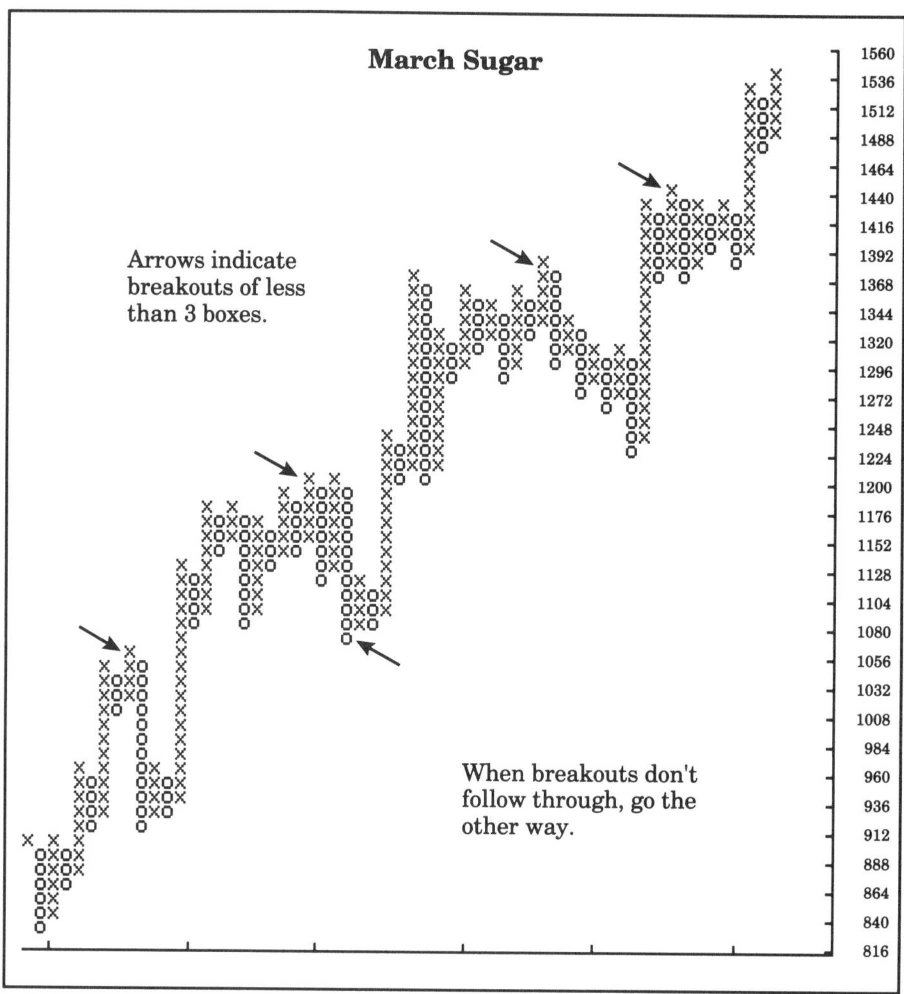

charts can be created or modified in an instant, we think the major drawbacks have been eliminated. We would suggest that our readers take the time to educate themselves further. We would recommend setting up a page for each commodity, which contains a point-and-figure chart based on weekly data, and one or more charts with daily data. Experiment with box sizes and reversals. We think you will be a better trader for the experience and will grow fond of the entirely different perspective of the markets that point-and-figure charts can give you. Often computers lead traders to zoom in on the markets and get them too involved in the minor price changes. Point-and-figure charts can be a nice way of stepping back and looking at the broader perspective.

Relative Strength Index

The relative strength index (RSI) is probably the most popular of all the countertrend oscillators. The index gives reliable overbought and oversold signals in most market conditions. The RSI also produces excellent

EXHIBIT 2–78

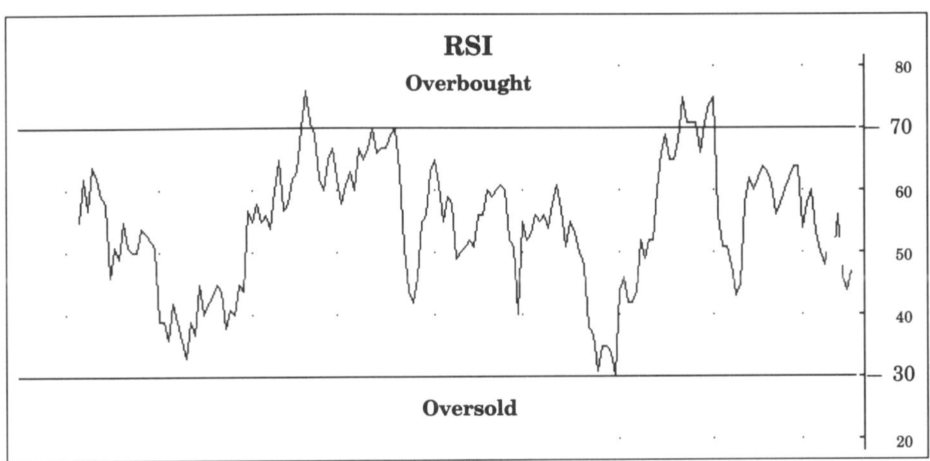

long-term divergence patterns, which can be used to give timely indications of major tops and bottoms. The RSI can be employed both as a profit-taking device and as a tool for fine-tuning market entries signaled by other methods.

The RSI formula was first devised by J. Welles Wilder, Jr., and explained fully in his 1978 book, *New Concepts in Technical Trading Systems*. The RSI calculates the ratio of up closes to down closes over the time period selected and expresses the result as an oscillator with a scale of 0 to 100. The formula is RSI = 100 – (100 / 1 + RS), where RS = average of the up closes of the last n days divided by the average of the down closes of the last n days. Readings near 0 indicate when a market is oversold, readings near 100 indicate overbought. Wilder recommended using a 14-day time period, equivalent to what he perceived to be a half-cycle for most commodities. (See Exhibit 2–78.)

Using 14 days as a default value, market tops and bottoms may be expected to occur sometime after the RSI goes above 70 or below 30. We do not recommend buying or selling at exactly these numbers, because, in a trend, the RSI often becomes stuck near one end of the range for days or even weeks, giving false indications of a top or bottom.

Wilder and others have advocated using a number of standard charting techniques on the RSI, claiming that specific patterns in the index will predict similar patterns in the underlying data. The following are some examples of the RSI signals that our experience and research have shown to be useful.

Failure Swings

The first of these formations is the failure swing, which is easier to observe in the RSI study itself than in the underlying chart. A failure swing consists of an RSI spike with a high over 70, followed by a second spike with a lower high than the first. The actual sell signal is generated when the low point between the RSI spikes is penetrated. A buy signal would be the reverse pattern, with two spikes downward followed by an upward penetration of the high point between the spikes. (See Exhibit 2–79.)

EXHIBIT 2–79

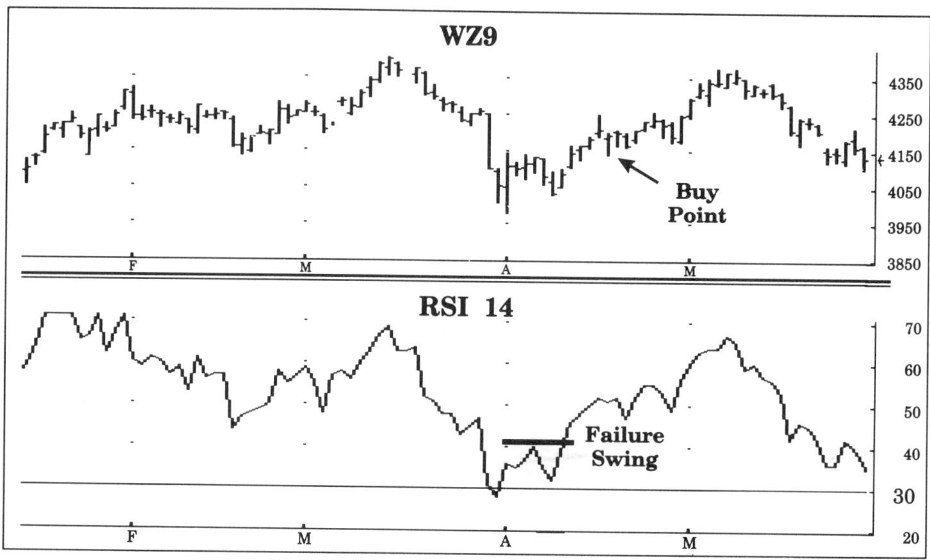

As you can see, failure swings can be powerful signals. Remember, the best signals will occur when the first spike goes well below 30 or above 70. You can't afford to ignore these failure patterns; they are usually signs of significant intermediate-term changes in market direction. Be careful of failure swings having so many little deviations that they take a long time to evolve. Our experience is that the best failure swings happen fairly quickly and are easy to spot.

RSI Divergence Patterns

Weekly Charts. We think the most significant and powerful RSI signals come in the form of divergences between formations in the index and formations in the underlying chart. We've found these divergences to be especially useful in spotting major long-term tops and bottoms on weekly charts. For example, take a look at the weekly chart of the S&P leading to the August 1987 top. (See Exhibit 2–80.)

Daily Charts. We recommend using a 10- to 14-day RSI to find daily divergence patterns. Examples are numerous. The first chart shows a divergence using a 14-day RSI. Note that the divergence is confirmed by the failure of the second RSI spike to reach a new low, showing that the market is technically strong. Make sure that your buy entry is after the up day that establishes the bottom of the second spike—not before. (See Exhibit 2–81.)

The next chart shows a 10-day RSI divergence that foretold the break in T-bonds in early August 1989. The sell entry was either the close of August 2 or the opening of August 3. (See Exhibit 2–82.)

While it's difficult to formulate a specific rule, we've found that divergences in which the tops are separated by only a few days, or by more than about 10 weeks, don't normally constitute good signals.

EXHIBIT 2–80

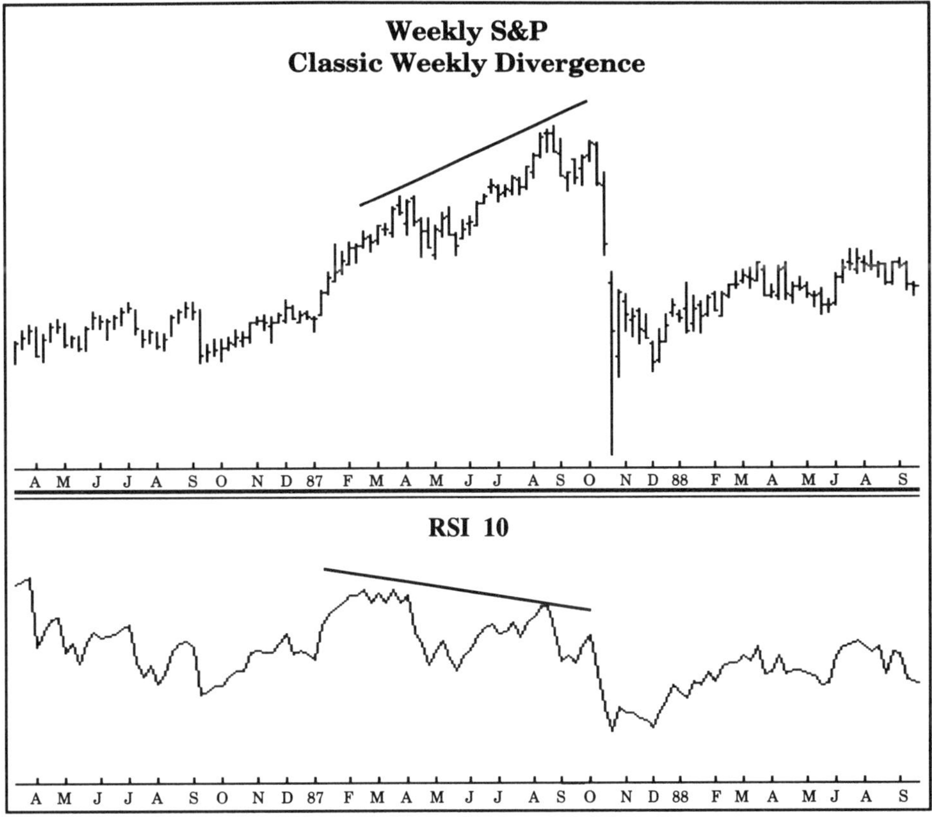

EXHIBIT 2–81

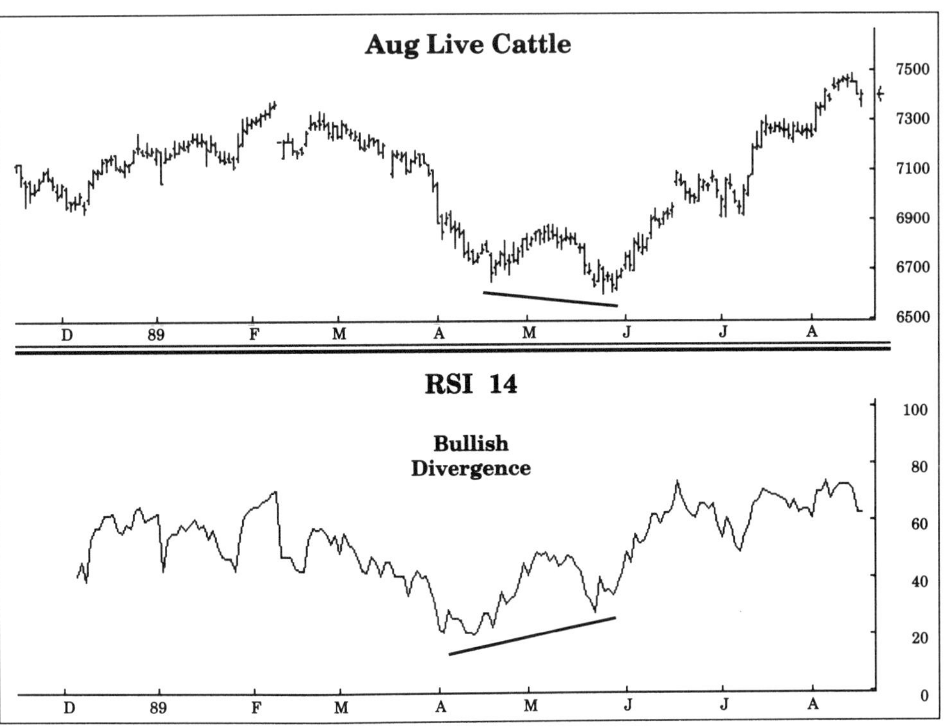

EXHIBIT 2–82

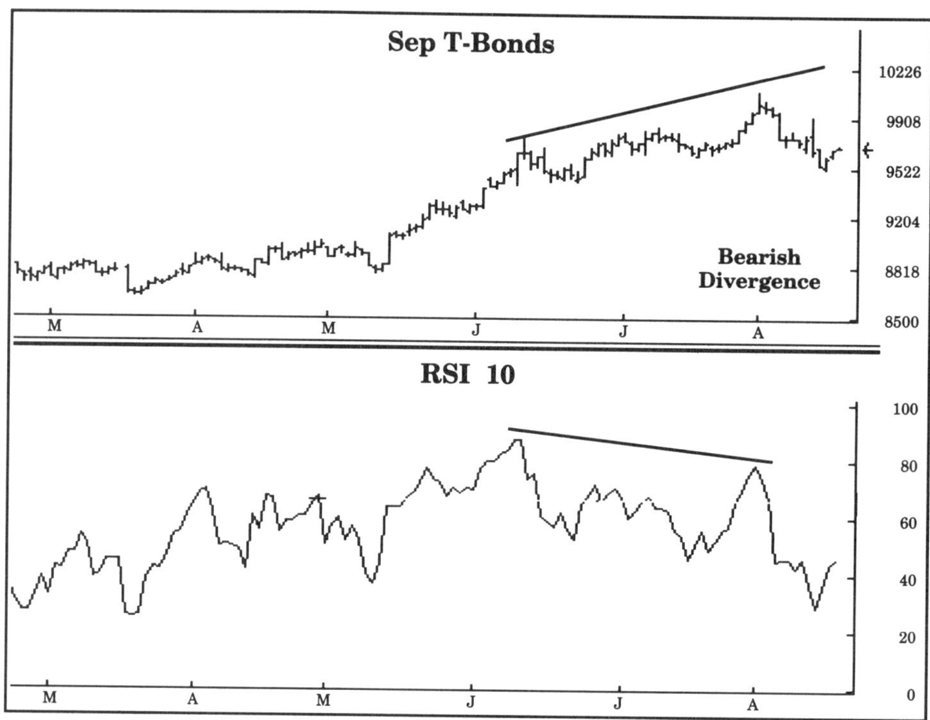

RSI Entry Filter

One of the most common problems trend-following systems face is entering a market after a strong reversal in direction. Entry is never precisely at the market turn, but after a significant price move in the new direction. Often, the short-term move that reverses the trend makes the market either overbought or oversold, leaving it vulnerable to a short-term correction. Nearly everyone has encountered the same problem after a trend-following signal has been generated by a powerful change in direction: Should you dare to risk entering the trade after three strong days up? Or five days up? Do you wait? If you wait, what are you waiting for?

An RSI filter can provide an excellent solution to this common problem. If the RSI value is greater than 75 (if you're buying), or less than 25 (if you're selling), then delay your entry. Enter only after the RSI pulls back to between 75 and 25. By definition, a minor market correction will have taken place and your entry will not be at overbought or oversold levels. (See Exhibit 2–83.)

Re-entry with RSI

Let's assume you've just been stopped out of a trade, but the trend is still intact. What's needed now is a precise way to so time your re-entry that your initial drawdown will be minimal.

EXHIBIT 2–83

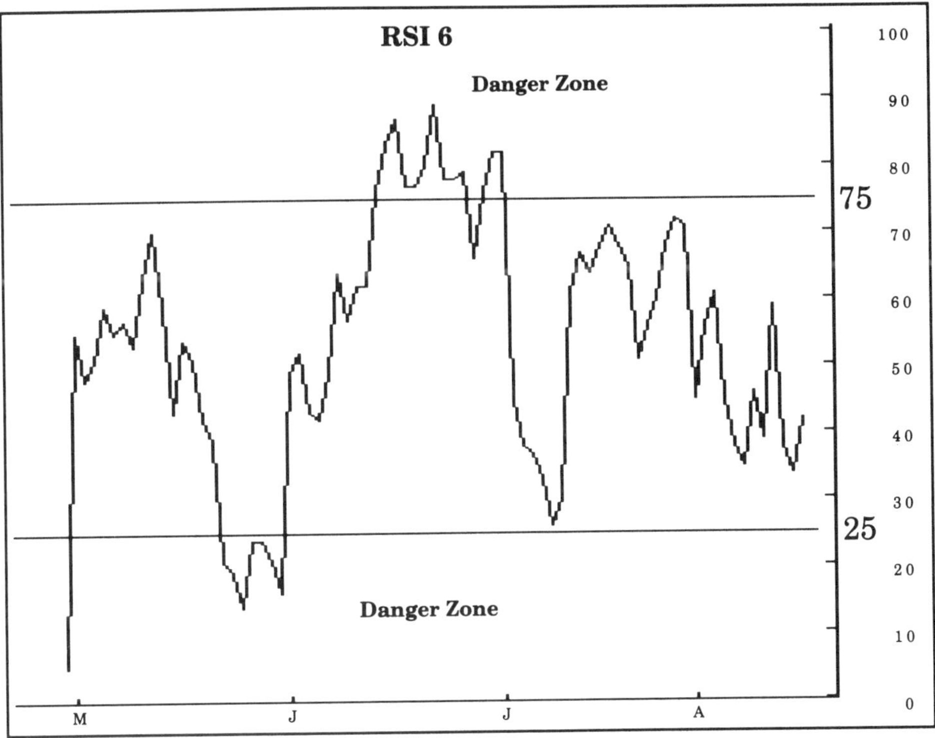

Use a short-term (for example, 3-day) RSI and wait for it to hook, entering only in the direction of the trend. To illustrate, let's assume your indicators say the market is going down and you need a re-entry point. Further assume that the RSI has been dropping and is now below 50. Try waiting for the RSI to move back above 50, then, when it hooks down, sell immediately. Waiting for the slight upward movement in the very sensitive short-term RSI has the effect of relieving any immediate overbought or oversold condition, allowing you to re-enter during a minor trend correction. (See Exhibit 2–84, November soybeans.)

Profit Taking with RSI

One of the most valuable of all applications of RSI is as an assist in profit taking. It's always nice to sit back and let profits run, but using relatively slow studies for profit-taking will inevitably give back an undesirable amount of profit before generating an exit signal. What's needed is an exit method that is quick to recognize when a market is at a peak, combined with a method of trailing stops that allows the profits to run as long as the market keeps going.

For profit taking, try a short-term RSI. A 10- or 14-day RSI is not normally responsive enough for profit taking. A profit-taking signal is completed when the RSI reaches 75 or higher (25 or lower, if you're short), and then retraces by 10 or more points. For example, let's say the

EXHIBIT 2–84

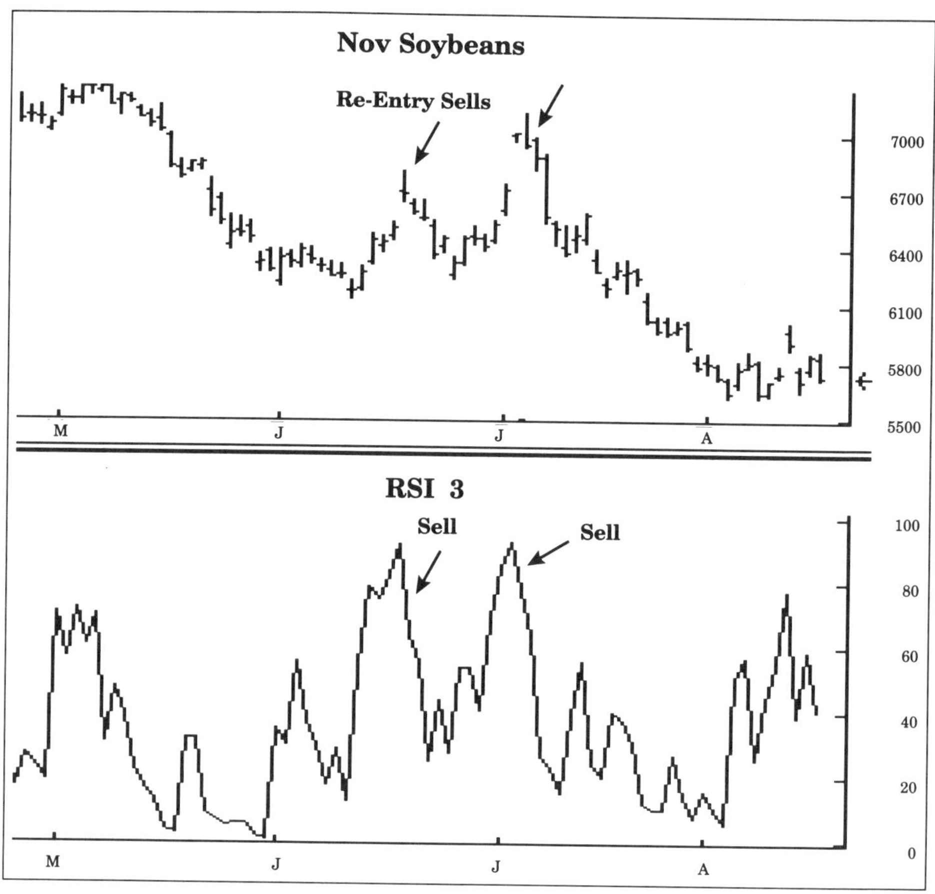

EXHIBIT 2–85

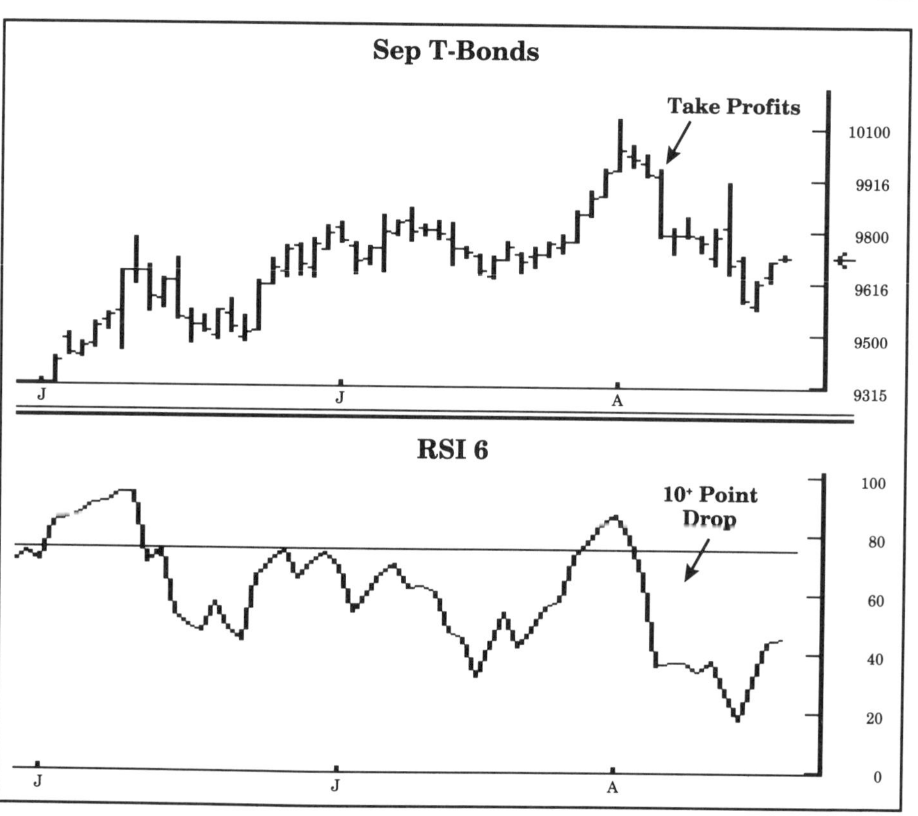

RSI goes up to 87 and then pulls back to 65. At this point the market is obviously pausing, and steps should be taken to protect your gains. Trail stops at either a recent *n*-day low or at a predetermined dollar amount, whichever is closer. (See Exhibit 2–85, September T-bonds.)

We've found the *n*-day low to be especially useful as a trail point. Quite often, the market will start back up without hitting your stop, and you can continue to trail your stop for a long while. Dollar trailing stops also work quite well (see "System Testing," Chapter 3).

Slow Stochastics

We believe that, in addition to the trend-following strategies employed by the majority of professional traders, consistency of performance can be enhanced by having technical indicators to use in the nontrending markets. Stochastics is one of the best of these tools. If you are careful to stay in the direction of the trend, it can be used in trending markets as well.

Stochastics have been popularized by George Lane, who has been using them in his investment educators courses since the 1950s. We have attended many of George's lectures and learn more about stochastics every time. He has perfected the use of stochastics over his many years of trading and can find innovative ways to make it perform well in almost any situation. We are indebted to him for most of our knowledge of stochastics. Much of the following information is from George's article on stochastics written for *Technical Traders Bulletin*.

The basic formula for stochastics is %K = today's close minus the low of the last *n* days, divided by the high of the last *n* days minus the low of the last *n* days. %D is a three-day moving average of %K. This %K and %D produce a so-called fast stochastic, which is rarely used because it is overly sensitive. (See Exhibit 2–86.)

Fast %K and %D smoothed by three again produce the slow stochastic, which is much more commonly used. (See Exhibit 2–87.)

Unless otherwise specified, we will be referring to the slower, smoothed version of stochastics in our ensuing discussion.

The stochastic calculation expresses the relationship between today's close and the range from high to low of the preceding *n* days. For example, if today's close is 30, and the range over the last *n* days is from 20 to 50, then fast %K = 30 − 20 / 50 − 20 = 0.33, a relatively low value. If today's close were 40, closer to the top of the range, then fast %K would be 0.66. %K and %D cannot be less than 0 or greater than 100. As days accumulate, %K and %D will be displayed as lines that range in value from 0 to 100, making stochastics an oscillator. Values closer to 0 theoretically indicate an oversold market. Values closer to 100 theoretically indicate an overbought market.

The basic stochastic signals are a crossing of the %K and %D lines, combined with a level of %K and %D that indicates overbought or oversold. Typically, oversold might mean a %D value less than 30,

EXHIBIT 2–86

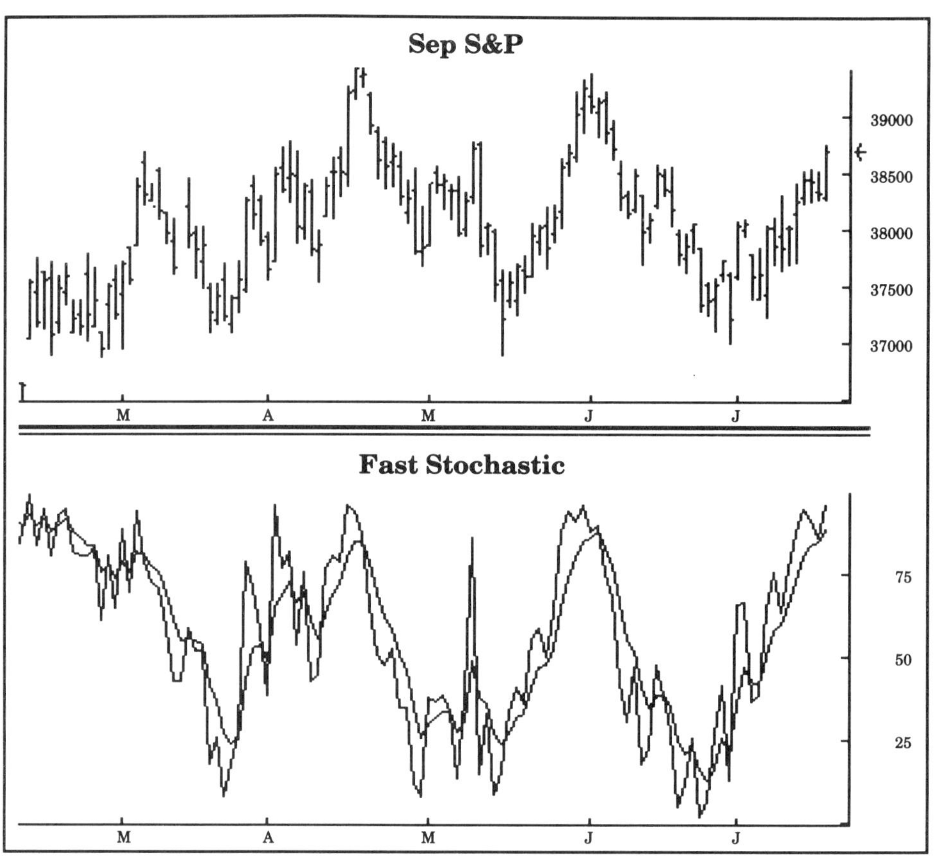

EXHIBIT 2–87

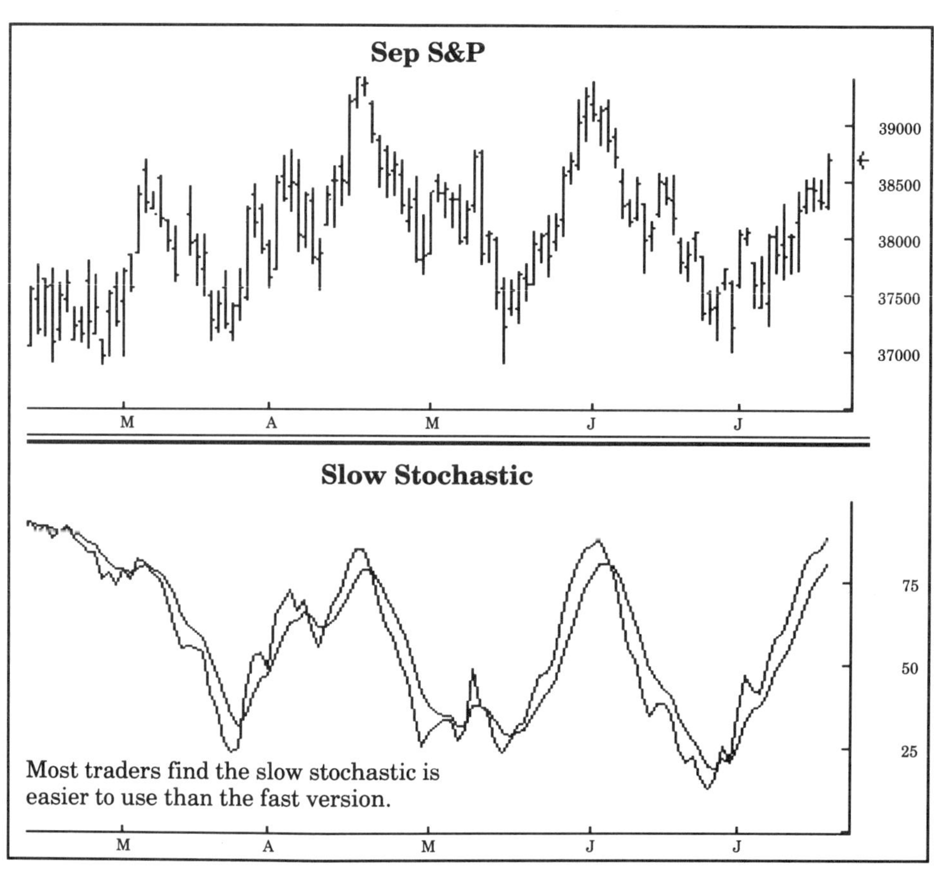

overbought greater than 70. Values of 80 and 20 are also commonly used. We have also seen traders disregard %K and watch for %D to reach an overbought or oversold level.

Time Periods

The commonly recommended time period for the slow stochastic is 14, although George Lane uses a broad range of values, finding what he perceives as the dominant cycle of the market he's trading and then using one half that amount for the number of bars in the stochastic. Technicians seem to have their own favorites. Our experience and testing show the 9 to 12 range to be the best compromise between the speed of the signals (%K crossing %D) and the validity or follow-through that produces the least amount of false signals. Like all other technical studies, stochastics are more responsive if a shorter time period is used and slower if a longer period is used. We will discuss some techniques that other technicians use to speed up the signals. We think that these methods are unnecessary. If you want faster signals, simply shorten the time period. Don't forget that faster is not always better. You should look for the most dependable signals, not the fastest.

When to Use Stochastics

Stochastics work best in broad trading ranges, or in a mild trend with a slight upward or downward bias. The worst market for normal use of stochastics is a persistent trending market that has only minor corrections. In such a market, the stochastics indicator will produce numerous countertrend entry points that will be quickly overpowered by the trend. A serious string of losses will result if you continue to use the standard methods of trading stochastics. Remember: The trader who coined the phrase "the trend is your friend" was not using stochastics. (For an example of stochastics whipsaws, see Exhibit 2–88.)

How do you identify and quantify a "strong" trending market? There are many methods; but, if it's not obvious that a "strong" trend is in progress, try measuring the trend with Wilder's ADX (as we explained in the section on DMI/ADX). It is possible to trade stochastics in a trend by ignoring the usual overbought and oversold levels of 70/30 or 80/20 and entering the market when the end of a reaction against the trend is signaled by a stochastic crossover from any level. There are better ways to be a trend follower, however, and we think the primary value of stochastics is as an indicator of bottoms and tops.

EXHIBIT 2–88

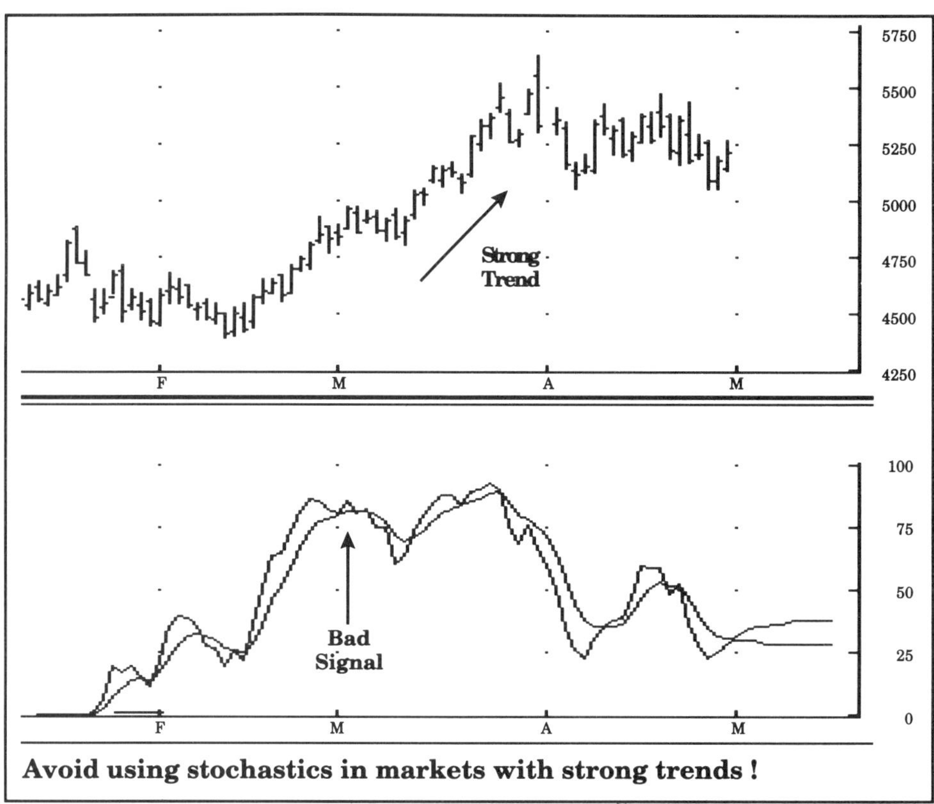

Avoid using stochastics in markets with strong trends !

Divergences

When a market makes a new high or low and the stochastic indicator fails to confirm by also making a new high or low, we have a divergence pattern. These can be simple divergences (see Exhibit 2–88) or George Lane's "classic divergence signal," which comes at triple tops. (See Exhibits 2–89 and 2–90.)

Note in Exhibit 2–90 that the second high (2) is lower than the first high (1), showing divergence. The third high (3), however, is higher than the second high but lower than the first high.

If the market does not behave as expected, we sometimes wind up with a "secondary divergence pattern" like the one shown in Exhibit 2–91. In this pattern, the prices also make three rallies to a top; but the stochastics makes a pattern of three descending tops, which create a divergence. In this "secondary" pattern, unlike the "classic" pattern, point 3 is lower than point 2. We find that these divergence patterns usually produce substantially better results than the ordinary stochastic signals. This seems to be true of most oscillators. We wish we could be more definitive about the results of divergences, but they are extremely difficult to test objectively.

EXHIBIT 2–89

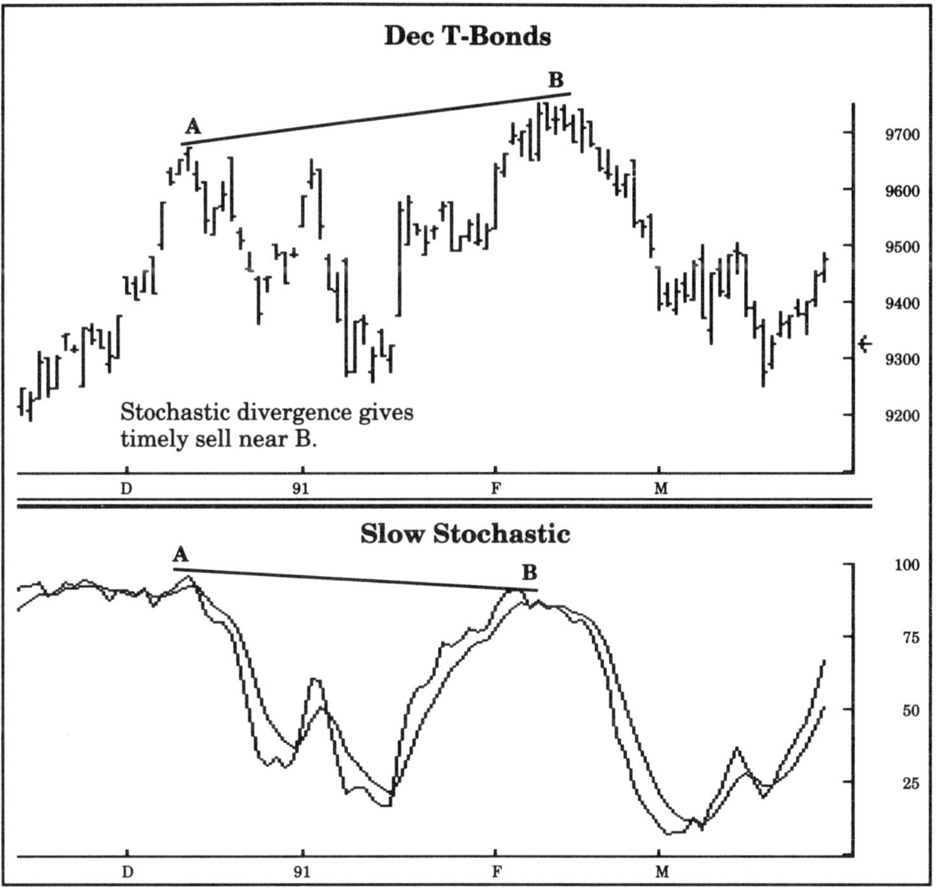
Dec T-Bonds
A
B
9700
9600
9500
9400
9300
9200
Stochastic divergence gives
timely sell near B.
D
91
F
M
Slow Stochastic
A
B
100
75
50
25
D
91
F
M

EXHIBIT 2–90

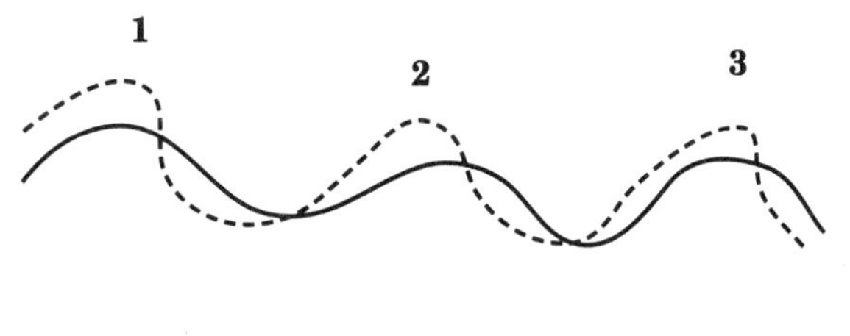
Classic Divergence:
The third stochastic high is higher than the second high while prices are making a pattern of higher highs.
1
2
3

EXHIBIT 2–91

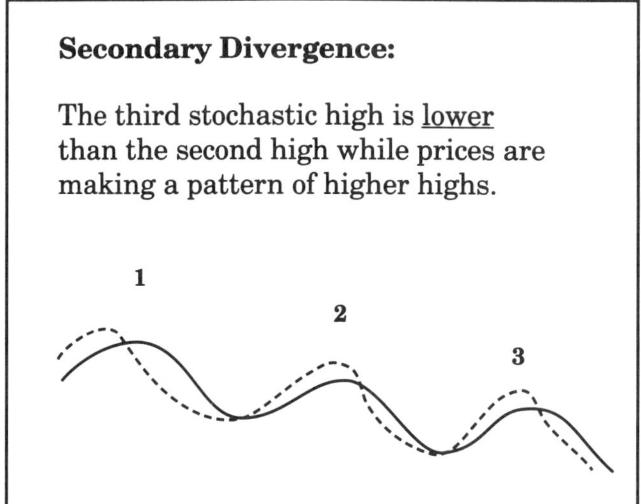
Secondary Divergence:
The third stochastic high is lower than the second high while prices are making a pattern of higher highs.
1
2
3

Left and Right Crossovers

Some technicians have proposed that a slow change in direction, as reflected in %D, is somehow more valid than a fast change in direction as measured by %K. What these traders look for is a pattern where %D has begun to change direction before the crossover, which would mean %K will cross to the right of the top or bottom (apex) of the %D line. This sequence produces the "right crossover," as opposed to the "left crossover" where %K crosses before the %D has begun to change direction. The premise is that the right crossovers produce better signals than the left crossovers. We fail to see the logic in this assumption. When we have been able to distinguish between left and right crossovers, which is difficult sometimes, we haven't noticed any correlation with the success of the trades. (See Exhibit 2–92.)

Knees and Shoulders

When %K has crossed up through %D and then pulls back a few percentage points at the next period but fails to repenetrate %D on the downside before turning up, Lane calls it a "knee." It supposedly denotes strength and a continuation of upward prices. If we have a similar pattern on the downside we call it a "shoulder." These knee and shoulder patterns normally occur when the prices are making a spike pattern like we described earlier. The rapid change in trend creates a "left-hand" crossover in the stochastics. In the knee and shoulder patterns, %K gives divergence at the spikes, even though %D cannot. (See Exhibit 2–93.)

EXHIBIT 2–92

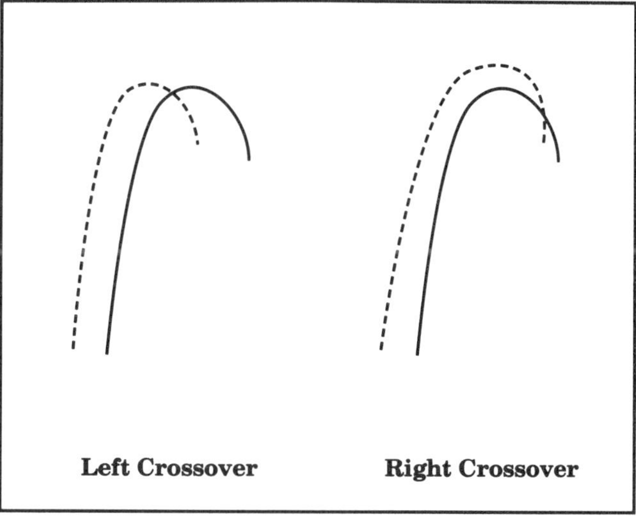

EXHIBIT 2–93

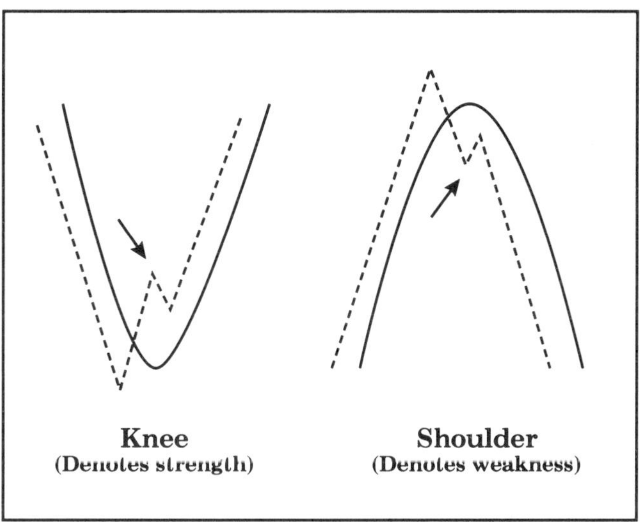

Hooks and Hinges: Patterns that Anticipate

Some close observers of stochastics have tried to design methods that will anticipate the actual crossovers and, thereby, get a head start on the signals. Two examples of these anticipatory patterns are the hinge and the warning hook.

The *hinge* pattern is merely an observation that the %D line is beginning to flatten out, thus forecasting an imminent change in direction prior to the actual crossover of %K.

The *warning hook* is an observation of an *extreme* hooking or changing of direction in the %K line prior to its crossing of the %D line.

EXHIBIT 2–94

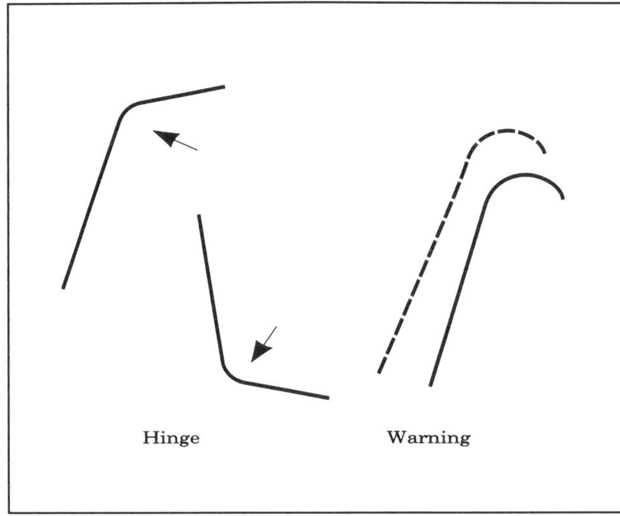

We think both of these patterns place too much emphasis on being early, instead of on being dependable. We advise waiting for a crossover. Be patient and avoid jumping at shadows. These anticipatory patterns may have more value if you use them for taking profits, rather than as entries. (See Exhibit 2–94.)

Bear and Bull Setups

Bear and bull setups are another of George Lane's special tools. Bear setups occur when prices are rising and making a series of higher highs and higher bottoms. The stochastics oscillator diverges and makes a pattern of lower lows while prices are still rising. This setup indicates that the next price swing to the upside may provide an important top. (See Exhibit 2–95.)

Bull setups occur when prices are declining and making a series of lower bottoms and lower tops. The stochastics oscillator diverges and makes a pattern of higher tops while prices are still declining. This setup indicates that prices will be making an important bottom soon. (See Exhibit 2–96.)

Bear and bull setups are really a sort of reverse divergence (called *convergence* by some). Several of our newsletter subscribers report success with this type of pattern.

EXHIBIT 2–95

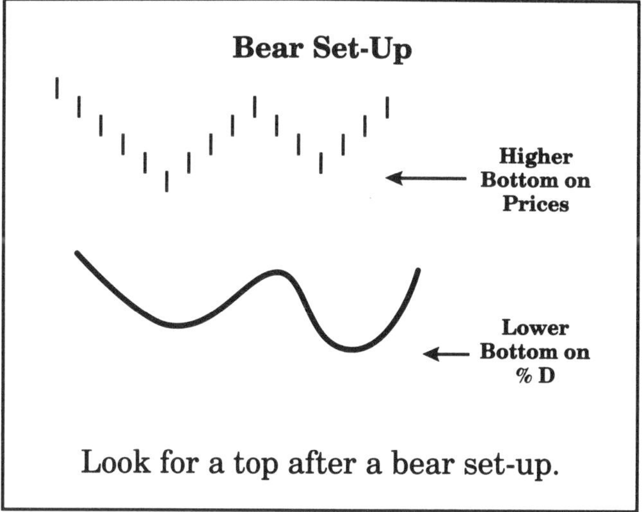

Look for a top after a bear set-up.

EXHIBIT 2–96

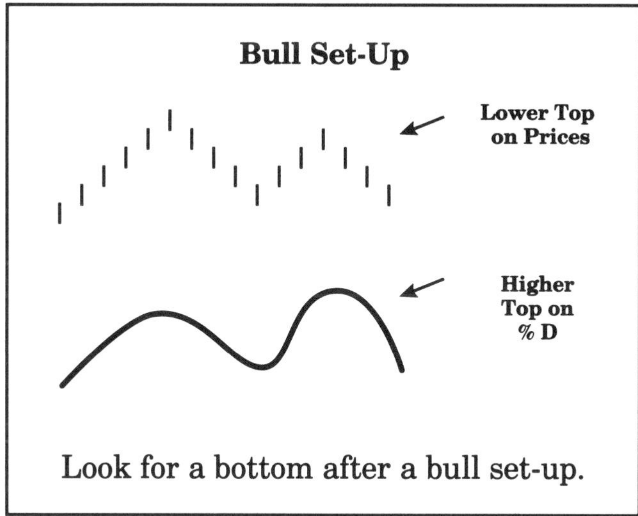

Look for a bottom after a bull set-up.

Taking Profits

Because of the countertrend nature of stochastics, profits must be taken quickly. Don't get caught waiting for a stochastics exit signal or you will probably wind up turning a winning position into a loser. You need to devise a method to take profits while the market is moving in your favor. Profit objectives or price targets work well. Don't get greedy—use hit and run tactics.

Sometimes a stochastic trade will develop into a trend. If you are fortunate enough to still be in the position, you might want to change your strategy and let your profits run. These trades are rare and, if you have followed our profit-taking advice, you will probably be long gone before the trend is confirmed.

Volatility

Some measurement of market volatility is part of more technical studies and trading systems than most readers might expect. Practically all of Wilder's techniques (RSI, DMI, CSI, Parabolics, and others) in some fashion incorporate the concept of volatility. Volatility is also part of various trading band or envelope studies available (Bollinger bands, for example), and volatility is even a key ingredient of point-and-figure analysis.

Unfortunately, simple volatility calculations are not a standard feature of most software packages, and the optional programs that offer volatility systems are usually of the "black box" variety, where their methodology is not fully disclosed to the user. We use a relatively inexpensive and fully disclosed program called the "Professional Breakout System" designed by Steve Notis and our System Writer Plus testing software for most of our work with volatility.

We prefer to use volatility as merely another tool and not as the foundation of a system. Most volatility based systems must rely on senseless optimizations that make them appear to work well over past data. During the periods when volatility is working well, the results are often spectacular, with instances of buying right at the bottom of a market as prices break out and selling at the top as prices peak out. When these volatile markets occur, the volatility systems receive high rankings for the results of trading that particular commodity over a short time. However, it is rare to see a volatility based trading system ranked high on a diversified portfolio basis over a long time.

Not surprisingly, volatility is the basis for a series of trading systems that have been sold by various vendors since the early 1970s, for prices ranging up to as much as $10,000. All of these systems used essentially the same methods. Most were derived from similar earlier systems, with minor changes that, in many cases, seem to have been added only to avoid possible copyright infringement. Many of these volatility based systems are reported to have been very profitable.

The Basics—Measuring Volatility

The volatility based trading systems all use the concept of range to define the extent of recent market movement. The simplest definition of range is the distance from high to low of any given time period. This is usually a day, but it could be a week or a month or even an intraday period measured in minutes.

This simple definition of range works fine most of the time, but it doesn't take into account days of extreme price movement. Limit days, for example, may have a very narrow range, but the market is obviously very volatile and volatility is increasing. Similarly, a day when there is a gap opening and the day's trading takes place outside the prior day's range is an example of increasing volatility, even if the actual range of the day is less than that of the prior day.

Wilder recognized this problem and defined the "true range" (TR) as the greatest of the following:

1. The distance from today's high to today's low.
2. The distance from yesterday's close to today's high.
3. The distance from yesterday's close to today's low. (See Exhibit 2–97.)

By itself, the true range is still just an isolated number. To make it meaningful, we must take a number of past days and find the mean, giving us an average true range (ATR). This is a direct measurement of market volatility. If the ATR is increasing, the market is becoming more volatile. If the ATR is decreasing, the market is becoming less volatile.

How many days to use to produce the "best" ATR is a matter of conjecture. Wilder's original volatility formula uses 14 days, but most of the modern system sellers have optimized this variable and found that anywhere from 2 to 9 days was better, with recent optimizations leaning toward the shorter time periods within that range.

How the Volatility Systems Work

All of the popular volatility-based trading systems work on the principle that a breakout or price spike outside of the recent range or the average true range is significant and should be used as a point at which to enter the market. For example, let us say that the ATR for the last five days in the NYSE Composite futures is 1.00 points. We would be interested in a price move that is a percentage, say 150 percent, of the ATR from the prior day's close. This means that we would be buying or selling if prices moved 150 percent × 1.00, or 1.50 points. If the prior day's close was 190.00, we would buy at 191.50 or sell short at 188.50.

EXHIBIT 2–97

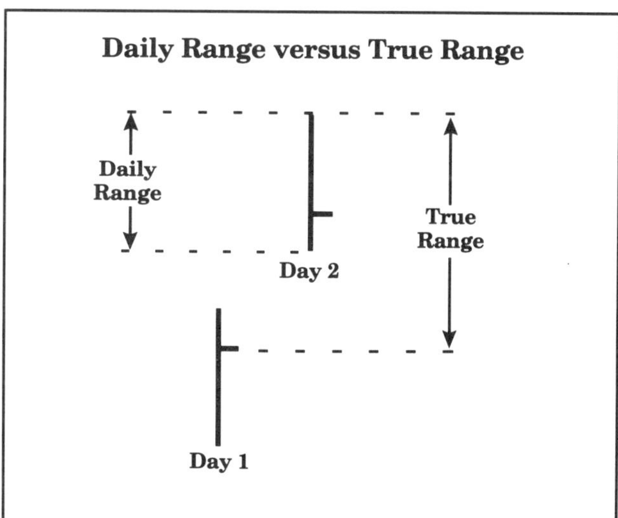

The two variables of the system are: (1) the number of days used to find the ATR; (2) the percent move from the prior day's close that constitutes a valid breakout.

These variables conveniently lend themselves to optimization, and the volatility calculations can easily be adjusted to make them fit the past data of any particular market. Most of the presently available software packages rely on optimizations to decide the precise values to be used for each variable.

As you may have deduced, the basic volatility breakout system is a reversal system always in the market. Each day after the close, calculate the ATR, and then multiply it by the percent move necessary to trigger a trade. Add the result to the close, and you will get the point at which a buy will be triggered the next day. Subtract the result from the close, and you will get the point at which a sell will be triggered. Enter both orders the next day and you are in business. (See Exhibit 2–98.)

Comments and Variations

One of the significant strategies of the basic system is that, since you are either long or short, there is no neutral area. The risk on any one trade is simply the difference between the entry point and the reversal point. If both are triggered on the same day or very close in time to one another, a whipsaw is the obvious result. Perhaps more important, the risk on a trade depends entirely on recent market volatility, which may or may not agree with a trader's wallet size or money management techniques.

Another interesting aspect of volatility systems is that the entry point and the reversal point will move away from each other if short-term volatility increases. How this could happen is easy to see: The market moves, the range increases, and the stops are positioned farther and farther away from each other. This might tend to reduce whipsaws, but it can also increase the initial risk on a trade after the trade has been entered. It can be disconcerting, and potentially disruptive, in a strict

EXHIBIT 2–98

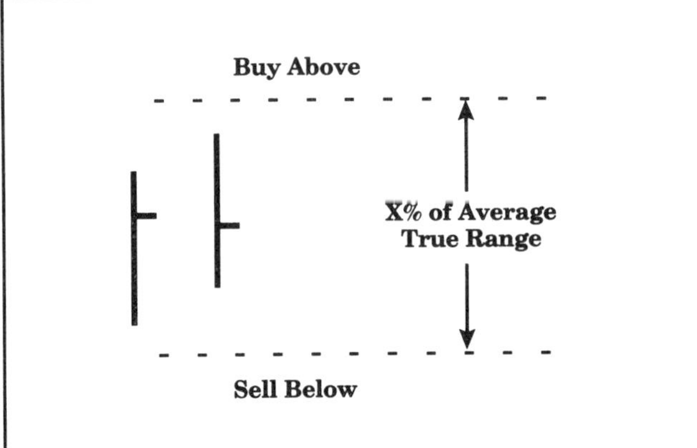

The average true range multiplied by the percentage factor creates a moving band above and below prices.

money management scheme, to plan to risk a certain dollar amount on a trade and then have that amount increase once the trade is underway.

It is also possible that a reversal point could be delayed almost indefinitely. For instance, let's assume that T-bonds are at 100, the system is long, and the reversal percentage is 150 percent of the two-day ATR. If the ATR remains the same, the move necessary to trigger a short will also remain the same. If T-bonds move slowly downward every day, with a daily range large enough to keep the ATR the same but yet the short is not triggered, theoretically the reversal point may never be hit. It will just keep moving away. This is obviously a rare occurrence but possible, and a sequence of this type could result in large losses (and, in fact, at least in test sequences, it has).

What's Wrong with Volatility Based Systems?

We think the volatility based trading systems are good over the short run but limited over the long run. Their trading results often show real promise in spurts, but they also tend to give back their gains over time and, in the long run, may be no better than a break-even system.

There are several areas of concern for us. First, all of the system vendors have optimized extensively to find the "best" values for the major system variables—the average true range, and the percentage move needed to trigger a trade. Apparently, the vendors assumed that, once the magic (optimized) numbers were found that produced spectacular hypothetical results, the system would continue to be profitable in the future. Any variations among volatility based systems appear to be minor and concentrate on only these two variables. For example, the definition of the average true range might be changed slightly, or a simple daily range might be substituted. Or, one vendor might elect to calculate the percentage move from the following day's open, rather than the prior day's close, to factor large overnight gaps into the system and reduce whipsaws. These minor variations haven't prevented large drawdowns in the system's trading results. In our opinion, the drawdown problems seem to be the result of two factors: overoptimization, and the perhaps invalid assumption that volatility works equally as well as an exit trigger as it does as an entry trigger.

By now, most of our readers are aware of our negative feelings about optimization and reversal systems. We believe that optimization is purely hindsight curve-fitting, giving a useless and grossly exaggerated illusion of potential profitability. However, properly conducted testing and subsequent forward-testing, followed by real-time tracking, can be a worthwhile and valuable exercise. But let's face it, if simple optimization really worked, by now a few die-hard computer addicts would have cornered or busted all the markets many times over.

Suggestions on Making It Work

Despite the problems we believe to be inherent in a volatility based approach, we still feel that these systems have the potential to be workable. There does seem to be a tendency for volatile moves to be in the direction of the trend. The real difficulty, which is common to most trend-following approaches, is frequent whipsaws when the markets have no trend and low volatility. Over a long period, markets will be alternately stagnant and dynamic, with most of the time spent in the stagnant mode. Similar to moving average systems, a volatility system fine tuned for a trending market will not work well in the sideways periods.

First, it is possible to cut down the considerable initial risk on each trade by creating a neutral zone between long and short entry points. The simplest way to do this is to set a percentage risk stop that is smaller than the percentage of the ATR triggering the entry. For instance, in our earlier example we had an ATR of 100 points in the NYSE Composite, and we would buy on a move upward of 150 percent of this, or 150 points. Once we have entered the trade, a tighter stop could be set by subtracting a smaller percentage of the ATR from the entry point. Logically, anything less than 100 percent of the ATR would be classified as too close and subject to almost random whipsaws; but using a number like 125 percent still requires the occurrence of a non-average event, and it gives a tighter stop level than our standard reversal point. If the risk stop is triggered, the system is now neutral until higher volatility triggers a new buy or sell entry.

Another possible improvement might be to avoid trades when a market is acting poorly, especially when the volatility is unusually low. There may well be "windows" of optimum profitability for the ATR of each commodity, where it is within acceptable boundaries, neither too high or too low. (See Exhibit 2–99.) It is safe to assume that a stagnant market with a relatively small range will result in losing trades, while a more volatile market will tend to be more profitable. The usual impulse is to reoptimize when the markets become stagnant, but it might be

EXHIBIT 2–99

Sample ATR Table for Bonds

ATR	Comments
1 22/32 +	ATR Values are too high -
1 20/32	Too much risk.
1 18/32	
1 16/32	
1 14/32	
1 12/32	Good ATR values -
1 10/32	Expect good trading results.
1 8/32	
1 6/32	
1 4/32	
1 2/32	
32/32	ATR values are too low -
30/32 –	Expect whipsaws

Editor's Note: The actual ATR values used above are for example only and not the result of research. (This is not a real ATR table for bonds.)

more profitable in the long run to sit out completely during the quiet markets and wait until the ATR becomes more in line with what your system normally needs to be successful. (Again, see Exhibit 2–99.)

A third possibility is to add an external filter, something that identifies conditions that must be met before a breakout is taken. There are at least two possibilities for this among readily available technical studies: DMI/ADX and CCI. We have mentioned repeatedly that an upturn in Wilder's ADX signals that a market is trending. Try trading volatility breakouts only when the 18-day ADX is rising. (See Exhibit 2–100.)

Similarly, a 20-period CCI based on either monthly or weekly signals will also tell you to what extent a market is trending over the longer term. Look for rapid acceleration of the CCI from its null or zero line; if this condition exists, the market is probably moving rapidly enough to make volatility based trading highly profitable.

Quick Exits. Perhaps the best way to make a volatility based system work over time is to use an exit method that is faster and more responsive than the entry method. Using a smaller volatility percentage to signal exits (as we described previously) should lessen the giving back of profits that is part of a normal volatility reversal system. It also provides a time period when the system is not in a trade. In theory, the market action avoided is after the peak of a trend, when prices are going against the trend but the volatility breakout that will reverse the trade has not yet occurred.

EXHIBIT 2–100

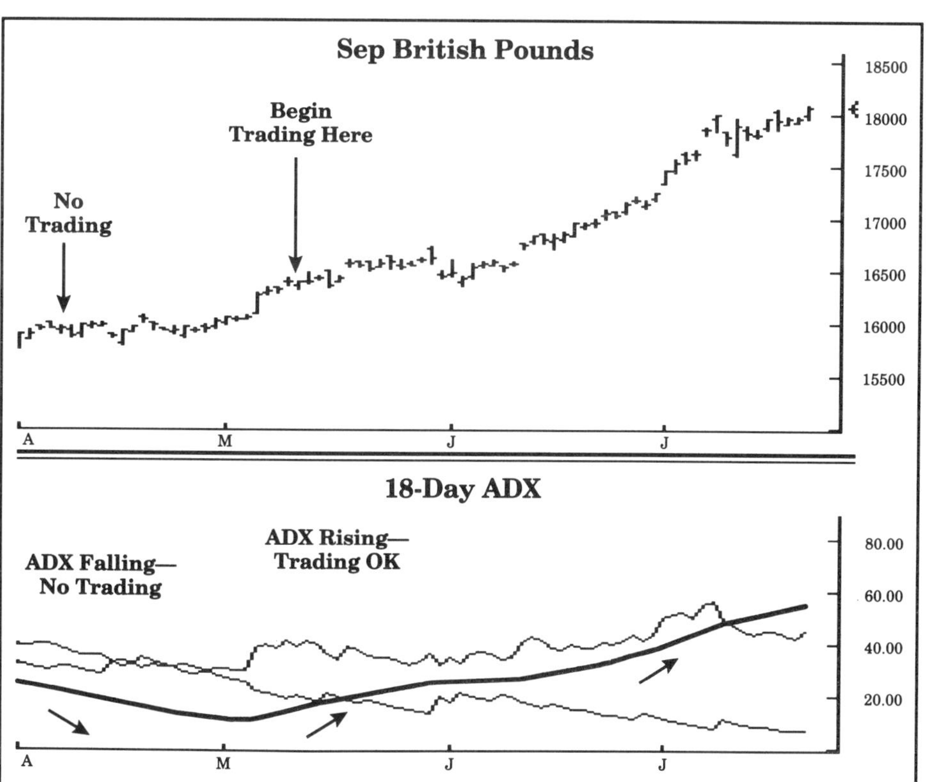

Other possible exit methods that we suggest are Wilder's Parabolic and a simple dollar stop or percentage trailing stop (by percentage we mean a percent of the underlying contract). It is true that quicker exits will mean missing part of the trend once in a while, but that is preferable to giving up a large portion of every profitable trade.

Volume and Open Interest

It is tempting to assume that a trading system based on volume and open interest would be workable. Anyone who has plotted volume or open interest, or both, has observed that they frequently coincide with or lead price action. Volume often increases when a market breaks out in either direction. A drop in open interest during a bull market will sometimes signal a near-term market top. It seems only logical that buying or selling pressure, as indicated by volume and open interest, should be at least as effective as techniques based on price alone. However, we fear that the value of volume and open interest as an indicator of any importance is an illusion.

Having said this, we will quickly concede that there may be occasional instances where studying the relationship between price, volume, and open interest can be useful. Volume and open interest can serve to bolster our opinions about the strength of a market breakout and warn us about the proximity of a market bottom or top. In spite of the many long-time advocates of volume and open interest, we don't believe that they can serve as the basis of a trading system. At best, they may have limited use as a confirmation or warning device.

A note before we start: Our previous comments and the comments to follow pertain only to futures volume, not stock market volume. Volume in the two types of markets is entirely different.

Trading with Volume

Volume analysis in the futures market has always had more than its share of operational difficulties. For one thing, volume figures are not released until near the end of trading on the day following the actual transactions. This means that, for the trader attempting to do a timely analysis, the information is at least a day late. It will be two days late if you don't get on-line information and must wait for the next morning's paper. Another obvious operational problem is the total distortion of volume created by limit days. Volume on lock-limit days is often negligible, yet this is when a market has its strongest or weakest price action. Here we have a clear case of an obvious preponderance of buyers or sellers, yet we are unable to measure it. (See Exhibit 2–101.)

Traditional volume analysis normally begins with the assumption that volume will expand as a market continues a trend and will contract as the market corrects. In a sideways market, volume will tend to be

EXHIBIT 2–101

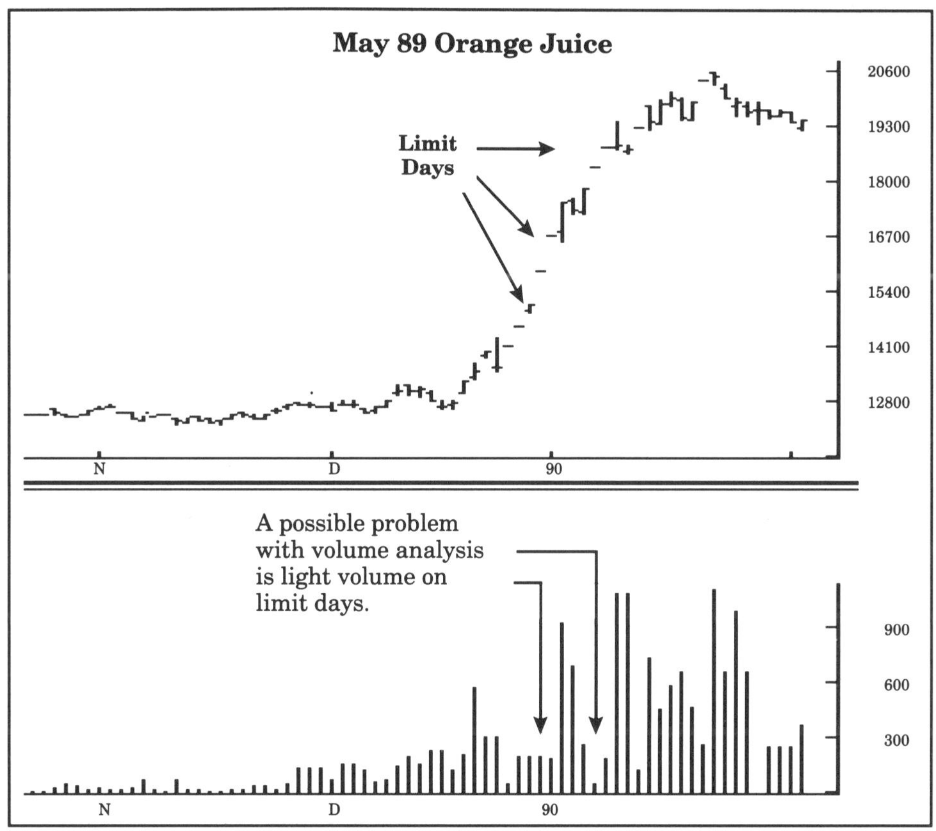

light. Volume will spike if the market breaks out (in either direction) and will rise as the market trends. We have observed that the heaviest volume will be on breakouts and in the areas where the market is trending upward.

Since these volume patterns are considered to be normal, any deviation from normal behavior can give rise to suspicion that the trend is not as strong as it appears and that perhaps it should not be followed. If, for example, a breakout occurs on light volume, many traders would not enter the market unless volume increased to confirm the breakout. Later in the trend, other traders might want to cover their positions, if volume began decreasing as prices continued to move in the trend direction. The overall assumption is that volume precedes price action (a highly questionable assumption), and that price action should be confirmed by volume changes.

We see serious flaws in this methodology. First and foremost, we are trading price, not volume. If a market is trending, and we are making profits, what does it matter if volume does not confirm? The volume indications are not nearly reliable enough in our opinion to warrant an exit from a profitable position. Prices are still moving—and that is the important thing. Reasonable risk control and carefully chosen trailing stops will take you out of the market in a more timely fashion than will volume analysis.

As we noted, we are not at all sure about the basic assumption that volume precedes price. It is just as logical to assume that price action precedes or attracts volume. Nothing gets the public's attention like an upside breakout. And remember, this is futures trading and not the stock market. For every buyer there must always be a seller. There is no upside/downside volume breakdown as there is in the stock market, and no specialists trying to maintain an orderly market at the risk of their own capital. In the futures markets, every buyer thinks he or she is correct, as does every seller. Volume by itself cannot push the market, because there cannot be more volume on one side of the market than the other. It is always exactly equal.

We have also observed that there is a great deal of hindsight involved in volume analysis. (Since it is always late being reported, it would be difficult to be a lead indicator.) If volume spikes during a breakout and the market continues to trend, everyone says that volume leads price and that the volume spike confirmed the beginning of a trend. If the trend doesn't continue, everyone says that the breakout was a blow-off or buying climax, confirmed by the spike in volume. Hindsight is always 20/20, and volume can conveniently confirm either outcome. (See Exhibit 2–102.)

The Basics—Open Interest

As most of our readers are well aware, open interest is the total number of outstanding contracts in the market at the end of the trading day. Because there is a buyer for every seller, and vice versa, total open interest also tells you the number of contracts long and the number of contracts short in the market. That number must always be exactly equal.

Open interest is usually plotted as a line chart just above the volume chart. Open interest figures are calculated by the clearing house in the same manner as the volume figures and are, therefore, also late. Open interest, in a more general sense than volume, measures the amount of money moving into or out of a futures market. If both sides of a trade are new to the market, open interest will increase. If one side is new and the other an old position closing out, open interest will remain the same. If both sides are closeouts, open interest will decrease. If these were the only possible variables, open interest interpretation would be much simpler than it is. The picture is often clouded, however.

Open interest in many markets, especially the agricultural commodities, varies seasonally. Hedging activities tend to be heaviest at harvest time, increasing open interest. The rise in open interest may be meaningful only if it differs significantly from the normal seasonal tendency. Commodity Research Bureau (CRB) charts conveniently plot a five-year average of open interest to make these seasonal comparisons easier.

Open interest will also change as speculative interest moves from one contract to another in the same commodity. If you are following the open interest only in the nearby contract, this can give false readings in a number of ways. For example, a drop in open interest in a rising market that is getting close to deliveries or expiration may not mean

EXHIBIT 2–102

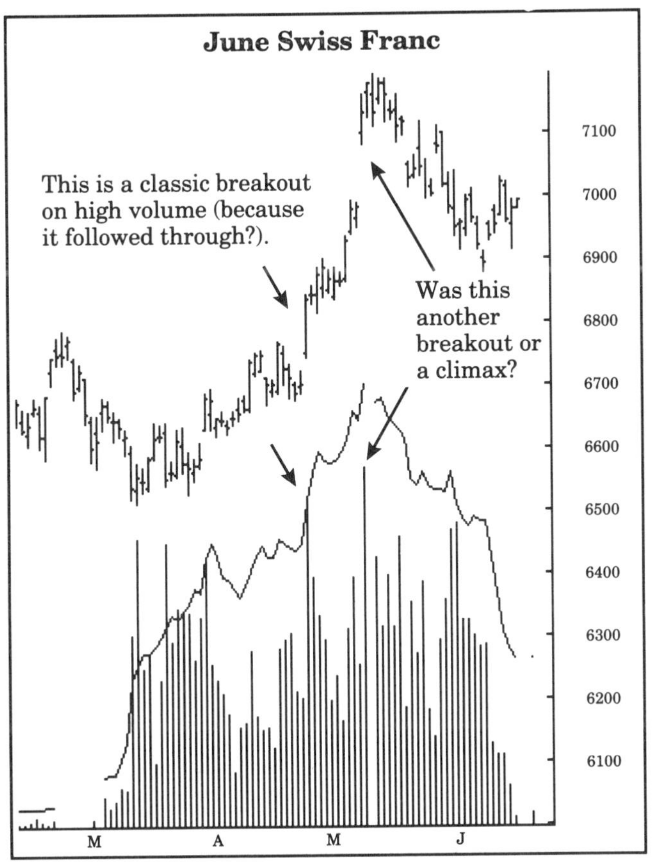
June Swiss Franc
This is a classic breakout on high volume (because it followed through?).
Was this another breakout or a climax?
7100
7000
6900
6800
6700
6600
6500
6400
6300
6200
6100
M
A
M
J

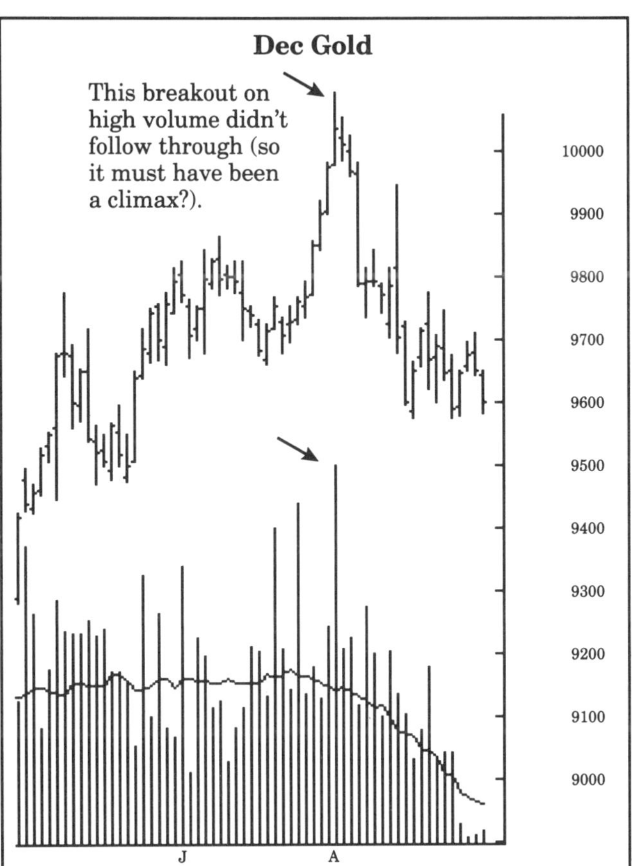
Dec Gold
This breakout on high volume didn't follow through (so it must have been a climax?).
10000
9900
9800
9700
9600
9500
9400
9300
9200
9100
9000
J
A

that speculators are abandoning the market and that the top is near. The drop in open interest may simply mean that they believe the market is strong and want to roll out of the nearby contract and into a contract that will give them longer staying power. (We suggest that watchers of open interest should follow total open interest, rather than month by month.) Spreading can also affect open interest on particular contracts, so be careful of reading too much into this data. In our opinion, the ideal chart for open interest would be a perpetual or continuous chart showing the total combined open interest plus the five-year average.

Volume and Open Interest Interaction

The simplest way to show the commonly accepted interrelationships between volume, open interest, and price action is to construct a table like the one below.

Price	Volume	Open Interest	Market Analysis
Up	Up	Up	Strong
Up	Down	Down	Weak
Down	Up	Up	Weak
Down	Down	Down	Strong

As you can see from the table, traditional open interest interpretation includes four possibilities.

1. Prices are going up, and open interest is going up. This means that new money is flowing into the market and there is buying pressure (Do not falsely assume there are more buyers than sellers, because there are not. The price rise indicates that the buyers are willing to pay higher prices and, of course, the sellers are willing to cooperate.) This situation is considered bullish.

2. Prices are going up, and open interest is declining. There are relatively few new buyers, and money is leaving the market. The rally is most likely caused by shorts who are giving up the ghost and covering their positions, thereby exiting the market. This is often bullish for the short term, because the shorts will normally pay any price to get out, and because they cannot afford to stay in and accept further losses. This action is ultimately bearish. Without new money coming into the market, the rally will fail as soon as the short covering is finished. However, short covering gets to be self-perpetuating and can last longer than one might suspect.

According to our friend George Lane, who is a very experienced trader and a strong advocate of volume and open interest analysis to confirm other indicators, the total open interest (meaning the open  interest of all contracts combined) always declines five to eight days before the final top.

3. Prices are falling, and open interest is rising. New money is coming into the market, and there is selling pressure. This is considered bearish.

4. Prices are falling, and open interest is falling. This is the opposite of situation **2.** Now the short sellers are making money and can afford to stay in the market. Much of the price drop is caused by discouraged longs closing out their positions. There is little new money coming into the market. This is initially bearish, but the market is considered ripe for a rally once the discouraged long liquidation is finished. The short sellers are generally notorious for their lack of patience and are likely to start covering as soon as the downward momentum subsides.

While we see nothing incorrect about these interpretations, we question their value. If your market opinion needs bolstering, the interpretations may be useful as a method of confirmation. We don't think that trading on open interest analysis will prove fruitful.

Having said that open interest changes do not appear to lead price changes, we must mention a significant observation about open interest that was pointed out to us many years ago. In a sideways or slightly downward market, a sudden drop in open interest is often followed by a market rally. (See Exhibit 2–103.) The conventional wisdom is that the large market participants are lifting their hedges in anticipation of an expected rally. The feeling is that "insiders" know which way the markets are going and position themselves in front of the anticipated move.

The "insider" theory runs throughout volume and open interest studies. It is difficult for us to believe that anyone ever actually "knows" which way any futures market is heading. In fact, contrary to popular perception, large commercials firms trade futures because they don't

EXHIBIT 2–103

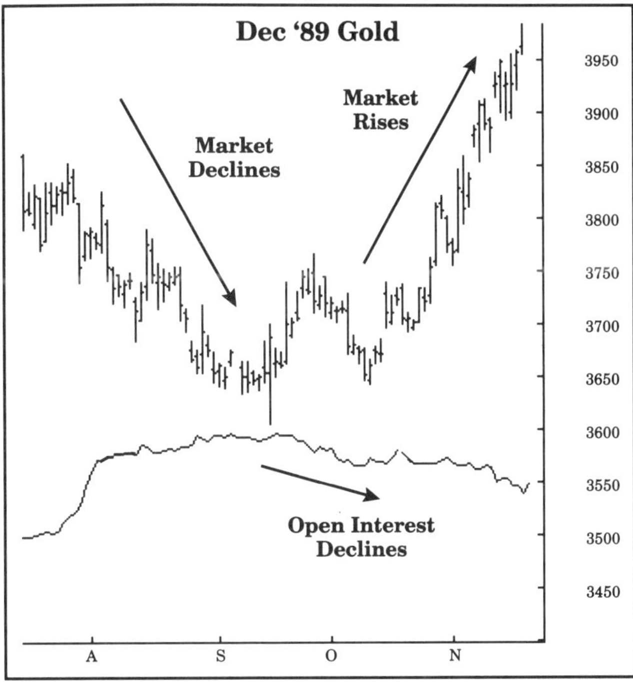

know which way the markets are going, not because they do. If they or anyone knew much of anything with any certainty, the futures markets would be nonexistent in a matter of months. (Again, see Exhibit 2–103.)

A more likely explanation for an open interest drop before a rally is a lack of conviction about market direction on the part of all traders. The shorts are not interested in the market, because of the low prices. The longs are not interested in a market that appears to be in a prolonged downtrend. However, rallies often seem to begin with very negative sentiment in a market that is already at low levels. In a situation like this, a sentiment indicator like Hadady's "Bullish Consensus" would probably be a better indicator than volume or open interest.

Volume and Open Interest Studies

The best-known readily available computer-generated technical study involving volume is on-balance volume (OBV), popularized in the early 1960s by Joseph Granville. The calculation is simple. Each day's volume is assigned a plus or minus, depending on whether the day's close was up or down. The resulting figures are added in a running total to become an OBV line. The actual value of the OBV line is not really important, but the formations it makes may be significant. Traditional volume/price logic applies to the OBV line, especially with regard to divergences between the OBV line and prices. We have our doubts about the validity of applying this stock market tool to the futures markets. There is no reason for all the volume for one day to be assigned to one side, since volume is always 50/50 in the futures markets.

There are additional sophisticated approaches to the volume question, most notably volume accumulation (VA), developed by Marc Chaikin, and the Demand Index devised by James Sibbet. Again it is our opinion that these stock market indicators are not well suited to futures trading, although they may be effective when applied to the securities markets. (Stock traders are fortunate they don't have to deal with open interest.)

Our summary, in case you haven't guessed by now, is that volume analysis works well in the stock market but not in futures. Open interest, at best, has only very limited uses as a confirming indicator.

Suggested Readings

DMI and ADX

Babcock, Bruce, Jr. *The Dow Jones-Irwin Guide to Trading Systems*. Homewood, Ill.: Dow Jones-Irwin, 1989.

Colby, Robert W., and Thomas A. Myers. *The Encyclopedia of Technical Market Indicators*. Homewood, Ill.: Dow Jones-Irwin, 1988.

Hochheimer, Frank L. *Computerized Trading Techniques, 1982*. New York: Merrill Lynch Commodities, 1982.

Wilder, J. Welles, Jr. *New Concepts in Technical Trading Systems*. Greensboro, N.C.: Trend Research, 1978.

Bands, Envelopes, and Channels

Babcock, Bruce, Jr. *The Dow Jones-Irwin Guide to Trading Systems*. Homewood, Ill.: Dow Jones-Irwin, 1989.

Gallacher, William R. *Winner Takes All: A Privateer's Guide to Commodity Trading*. Toronto: Midway Publications, 1983.

Hochheimer, Frank L. "Channels and Crossovers: An Explanation and Computerized Testing of Commodity Trading Techniques." In *Technical Analysis in Commodities,* P. J. Kaufman, ed. New York: John Wiley & Sons, 1980.

Irwin, Scott H., and J. William Uhrig. "Do Technical Analysts Have Holes in Their Shoes?" *Review of Research in Futures Markets* 3, no. 3 (1984), pp. 264–81.

Lukac, Louis P.; B. Wade Brorsen; and Scott H. Irwin. *A Comparison of Twelve Technical Trading Systems*. This paper was essentially a revision of Lukac's M.S. thesis at Purdue University. The study of trading systems was retrieved from the university archives and reprinted in 1990 by Edward Dobson of Traders Press in Greenville, S.C.

Commodity Channel Index

Colby, Robert W., and Thomas W. Meyers. *The Encyclopedia of Technical Market Indicators*. Homewood, Ill.: Dow Jones-Irwin, 1988.

Lambert, Donald R. "Commodity Channel Index: Tool for Trading Cyclic Trends." *Commodities,* October 1980.

Momentum and Rate of Change

Babcock, Bruce, Jr. *The Dow Jones-Irwin Guide to Trading Systems.* Homewood, Ill.: Dow Jones-Irwin, 1989.

Colby, Robert W., and Thomas A. Meyers. *The Encyclopedia of Technical Market Indicators.* Homewood, Ill.: Dow Jones-Irwin, 1988.

Eng, William F. *The Technical Analysis of Stocks, Options and Futures.* Chicago: Probus Publishing, 1988.

Kaufman, Perry J. *The New Commodity Trading Systems and Methods.* New York: John Wiley & Sons, 1987.

Murphy, John J. *Technical Analysis of the Futures Markets.* New York: New York Institute of Finance, 1986.

Pring, Martin J. *Technical Analysis Explained.* New York: McGraw-Hill, 1985.

Moving Averages

Maxwell, J. R., Sr. *Commodity Futures Trading with Moving Averages.* Red Bluff, Calif.: Speer Books, 1976.

"TTB Interviews Joe DiNapoli." *Technical Traders Bulletin,* February 1990, pp. 1–7.

MACD Trading Method

Appel, Gerald. *The Moving Average Convergence/Divergence Trading Method—Advanced Version.* Toronto, Ontario: Scientific Investment System, 1985.

Babcock, Bruce, Jr. *The Dow Jones-Irwin Guide to Trading Systems.* Homewood, Ill.: Dow Jones-Irwin, 1989.

Parabolic

Kaufman, Perry J. *The New Commodity Trading Systems and Methods.* New York: John Wiley & Sons, 1987.

Wilder, J. Welles, Jr. *New Concepts in Technical Trading Systems.* Greenboro, N.C.: Trend Research, 1978.

Percent R

Williams, Larry R. *How I Made One Million Dollars Last Year Trading Commodities.* Carmel Valley, Calif.: Conceptual Management, 1973.

Point and Figure

Cohen, A. W. *How to Use the Three-Point Method of Point-and-Figure Stock Market Trading.* Larchmont, N.Y.: Chartcraft, 1972.

DeVilliers, Victor. *The Point-and-Figure Method* of Anticipating Stock Price Movements. New York: Trader Press, 1966.

Kaufman, Perry J. *The New Commodity Trading Systems and Methods.* New York: John Wiley & Sons, 1987.

Whelan, Alexander. *Study Helps in Point-and-Figure* Technique. New York: Morgan, Roberts and Roberts, 1962.

Wyckoff, Richard D. *Stock Market Technique Number One.* New York: Wyckoff Associates, 1933.

Zieg, Kermit C., and Perry J. Kaufman. Point-and-Figure Commodity Trading Techniques. Larchmont, N.Y.: Investors Intelligence, 1975.

Relative Strength Index

Wilder, J. Welles, Jr. *New Concepts in Technical Trading Systems.* Greensboro, N.C.: Trend Research, 1978.

Slow Stochastics

Elder, Alexander. "Using Stochastics to Catch Early Trend Reversals." Futures, June 1987, pp. 68–70.

Kaufman, Perry J. *The New Commodity Trading Systems and Methods.* New York: John Wiley & Sons, 1987.

Lane, George C. "Lane's Stochastics." *Technical Analysis of Stocks and Commodities, Investment Techniques* 2, pp. 87–90.

Murphy, John J. *Technical Analysis of the Futures Markets.* New York: New York Institute of Finance, 1986.

Schirding, Harry. "Stochastics Oscillator." *Technical Analysis of Stocks and Commodities* 2, pp. 94–97.

Stein, Jon. "Learning to Swing to Momentum with Stochastics Signals." *Futures,* May 1989, pp. 36–37.

Volatility

Kaufman, Perry J. *The New Commodity Trading Systems and Methods.* New York: John Wiley & Sons, 1987.

Notis, Steven. *User's Manual for the Professional Breakout System.* Nesconset, N.Y.: Byte Research and Trading, 1989.

Wilder, J. Welles, Jr. *New Concepts in Technical Trading Systems.* Greensboro, N.C.: Trend Research, 1978.

Chapter

3 System Testing

The Basics

Why Test?

We are often asked, "Why test a trading system? You're only going to get hypothetical results. How do you know the system will work in real time?" The real answer to the last question is that you never truly know if your system will work in the future, but there are only two ways to find out if it has any validity. The first is to trade it in real time, and the second is to test it. Since the time and expense of real time testing of a new trading system is prohibitive, it follows that computer testing is at least an easy way to see how your pet system design would have worked in the past. You learn the good and the bad about your system—and, if you test correctly, you know about what to expect in real time trading.

Above all, you accomplish two things. First, to test a system, you must make your system mechanical, so the only discretionary element is "Do I take this next trade—or don't I?" We believe that mechanical trading systems are best for the vast majority of traders. Second, you find out if your system has what Ralph Vince in *Portfolio Management Formulas* (see "Suggested Readings" at end of chapter) calls a "positive expectation." Others have called this the "trader's edge." It may sound simplistic, but if your system is not profitable in testing, it will not be profitable in real time. With all of the talk about money management schemes recently we have noticed there is an illusion that a mediocre system can be turned into a winner by somehow managing the trades and the cash differently. This is not true. No money management or betting scheme will turn a losing system into a winner. You can use any gambling strategy you care to try, and if you don't have a positive expectation, over the long run money management won't change your results at all. You must have an edge at the outset. The only way to see if you have this advantage is to test or trade your system.

Don't expect to find definitive results establishing that any technical study or trading system is superior to any other. We also hope you won't be overly disappointed if you follow all the rules, test correctly, and still don't find success. Every test ever done is only valid in the context of its internal structure and in relation to the data included in the test. If we test a trading system over 20 different markets from 1980 to the present, the results say nothing about 1975. More important, they are limited in what they say about the future. We haven't "proven" anything, nor should we expect to. The best we can do is to be as rigorous and thorough in our testing as we possibly can. There are no easy answers. Nothing is definite in futures trading.

Software

Computer testing of mechanical trading systems has been around for over 20 years but has only become popular in the last several years with the introduction of PC-based software packages that make the process possible without a great amount of programming knowledge. Almost anyone can now create a "profitable" trading system that shows fantastic hypothetical results over historical data. Most of the trading systems that sold for large sums over the past 20 years or so have been created by this method. Unfortunately, as thousands of disappointed investors can testify, commercial "black box" systems rarely if ever work as expected. As far as we know, the same can be said of the great majority of trading systems generated by the use of testing software. The reasons for this apparent lack of success don't lie in the testing software but in the testing and evaluation methods used by the testers. We use System Writer Plus and Computrac/SNAP for our testing, and both are excellent programs, which we can recommend without hesitation. Neither of them shows any bias or lack of flexibility that might tempt a researcher to adopt inadequate testing methods. The problem, as we pointed out, is the testing methodology itself and not the software.

We realize that not everyone owns system testing software. It is expensive and complex, with a steep learning curve. It is not necessary to possess it to create a viable trading system. The elements of any system should be the same, whether you have expensive testing software or are doing your own programming. It is even possible to test a trading system without expensive software, simply by sitting in front of a computer screen and objectively trading your system over past data. In fact, there are advantages to doing it this way. One advantage is that, without the extensive optimization capability of the software packages, your system is less likely to be overly curve-fitted. However, the pros of the testing packages far outweigh the cons. We strongly recommend that you either obtain some system testing software or program your own, if you have the skills and feel that the commercially available systems don't meet your specific needs.

Elements of a Trading System

At the risk of being redundant, we'd like to cover the attributes that a trading system must possess if it is to be successfully tested. Some (or all) of these things may seem obvious; but we have spoken to literally thousands of traders over the past two years in the course of putting out our newsletter and writing this book, and we can say with some confidence that many people don't fully understand what a trading system should or should not do.

The first prerequisite of a trading system to be seriously tested is that it must be purely mechanical. The only discretionary component should be the decision to trade the system fully or not. All other decisions must be built into the system. We realize that many, if not most, speculators are currently trading systems that are at least partly discretionary. Also, we're aware that most truly successful traders consider some degree of discretion a necessary component of their trading. We have no quarrel with this—but it's impossible to test, because it's hopelessly subjective. Discretionary elements have no place in a mechanical trading system that is being prepared for testing.

Expect the Worst

The system you design for testing should attempt to anticipate all contingencies. It is very common for us to hear a trader downplay a missing element of a favorite trading system. The typical response is, "It's never happened to me, so why plan for it? Why should I use stops, if my system always seems to catch tops and bottoms and there's never been a drawdown that I couldn't handle?"

This is not only naive but dangerous. Always assume that what can happen will happen. A system must always expect the worst and be prepared to cope with it. You must always seek to achieve complete risk control. Don't assume that, because it hasn't happened in the past, it won't happen in the future.

Here is a typical example: Many traders prefer to use close-only stops to avoid taking whipsaw-type losses on intraday stops. It can well be rationalized that intraday price movement is inconsequential and that only the close is significant. (Actually, close-only stops are usually adopted by traders who have been stopped out of potentially profitable trades and are attempting to make sure that it won't happen again.) Can you imagine anyone foolish enough to be long the S&P on October 16 or 19, 1987, with a close-only stop! It should only take the possibility of situations like this to convince anyone that it's better to have an ordinary stop and a re-entry strategy. Anticipate the awful, then you won't be quite as surprised and unprepared when it happens.

The Perils of Optimization

Unfortunately, the somewhat misguided objective of many testing projects is to develop trading strategies that squeeze the greatest possible profit out of the historical data. The assumption is, the better it worked in the past, the better it will work in the future. If this were true, everyone who designed a historical model that worked well in the past (meaning essentially everyone who has ever used system testing software) would be very wealthy by now. Obviously, this isn't what has happened to the majority of system testers.

Most testing we've observed seems to follow a standard scenario. A trader buys the latest software package and some data. He or she puts together a few favorite technical studies or chart patterns that seem to have worked in the past, and runs the computer hour after hour to find precise values for each parameter that produce the most profit. Impressed by the fantastic results, greed takes hold and he or she starts trading right away. Inevitably, the trader runs into a series of losses and decides that something is wrong with his or her trading methods. The most obvious thing to do is to optimize again and to get rid of the losing components of the system. The trader reoptimizes and is gratified to see that the modifications have, in hindsight, eliminated most of the losing trades. Confident again in spite of the previous losses, he or she resumes trading, only to suffer another surprising series of losses. Many traders repeat the process until either their money or patience runs out. Usually it's the money that gives out, leading them to believe that they would surely succeed if only they could afford to optimize and trade one more time. Other traders conclude that the fault lies in using mechanical trading systems, and they switch to a subjective trading method that can never be tested. The losses, of course, continue—but now they are merely the result of bad luck, bad fills on orders, raids on stops, manipulation by insiders, or the lack of attention of their broker.

What Really Went Wrong?

It is useful to dissect the above process and to review what went wrong and why before exploring more correct procedures. First and most obvious, be wary of optimization in almost any form. Literally any technical indicator or set of indicators will show tremendous profits when optimized for the best combination of parameters, even over a random data set. The computer is analyzing millions of combinations, so the probabilities are very good that some of these will, at least in hindsight, make money.

Faced with the lure of almost instant riches as indicated by the amazing optimized results, the temptation to begin trading immediately is overwhelming. The belief in this optimization process is so strong that traders will optimize again and again, even though the status of their trading accounts should be telling them that they are doing something wrong. This is exactly what happened to the trader in our previous example. You can hear the trader saying, "Just one more optimization, and I'll have it made." Unfortunately, one more optimization will never solve the problem.

To Optimize or Not to Optimize

Anyone who believes that full optimization works as well as touted by some system vendors would do well to read "The Usefulness of Historical Data in Selecting Parameters for Technical Trading Systems" by Louis B. Lukac and B. Wade Brorsen. Their work is systematic and complete. They tested two trend-following systems, the Channel Breakout and

Wilder's Directional Movement System, using 20 years of data. The only variable that was optimized was the number of days used in each calculation. That parameter was stepped through a time period of 5 to 60 days, in 5-day increments.

They compared three different optimization schemes with a random test, which used parameter values randomly chosen from the 5- to 60-day set. The most significant finding was that the re-optimization strategies did nothing to increase system performance. Each optimization method produced results not significantly different from the random test. With or without optimization, profits were on the order of 50 to 65 percent for the Channel Breakout System, and 30 to 54 percent for Wilder's Directional Movement System. They stated, "The results of all the tests suggest that the forecasting ability of optimization is limited. Optimization was not able to forecast parameter sets which would produce portfolio profits better than a random selection strategy."

Let us stress that this was a rigorously formal test done with great attention to detail. Anyone who claims that full optimization works better than a simple blind simulation will have to produce contrary results that are just as rigorously attained.

How to Avoid Curve-Fitting

Some curve-fitting is unavoidable. It would be difficult and undesirable to design a technical study without it. When a trader "eyeballs" a chart and sees that a 9-day RSI seems to fit that particular market better than the standard 14-day, he or she is curve-fitting. Because that seems so simple and effective, it is only a small step from there to testing every possible RSI parameter. Once this process begins producing profitable results, the permutations become almost endless: "We'd better add a few more technical studies to make sure we don't miss anything. While we're at it, let's optimize for the correct initial risk and best trailing stops, so our system is as complete as we can make it." The ultimate product is a system contrived with all the best intentions that has been curve-fitted to the *n*th degree. As good as it looks on paper, the odds against it working in the future have become astronomical. The effects of optimization are exactly the opposite of what might seem obvious. The better it looks, and the more complete and complex the system is, the less likely it is to succeed at all.

There is a rigorous explanation of why optimization and curve-fitting can go wrong. Frankly, it's such a simple and easily described concept that we can't believe that more traders aren't paying more attention to it. Any statistician knows about the notion of freedom loss. In layman's terms, it means that each parameter added to a trading system represents a degree of control lost over the final outcome of the testing procedure. The more technical studies or trading rules that you introduce, the less robust and reliable will be the results. The more you try to improve a system, the less likely it is to work as tested.

You should have two to five variables at the most. The fewer variables, the more reliable the results. An interesting corollary is that it allows you to look at your own past work and that of others and quickly decide if any of it is curve-fitted. The likelihood of the system being curve-fitted varies directly with the number of variables used to test the system. The greater the number of technical studies and rules (especially exceptions to rules) the more curve-fitted the model is. Watch out for systems that are so complex that it takes a computer to run them.

Another way to avoid curve-fitting is to avoid creating systems that are custom tailored to specific markets. This is an easy trap to fall into, but it is the ultimate in curve-fitting. A good system does not have to work historically in all markets to be successful, but it should work in most markets, with few if any changes from market to market. If you have to change the system to make it adapt to each market, something is very wrong with the basic system. We are well aware of the argument that each market has its own unique character, but we also remember the times when currency futures had almost no volatility and grain contracts fluctuated thousands of dollars per day. Markets change, and the best way to make sure your trading system will be in step is to test it in static form over as many varying markets as possible.

Before we leave the subject, there is another more subtle form of optimization creeping into popularity. We are referring to the practice of running historical data through a computer to find "seasonals." There are a handful of well-known traders/authors who are providing test data to show that, if you bought a particular commodity on a particular date each year and then sold it on a particular date, you would have had a profit x number of times. This is pure nonsense, with absolutely no statistical validity or application to trading. If we want, the analytical powers of the computer will allow us to optimize the data, rather than the system. The data is examined in very small segments to extract exact dates that would have fit the system. Instead of curve-fitting the system, we can curve-fit the data. Of course, there are many obviously logical and sometimes valid longer-term seasonals (like annual harvest lows in the fall, for example), but beware of carrying seasonals to the point of absurdity. Any seasonal trading advice that is more specific than suggesting the best month for a trade should be highly suspect.

Selection of Test Period

Another critical area often overlooked is the period of test data to be selected. At the barest minimum, the test period should be long enough to generate at least 30 trades in each market. Having less than 30 trades violates one of the basic rules of sampling theory, which dictates that at least 30 data points must exist for a data set to indicate a normal distribution. Note that this doesn't refer to days, weeks, or months of data but to actual trades. Anything less than 30 will generate statistically unreliable results. The more trades over 30 the better.

Just as important, the market periods you are testing must contain as many occurrences of each possible market condition as possible. Up, down, and sideways are the simplest (albeit subjective) definitions of possible market conditions; your study period should contain as many of each as possible. The intent is to simulate potential future conditions by including as much of the past as possible. Measuring this only in years can create problems. For example, the stock market has not had a serious down period since stock index futures were introduced, so testing with this data would tend to favor systems with a bullish bias. The full life of the stock index markets doesn't really contain enough data to reflect potential future market conditions. The petroleum complex, on the other hand, has shown us a great deal more variability and might be expected to produce a more robust trading system as a result. To explain it another way, the results of a short time period of testing in the crude oil market might give truer results than a longer period of testing in the stock indexes, because the stock index data contains an obvious upward bias so far. A buy-only system in the stock index market would have been likely to produce much better results than a sell-only system. As Yogi Berra once observed, "The future ain't what it used to be."

An interesting corollary is that, as tempting as it might seem at times, a system should never be biased toward one side of the market. Obviously, with a few notable exceptions, most of the profits in the stock indexes will have been on the long side. This doesn't mean that a trading system should favor that side of the market. The system should have no opinion or bias toward one side or the other. If this seems obvious, recall that in the 1970s most of the profits made in the commodity markets were on the long side. Many of the trading systems devised during that period became, essentially, bull market systems. The easiest way to improve your results during that period was to restrict or eliminate short sales. We suspect that this bullish bias was a principal reason for the poor performance of many commodity advisors in the early 1980s.

Our conclusion: There is no firm definition of how much data a test should include. If we assume that the average trend-following system trades about once a month per market, at least three years would seem to be a minimum, at least for an initial test to produce the 30-trades minimum mentioned earlier. Then add two or more years for forward testing (we'll explain this later) and you have five years, which, only by coincidence, is the generally accepted minimum. Add more time if the market has been only one- or two-dimensional during the period studied. You will want to include as many different market conditions as possible in your study.

We like to use lots of data and to test over varying time periods. Unless you've done this, you can never fully appreciate how elusive a profitable trading system can be and how time-dependent the testing results are. We are very wary of systems that have not been tested through time periods that reflect a representative sample of market conditions.

Notice how in the following table (see Exhibit 3–1) the results are affected by changing the time frame, especially with regard to drawdowns. The return is similar, which brings up an interesting point. Just about all of the optimization/testing procedures we've seen focus on total return as the sole criterion for choosing the most optimal parameters to use in subsequent tests or in real time trading. In our simple example, the returns seem to be in line with one another. The drawdowns, however, are vastly different. How many traders would be willing to ride out a $10,000 drawdown while trading a contract with an average margin of only about $2,500? That's asking a great deal.

EXHIBIT 3–1

20-Day Channel Breakout System, Crude Oil		
	1/87-1/90	1/86-1/90
Total Return	16,225	19,690
% Winners	41	38
Ratio Avg. Win/ Avg. Loss	4.96	3.31
Maximum Drawdown	-3,090	-10,595

The example in Exhibit 3–1 illustrates one of the seldom-mentioned perils of testing (in general) and optimization (in particular). When you test for only one result (usually total return) you are probably ignoring other equally important data. We recommend that you test for a matrix of attributes, rather than just for one. We realize this complicates the procedure and may in many ways make it subjective, but testing only for total return is often misleading and can be harmful to your financial health.

Selection of Test Data

As far as we know, no publicly offered testing software incorporates the ability to roll a trade from one contract month to another without causing a break in the values of any technical study it is calculating at the time. The break invalidates the study and, therefore, the test. Of course, it is theoretically possible to feed the computer a series of contract months for a given commodity, test each month separately, and then consolidate the results, but we can't imagine a more tedious and error-prone procedure.

The solution is to arrange your data into a continuous stream that has no breaks and, therefore, allows continuous testing. We won't go into detail about the calculations to ensure a smooth transition from one contract to the next; but we are satisfied that, given that testing is hypothetical anyway, the results are reasonably accurate.

We have data from two sources: FutureSource and Technical Tools. The Technical Tools data comes with software to create your own continuous (or other) contracts. If you have a number of different analytical software packages (as we do), Quote Butler from Technical Tools is an excellent way to switch data from one to another without having to buy data for each specific application. We have no recent experience with any other data vendors, but there are several reliable sources of inexpensive and clean data.

Slippage and Commissions

Don't trust any testing results that don't include a liberal allowance for slippage and commissions. They make an incredible difference in your results. A lot of trading systems make small steady profits when tested without allowing for slippage and commissions and turn into steady losers when transaction costs are factored in. This is especially true of short-term or day-trading systems. The more frequently a system trades, the more critical transaction costs become.

A particularly glaring example was in a recent national publication. The article explained an indicator that purported to call intraday turns in stock index futures. Although the volume of trades was high, there was no allowance for transaction costs. We calculated that, given very discounted commissions and only occasional slippage, the system was at best a break-even method, at worst a steady loser.

Everyone has favorite numbers for transaction costs. We allow $75 for slippage and $50 for commission per round turn, for a total of $125 per trade. This number may seem high, but we prefer to err on the conservative side. When we are testing portions of a trading system, we may elect to intentionally leave out slippage and commissions just to simplify the operation, but we make sure they are back in before we start looking at potential bottom-line results.

Testing Protocols

We'll explain a few of the most common optimization and testing schemes.

Simple Optimization

This is as easy as it sounds. You create a trading system, then optimize it over a comprehensive set of parameter values until you find the ones that yield the best return. In our opinion, this is the least-productive system testing method. It is curve-fitting of the worst kind.

Cumulative Forward Testing

This is also called "roll-forward" optimization. Cumulative forward testing requires that you optimize a system over a period at the beginning of your data, then test the results over a relatively short subsequent period. You then reoptimize over a period that includes both data sets and continue the cycle. For example, if you have 10 years of T-bond data, you might optimize over the first 3 years, then test over the next one. If the results are still good, you then optimize over the full four years, then test the fifth year, and so on. This is one of the forms of optimization that was tested by Lukac and Brorsen and found to be no better than random (see above).

Simple Forward Testing

This is also called "blind simulation" or "out of sample testing." You develop your system over the beginning of your data (say for the first 5 years of a 10-year data set), and then test what you believe is your best combination of parameters and rules over the more recent time period, with no modification. If it doesn't work, it's back to the drawing board. Whether you optimize or not in the first phase of testing is not as important as keeping the number of variables low. The most important point is that any trading system subjected to simple testing or optimization without forward testing is, most likely, doomed to failure.

Forward testing is the most elegant solution to the system testing muddle. It offers some of the advantages of optimization with none of the disadvantages. If your system doesn't prove profitable with this forward testing procedure, throw it out.

Measuring Performance

The most obvious testing goal is profitability. How much money did my model make? Another way to calculate this might be percent return, which is the annualized return based on the amount of money needed to trade the account. The percent return should be looked at over the entire testing period and then broken down into small segments, so negative periods can be isolated. Keep in mind that percent return is simply a function of the amount of capital used. You can double the percent return by starting with only half as much capital, but you have not improved the system. You may actually improve a system by starting with more capital, but percent return will suffer accordingly. Frivolous and meaningless trading contests are won by making big returns with small amounts of capital. This overleveraged trading seldom results in a viable or sustainable track record, as evidenced by the dismal performance of the commodity mutual funds managed by some well-known contest winners.

The Sharpe Ratio

A popular measure of performance derived from the percent return is the Sharpe ratio, devised by William Sharpe, which is defined as the annualized return (a profitability measure) minus the risk-free rate of return divided by the annualized standard deviation of return (a volatility measure). Some practitioners eliminate the risk-free rate of return, so check this if you're comparing results. The higher the Sharpe ratio, the higher the return and the lower the volatility. The industry standard for commodity trading advisors is to calculate the Sharpe ratio based on monthly data. We realize that the Sharpe ratio has limitations (for example, increased upside volatility will result in a lower Sharpe ratio) but it is still the most common index of its type. It may be helpful for you to compare the results of one system versus another and to compare your results with those of professional advisors. The best system for you may not be the one that makes the most money but the one with the highest Sharpe ratio.

The Sterling Ratio

Because the Sharpe ratio has its shortcomings, other statistics have been developed to fairly compare performance. The most popular of these are ratios of drawdown to rate of return. The Sterling ratio was designed by Deane Jones of Jones Commodities. The formula is:

> Sterling ratio = (3 yr avg rate of return / ((-1×3 yr avg max drawdown) + 10))

The main criticism of the Sterling ratio is that it is usually calculated yearly and, therefore, reacts too slowly to changes in performance.

The Calmar Ratio

The Calmar ratio, devised by Terry Young of CMA Reports, takes the average rate of return for the past 36 months and divides it by the maximum drawdown over the same period. It is calculated monthly, which makes it more sensitive than the Sterling ratio. Because the Calmar ratio carries negative performance numbers as zero, a ratio of less than zero means negative performance over the last three years. Any downtrend in the Calmar ratio should be monitored closely.

The Geometric Mean

Probably the most mathematically accurate measurement of a trading system's potential is Ralph Vince's geometric mean. The geometric mean measures the growth factor of your trading system. The higher the geometric mean, the more potential your system has to make high returns when reinvesting. For any system with a geometric mean greater than 1, you can maximize the return on your account by calculating optimal *f*, the optimal fixed fraction of your largest perceived loss to bet on each trade. We don't have space to do justice to the complex derivation of the geometric mean and optimal *f* here, nor could we explain it as elegantly as Vince does. We believe that his book is one of the most significant accomplishments in the field of money management in the futures markets.

Note that it is entirely acceptable for your system to be profitable in most of the markets you're testing and a loser in a few of them. One successful commodity trading advisor of our acquaintance trades in all the markets he has tested (winners and losers), and claims that his equity curve is smoother as a result of this diversification. He deliberately seeks some negative correlation between commodities in the portfolio. He has found that the profitable periods in his losing markets usually coincide with losing periods in the winning markets . A trading system will not be profitable in all markets all the time. If you have designed it correctly, the drawdowns will be minimal in the losing markets, and they will eventually have profitable periods.

Be careful about testing lots of commodities and then constructing a portfolio of only the winning contracts. This is a popular device of system vendors, and the results are pure fantasy, although it does help to produce an impressive track record. It's obviously just another form of curve-fitting.

Testing for Specific Results

A trading system should be designed from the beginning to achieve a predetermined set of performance measures. Perhaps the most important of possible objectives are: *percent winners* and the *ratio of average win to average loss.* These can be used to calculate probability of ruin (POR), giving you some idea of the reliability of your system. Most testing software gives other useful data also. Here is a list, with comments.

Net Profit

Net profit is an overrated measure of success for several reasons. First, check to make sure that a few large trades haven't skewed your results. You don't want to use a system whose success depends on nonrecurring events (like the Hunts' corner of the silver market or sugar futures going back to 63 cents).

Next, don't assume that in real time your system will reproduce anything like the net profits from your tests. Future results depend on the markets performing as they did in the past—and we know that they won't. You cannot predict what the markets will do in the future. You can only try your best to make sure that your system is prepared to deal with most of the foreseeable future market conditions.

Number of Trades in the Test Sample

The total must be over 30 to be sure of statistically significant results. Even if you tested 25 years of data, and didn't have at least 30 trades, the results would be highly suspect. We once heard a lecture about the validity of a stock market indicator that only averaged one trade every 40 years. We would have wanted to see 1,200 years of results to be impressed by this method. The more trades you have, the better. Hundreds of trades is much better than 30.

Largest Winning and Largest Losing Trade

The largest winner is important if it has skewed the net profit unreasonably. Many conservative systems testers will throw out the largest winner in each commodity and reevaluate the results. The largest loser can be especially important if it exceeds your normal risk-control measures. Perhaps there is some problem or contingency you've overlooked. Be careful of measures to eliminate the biggest losers; this is where most traders stumble into curve-fitting. Don't make special rules that skip the big losers, just review your stop and risk-control procedures. Controling the largest loser can be critical, if you're trading on an aggressive reinvestment basis using any form of pyramiding or even a more sophisticated method like optimal *f*. You want to avoid surprises that can invalidate your whole strategy.

Maximum Consecutive Winners and Losers

Maximum consecutive losers can be useful. It gives you an idea of how much emotional pain you might have to endure while trading your system. A forecast of this number could help prevent panic when it actually happens.

Peak-to-Valley Drawdown

A very important yet commonly overlooked statistic is percent equity drawdown, measured peak to valley. A system that generates an annualized percent return of 100 percent over five years will be difficult to follow, if it has allowed peak-to-valley drawdowns of 50 percent several times during the five years. It would take a strong stomach and deep pockets to trade such a system with confidence. In our experience, a smooth equity curve is much more desirable and harder to obtain than a high annualized return.

This curve is very important as a measure of how practical your trading system will be with real money on the line. Most often, the systems that give the largest net profits have the largest drawdowns. Combine a large drawdown with a string of losses and you have the reasons why most people prematurely abandon a potentially good trading system. Again we emphasize: A system must be designed within the personal stress tolerance of each individual trader. Much like the anticipation of consecutive losses, anticipation of the potential drawdown that we must endure can generate a vital element of confidence, which will allow us to trust the system and survive inevitable losing periods.

For professional money managers, there is another reason for calculating maximum drawdown. Commodity trading advisors and the people who market them tell us that the public is getting smarter (about time) and is more interested in those rare CTAs whose record shows steady growth and small drawdowns, rather than in the high-fliers who show big short-term gains with large peak-to-valley drawdowns. Those of you who are interested in becoming CTAs and managing public money would do well to create a system whose largest peak-to-valley portfolio drawdown (measured daily) is under 20 percent. This really requires a combination of good money management (including proper capitalization) and a sound, risk-controled trading system.

Some commercially available software displays drawdown as total equity minus any open equity that is at a loss. The rationale for this is that open profits will eventually end up as closed profits and, therefore, there is no risk in profitable positions. This is not true. Futures positions are marked to the market every day. Rarely if ever is a profitable trade closed out at its equity high. Equity that is given up in taking a profit and equity that is given up in taking a loss are subtracted from your account in the same manner. The most accurate way to calculate maximum drawdown is to take the difference between a peak high in daily total equity and a subsequent valley low in daily total equity. This calculation mirrors what would actually happen in your account. Any other method of calculating drawdown is misleading. If your software doesn't have the proper calculation available, print out the daily total equity figures and do the subtraction yourself. If you can, do it for each market separately and then for the total portfolio if you've tested one. The results can be very revealing.

Don't throw away your testing results. They provide an early warning system to alert you if your system is beginning to self-destruct in real trading. Any results approaching the maximum drawdown, or maximum consecutive losers, should be viewed with caution, as should any downtrend in winning percentage or win/loss ratio.

Here are some general guidelines that will help focus your testing goals:

Percent Winners

Most successful trend-following traders have 35 percent to 45 percent winners. It is difficult to get much over 55 percent, as you will see when we do some actual testing. Be especially aware of the effect that stops have on winning percentage.

Ratio of Average Win to Average Loss

This should be well over 1 : 1 (break-even). Obviously a ratio of 3 : 1 or 4 : 1 is nice; but, given a decent percentage of winners, 2 : 1 or even less will make you plenty of profit.

Total Return and Maximum Drawdown

These are either contract-specific or portfolio measurements expressed in dollars. For example, the total return on S&P contracts should only be compared with the maximum drawdown on S&P contracts. Total return and maximum drawdown are the ultimate expression of risk/reward. Of the two, drawdown is more important. It is possible to express both as a percent of margin; but margin is a moving target related to contract months and can change frequently and abruptly, so it doesn't always give a precise measurement.

Volatility and Probability of Ruin

Calculating two key figures will give you some idea of how reliable your trading system will be in real time. The first figure to calculate is the standard deviation of your trading results. The higher the standard deviation, the more volatile your trading results will be. The lower the standard deviation, the less volatile your results will be. All other things being equal, choose the system that has the least volatility (lowest standard deviation) in terms of individual trading results. This should help ensure the highly desirable smooth equity curve.

The second key figure is probability of ruin (POR). The POR gives the trader the exact probability, expressed as a percentage, that his or her account equity will decline to a specified point before rising to a specified higher point. Six figures go into the calculation: percent winners, average profitable trade in dollars, average loss in dollars, initial account equity, level at which an account can be said to be at ruin, and level at which account can be said to be successful.

The POR is based on the notion that, within any trading system, events will routinely occur and may appear abnormal but are really within the realm of probability. For instance, a coin flipped an infinite number of times will have a heads/tails ratio of 1 : 1; but approximately once every 1,024 coin flips either heads or tails will show up 10 times in a row. Every trading system, therefore, lives with the possibility that, independent of changing market conditions, it will to some extent self-destruct. POR is the probability of that self-destruction. The extent to which we can control percent winners and the profit/loss ratio dictates the degree of control we have over our trading system. We may not be able to control changing market conditions, but we can at least make sure that our trading system won't self-destruct of its own accord. There are a number of ways to calculate the probability of ruin (or risk of ruin). We'll be using the simplest formula found in *The Theory of Blackjack* by P. Griffin. The following table shows the POR figures for a representative variety of winning percentages and average profit to average loss ratios. Just to keep the numbers simple, we've assumed an initial account equity of $25,000, a profit target of $50,000, and a loss level (ruin) of $12,500. (See Exhibit 3–2.)

As you can see in the table, the POR changes drastically as the winning percentage and profit/loss ratios change. A small system adjustment that results in a positive change in either ratio can make an enormous difference in our confidence in the system's future capabilities.

The POR can be very revealing. For example, the average CTA managing public funds today probably has a winning percentage of from 35 percent to 45 percent, with most of them under 40 percent. A 35 percent winning percentage demands a high average profit to average loss ratio to be successful, as you can see. This is fine and readily attainable when the markets are trending; but, if they get choppy, the profit/loss ratio will quickly drop and the POR will increase to frightening levels. Monitoring these two statistics closely and perhaps altering your trading system to take into account nontrending markets may be necessary to ensure survival.

EXHIBIT 3–2

Probability of Ruin Matrix $25,000 Account

	% Winners									
$Profit:$Loss	**25**	**30**	**35**	**40**	**45**	**50**	**55**	**60**	**65**	**70**
750:1000	100	100	100	100	100	98	77	15	1	0
1000:1000	100	100	100	99	92	50	7	1	0	0
1500:1000	100	99	90	50	12	2	0	0	0	0
2000:1000	97	79	35	9	2	1	0	0	0	0
2500:1000	79	38	12	4	1	0	0	0	0	0
3000:1000	50	19	6	2	1	0	0	0	0	0
3500:1000	31	12	5	2	1	0	0	0	0	0
4000:1000	21	9	4	2	1	0	0	0	0	0

Testing Entries, Exits, and Stops

Once you've assembled the elements of your trading system, the temptation is to immediately test it as a unit. After all, if a system is by design and definition a group of interrelated parts, it seems logical that it should be tested as one entity. The problem with this is the great possibility that one element of the system is enhancing or hindering results out of proportion to the others. Your entry method might be excellent; however, if your exits are weak you'll discard your entries along with the rest of your system, if the overall results aren't up to your standards. It is also good to know how often one element is used versus another. If your risk control consists of two types of stops, one a simple dollar stop and the other a recent high or low, the design and testing process would be helped if you knew how often each is triggered.

For these reasons, we've created methods that separate portions of a trading system and allow them to be tested in isolation. They aren't perfect, because a system's parts are often inescapably connected, but we have found them to be very useful. Please note that any testing results we show are not intended to be definitive statements about the prowess of one method over another. We are attempting to demonstrate procedure, not be the arbiter in the ongoing dispute over which technical studies are better than others. We strongly urge that you attempt these procedures on your own, within the context of your own needs, and draw your own conclusions.

Testing Entries

It can be very revealing (and humbling) to test your favorite entry methods. We have all too frequently found that many of our cherished assumptions about the right way to enter a market have been mediocre at best. As you become adept at testing systems, you will probably find that the importance of your entries will diminish, and that the way you exit the markets becomes the more critical factor. All that you can ask of an entry is that it give you a better than random potential for profit. Once you have that, it is up to your exit strategy to capture as much of the profits as possible while keeping the losses within reason.

One of the most critical statistics derived from system testing is the percentage of winners versus losers (% winners). Everything else being equal, a high winning percentage is obviously preferable to a low winning percentage. Fortunately, if the average profit to average loss ratios are adjusted correctly, long-term profits can result even if the winning percentage falls to a very low figure. Most long-term traders manage to survive by catching some very large profits now and then and wind up with a winning percentage of only 35 percent to 45 percent. The problem is that, in spite of small losses and big profits, the lower the winning percentage, the more volatile the trading results will be. At some point, the peak-to-valley equity swings will become intolerable for all but the most stout-hearted traders.

An even more difficult task is faced by day traders who must develop a method that wins well over 50 percent of the time. These traders can't let their profits run, because they have to exit before the market closes. Their ratio of transaction costs to trade profits is typically very large, and it is extremely difficult to sustain an average profit to average loss ratio of more than 1 : 1. Whether you are a long-term trader or a short-term trader, it is impossible to have a high percentage of winners without entering the markets correctly. While it is true in the overall scheme of things that exits are more important than entries (after all, it's the exit that ultimately determines the outcome of a trade), good exits are a lot easier to find when the entries have been done correctly.

The Methodology of Entry Testing. The best way to effectively test any single element of a trading system is to isolate it as much as possible. However, isolating elements of a trading system is much more difficult than it would seem, because trading systems by definition consist of a set of interdependent parts. Changing one element by even the smallest amount may drastically change your trading results in unexpected and unpredictable ways. We have often made very carefully thought-out minor modifications to a system we were testing that created incredible disarray in our carefully crafted strategy. After this had happened an embarrassingly large number of times, we decided to adopt a stepwise approach that would allow us to isolate the entries from the other elements of our system. We won't assert this is the only or even the best way to properly test entries, but it seems very logical and it works for us.

The method is simple. Set up your trading system and then delete your normal exits. Replace them with a method that automatically exits the market a given number of days after each trade has been entered. In our testing we are usually looking for entry signals that put us on the correct side of intermediate-term trends, so we set up the test to exit after a range of 5, 10, 15, and 20 days. The range of days approach allows some insight into the direction and strength of the market after the entry. For example, if our 5-day exits show a poor percentage of profitable trades while our 10-day exits produce good results, we might conclude that we have room for some improvement in the timing, although our direction seems correct. If the five-day exits produce the best results, we might have a good entry method for short-term trading but not for our longer-term objectives. You should adjust the time periods of the exit days to suit your own style of trading. For example, you might find it valuable to test exits after only 1 day or you might want to show exits after 30 days.

Analyzing the Test Results

We want the test to show a winning percentage that is based as much as possible on the correctness of the entry direction and timing without any other considerations. Eliminate all slippage and commission costs and use no stops. There will be plenty of opportunity to factor back in the appropriate costs once we are farther along in putting together a complete system for testing. Because you're not using stops or any other realistic exits, net profit figures derived from this type of testing are essentially meaningless. For now we have to regard profits and losses as an accident of the markets. The same is true of average profit to average loss ratios. When we finish putting together our complete system, our actual stops and profit-taking exits will determine these numbers. At this point, the critical figure to consider when comparing entries is the winning percentage.

If an entry method is worthwhile, it should get you into markets in the correct direction with a winning percentage that is significantly better than random. We're not going to go into statistical tests of significance; but, as a rule of thumb, for any entry method to be better than random it should be profitable at least 55 percent of the time over a range of markets. Also, if you are trying to be a trend follower, the trades should show higher winning percentages as the time span increases.

It is extremely important that any entry method you select should yield better than random results at first, because adding stops and attempting to let profits run will invariably reduce the winning percentage substantially. The better your entry percentage is initially, the tighter your stops can be. If you prefer your stops relatively loose, you can maintain a higher winning percentage at the expense of more risk per trade.

It is possible to make adjustments to a trading system by changing various elements and seeing what the results are on an iterative basis; but we've found that it's a lot easier if you work from a base of knowing exactly how effective your entries are, so you can clearly see the effect of your exit strategies. If you start with a 75 percent correct entry method that winds up with only 30 percent winners after adding all the necessary stops and exit strategies, you can proceed to correct only the faulty elements of the system, instead of modifying the entries as most traders would be inclined to do. Most traders would look at the system just described and blame the entries. Unfortunately and very incorrectly, entries tend to get the credit or the blame for system results. Our independent testing of entries allows us to decide how much credit or blame is actually deserved. Most testing of technical studies seems to have been done on a reversal basis, where the same indicator is used for both entries and exits. We'll stay away from boring everyone with these useless test results. The study could be excellent at one task or the other and the results would never be known, because of the failure to isolate the ability to perform each function.

Testing Procedures

All of the test results shown in this section reflect the period from January 1986 to December 1990 (five years). The tests used daily data—specifically open, high, low, close. Entries were intraday in the case of channel breakout and volatility entries, the next day's open in the case of the others. No stops were used. Slippage and commission were set at zero. Exits were on the close of days 5, 10, 15, and 20 after entry.

We tested five markets: D-mark, gold, soybeans, T-bonds, and crude oil. We've limited the testing to these markets because they represent five different commodity groups and give us a general idea of entry performances. If we were to find an indicator that had particularly good results, we would expand the scope of the testing to more markets. The entry methods we selected for testing were popular strategies that we hope will be of interest.

Moving Average Crossover

Moving average crossovers are probably still the most commonly used entry technique. However, the smoothing effect that makes them desirable as entries is exactly what makes them relatively ineffective as exits. We've chosen to test one of the standard moving average studies: the 9-18 crossover. As with most moving average studies, a long entry is generated when the 9 crosses above the 18. A short entry occurs when the 9 crosses below the 18. (See Exhibit 3–3.)

EXHIBIT 3–3

TABLE 1
Moving Average Crossover

Day of Exit:	5	10	15	20
Beans	62	50	59	60
D-Marks	64	63	57	63
Gold	43	54	70	54
T-Bonds	40	45	56	47
CrudeOil	43	45	43	41

(% Winners)

Channel Breakout

We've tested the basic method, which is to enter the market on a new intraday high or low of the last *n* days. We've chosen 10 days as our time period. (See Exhibit 3–4.)

EXHIBIT 3–4

TABLE 2
Channel Breakout

Day of Exit:	5	10	15	20
Beans	46	47	49	38
D-Marks	53	57	50	55
Gold	52	59	50	51
T-Bonds	47	48	50	48
CrudeOil	61	57	55	64

(% Winners)

Stochastic Crossover with Boundaries

This is the standard countertrend stochastic entry: Buy when %K crosses above %D after the oscillator has been below 25. Sell short when %K crosses below %D after having been above 75. Crossovers between 26 and 74 are ignored. (See Exhibit 3–5.)

EXHIBIT 3–5

TABLE 3
Stochastic Crossover With Boundaries

Day of Exit:	5	10	15	20
Beans	56	61	61	59
D-Marks	41	43	49	41
Gold	41	48	47	61
T-Bonds	44	45	48	52
CrudeOil	46	39	39	46

(% Winners)

Stochastic Pop

The stochastic "pop" was described by George Lane. It attempts to cash in on the tendency of markets to trend in the direction of a 14-bar slow stochastic that is advancing through the 75 level or declining through the 25 level, making this application of stochastics a trend-following method. (See Exhibit 3–6.)

EXHIBIT 3–6

TABLE 4
Stochastic Pop

Day of Exit:	5	10	15	20
Beans	50	47	50	47
D-Marks	53	57	58	50
Gold	51	50	52	44
T-Bonds	50	53	49	50
CrudeOil	53	55	59	55

(% Winners)

Relative Strength Index

Wilder's relative strength index is another popular countertrend method. We've used the common 14-bar RSI, selling when it is overbought (above 75) and buying when it is oversold (below 25). (See Exhibit 3–7.)

EXHIBIT 3–7

TABLE 5
Relative Strength Index

Day of Exit:	5	10	15	20
Beans	66	55	55	75
D-Marks	56	36	25	20
Gold	60	50	43	53
T-Bonds	52	60	46	53
CrudeOil	34	21	21	28

(% Winners)

Commodity Channel Index

We've used the CCI here as a trend-following indicator, buying or selling when it crosses the zero line, the direction being determined by the CCI's direction. We used a 10-bar CCI. (See Exhibit 3–8.)

EXHIBIT 3–8

TABLE 6
Commodity Channel Index

Day of Exit:	5	10	15	20
Beans	50	48	57	42
D-Marks	43	54	42	48
Gold	40	46	53	57
T-Bonds	55	41	55	47
CrudeOil	51	43	51	40

(% Winners)

Momentum

The momentum study uses a simple calculation that plots the difference between today's market close and the close *n* days ago. We used 10 days and entered when the zero line was crossed. (See Exhibit 3–9.)

EXHIBIT 3–9

TABLE 7
Momentum

Day of Exit:	5	10	15	20
Beans	55	64	55	47
D-Marks	48	50	61	58
Gold	46	54	58	46
T-Bonds	52	46	60	31
CrudeOil	40	40	50	35

(% Winners)

Volatility

A market is entered intraday on a breakout in either direction of *p*% of *n* day's average true range (ATR). This type of entry has been the basis of many widely marketed trading systems. The first table (see Exhibits 3–10, 3–11, and 3–12) shows the results of a 150 percent breakout of the average true range of the last 10 days. The second table shows the results of a 100 percent breakout of the last 10 days. The third table shows the results of a 100 percent breakout of the last five days.

EXHIBIT 3–10

TABLE 8
Volatility Entry (150%-10 days)

Day of Exit:	5	10	15	20
Beans	53	46	33	42
D-Marks	41	41	44	44
Gold	36	58	55	51
T-Bonds	63	72	72	58
CrudeOil	60	60	47	54

(% Winners)

EXHIBIT 3–11

TABLE 9
Volatility Entry (100%-10 days)

Day of Exit:	5	10	15	20
Beans	52	45	32	36
D-Marks	56	56	55	54
Gold	35	51	54	48
T-Bonds	69	68	66	58
CrudeOil	58	52	46	46

(% Winners)

EXHIBIT 3–12

TABLE 10
Volatility Entry (100%-5 days)

Day of Exit:	5	10	15	20
Beans	42	46	27	25
D-Marks	60	54	56	52
Gold	39	47	52	51
T-Bonds	62	64	61	51
CrudeOil	54	50	48	42

(% Winners)

EXHIBIT 3–13

TABLE 11
Random Entries

Day of Exit:	5	10	15	20
Beans	48	46	53	46
D-Marks	55	53	46	45
Gold	43	53	60	55
T-Bonds	48	55	51	55
CrudeOil	45	38	51	53

(% Winners)

Random Entries

We could go on forever, but we think at least one point is clear: It doesn't take a lot of sophisticated analysis to see that none of the above entry methods are much better than random. Just to prove the point, here are the results of a test that uses a random number generator to decide whether to buy or sell. The entries are on the open the day after the exit of the prior trade. There are no technical studies involved. (See Exhibit 3–13.)

The results are what you might expect. The discouraging thing is that none of the technical studies we tested did much better than the random tests. Incidentally, a series of these random entry tests is sure to produce an occasional astoundingly good result. These are fun to look at, but they also make you realize how careful you must be when you're designing and testing a trading system.

The Importance of Exits

Obviously, we don't recommend you actually trade without stops, exiting the market after an arbitrary number of days. The exercise does point out, though, how difficult it is to find an entry method that, when separated from an exit strategy, gives nonrandom results. The purpose of an entry, as we stated, is to give you an opportunity for profit that is better than coin flipping. You need to test your entries, and, if your present method doesn't do better than random, you'd better find a new one.

Perhaps more to the point, this study also highlights the importance of exits. We assert that it is entirely possible to create a profitable trading system using random entries and a combination of stops and profit-taking exits. It is not possible to create a profitable system using near-perfect entries and random stops and exits. Concentrate your efforts where they are important: on risk control, good exits, and money management, rather than on chasing the Holy Grail of the ultimate entry method. The next time you hear about someone making big profits because of the latest high-tech entry method, ask them for their exit strategy and write it down because it's probably the real secret to their success.

Testing Exits

In the last section, we isolated a number of entry methods and tested them. As we saw, testing entries that are independent of exits is relatively simple and straightforward; the results are objective and easy to evaluate. Testing exits independently is much more difficult. Since entries and exits often interact in unexpected ways, tests that are designed to show us the relative merits of various exit strategies will be affected by the entry method. We have done our best to devise a testing procedure that will give us some insight into the relative merits of various popular exit strategies. Although we are not entirely satisfied with the testing methodology, we think it is good enough to allow us to fairly compare various exits over uniform market conditions. The results were most interesting.

The Methodology of Exit Testing

It is probably impossible to isolate an exit for testing as effectively as you can an entry. The best method we've come up with is to test all of the exit strategies using the same, simple entry method. We selected an entry method that gives reasonable results as a reversal system, and then we tested each of the various exit methods over the same data with identical entries. If each exit method is tested using the same entries, we should be able to make some valid comparisons of the results. Admittedly, exits that work well with one entry system won't necessarily work well with another; but if the entry is as generic as possible, at least you will get some feeling for the comparative effectiveness of a number of different exits. Similar to entry testing, you may be dismayed when you view the test results of your favorite exit strategies and find they are no better than a simple reversal system. We certainly have been surprised by many of our test results.

As an entry method for our tests, almost any simple trend-following reversal system will do. We've chosen to use a simple dual moving average crossover system (5 days/10 days, 5/20, 5/30, and 5/40) as the static entry timer. A long entry will be signaled when the shorter-term moving average crosses over the longer-term moving average, and a short entry will be generated by the opposite crossover. The exits for the initial benchmark test will be the moving average reversals. On the opening of the day after the moving averages cross, we will close out one trade and immediately initiate another in the opposite direction. Because we want to keep the entry points as fixed as possible, so as to directly compare exits, we will trade only at the crossovers and not in between.

In our tests, we have adjusted the sensitivity of the exit timing methods so that an exit will usually be generated before the next moving average reversal. If an exit isn't triggered, the trade will be closed out by the moving average crossover and a new trade initiated on the same date and at the same opening price as the benchmark reversal system. All of the tests should thus generate the same number of trades per market as the benchmark system. Each exit will have to contend with identical market conditions, including the same reversals of the benchmark system. This allows us to compare exits against exits. All other things being equal, the exit strategy that performs the best should be easy to find.

One caveat: It is difficult to find an exit that always gets us out of the market before the moving average reversal. The more trades that use the nonreversal exits, the better for our test. We want as many of the exits as possible to be signaled by the exit method being tested and not by the moving average reversals. Unfortunately, we can't get rid of the benchmark reversals, because then the number of trades and the entry dates will be entirely different from one exit test to another.

We mentioned that we were not entirely satisfied with our testing procedures. When we are testing entries we can reasonably determine how effective the entry is by simply measuring the winning percentage. In our tests of exits, the percentage of winners and other results are kept somewhat constant by the common entry method and by the fact that a significant number of exits are signaled by the benchmark reversals, rather than the exits actually being tested. Because the winning percentage tends to stay relatively constant throughout the tests (with one notable exception, which we'll explain) we need to look for additional measures of exit performance.

The average profit to average loss ratio is not very meaningful, because we're testing without stops and without slippage and commissions. The statistic that does show the most meaningful variation with different exits is net profit. We have pointed out that, as a measure of the overall efficiency of a trading system, net profit is not the best indicator. However, in this case we will use net profit and winning percentage as our measures for comparison.

The Benchmark System

All of the test results shown in this section reflect the period from January 1986 to December 1990 (five years). The tests used daily open, high, low, and close. All of the entries were on the open of the day following the moving average crossover. Although initial stop losses are a form of exit, they would cloud the issue here, so we used no risk control stop losses in our tests. Slippage and commission were set to zero. We tested the same five markets we used in the previous section: D-mark, gold, soybeans, T-bonds, and crude oil. The exit methods we selected for testing are some popular and logical strategies, which we assumed would interest most traders.

As you can see, the results of the benchmark system itself are less than spectacular, but adequate for our purposes. In our tests, we will look for exits that improve the system. Generally speaking, a moving average system's main vulnerability is its exits; as prices change direction, we can expect to give up a large portion of profits before a reversal is signaled. Theoretically, exits that are more sensitive than the entries should capture more of each market move. Here is a description of the exit strategies we tested.

Parabolic Stop and Reverse. The Parabolic we tested is not calculated exactly according to Wilder's original formula. We used System Writer Plus for our testing, and the Parabolic formula they provide differs from the original. The System Writer version allows the user to select the number of days back to scan for the extreme high or low starting point. The calculation is otherwise identical. We did two tests, one using a 5-day Parabolic and the other using a 10-day Parabolic.

Support/Resistance. One of the most common exits we've come across is a stop that trails at the high or low of the last *n* days. The stop is triggered when the market corrects to the stop point. We did two tests, one using a high or low of the last 3 days, the other a high or low of the last 10 days.

RSI Trail. We've used Wilder's RSI here to indicate when the market becomes overbought or oversold. When a 9-day RSI gets above 75 or below 25 and the market closes against the direction of the trade, we exit on the opening the next day. The idea is to exit the market on strength, rather than wait for a serious correction.

Key Reversal. Of the various patterns that are supposed to indicate turning points in the markets, probably the most commonly known is the key reversal. The general definition of a key reversal (to exit a long position) is a new market high followed by a close lower than the prior day's close. For our test we've defined our key reversal as a new high for the last 10 days, followed by a close lower than the previous day. A key reversal to exit a short position is a new low for the last 10 days, followed by a close higher than the previous day. (See Exhibit 3–14.)

Trailing Stops

Risk in an open trade can be defined in two ways. *Initial risk* is the difference between market entry and a risk-control stop. *Equity risk* is the difference between an open position's market price and the price your exit strategy dictates. Most trend-following reversal exits, such as those of our benchmark system, tend to be relatively far from the market, making the risk on open positions considerable. This equity risk multiplies as trading proceeds over a portfolio of markets. It can be argued that equity risk is a "nice" problem to have because it increases with profitable positions. But a loss is a loss, whether it occurs from an equity high or not. In either case, money disappears from your account.

One simple way to control this kind of risk is to trail a stop behind the trade. The stop can be calculated in a number of ways; but for this

EXHIBIT 3–14 Part A

EXIT		SOYBEANS				D-MARK				GOLD			
		5/ 10	20	30	40	5/ 10	20	30	40	5/ 10	20	30	40
Benchmark	W%	39%	37%	31%	26%	36%	52%	34%	39%	39%	37%	31%	32%
	$P/L	4525	2525	(2075)	(50)	4700	47337	29275	21087	830	17750	10470	9030
5-Day Parabolic		37%	37%	29%	36%	34%	44%	38%	34%	36%	33%	31%	34%
		(4737)	(2506)	(10212)	(850)	5112	8862	5675	(1200)	1163	(1141)	(5393)	5202
10-Day Parabolic		39%	40%	34%	36%	36%	50%	44%	41%	36%	37%	31%	34%
		1900	(2156)	(5862)	(6137)	4475	22237	16987	7062	(2231)	14424	960	8027
3-Day High/Low		34%	36%	39%	44%	33%	36%	36%	32%	32%	30%	19%	22%
		3237	2237	(4350)	2512	5137	13162	7250	(1112)	(4710)	(2980)	(10400)	(6420)
10-Day High/Low		38%	34%	31%	36%	34%	45%	32%	34%	36%	27%	19%	28%
		8037	4125	(8275)	(3062)	2075	27700	16612	14800	(2770)	1930	(9010)	(1590)
RSI Trail		39%	37%	32%	28%	37%	54%	38%	41%	40%	37%	33%	32%
		(100)	4725	(750)	2775	562	34250	13387	2187	(2770)	7460	2670	2210
Key Reversal		44%	51%	49%	46%	37%	57%	48%	50%	42%	43%	35%	42%
		2600	6937	(6400)	(887)	(7837)	33787	21112	20950	1650	4700	1860	5560
$500 Trail. Stop		48%	58%	55%	59%	52%	69%	63%	54%	47%	57%	54%	63%
		3600	13459	3625	5737	(1462)	16650	3887	(4212)	6310	12150	3220	9990
$1000 Trail. Stop		44%	44%	44%	38%	40%	60%	51%	47%	43%	49%	43%	44%
		962	10425	1387	87	(2062)	25312	16162	4512	6480	25140	14300	14150
Volatility		38%	39%	40%	44%	42%	57%	48%	45%	34%	37%	25%	34%
		12375	2556	(3762)	6675	10287	20175	6812	6987	(372)	2124	(4762)	5748
Stochastic Cross		41%	48%	49%	51%	35%	52%	46%	45%	44%	43%	29%	42%
		50	5225	500	5362	(8987)	11825	4112	(5000)	(5050)	(2060)	(6820)	(2020)
$1000 Profit Target		45%	51%	50%	44%	50%	64%	59%	56%	44%	52%	47%	51%
		(6187)	12475	4462	1650	6125	19350	10487	1262	6630	8420	200	5010
$2000 Profit Target		40%	41%	36%	30%	36%	54%	36%	41%	39%	39%	35%	34%
		(6987)	13675	(4312)	(2150)	(2200)	23512	4537	(1150)	6870	11170	3970	4960
Random		42%	44%	34%	40%	42%	60%	46%	41%	43%	46%	21%	42%
		7812	12537	(5625)	7875	2712	17975	12962	16225	3540	(380)	(17700)	850

EXHIBIT 3–14 Part B

T-BONDS				CRUDE OIL				TOTAL
5/10	20	30	40	5/10	20	30	40	EXIT P/L
38%	34%	35%	38%	43%	40%	37%	40%	
(17812)	2843	16937	12531	21030	19980	17000	33480	251,393
36%	35%	35%	40%	39%	40%	37%	40%	
(14031)	3875	375	3031	16750	14900	16550	13630	55,055
39%	36%	48%	54%	44%	37%	38%	46%	
(5843)	10687	19906	19031	18520	11270	11370	18080	162,707
33%	36%	33%	30%	34%	33%	33%	34%	
(11968)	(6093)	(3468)	6562	5110	1181	3230	870	(1,013)
35%	34%	37%	33%	40%	36%	38%	43%	
(4625)	18531	22125	781	23820	9160	8320	8950	137,634
38%	35%	35%	35%	44%	42%	38%	46%	
(20781)	6375	19968	16750	8140	12230	4930	8450	122,668
38%	41%	39%	47%	45%	43%	46%	56%	
(29000)	(9187)	(13593)	(6000)	(6640)	(11230)	(790)	10100	17,692
52%	59%	66%	66%	54%	54%	44%	59%	
(18187)	9906	5750	7718	12370	11670	(2380)	9680	109,481
47%	51%	58%	66%	47%	46%	38%	50%	
(12531)	(4343)	3187	16968	18920	21900	12240	19230	192,426
40%	42%	44%	42%	47%	39%	38%	43%	
6062	17312	14593	18687	14230	2760	8080	6970	153,537
41%	46%	50%	45%	43%	40%	46%	46%	
(12468)	2625	6437	9468	(4670)	(5300)	(5070)	(3640)	(15,481)
52%	54%	60%	66%	49%	48%	44%	56%	
(27937)	(5406)	4156	7031	(7460)	(3270)	(7200)	3790	33,588
43%	42%	53%	57%	45%	43%	38%	43%	
(10156)	(4125)	13656	18000	9910	15130	3500	10850	108,660
41%	45%	48%	47%	48%	40%	42%	43%	
(8843)	2656	11468	531	22850	8790	10200	23370	129,805

test we've chosen a constant dollar stop, calculated from the highest or lowest close in the direction of the trade. We tested a $500 and a $1,000 trailing stop.

One factor jumps out at you as you look at the results of these exits: The winning percentages are much higher than we've been seeing in the other tests. The explanation: As the markets are correcting, the trades are being closed out before they have a chance to become losers. The trade-off is that total profits can be adversely affected, because some trades will be closed out far short of their maximum profit potential. Everything else being equal, we like trailing stops, especially when used in combination with another type of exit. They provide a relatively fail-safe way to protect profits. (Yes, we know about gaps and limit moves—but they affect any type of exit, not just trailing stops.) The trailing stops will also tend to lower the variability of trade results, as measured by standard deviation. The smaller the standard deviation of trades, the smoother the equity curve.

Volatility

The market is exited on a volatility breakout against the direction of the trend. We used 100 percent of five day's average true range to define our volatility exit signal. The basic theory is that a change in trend is often signaled by a significant one-day price movement in the opposite direction.

Slow Stochastic

The stochastic test is as simple as we could make it. We exit a long when %K crosses below %D, and exit a short when %K crosses above %D. We used a 14-day slow stochastic. This should get us out of a market when it begins to correct or change trend.

Profit Targets

Many of the arguments that apply to trailing stops apply to profit targets. Taking profit at a given dollar amount will have the effect of smoothing the equity curve. In theory, the large profits that will be missed occasionally are made up for by not giving back some of the profit on every trade.

Random Exits

When we tested entries, we discovered that most popular methods were really no more effective than entry points selected randomly. We thought it would be interesting to come up with a random exit and test it. For this test, our random exit has two steps. First, a number between 5 and 20 is randomly selected to determine the minimum number of days to keep the trade open. After the minimum number of days, the first close against the direction of the trend will result in the trade being exited on the next day's open. (Although the minimum number of days is random, there is still an element of trend following involved.) As you can see, the results aren't a lot different from the other tests, although, if we had run a thousand random tests, we may well have come up with some tremendous results. (See Exhibit 3–14.)

Conclusions

While the real purpose of this section is to demonstrate a testing procedure, not to definitively compare exits, some observations are inescapable. While the exits made dramatic differences in the results, none improved the benchmark system. Here are some tentative conclusions:

1. Test the entry and exit strategies separately before you integrate them into a system. If we had tested our moving average entries using stochastic exits, we might have concluded that moving averages were not profitable.
2. The choice of exit strategies can have a dramatic impact on the profitability of an entry system.
3. The exit with the best winning percentage is not necessarily the most profitable.
4. Specific entries might determine the range of profitability, but the exits are responsible for the final result.
5. Trailing stops produced the highest winning percentages.

Remember that winning percentage and average profit to average loss ratio are the critical elements in the probability of ruin formula. If we can adjust both of these criteria in our favor, we are more likely to achieve our trading goals.

We're sure that if you inspect the test data closely you will come to other meaningful conclusions. We have just scratched the surface of a topic that deserves further research and attention.

Testing Stops

We've seen that testing market entries independently is relatively simple, while testing exits is more difficult. Probably the most significant result of the previous tests on exits was that using trailing stops substantially increased the winning percentage.

The basic difference between the exits we tested previously and the stop losses that we will be testing in this section is that the exits were intended to capture profits while stops are primarily intended to control risk. But, as you will observe, in many cases the lines of distinction are blurred. The real objective of both sets of tests is to see how effective various stops and exits are as part of a simple trend-following system. We think you'll be as surprised, as we were, at some of our results.

Methodology

Since stops are a form of exits, there is no reason to change our methods, and we will use the same testing procedures as we did in the previous section. For our benchmark system, we've used the same dual moving average crossover method (5/10, 5/20, 5/30, 5/40). Entries and exits are on crossovers only. This is a reversal system; on the opening following a moving average crossover, we will close out the existing trade and immediately initiate another in the opposite direction. One of the important reasons for selecting a reversal system like this one is that the entry points are fixed no matter what the exit. Therefore, it allows us to uniformly compare how various stops and exits affect results.

Similar to our previous tests, some of our stops will not be triggered before the moving average reversal takes place. Depending on the nature of the stop, this may or may not be significant, but in any case it is unavoidable.

The time period tested is from January 1986 to December 1990. Entries were all on the open of the day following a moving average crossover. Slippage and commission were set to zero. The markets are the same as before: D-mark, gold, soybeans, T-bonds and crude oil.

Analysis of stop testing results is subject to the same limitations as analysis of normal exit testing. Winning percentages will vary somewhat, but they will primarily be determined by the entry method we selected. Therefore, we can only reach limited conclusions about the effect of stops on the winning percentage. We are forced to rely on net profit as the fairest and most accurate measurement of the different stop methods. As we've pointed out before, net profit is well down the list of statistics to monitor when you are testing a system—but in this case, it's the best measure we have.

We'll mention one other possibility for comparing the effectiveness of stops. Protective stops, if used correctly, should reduce drawdown. It's something to monitor if you are doing this type of testing yourself.

Initial Risk Stops

We have grouped the stops we intend to test into three major categories: initial risk stops, break-even stops, and trailing stops. An initial risk stop can be defined as a stop that in some way limits the amount of loss a trade can accumulate from the entry point. When a trade goes against us immediately, the initial risk stop is normally triggered before any other type of exit. It is your most basic "stop loss" order. We tested three types of stops that can be classified as initial risk stops.

Dollar Stops. The first initial stop we will look at is the simple dollar stop. When a trade goes against us by a given dollar amount (measured from the entry point) we immediately exit the market. The stop stays in effect until it is triggered or until the trade is closed out. We tested four dollar amounts: $500, $1,000, $1,500 and $2,000. Obviously, these figures don't begin to cover all the possibilities, but they will give us an idea of the general effectiveness of this method. To some extent, the amounts we selected for testing are subjective. However, in previous testing we've found that stops tighter than $500 usually result in a considerably lower winning percentage and stops larger than $2,000 result in too much drawdown.

Be careful about being too precise about dollar stops. If $781.25 works best in T-bonds and $425 works best in soybeans, it is tempting to find an "optimum" stop for every market and trade accordingly. It is much better to find a round number that you're comfortable with and use the same dollar stop in every market.

Support/Resistance. Many traders are uncomfortable with a simple dollar stop, because they feel it isn't reflective of a particular market or of recent market conditions. Perhaps the most common alternative is to place a stop at a recent swing high or low, reasoning that these swing points become important support and resistance levels. We used recent swing highs and lows that occurred within the 20 days prior to our entries.

No-Profit Exit. We tested this method because of comments we've often heard from experienced traders. They observed that the best trades seem to be profitable right away. If this is true, then the obvious way to eliminate most of the losers is to test each trade a given number of days after its entry and see if the trade is profitable. We used 1, 5, and 10 days in our testing. If there is no profit after the specified number of days, the trade will be closed out on the opening the following day. If the trade is profitable, it will be allowed to continue to its normal conclusion. This isn't really an initial risk stop, but it fits best into this classification.

Break-Even Stops

A break-even stop is defined as a stop that is placed at the entry point of the trade once a certain amount of profit is reached. The obvious purpose of such a stop is to prevent a reasonable profit from turning into a loss. We've read in recent literature a few negative comments about break-even stops, the primary concern being that they may have a tendency to prematurely exit from potentially good trades. In our testing, we set break-even stops after profit levels of $500, $1,000, $1,500, and $2,000.

Trailing Stops

Trailing stops are stops that are continuously calculated after some logical price points have been reached. They can serve as initial risk stops or profit-taking exits, or both.

Dollar Trail from Close

This calculates a stop point from the highest close or lowest close in the direction of the trade. The stop does not trail until the trade is in profit by the amount of the stop. We trailed stops of $500, $1,000, $1,500 and $2,000.

Dollar Trail from High or Low

This calculates a stop point from the highest high or lowest low reached during the course of the trade. On the profit side, the theory is that, once a profit high has been reached, some of the profit should be protected by trailing a stop. Any loss on the trade will be limited to the difference between the high or low the trade has reached and the trailing stop. This stop begins to trail immediately and serves as an initial risk stop as well as a trailing stop. We trailed stops of $500, $1,000, $1,500 and $2,000. (See Exhibit 3–15.)

Conclusions

1. None of the stops we tested improved the benchmark results.
2. Smaller, tighter stops lowered the winning percentage while wider stops raised the winning percentage.
3. As a general rule, stops with a small dollar risk that trailed too closely or that closed out a trade too early were not as successful as stops that allowed the trades to fully develop.
4. There is a tendency toward mediocre performance as tighter stops are used and toward improving performance as stops are widened. As stops become too large, improvement lessens, and we may even begin to lose ground as the large losses take their toll.
5. As far as initial risk is concerned, the simple dollar stops perform as well as so-called logical stops. This is probably also true for stops that are used as profit-taking exits. The highest total profit figures come from trailing stops from prices that are very far away, but we think that to follow such a system in actual practice would be difficult. However, many successful trading advisors use this approach.
6. Break-even stops performed extremely well.

We have often asserted that market exits are more important than market entries. We've seen how changing the exits of a simple trend-following system can substantially change the trading results. Our tests have shown the effects of a number of different exits, some that reduce risk, some that capture profit, and some that do both.

Creating a Simple Trading System

In this section we are going to chronicle the evolution and testing of a simple but effective trading system, beginning with an appropriately sized account and continuing through the phases of selecting a portfolio to trade, establishing risk control, and building the system itself. We'll explain the reasons for each decision we make along the way. We believe in simple systems and simple testing procedures, so we won't be using complex optimization techniques. We want to emphasize that our goal in this section is simply to show the procedures for building and testing a system. The system produced as a result is not necessarily a system that we would recommend. We make no claims whatsoever that the system will be profitable in the future.

EXHIBIT 3–15 Part A

STOP		SOYBEANS 5/10	20	30	40	D-MARK 5/10	20	30	40	GOLD 5/10	20	30	40
Benchmark	W%	39%	37%	31%	26%	36%	52%	34%	39%	39%	37%	31%	32%
	$P/L	4525	2525	(2075)	(50)	4700	47337	29275	21087	830	17750	10470	9030
$500 Init. Risk		34%	32%	27%	22%	27%	33%	24%	40%	32%	18%	9%	18%
		1546	7600	7712	7375	12837	34675	25900	22525	830	(6000)	(5180)	7590
$1000 Init. Risk		38%	35%	29%	24%	36%	45%	28%	32%	39%	36%	27%	32%
		5000	(1212)	(187)	1512	7437	41100	19175	19837	520	15830	7730	9370
$1500 Init. Risk		39%	36%	29%	26%	36%	50%	34%	39%	39%	37%	31%	32%
		8512	(375)	(3262)	3112	4187	41937	28700	23887	(2860)	16020	8350	7010
$2000 Init. Risk		39%	36%	29%	26%	36%	52%	34%	39%	39%	37%	31%	32%
		5600	(2350)	(5975)	(500)	3700	47525	29637	22850	(460)	17300	10120	9210
Support/Resist.		38%	37%	34%	36%	35%	48%	36%	36%	37%	28%	23%	26%
		9000	3300	(8587)	(1562)	(1512)	28375	11350	2787	600	4750	(6110)	200
1 Day No-Profit		36%	32%	22%	22%	32%	42%	28%	41`%	38%	26%	23%	28%
		12275	750	(662)	3637	1625	37625	18875	20362	(9330)	(9360)	(800)	990
5 Day No-Profit		38%	32%	32%	30%	38%	50%	30%	34%	36%	31%	17%	26%
		3725	3225	3762	5762	9462	44025	19762	20237	(7560)	11980	5240	7590
10 Day No-Profit		39%	37%	31%	24%	36%	48%	30%	32%	39%	37%	31%	26%
		5750	(475)	50	162	4600	40687	20900	15425	80	19480	6140	5310
$500 Break-Even		46%	55%	59%	55%	49%	60%	57%	47%	44%	60%	49%	57%
		18487	14725	9837	7712	3287	35150	30812	16212	(5920)	40	6120	12530
$1000 Break-Even		44%	45%	45%	38%	42%	61%	48%	45%	42%	49%	43%	48%
		10650	3750	5837	3962	4537	34987	30300	16025	(2440)	21470	14060	12270
$1500 Break-Even		42%	43%	39%	32%	37%	57%	42%	36%	41%	46%	39%	40%
		8625	4362	3275	4312	(2087)	40275	32225	21637	(1410)	20210	12780	10200
$2000 Break-Even		40%	40%	36%	28%	36%	54%	36%	34%	39%	39%	35%	34%
		4750	3650	(262)	1475	4250	40412	29437	20625	(2320)	17530	11180	9100
$500 Trail		48%	58%	55%	59%	52%	69%	63%	54%	47%	57%	54%	63%
		3600	13459	3625	5737	(1462)	16650	3887	(4212)	6310	12150	3220	9990
$1000 Trail		44%	44%	44%	38%	40%	60%	51%	47%	43%	49%	43%	44%
		962	10425	1387	87	(2062)	25312	16162	4512	6480	25140	14300	14150
$1500 Trail		42%	43%	36%	30%	36%	55%	38%	39%	39%	43%	37%	38%
		(175)	4550	(5825)	(2112)	(1400)	34950	17100	1512	(2330)	14700	11000	12140
$2000 Trail		40%	37%	32%	30%	36%	54%	36%	39%	39%	39%	33%	32%
		1675	9337	3825	10212	2312	41037	24050	12575	(4300)	12920	7080	7780
$500 H/L Trail		50%	62%	63%	61%	55%	69%	73%	56%	50%	63%	56%	63%
		4737	11875	1412	5362	2600	14962	13750	(212)	1040	4550	3000	4460
$1000 H/L Trail		45%	51%	50%	42%	46%	64%	57%	52%	44%	52%	47%	48%
		2275	15050	950	2300	600	22537	11187	5312	9210	22860	8200	11030
$1500 H/L Trail		42%	44%	39%	34%	37%	57%	44%	41%	41%	46%	39%	40%
		(3362)	5575	(3912)	800	(3137)	34812	19912	9525	2420	1940	8910	8820
$2000 H/L Trail		40%	41%	36%	30%	36%	54%	36%	39%	39%	39%	35%	34%
		(8062)	2012	(6187)	(2512)	2862	35362	17700	15500	(2440)	15580	11450	11130

EXHIBIT 3–15 Part B

T-BONDS 5/10	20	30	40	CRUDE OIL 5/10	20	30	40	TOTAL P/L
38%	34%	35%	38%	43%	40%	37%	40%	
(17812)	2843	16937	12531	21030	19980	17000	33480	251,393
23%	18%	12%	14%	34%	24%	27%	25%	
7250	3468	3750	(4031)	11690	5830	22660	19600	187,627
33%	26%	19%	23%	40%	34%	35%	34%	
10625	(4562)	(4593)	(7031)	26210	7270	22150	29960	206,141
37%	30%	33%	33%	40%	37%	37%	34%	
4281	3437	24281	5750	17100	12040	21170	27330	250,307
38%	30%	35%	35%	42%	40%	37%	37%	
(7156)	(2593)	24531	9625	22080	18790	17080	29360	248,374
37%	35%	41%	47%	42%	39%	37%	43%	
(5281)	14843	18500	14562	27860	15220	19380	17290	164,965
32%	25%	32%	28%	35%	31%	31%	31%	
(10312)	(21843)	8843	2062	11970	11040	22110	13250	113,107
36%	32%	30%	33%	41%	33%	37%	31%	
(7406)	8750	18656	2312	17630	12110	15520	12620	207,402
38%	35%	35%	35%	42%	37%	35%	37%	
(16375)	7718	17093	4843	20840	17390	17800	27880	215,298
52%	57%	55%	57%	45%	48%	42%	53%	
(5687)	(906)	(1875)	(2375)	6840	12760	19060	33160	209,969
48%	47%	50%	57%	45%	45%	37%	43%	
(17812)	(6031)	(3562)	(6875)	13720	16010	20500	28230	199,588
42%	45%	46%	52%	45%	45%	37%	40%	
(17812)	(7343)	(6687)	10125	23270	23210	20230	31370	230,767
39%	37%	42%	42%	44%	42%	37%	40%	
(16406)	(3687)	17875	12218	24440	22740	17000	33380	247,387
52%	59%	66%	66%	54%	54%	44%	59%	
(18187)	9906	5750	7718	12370	11670	(2380)	9680	109,481
47%	51%	58%	66%	47%	46%	38%	50%	
(12531)	(4343)	3187	16968	18920	21900	12240	19230	192,426
42%	46%	53%	61%	45%	43%	38%	43%	
(13781)	12437	14781	21406	17690	26350	13500	19020	195,513
41%	39%	46%	50%	43%	40%	38%	43%	
(12125)	7500	14906	25843	17940	21510	9680	26470	240,227
56%	65%	67%	73%	52%	56%	53%	65%	
(19000)	4906	2375	12375	(500)	4310	(6260)	4710	70,452
50%	53%	58%	61%	49%	48%	40%	53%	
(26906)	(2406)	4093	12187	14290	13540	8020	10080	144,409
44%	48%	53%	61%	45%	43%	38%	43%	
(2906)	16031	(2031)	17437	15270	19770	13810	18440	178,124
41%	40%	51%	54%	45%	43%	38%	43%	
(15125)	(8125)	13312	19156	17770	28320	12610	19670	179,983

Goals for the Trading System

Our first requirements are that the system should be mechanical, easy to maintain, and easy on the trader's ulcer. By easy to maintain we mean that the trader doesn't have to be glued to a quote machine all day, and, in fact, can dispense with real-time quotes altogether if he or she wants. It also means that all necessary calculations can be done (using the right software) in a matter of minutes per day, with all orders entered only once per day, preferably just before the opening. The turnover rate of the system (what we call the "pace") must be low enough that the part-time trader will feel comfortable and in control.

It is obviously difficult to project a rate of return for any investment scheme (never mind for a futures trading system), but the opportunity for return must be commensurate with the degree of risk. We would like to see our testing show an annualized rate of return of at least 20 to 30 percent. Just as important, we would like a winning percentage of at least 40 percent and an average win/average loss ratio of at least 2 : 1, which would give us a statistical probability of ruin of nearly zero. We would like to limit our maximum potential peak-to-valley drawdown to about 40 percent or so. If this drawdown sounds high, check the track records of a few successful commodity trading advisors. Even though they are professionals and working with much larger accounts than the average trader, you'll find that very few of them have avoided drawdowns of 40 to 45 percent. Given the low success rate of part-time traders and our restricted account size, 40 percent is realistic.

Account Size

Choosing the size of a futures trading account is obviously up to the individual trader's wallet size and fear quotient, but there are boundaries below which it is very difficult to operate effectively. It is our experience, backed by considerable industry research, that relatively small accounts, meaning under $25,000, have a much lower probability of success than larger accounts. With this in mind we've chosen $25,000 as our account size. Even with this amount, significant drawdowns will be hard to avoid. All else being equal, the larger the account, the easier it should be to keep the percentage drawdown small.

Portfolio

Choosing a portfolio to trade is always a subjective task. We want to be sure that we're diversified and in markets that aren't so continually volatile that the risk becomes impossible to control. We're creating the system with the idea that it can be maintained in about 20 minutes a day, which precludes day trading. It is difficult if not impossible to trade the stock indexes for $25,000 if we're holding trades overnight, so they are effectively eliminated. We don't want to be in a situation where one bad market day will erase most of our account. Also, just to be conservative, we want to keep our maximum margin requirements to about 30 percent of the account. We can't do this if we're trading the stock indexes. We could just monitor a lot of markets and take the first trade that comes along, staying within our margin limit, but if we do this we aren't trading what we've tested.

We'll trade the usual fixed portfolio of five markets, each in a separate market group. In currencies we'll trade the D-mark, in precious metals gold, in interest rates T-bonds, in agriculturals soybeans, and in the petroleum complex crude oil. We'll leave out the food and fiber group, because adding a market from that group would bring our total margins above $10,000 (at present rates) and of all the complexes these markets are in our opinion the most likely (after stock indexes) to cause sudden large losses.

Software and Data

We use both CompuTrac/SNAP and Omega Research's System Writer Plus for testing. For this application, we used System Writer Plus, partly because of the existence of a very handy piece of software called Portfolio Analyzer, written and sold by Tom Berry. Portfolio Analyzer takes individual files created by System Writer Plus and combines them to display test results on a portfolio of markets, rather than one market at a time. It also calculates daily, monthly, quarterly, or yearly equity, so you can see the effects of system or portfolio changes across the spectrum of markets you are trading. It allows you to test for portfolio drawdown and rate of return directly, rather than by estimating or building a spreadsheet and entering individual market results to get a composite report. It often happens that a market that is a net loser adds significantly to a portfolio by showing returns that are negatively correlated with those of other markets. If that market (or markets) wins while others are losing, the effect is to soften total drawdown and smooth out the equity curve. We should, therefore, not be dismayed if one or two of the markets we've chosen turn out to be net losers as a result of our testing, as long as the equity curve is smooth and the overall result is as desired.

Six and a half years of daily data will be used for testing, starting with January 1, 1984, and ending with June 29, 1990. The data are arranged as continuous contracts. We really can't go back farther and still test the full portfolio; crude oil didn't start trading until late 1983. We'll be especially interested in the years 1986, 1988, and 1989. These were particularly tough years for trend followers. If we can survive them, it lends credibility to our trading system.

Curve-Fitting and Optimization

We've discussed this in great detail previously, but since some curve-fitting is impossible to avoid it's worth mentioning again. We will be curve-fitting to the extent that the technical studies, their values, and our stop values will be items with which we have had actual trading experience. Trading gives you a feel for some things that are difficult to acquire in any other way. We've also had a lot of testing experience, which interestingly enough has in most (but not all) cases supported observations derived from actual trading.

We will not optimize. We will test our system, and if it doesn't work we will modify it. We will not test endless combinations of study values and risk levels to find an optimum solution. We will use exactly the same study values and stops for every market, further ensuring that we are doing as little curve-fitting as possible. If the system works in most of the markets we've chosen and the losing markets buffer equity drawdowns, we will have done our job satisfactorily. Remember, it is the markets and our wallets we have to live with; we aren't doing this to satisfy the computer's insatiable need for perfection at the cost of reality.

Risk Control

There is no such thing as a successful trading system that doesn't adequately control risk. For testing purposes, we define risk in two ways: *initial risk,* which is the difference between an entry point and a protective stop, and *equity risk,* which is the difference between marked-to-the-market equity and a trailing stop. These two categories can be further divided into initial and equity risk in a single trade, and initial and equity risk across a portfolio of simultaneous trades.

Initial risk is controlled by protective stops. In our own trading we try not to risk more than 1.5 percent on a $100,000 account, which means a $1,500 stop. Since we are trading the same markets as we would with a larger account, and since our experience is that smaller stops in these markets cause a larger number of losing trades, we will stick with this number. We may consider trying different values if our winning percentage is less than we had hoped. Remember the exit testing: As a general rule, the smaller the stop, the lower the winning percentage.

Equity risk is controlled by trailing stops. There are several ways to do this, but we prefer trailing by a simple dollar amount. This is a technique that is somewhat out of favor; but we like it because it allows you to quantify portfolio risk—that is, the sum of the differences between open equity and trailing stops. If portfolio risk is too large, equity swings will be unlivable. This is a phenomenon familiar to commodity trading advisors and their clients. Profit builds up in a group of positions over a period of months, and then the markets reverse and a sudden, sharp equity loss occurs. This happens even though there have been no losing trades! A client of a CTA can easily find himself or herself in a position of paying incentive fees or even taxes on profits that have vanished. The only way to control this type of risk is with trailing stops. We will trail a $1,500 stop. If we weren't using a trailing stop, we would use a break-even stop; but, since their functions are relatively similar, we'll use the trailing stop only.

It is possible to optimize these stop values one at a time or together, but we won't do that. We want a robust trading system that will work tomorrow, not an optimized one that worked yesterday.

Technical Studies—Entries

The most common trend-following study is the simple moving average. We've been using them for many years and have tested vast numbers of combinations. A few favorites have emerged. We normally favor a dual moving average approach, with some of our favorite combinations being 3/12, 9/18/,10/18, and 10/20. You'll remember that a 5/10, 5/20, 5/30, and 5/40 worked well as a benchmark system for our exit testing, but we normally favor something a little more sensitive than that. We'll try a dual 3/12 moving average, for entries only.

Technical Studies—Logical Exits

Wilder's Parabolic is a common exit technique, and it tested fairly well as a separate exit versus our benchmark system. We'll use that as our exit, using Wilder's original values to increment the SAR points. The Parabolic starting point will be different, because System Writer Plus does not have Wilder's original formula as an available function. Wilder's formula uses the high or low of the prior Parabolic trade as a starting point. SWP's formula uses the high or low of the last *n* days, leaving you to select the *n*. A relatively short *n* period has the advantage of bringing the initial stops closer. When we've tested the Parabolic previously, the number of days selected was not especially important as long as it was within a range of about 4 to 15. We'll use 10 days, as we did in our exit testing.

First Test

For this test, we want to keep it as simple as possible with as little degree of freedom loss as we can manage. We're using a 3/12 moving average crossover for entries, a 10-day Parabolic for exits, and $1,500 initial risk and trailing stops.

Our procedure will be to test the entire six and a half years of data to see how the entries are working. If they are obviously not working well, we'll break the testing period into two parts, the first part being four years and the second part two and a half. Then we'll test some other combinations over the earliest section of our data and affirm our final combination over the later data. (See Exhibit 3–16.)

EXHIBIT 3–16

PERFORMANCE SUMMARY
TEST NUMBER ONE

	Soybeans	D-Mark	Gold	T-Bonds	Crude Oil	Portfolio
Net Profit	-$8,981	$16,187	-$26,860	$29,156	$14,525	$24,027
Number of Trades	81	61	76	94	59	371
% Profitable	33	40	19	44	35	35
Avg. Win/ Avg. Loss	1.63	2.09	1.95	1.80	2.47	2.06
Maximum Drawdown	-$16,256	-$14,512	-$30,701	-$9,937	-$8,900	-$22,259

Actually, the results are pretty encouraging. As we might have expected, soybeans and gold are losers; but it's surprising to see how well the system has handled T-bonds, D-marks, and crude oil. It's possible that, with a little help, we may have a workable trading system.

The next step is to run the results through Portfolio Analyzer. We see that the profits average $3,282 per year (we're always assuming no pyramiding or compounding), which is an annualized yield of 14.8 percent. We know a lot of traders who would be happy with that. But look at the drawdown, $22,259! If it happened early on in our trading, it would wipe us out. A quick calculation shows us that our winning percentage of 35 percent and ratio of average win to average loss of 2.06 gives us a high probability of ruin. The chances of the portfolio declining to $15,000 (down 40 percent) before it rises to $50,000 are 45 percent.

As we can see, the predictable has happened. We have managed to design a profitable but unacceptable trading system. This exercise is a good example of why we should never use net profitability as the sole criterion for judging the effectiveness of a trading system. As we've stated previously, test for a specific matrix of criteria that in your judgment is going to yield the best solution.

The Next Step

The next step, admittedly, is subjective and judgmental. We're going to look at the individual trade listings for each market to see if the entries have been successful or not. This is subjective and judgmental for two reasons. First, if you analyze a single element in a group of interdependent parts of a trading system, you never really know how important each element is to each trade. Often making one small change that you think is innocent will disrupt the chain of events and the change will ripple throughout the system. Second, there really aren't, and probably shouldn't be, any objective criteria to aid your decision. Perhaps this is where art and experience come in.

We're looking at strings of trades to see how quickly and by how much the trades have been in profit. Obviously, it's a waste of space to print the results of 367 trades, but two common phenomena emerge as we look at all five markets. First, as you might expect, the good trades were in profit quickly. Second, the bad trades lost quickly and were in clusters. Looking at the trades on a chart, one at a time, a pattern becomes clear. Our moving average entry does well when the markets are making wide swings, but there are large strings of losses when they are choppy.

ADX as a Filter

We frequently use Wilder's DMI and its ADX derivative. Most of the tests in which we've used it as a filter to objectively decide whether a market is trending have shown it to be effective. We've found that good results normally cluster in a range between about 10 and 25 days, depending on the application. We'll use an 18-day ADX, since 18 is in the middle of the range.

We must use some care in the way we test ADX. If we're not careful, it will not act as a filter but as an entry trigger by itself. We'll code the entry so that we only buy or sell when an ADX uptick and a moving average crossover occur on the same day. If the ADX is trending downward, the market is directionless and our look at the trades has shown us that these are big losing periods.

As you can see in the exhibit below, the changes are dramatic. All of the markets are now profitable, although we might wish to make more money in gold after six and a half years of trading. Surprisingly, T-Bonds and crude oil are not as profitable as before. The winning percentages are higher, though, and the number of trades is considerably less. It appears our filter is doing its job. Let's run Portfolio Analyzer. (See Exhibit 3–17.)

EXHIBIT 3–17

PERFORMANCE SUMMARY
TEST NUMBER TWO (with ADX)

	Soybeans	D-Mark	Gold	T-Bonds	Crude Oil	Portfolio
Net Profit	$6,687	$23,625	$1,219	$19,187	$10,615	$61,333
Number of Trades	34	22	34	32	29	151
% Profitable	38	59	38	46	41	44
Avg. Win/ Avg. Loss	2.27	3.01	1.72	2.15	2.36	2.32
Maximum Drawdown	-$5,125	-$2,600	-$12,529	-$6,187	-$6,235	-$9,414

The total net profit using ADX is $61,333, more than double the profit of the previous test. The simple annualized rate of return is now 37.7 percent. The number of trades is down to 151. Even better, our winning percentage has increased to 44 percent, and the ratio of average win to average loss has also increased—to a healthy 2.32. Our probability of ruin is now only 2.9 percent. The maximum peak-to-valley drawdown is $9,414, well within our original guidelines. The monthly equity figures are on the following pages. Notice that we have withdrawn profits or deposited losses at the beginning of each year, so we start every year with $25,000. (See Exhibits 3–18 and 3–19.)

Further Testing

If we wanted to carry our exercise to its logical conclusion, we would take more steps. Most important, we would test each variable parameter over a range of values, to make sure that we haven't coincidentally curve-fitted our system. The results should be acceptable over a range of values. Following this, we could optimize for the "best" values over the

EXHIBIT 3–18 Part A

$25,000 Hypothetical Account - Jan. 1984 to Jun. 1990

($125 per trade deducted for commissions and slippage)

Period Ending	Beginning Equity	Additions*	Withdrawals *	Net Performance	Ending Equity	Rate of Return
Jan-84	$0.00	$25,000.00	$0.00	-$386.25	$24,718.75	-1.13%
Feb-84	$24,718.75	$0.00	$0.00	$1,000.50	$25,719.25	4.05%
Mar-84	$25,719.25	$0.00	$0.00	-$1,178.75	$24,540.50	-4.58%
Apr-84	$24,540.50	$0.00	$0.00	$2,627.50	$27,168.00	10.71%
May-84	$27,168.00	$0.00	$0.00	$4,072.50	$31,240.50	14.99%
Jun-84	$31,240.50	$0.00	$0.00	-$197.50	$31,043.00	-0.63%
Jul-84	$31,043.00	$0.00	$0.00	$8,807.50	$39,850.50	28.37%
Aug-84	$39,850.50	$0.00	$0.00	-$4,517.00	$35,333.50	-11.33%
Sep-84	$35,333.50	$0.00	$0.00	$1,375.00	$36,708.50	3.89%
Oct-84	$36,708.50	$0.00	$0.00	$2,506.25	$39,214.75	6.83%
Nov-84	$39,214.75	$0.00	$0.00	$1,595.00	$40,809.75	4.07%
Dec-84	$40,809.75	$0.00	$0.00	$1,252.50	$42,062.25	3.07%
				$17,062.25		68.25%
Jan-85	$42,062.25	$0.00	-$17,062.25	-$2,726.50	$22,273.50	-10.91%
Feb-85	$22,273.50	$0.00	$0.00	$1,275.00	$23,548.50	5.72%
Mar-85	$23,548.50	$0.00	$0.00	$105.00	$23,653.50	0.45%
Apr-85	$23,653.50	$0.00	$0.00	-$171.25	$23,482.25	-0.72%
May-85	$23,482.25	$0.00	$0.00	$6,302.25	$29,784.50	26.84%
Jun-85	$29,784.50	$0.00	$0.00	$326.25	$30,110.75	1.10%
Jul-85	$30,110.75	$0.00	$0.00	$3,027.00	$33,137.75	10.05%
Aug-85	$33,137.75	$0.00	$0.00	-$417.50	$32,720.25	-1.26%
Sep-85	$32,720.25	$0.00	$0.00	$1,110.00	$33,830.25	3.39%
Oct-85	$33,830.25	$0.00	$0.00	-$412.50	$33,417.75	-1.22%
Nov-85	$33,417.75	$0.00	$0.00	$480.00	$33,897.75	1.44%
Dec-85	$33,897.75	$0.00	$0.00	$692.00	$34,589.75	2.04%
				$9,589.75		38.36%
Jan-86	$34,589.75	$0.00	-$9,589.75	$662.50	$25,662.50	2.65%
Feb-86	$25,662.50	$0.00	$0.00	$3,095.00	$28,757.50	12.06%
Mar-86	$28,757.50	$0.00	$0.00	-$762.50	$27,995.00	-2.65%
Apr-86	$27,995.00	$0.00	$0.00	-$1,456.25	$26,538.75	-5.20%
May-86	$26,538.75	$0.00	$0.00	$0.00	$26,538.75	0.00%
Jun-86	$26,538.75	$0.00	$0.00	-$1,323.00	$25,215.75	-4.99%
Jul-86	$25,215.75	$0.00	$0.00	$2,792.50	$28,008.25	11.07%
Aug-86	$28,008.25	$0.00	$0.00	$75.00	$28,083.25	0.27%
Sep-86	$28,083.25	$0.00	$0.00	-$2,850.00	$25,233.25	-10.15%
Oct-86	$25,233.25	$0.00	$0.00	-$1,025.00	$24,208.25	-4.06%
Nov-86	$24,208.25	$0.00	$0.00	$1,801.25	$26,009.50	7.44%
Dec-86	$26,009.50	$0.00	$0.00	-$3,558.75	$22,450.75	-13.68%
				-$2,549.25		-10.20%
Jan-87	$22,450.75	$2,549.25	$0.00	-$2,313.75	$22,686.25	-9.26%
Feb-87	$22,686.25	$0.00	$0.00	-$1,375.00	$21,311.25	-6.06%
Mar-87	$21,311.25	$0.00	$0.00	$2,218.75	$23,530.00	10.41%
Apr-87	$23,530.00	$0.00	$0.00	$6,481.25	$30,011.25	27.54%
May-87	$30,011.25	$0.00	$0.00	-$1,470.00	$28,541.25	-4.90%
Jun-87	$28,541.25	$0.00	$0.00	$0.00	$28,541.25	0.00%
Jul-87	$28,541.25	$0.00	$0.00	$987.50	$29,528.75	3.46%
Aug-87	$29,528.75	$0.00	$0.00	-$585.00	$28,943.75	-1.98%
Sep-87	$28,943.75	$0.00	$0.00	-$1,448.75	$27,495.00	-5.01%
Oct-87	$27,495.00	$0.00	$0.00	$2,042.50	$29,537.50	7.43%
Nov-87	$29,537.50	$0.00	$0.00	$4,553.75	$34,091.25	15.42%
Dec-87	$34,091.25	$0.00	$0.00	$800.00	$34,891.25	2.35%
				$9891.25		39.57%
Jan-88	$34,891.25	$0.00	-$9,891.25	-$2,615.00	$22,385.00	-10.46%
Feb-88	$22,385.00	$0.00	$0.00	-$310.00	$22,075.00	-1.38%
Mar-88	$22,075.00	$0.00	$0.00	-$4,188.50	$17,886.50	-18.97%
Apr-88	$17,886.50	$0.00	$0.00	$718.75	$18,605.25	4.02%
May-88	$18,605.25	$0.00	$0.00	$3,903.75	$22,509.00	20.98%
Jun-88	$22,509.00	$0.00	$0.00	-$1,992.25	$20,516.75	-8.85%
Jul-88	$20,516.75	$0.00	$0.00	-$770.00	$19,746.75	-3.75%
Aug-88	$19,746.75	$0.00	$0.00	$2,410.00	$22,156.75	12.20%
Sep-88	$22,156.75	$0.00	$0.00	$8,022.50	$30,179.25	36.21%
Oct-88	$30,179.25	$0.00	$0.00	-$45.00	$30,134.25	-0.15%
Nov-88	$30,134.25	$0.00	$0.00	$2,427.50	$32,561.75	8.06%
Dec-88	$32,561.75	$0.00	$0.00	$3,621.50	$36,183.25	11.12%
				$11,183.25		44.73%

Profits withdrawn or losses added at start of each year.

EXHIBIT 3–18 Part B

$25,000 Hypothetical Account - Jan. 1984 to Jun. 1990

($125 per trade deducted for commissions and slippage)

Period Ending	Beginning Equity	Additions*	Withdrawals *	Net Performance	Ending Equity	Rate of Return
Jan-89	$36,183.25	$0.00	-$11,183.25	$763.00	$25,763.00	3.05%
Feb-89	$25,763.00	$0.00	$0.00	-$2,261.75	$23,501.25	-8.78%
Mar-89	$23,501.25	$0.00	$0.00	$1,212.50	$24,713.75	5.16%
Apr-89	$24,713.75	$0.00	$0.00	$3,248.75	$27,962.50	13.15%
May-89	$27,962.50	$0.00	$0.00	$3,361.25	$31,323.75	12.02%
Jun-89	$31,323.75	$0.00	$0.00	-$825.00	$30,498.75	-2.63%
Jul-89	$30,498.75	$0.00	$0.00	$612.50	$31,111.25	2.01%
Aug-89	$31,111.25	$0.00	$0.00	-$1,257.50	$29,853.75	-4.04%
Sep-89	$29,853.75	$0.00	$0.00	$3,912.50	$33,766.25	13.11%
Oct-89	$33,766.25	$0.00	$0.00	-$2,998.25	$30,768.00	-8.88%
Nov-89	$30,768.00	$0.00	$0.00	$5,127.50	$35,895.50	16.67%
Dec-89	$35,895.50	$0.00	$0.00	$5,332.50	$41,228.00	14.86%
				$16,228.00		64.91%
Jan-90	$41,228.00	$0.00	-$16,228.00	$2,713.75	$27,713.75	10.86%
Feb-90	$27,713.75	$0.00	$0.00	-$1,050.00	$26,663.75	-3.79%
Mar-90	$26,663.75	$0.00	$0.00	-$1,240.00	$25,423.75	-4.65%
Apr-90	$25,423.75	$0.00	$0.00	$900.00	$26,323.75	3.54%
May-90	$26,323.75	$0.00	$0.00	-$1,325.00	$24,998.75	-5.03%
Jun-90	$24,998.75	$0.00	$0.00	$35.00	$25,033.75	0.14%
				$33.75		0.14%

Hypothetical or simulated performance results have certain inherent limitations. Unlike an actual performance record, simulated results do not represent actual trading. Also, since the trades have not actually been executed, the results may have under–or–over compensated for the impact, if any, of certain market factors such as lack of liquidity. Simulated trading programs in general are also subject to the fact that they are designed with the benefit of hindsight. No representation is being made that any account will or is likely to achieve profits or losses similar to those shown.

EXHIBIT 3–19

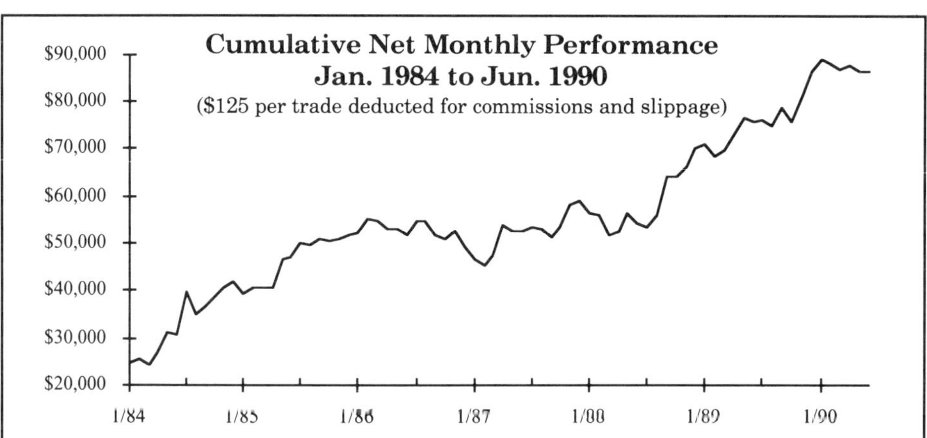

first several years of data and then test these values over the subsequent years. This is difficult to do in this case, because of the scarcity of trades; but if your system generates a large enough sample, we recommend it. Defining the best values is a little difficult. The safest way is to choose the values that give results in the middle of the range over which the variable has been tested. If the most optimum value is at one end of the range, it is probably better to ignore it and pick something in the center of the distribution. For example, let us say you've tested over a range of initial risk stops from $500 to $2,000, in increments of $100. The so-called best stop value is $900, but results fall off sharply below $800. They continue to be evenly distributed right up to $2,000. It is better to use a value midway between $800 and $2,000, rather than the best stop of $900.

Conclusion

Computer testing of trading systems is still in its infancy. Traders seem to be moving toward more productive testing methods, but there is still not much written about the subject. Perhaps this is because there are no absolutes in testing, just as there are none in trading. Still, there is a misconception that testing "proves" something, which we've tried to dispel. We hope that we have stimulated some debate on the subject, and that some of the excellent work being done in futures management firms and by some talented private traders will be made public.

Suggested Readings

Griffin, P. *The Theory of Blackjack.* Las Vegas: Gamblers Press, 1981.

Lukac, Louis B., and B. Wade Brorsen. "The Usefulness of Historical Data in Selecting Parameters for Technical Trading Systems. *The Journal of Futures Markets* 9, no. 1 (1989), pp. 55–65.

Vince, Ralph. *Portfolio Management Formulas.* New York: John Wiley & Sons, 1990.

Young, Terry W. "Introducing the Calmar Ratio." Technical Traders Bulletin 3, no. 9 (September 1991), pp. 1–10.

Chapter

4 Day Trading

Introduction

Costs of Doing Business

The day trader enters and exits trades during the same market session, normally a period of only four to six hours from opening to close. The very short-term nature of day trading presents advantages and disadvantages to the trader. The major advantages are the lower margin requirements and the absence of overnight risk. The disadvantages are the bad odds, the time and effort required, the limited profit potential, and the burdensome costs of frequent transactions.

The transaction costs consist of commissions and slippage. The trader might have a mental image of trading at the prices shown on a computer screen, but in reality she must continuously buy at the offered price and sell at the bid price. The spread between the bid and offer becomes a substantial hidden cost of doing business. It is also unrealistic to expect stop orders to be filled at the stop price all of the time. The commissions are a large and much more obvious cost. In the meantime, to offset these unavoidable costs, the day trader is limited to only very small profits. Under even the most optimistic scenario, the day trader's potential profits are limited to only a portion of the price range occurring within one day of trading.

Let us assume that our day trader is paying $20 per trade in commission, and the spread between the bid and offer amounts to $10 buying and $10 selling. For the trader to complete a trade that nets $100, she must be smart enough to identify a move of $140 on the price screen that she watches. On the other hand, when her timing is wrong by only $140, she is going to lose $180. It doesn't take a Ph.D. in mathematics to figure this isn't an ideal business environment. In fact, even the professionals on the floors of the exchanges must be excellent, highly disciplined traders just to survive. The public does not realize how many of these professionals fail, in spite of the advantage of being on the floor and paying only minimal costs per trade. Imagine how small the odds for success must be for an off-the-floor trader faced with the costs we have described.

To have any hope of success, the day trader must strive to maximize the profits on each trade so that he can overcome the tremendous disadvantage of the transaction costs. Unfortunately, the day trader has very little control of the potential profit to be obtained, because the price range during the day so severely limits the maximum profit to be realized on an average trade. No trader can reasonably expect to buy at exact bottoms or sell at exact tops. A very good trader might hope to be able to capture the middle third of an intraday price swing. This means that to make $180 the total price swing must be three times this amount, or $540. How many futures markets have a daily price range of $540 or more? Very few. How many futures markets can produce a $180 net loss? Almost any of them.

Don't forget, the trader who is smart enough to find markets with $540 price swings and then smart enough to trade them so correctly that he nets $180 is only going to break even unless he has more winners than losers. To make money in the long run, the day trader must have a percentage of winning trades that is far better than 50 percent or he must somehow figure out how to make more than $180 on a $540 price swing. (Or best of all, do both.) This also assumes that the trader is smart and disciplined enough to harness his instincts and emotions and carefully limit the size of the losses.

Tough Odds

As you can see, a day trader is faced with an almost impossible task. We would venture a very educated guess that less than one out of a thousand day traders makes money over any sustained time. Our advice is to not even attempt it. Your time and energy will be much better spent perfecting your longer-term trading skills. Even if you should succeed at day trading, it is difficult to reinvest the profits and continue to compound them. Day traders can only operate efficiently in small size, so don't expect to make your fortune at it—it's only a hard-earned living at best.

In spite of our sincere warning, we know many traders will attempt to beat the odds and become day traders for a while. Fortunately, the lessons learned can be applied to more serious and productive trading later on. We will do our best to teach you as much as we can about day trading and make the learning process less costly. Obviously, we don't have all the answers or we wouldn't have such a negative outlook on the probability of success. We have learned a great deal about this subject over many years of trading, and the fact that we have elected to no longer play this game simply demonstrates our personal preferences in the allocation of our productive time. We hope whatever hard-earned information we pass along proves helpful.

Selection of Markets for Day Trading

As we pointed out earlier, very few markets have wide enough intraday price swings to make them suitable candidates for day trading. Day traders generally prefer to concentrate their efforts on only one or two markets. The prices must be watched closely, and there are very few markets that are suitable even if we had the capacity to follow lots of them. Presently, day traders tend to favor the stock indexes, bonds, currencies, and energy markets. From time to time other markets may become candidates for day trading, because of temporary periods of high volatility.

We ran a test to see what percentage of the time various markets had a total daily range of $500 or more between the high of the day and the low. Here are some sample results over our most recent 1,000 days of data: S&P Index 69 percent, NY Composite 64 percent, British pounds 53 percent, T-bonds 50 percent, Swiss francs 50 percent, Japanese yen 38 percent, heating oil 37 percent, D-marks 35 percent, crude oil 31 percent, soybeans 28 percent, silver 23 percent, gold 21 percent, and sugar 13 percent. As you can see, only five markets had a $500 range 50 percent of the time.

Consider Tick Sizes

In addition to looking for a wide daily range, the liquidity and the size of the minimum spread should also be factors to consider when selecting markets for day trading. Our example of costs included paying a spread of only $10 on each side of a trade. In the S&P market, a minimum spread would be $25 each side, while in the bond market a 1/32 spread is $31.25. If you are day trading bonds with $20 commissions, you must overcome total costs of $82.50 added to losses and subtracted from gains. Your average winning trade must run $165 farther than your average loss just to break even. This assumes a one tick spread, which is the best case possible. The element of liquidity comes in to play in determining the number of ticks in the spread between bid and offer. A one tick spread is the best you can hope for, and most markets have a wider spread than that. You can usually assume that the higher the average daily volume, the tighter the spread. For that reason, you will want to concentrate your day trading in only those markets with very high volume. Otherwise, you can be making good timing decisions and still be assured of losing money.

Maximizing Profits

Day traders are constantly faced with the problem of capturing as much profit as possible from a relatively small range of prices. This situation naturally leads traders into the strategy of buying dips and selling rallies, rather than attempting to follow trends. Most trend-following strategies tend to be much too slow for day trading. Countertrend strategies offer the potential of extracting the greatest profit from a small range of prices. However, countertrend strategies tend to be less reliable than trend-following strategies, because quickly spotting turning points in prices is much more difficult than simply trading in the direction of a trend.

We have observed that the best day traders incorporate elements of both methods. Successful day traders try to buy dips within an uptrend and to sell rallies within a downtrend. The day trader who consistently makes money must be good at following trends and be good at finding short-term turning points. Most traders lose money because they are never very good at either task. As we look at some examples of possible day-trading strategies, keep these two steps in mind: First find the intermediate trend and then find the short-term turning points. Both steps need to be done quickly and accurately to produce a winning day trade.

Our Disclaimer

The day-trading methods that follow are a few of the many methods that have been shared with us over the last few years. We seldom attempt to day trade, so we have very little first-hand experience with any of these methods. The various traders who shared these methods with us claimed success with them. We tried to select the ones that seemed most logical and the ones that seemed to hold up under a cursory examination over very limited data. The inclusion of these methods should not be considered an endorsement or recommendation. At best they should give the reader some food for thought—and a representative sample of the many methods and tools that can be used for day trading. Use them at your own risk.

The 5-25 Envelope Method

This day-trading method is based on a very unusual way of using a moving average envelope. Most envelope systems call for trading in the same direction as the envelope breakout. The 5-25 method does just the opposite.

We assume that the market will traverse back and forth between the extremes of the envelope. We treat the excursions beyond the boundaries as overbought or oversold levels. After a move outside the envelope, we expect the market to re-enter the envelope and traverse to the opposite side. Here are the rules:

1. Use 30-minute bars on the S&P futures.
2. Set up an envelope study for five periods, normal (no smoothing), and at a distance of 25/100 of 1 percent from the closes.
3. Look for trades only when the boundaries of the envelope are at least 150 points apart. When one of the 30-minute bars closes at least 5 points outside the envelope, look to initiate a trade in the opposite direction as soon as the next bar closes back inside the envelope.
4. Use an initial stop loss at the extreme high or low point just before your entry. After the market has moved 75 points in your favor, the stop loss should be changed to at least your break-even point.
5. Take profits when the market reaches the opposite side of the envelope. If you want to simplify the profit taking, use the boundary of the envelope at the time you enter the trade as the target, otherwise you might have to adjust your exit point every half hour. (See Exhibit 4–1.)

EXHIBIT 4–1

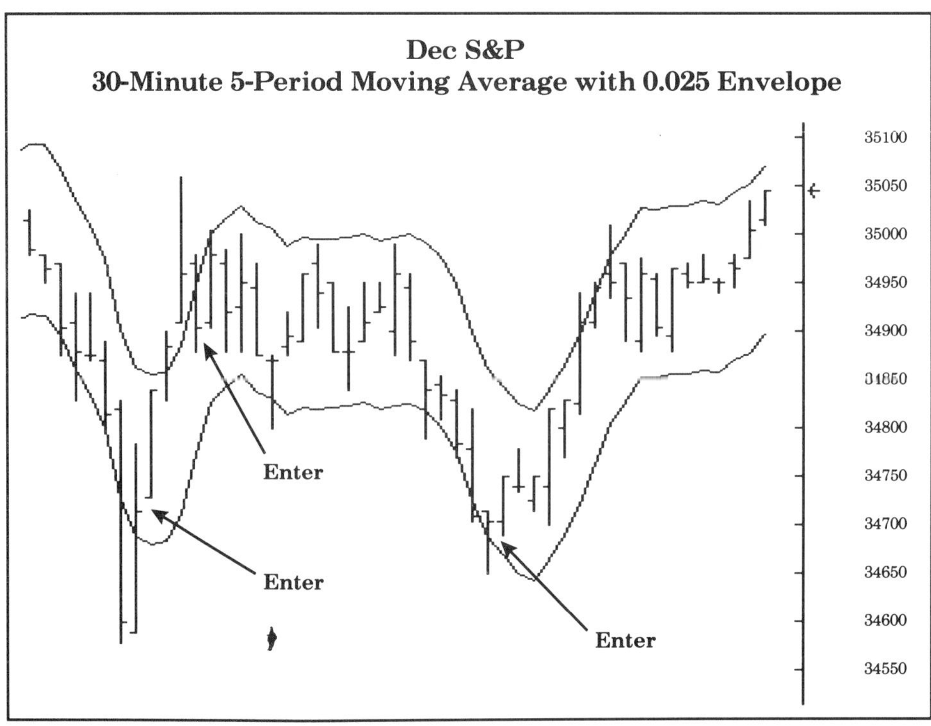

With some modifications to the envelope, this system can be used for regular trading instead of day trading. We used to have good results using it to trade soybeans.

The "Hi MOM" System

We call this day-trading strategy the "Hi MOM" system, because trades are signaled only when there is a high momentum reading. Here is how it works:

1. Use 9-minute bars on the S&P futures. We picked the 9-minute interval because the system must be sensitive to minor price patterns. The 9-minute bars also divide the trading day into 45 equal time periods. Ten-minute bars would probably work just as well; but we have a slight preference for the logic of having all bars represent an equal time period, rather than having an odd bar at the end of the day. The 9-minute bars also give us a head start on traders using the more common intervals of 10, 15, 20, and 30 minutes.

2. Directly underneath the 9-minute S&P bars, set up a six-bar momentum study. Scale the study so you can easily tell when the momentum reaches +/− 150.

3. Look for divergences between the MOM study and the S&P bar chart. The first spike of the particular divergences we are looking for will have to have penetrated the +/− 150 level on our MOM chart. The second or third divergence spike does not have to reach the 150 level.

4. After a Hi MOM divergence, enter the market as soon as possible after the hook that completes the divergence pattern. Place an initial stop loss 20 points beyond the recent high or low of the bar chart. (Point B of an AB divergence). Trail the stop using peaks and valleys on the bar chart as support and resistance levels.

EXHIBIT 4–2

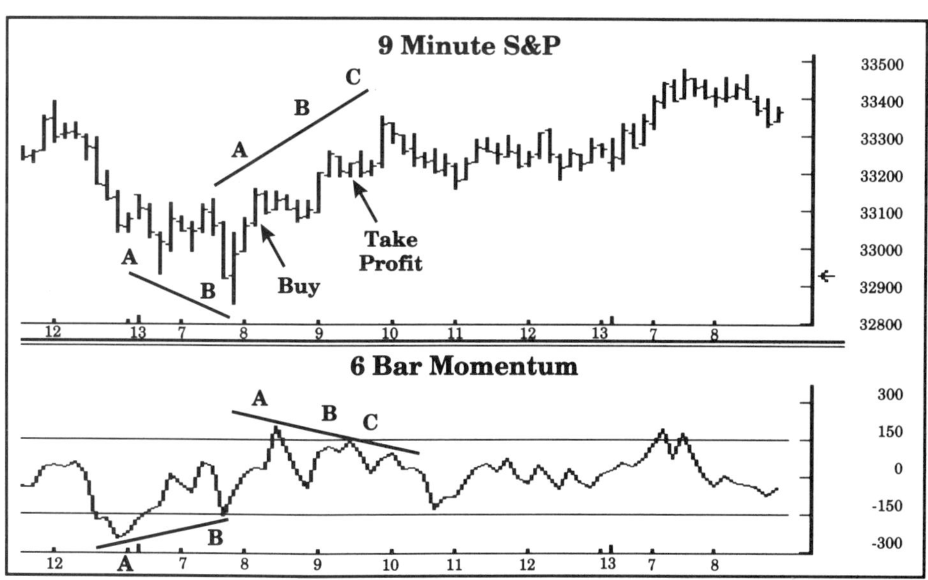

5. Take profits when there is a divergence in the opposite direction, but do not reverse the trade. We want to only trade the first divergence of the day. The exception to the one trade per day rule is when the divergence sets up as an ABC divergence with three spikes instead of two. If we entered after the second peak and were unfortunate enough to get stopped out on the third spike, we will want to initiate a second trade in the same direction if the divergence continues. Close out any remaining open positions at the end of the day. (See Exhibit 4–2.)

The "Hi MOM" system is simple but very effective, because it combines the patience of waiting for volatile periods (indicated by the +/− 150 MOM) with the excellent entry timing provided by divergences.

Intermarket Divergences, Ohama's 3-D Technique

One of our subscribers in the Los Angeles area, Gary Inouye, worked closely with Bill Ohama for several years prior to Bill's death in 1990. Gary has been very successful in applying Bill's well-known "3-D" techniques to day trading. Here is an explanation:

1. Make a page of five-minute charts on two or three related commodities. For example, compare the five-minute charts of the S&P, the NY Composite, and the Major Market Index. You might also compare the T-bonds, the T-notes, and the muni bonds. There are other possible related groups, like currencies, energy futures, or the soybean complex, but the best day trades are usually in stock indexes or bonds.
2. Carefully compare the five-minute charts for divergences where one commodity makes a new high or low and where one or more of the other commodities in the group fails to confirm by also making a new high or low. (See Exhibit 4–3.)
3. When a divergence is spotted, the trade should be implemented in the most tradeable (most liquid) commodity in the group. For example, in the stock indexes you would trade the S&P, not the Major Market Index.
4. Once a trade has been entered, some method of trailing stops would be advisable. For example, a trailing stop of about 125 points in the S&P would be a starting point. It would be logical to use wider stops during volatile periods and tighter stops when the markets are quiet.
5. If you get a quick profit of $500 within a half hour, just take it. If the trade moves more slowly, hold on as long as it seems to be trending in the right direction. Gary does not wait for a signal to close out the trade but uses his judgment on when to take profits or losses.

This method is not a complete system, because of the lack of specific stops and the lack of a more specific exit strategy. Your results might be better or worse depending on your skill at exits. We like the entry method.

EXHIBIT 4–3

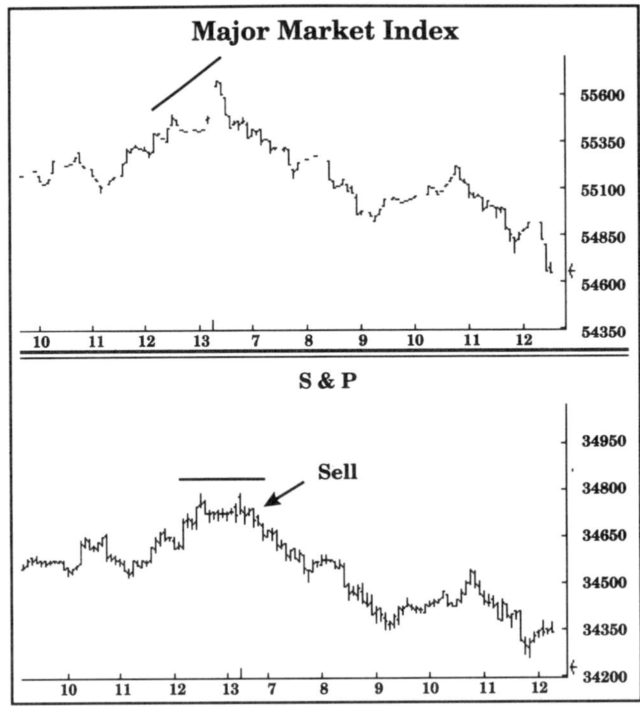
Major Market Index
55600
55350
55100
54850
54600
54350
10 11 12 13 7 8 9 10 11 12
S & P
Sell
34950
34800
34650
34500
34350
34200
10 11 12 13 7 8 9 10 11 12

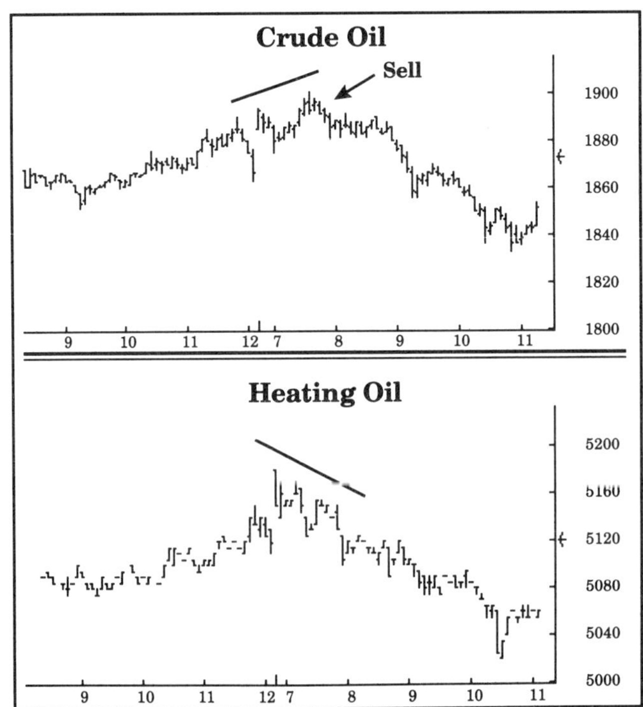
Crude Oil
Sell
1900
1880
1860
1840
1820
1800
9 10 11 12 7 8 9 10 11
Heating Oil
5200
5160
5120
5080
5040
5000
9 10 11 12 7 8 9 10 11

Kane's %K Hooks

The following S&P day-trading strategy was related to us by Steve Kane, who was a fellow speaker at Fred Brown's Technical Analysis Conference in Austin, Texas, in 1990. When we returned from the seminar, we started watching the system and we have been encouraged by its effectiveness over recent data. Here is how it works:

1. Determine the trend using one-hour charts. Trade only when the hourly chart has made a higher high or lower low within the last two hours. When the trend is up, look for buy signals only. When the trend is down, look for sell signals only.
2. Entries: Use a five-minute chart with a 12-period slow stochastics. Buy when the %K (the faster moving line) goes below 20 and turns up. Sell short when the %K goes above 80 and turns down. (Don't forget to trade only in the same direction as the hourly trend.)
3. Stops: Use an initial stop of 100 points, or put a closer stop just beyond a recent trading range. When the trade is 100 points ahead, it is a good idea to raise the stop to break even.
4. Exits: Take profits when the %K hooks in the opposite direction from +80 or −20. Another strategy is to watch the one-minute stochastics and exit whenever there is a divergence against the current trend. (See Exhibit 4–4.)

Steve had a few additional comments worth passing along. He has observed that, when the %K entry signals are also divergences from the price action, the resulting moves are particularly strong. He also suggests that, when there is a very sudden profit move of 100 points or more, it is often a good idea to take the profit immediately. Finally, he cautions that, whenever there are two consecutive losses in a day, it is time to stop trading and try again tomorrow. This is good advice for almost any day-trading method.

We like the idea that this is a method that buys dips in an uptrend and vice versa. We also like the idea of buying when the %K hooks, rather than waiting for the usual crossover signal. We think Steve's strategy might also be applied to day trading in other markets as well as S&Ps.

EXHIBIT 4–4

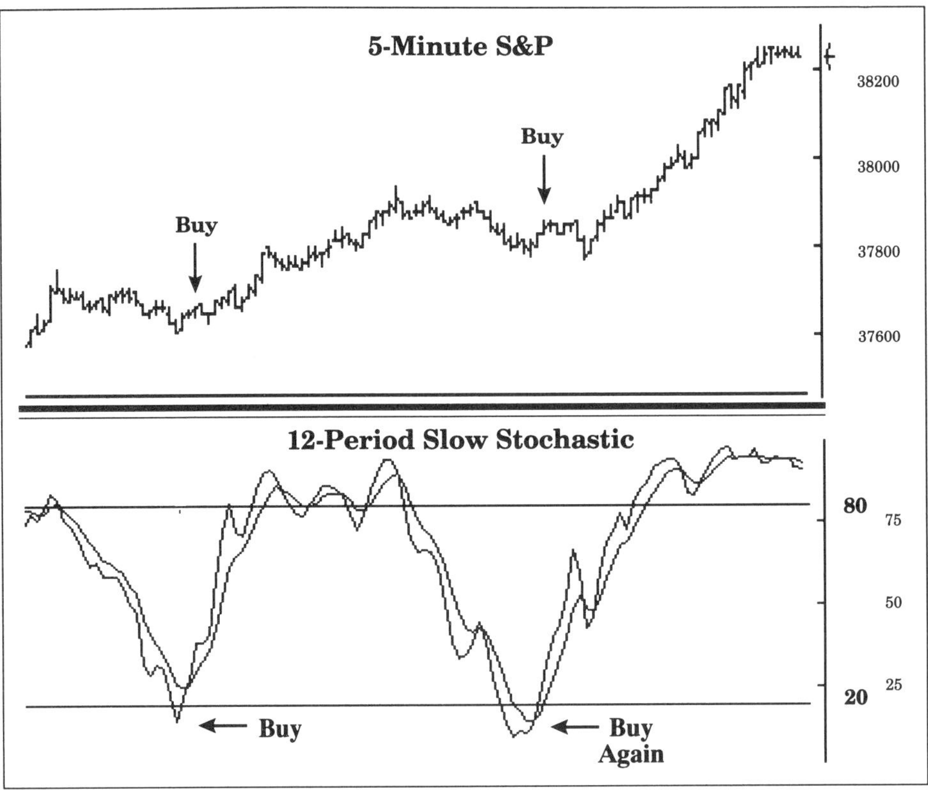

5-Minute S&P
Buy
Buy
38200
38000
37800
37600
12-Period Slow Stochastic
80
75
50
25
20
Buy
Buy
Again

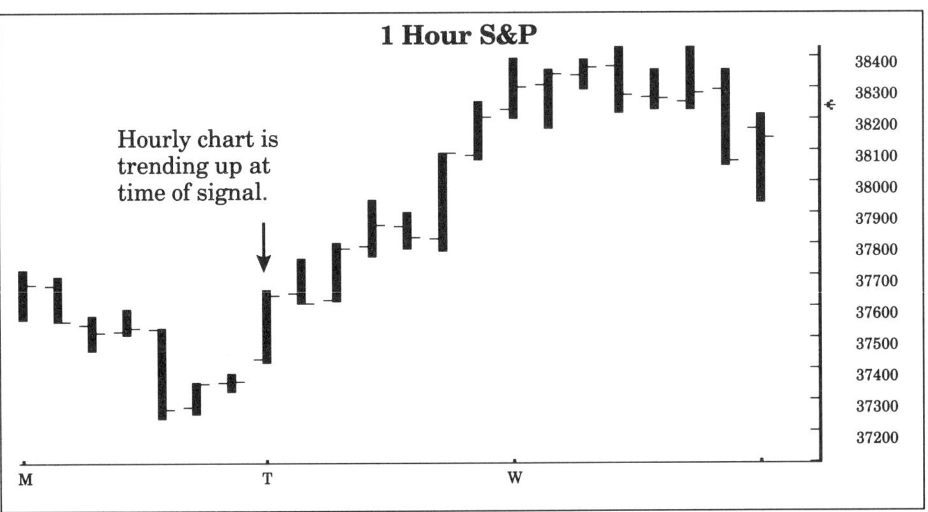

1 Hour S&P
Hourly chart is
trending up at
time of signal.
38400
38300
38200
38100
38000
37900
37800
37700
37600
37500
37400
37300
37200
M
T
W

One-Minute Charts with Stochastics

This is a day-trading method developed by Humphrey Chang, a trader and former futures broker in California. Humphrey explained that the method works best for day trading S&P futures, but mentioned that he sometimes uses it for day trading yen and Swiss franc futures. Here is the method:

1. Use one-minute bars for the S&P futures and a 21-period stochastic.
2. One of the most important rules is that entries are done only in the first hour of trading. After the opening, wait until both stochastics lines go to an extreme level (above 80 or below 20) and then cross. Enter as quickly as possible after the cross. Ignore all other stochastics signals after the first hour.
3. Trail stops using swing patterns. Look for patterns of higher lows, or, if you are short, look for patterns of lower highs. Humphrey cautioned not to have any stops at the exact high or low of the day. He has observed these are points that the floor traders are watching and seem to raid as frequently as possible.
4. The trade is left on until stopped out by the trailing stop or exited at the close of the market. (See Exhibit 4–5.)

EXHIBIT 4–5

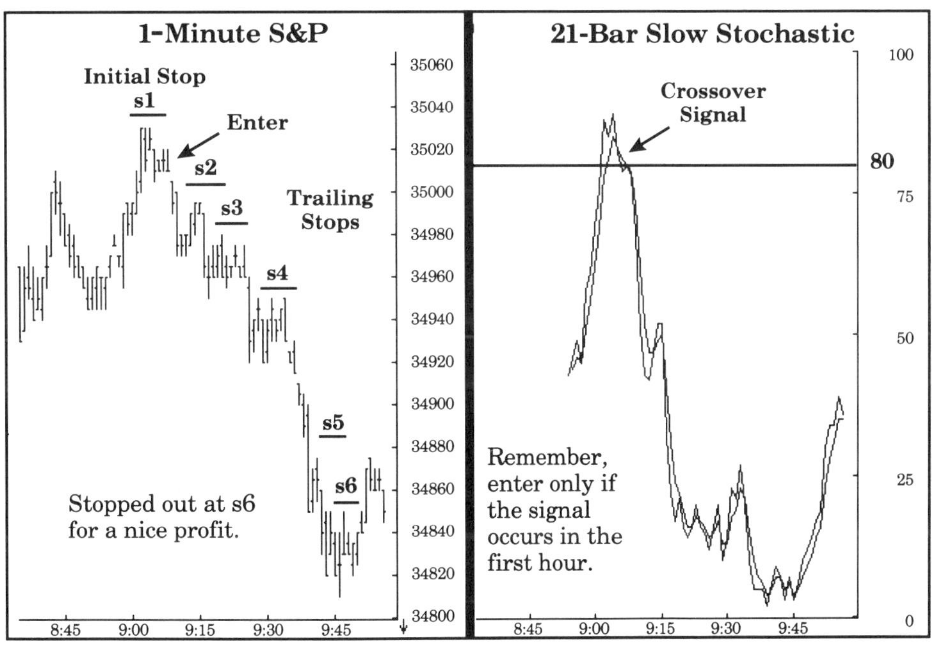

Humphrey suggested that the method can be made more reliable by trading only in the direction indicated by the half-hour stochastic with 14 periods. For example, if the half-hour %K is above the %D, you would use the one-minute stochastic for buy signals only.

Pivot Points

As we have explained in our previous chapters, we don't believe in the general practice of forecasting specific prices. However, if enough people use exactly the same method and wind up looking at the same forecasted prices, perhaps they do start to have some predictable impact on trading. We suspect that the popularity of these pivot points is causing them to act as self-fulfilling prophecies. The formula for figuring pivot points (or support and resistance levels) was explained to us by one of our newsletter subscribers, Neal Weintraub, author of *The Weintraub Daytrader* and a floor trader in Chicago, who conducts some unique training seminars for traders, which he calls "Commodity Boot Camp." Neal explained to us that the formula is very widely followed, particularly by many floor traders who make a note of the pivot points before entering the pit each day. Neal suggested that knowledge of the calculations might be especially useful for S&P traders.

We start the pivot point calculations by adding together the previous day's high, low, and close. Then we divide by three to get an average price. Example:

Yesterday's high = 365.30

Yesterday's low = 361.30

Yesterday's close = 364.40

Total = 1091.00 divided by 3 = 363.66 avg. price)

Now to find today's pivot point high (or resistance level) we simply take the previous day's average price, multiply it by two, and then subtract the previous day's low. Example:

363.66 (yesterday's average price) × 2 = 727.32

727.32 − 361.30 (yesterday's low) = 366.02 (expected pivot point high)

Next, to find today's pivot point low (or support level) we simply take the previous day's average price, multiply it by two and then subtract the previous day's high. Example:

363.66 (yesterday's average price) × 2 = 727.32

727.32 − 365.30 (yesterday's high) = 362.02 (expected pivot point low)

These numbers represent the nearby support and resistance levels that for many years have been very widely circulated among day traders and floor traders. Since they are not chart points but are calculated numbers, the chartists will probably see them only after the fact, while the floor traders have the numbers noted on their trading cards.

Neal goes on to explain that we can carry the calculations another step further if we want and calculate a "highest high" (or extreme resistance point) as well as a "lowest low" (or extreme support level).

To calculate the highest high, we take yesterday's average price of

363.66, subtract the expected pivot point low of 362.02, and add the expected pivot point high of 366.02.

Our answer, 367.66, might be a good target on the upside if the resistance at 366.02 is broken. It would also indicate the next possible resistance level as the market advances.

To calculate the lowest low, we take yesterday's average price of 363.66, then we subtract the difference between the expected pivot point low of 362.02 and the pivot point high of 366.02 (a difference of 4.00). Our answer of 359.66 represents a possible target or low point on the way down if our first support level of 362.02 doesn't hold.

We used real numbers for our examples, so we couldn't resist checking the S&P after the close to see how we did. The low of the day was 362.10 versus our projected pivot point low of 362.02. Not bad. (Sep S&P 6-21-90)

Again we caution that we think these points only work because they are popular and that popularity may be short-lived. If they should stop working for a while, because of some more important factors, they may never work again and you can throw this method away forever. On the other hand, if more people follow them, as time goes on they will work better than ever. In the meantime, we thought they were an interesting phenomenon worth passing along. We would be inclined to give more weight to the nearby numbers than to the "highest high" or "lowest low" calculations.

Price Gaps on Openings

At a meeting of the Technical Analysts of Southern California in 1989, Bruce Babcock, Jr., was the guest speaker and described a day-trading strategy that he was developing. Bruce is the publisher of *Commodity Traders Consumer Report* and author of several commodity trading books. His book, *The Dow Jones-Irwin Guide to Trading Systems,* which has been referenced here many times, contains a great deal of useful information, and we recommend both his book and his CTCR newsletter to our readers.

Here are the highlights of the day-trading strategy that Bruce described to us:

1. Trading nearest month S&P futures, wait for an opening price that gaps noticeably from the previous day's close. You will then be looking for a trade in the direction of the gap. If the opening price gaps up, look for an entry on the buy-side. If the opening gaps down, look for an entry on the sell-side.
2. Tack on a few points above or below the opening price range and enter the market on a buy stop or sell stop as the market begins to trend in the direction of the gap.

EXHIBIT 4–6

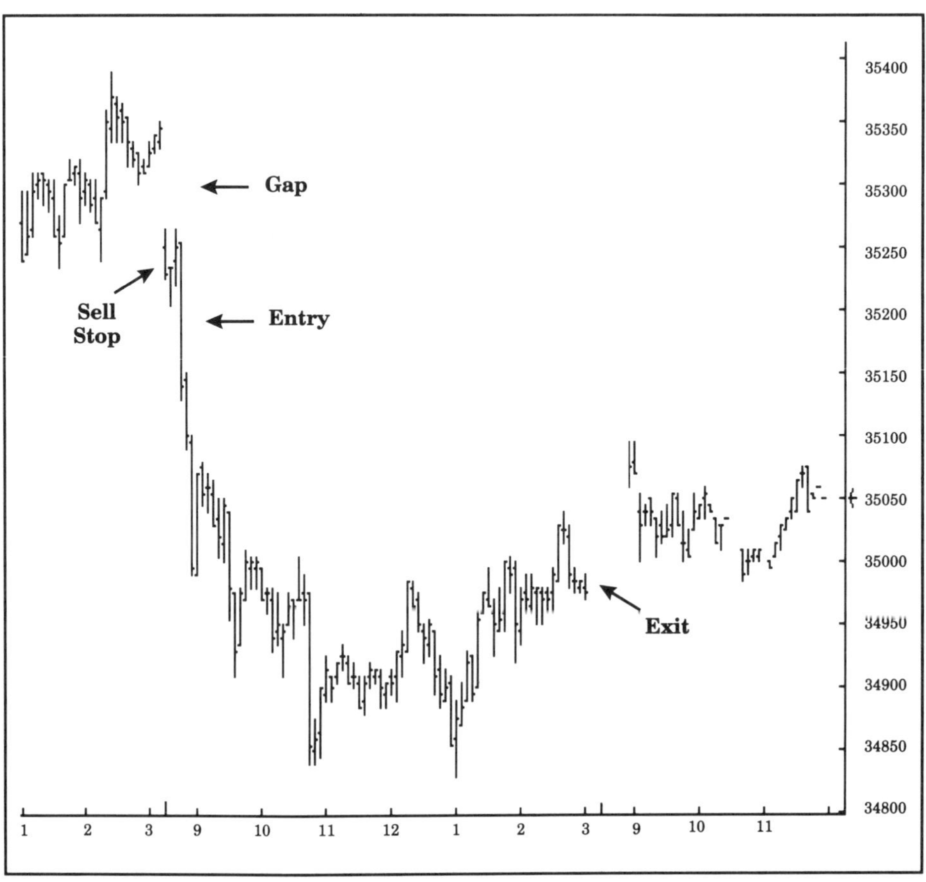

3. Use a stop loss of about $500 and exit the trade on the close. (See Exhibit 4–6.)

Bruce was probably intentionally vague about defining some of the instructions in specific terms. His gap strategy can be tailored to suit your individual trading style. Bruce indicated that he had done a considerable amount of testing with various gap and follow-through parameters. Generally, the bigger the gap and the more points you tack on to the opening range, the more likely you will be to have a winning trade. However, waiting for bigger gaps and more follow through means fewer trades.

Remember, profitable day trading requires high volatility, so we advise keeping the parameters toward the higher side, rather than the low side. That way you will be trading only after the market has demonstrated some volatility. As a starting place, try waiting for gaps of 75 points and tack on 25 points for follow through. If you want more trades, make the numbers smaller; if you want fewer trades, make the numbers bigger.

RSI Divergences

Here is a simple day-trading method that uses a short-term RSI to find potential tops and bottoms in the S&P market. It is a logical approach that should work in any market and could be modified to use in longer-term trading as well. It is one of our favorite day-trading strategies for someone who does not need a trade every day. This method may go several days between trading signals, but, when the signals occur, it has a better winning percentage than some of the more active strategies. Since it doesn't trade every day, it could be a supplemental method to be followed in addition to a more active system.

This method works best when trades are signaled in the direction of a longer-term trend. When there is no prevailing trend, the signals can be taken in either direction. You might want to review the use of ADX as a trend-measuring tool. When the daily ADX is rising, the day trades should be done only in the direction of the trend. When the ADX is declining, the trades can be in either direction. Be patient and don't anticipate the divergences.

Here are the specific rules:

1. Use a 30-minute bar chart on the S&P with a six-period RSI based on closes.

EXHIBIT 4–7

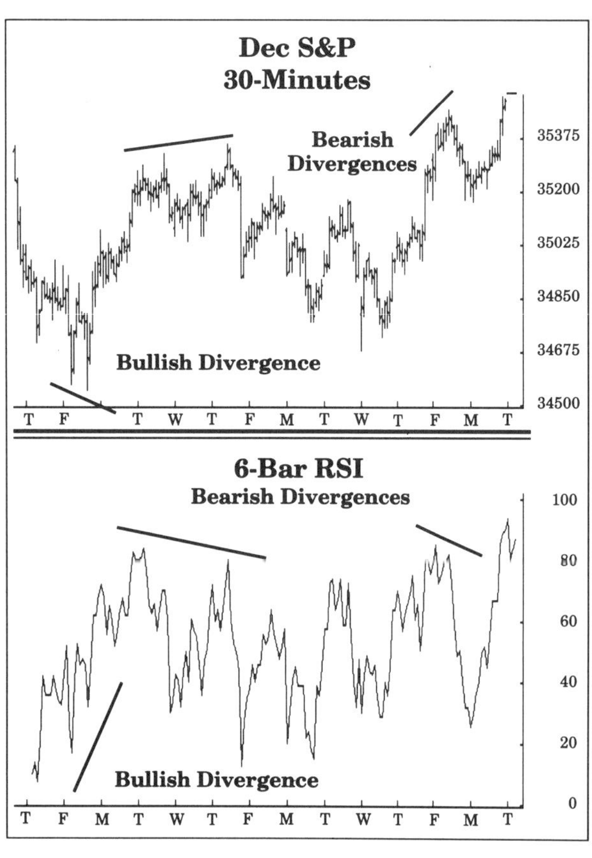

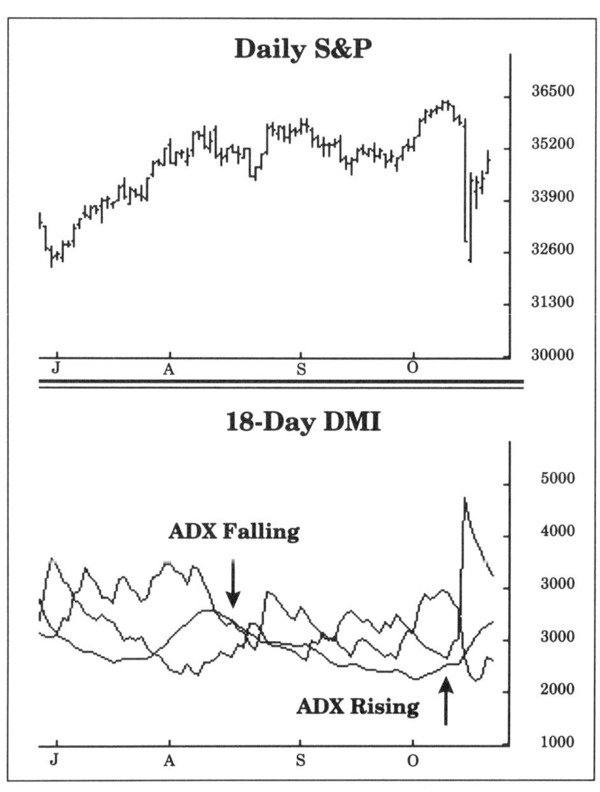

2. Look for divergence patterns in which the first RSI spike has penetrated the 80 or 20 levels on your screen. The second RSI spike doesn't need to reach these levels. Buy or sell immediately after the divergence is confirmed by a 30-minute close in the direction of the signal.
3. Use an entry stop of 100 S&P points or two ticks above or below a recent high or low, whichever is closer.
4. Exit at the stop or at the close of the day.
5. Don't enter any new trades in the last 45 minutes of the market. (See Exhibit 4–7.)

In markets other than the S&P, this day-trading method could be modified by changing the 30-minute bars to a shorter time period. If that were done, the 80/20 levels of the RSI might have to be adjusted to a higher or lower level.

It is worth noting that, in periods when the market is less volatile, 70/30 works better than 80/20, because the RSI doesn't get as overbought or oversold. However, one of the important virtues of this system is that it takes a fairly volatile market to make the RSI reach the 80/20 level, and trades don't get signaled unless there is enough volatility to make trading worthwhile. Don't be tempted to defeat that valuable feature of the system by adjusting the levels downward beyond 70/30 just to get more frequent trades.

Sibbet's "Knife" System

The following is a system for day trading the NYSE Composite Index (commonly referred to by traders as the "Knife," because it trades on the New York Futures Exchange). It is brought to us by our old friend and mentor of 25 years ago, Jim Sibbet, who is probably best known for his "Demand Index" and his newsletters on silver and gold. Jim says he prefers to trade the NYFE, instead of the S&P, because on a per dollar of margin basis he can make more money using the NYFE. He also believes it is a more orderly market with less risk. Here is his explanation of the strategy:

1. Use 5-, 10-, or 15-minute charts on the nearest NYFE contract. You just need price data, not patterns of any kind—so the time intervals don't matter.

2. Identify a fairly recent significant high or low point on the chart. (Just eyeball it for now.) If the point was a high, we will be looking to go short as soon as the market has declined by 0.70 from the high. If the significant point was a low, we will be looking to buy as soon as the market goes up by 0.70 from the low. Once the market has moved 0.70 from a high or low, we want to follow the current direction under the assumption that it's going farther. You should use a buy stop or sell stop at the 0.70 change in direction to automatically put you into the trade.

EXHIBIT 4–8

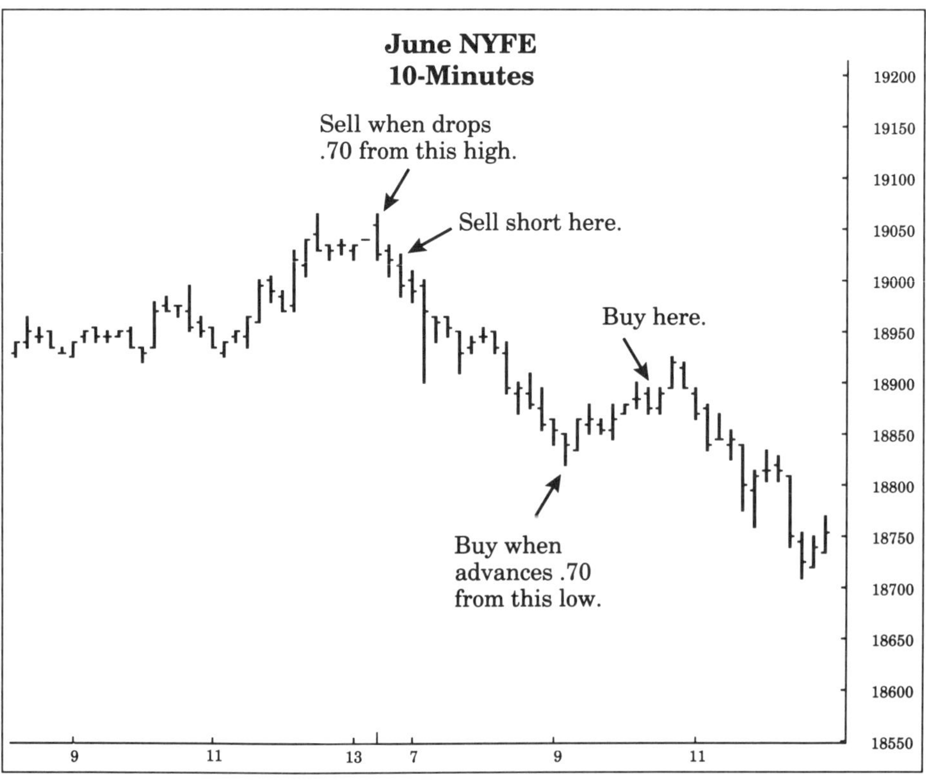

3. Once you have started a trade, protect yourself with a very close stop loss order at 0.30 from your entry point.

4. If the trade goes in your favor, as soon as you are ahead by 0.30 move your stop up to your entry point. As soon as you get ahead by 0.70 move your stop again to 0.50 points away, so you lock in a 0.20 profit. When you are ahead by 0.90, use a 0.70 trailing stop and be prepared to not only exit but to reverse the trade. (You may not want to reverse late in the day, unless you are prepared to carry the trade overnight. Jim will carry the trade overnight only if he is on the right side of his other indicators.)

5. If you are unlucky and get stopped out before you reach the point where your stops are 0.70 away, you should try and re-enter the market in the same direction. On the re-entry, you will put the trade back on as soon as the market moves 0.20 in the direction of your first trade. (The fact that the market has not reversed by 0.70 since the previous signal indicates there is still a trend in the same direction you attempted to trade before.) Jim says he often is able to re-enter the market at a better price than his exit and make money on the second try. (See Exhibit 4–8.)

We were more than a little worried about the potential activity and market watching that are required by Jim's methods. If we go out for coffee we might miss two or three stop changes and a couple of reversals. We would also need a very patient and understanding broker, one who would put up with the frequent stop changes. However, there is some basic merit to the system, and we thought it was worth passing along as food for thought. It might be the basis for a more practical system with wider parameters.

Stochastic Divergences

This day-trading method combines the ADX, half-hour stochastics, and three-minute stochastics. This system works best in S&P futures and currencies.

1. Use the 18-day ADX/DMI to measure the strength of the daily trend. If the ADX is rising, trades should be done only in the direction of the trend. If the ADX is declining, trades can be done in either direction.

2. Check the direction of the short-term trend using half-hour bars on the slow stochastics as an indicator of the direction of the trend. It is O.K. to trade either with or against the stochastics trend as long as the 18-day ADX/DMI is declining.

3. Use three-minute bars on the futures contract. Set up another chart using three-minute bars with a 21-period slow stochastic.

4. Trades are entered after a divergence between the three-minute futures chart and the three-minute stochastic chart. The first point of the divergence must occur with the stochastic either above 80 or below 20.

Look for occasional three-point divergences. These are less frequent than the two-point divergences, but they are particularly good signals. In fact, you can take the three-point divergence trades regardless of the daily ADX or stochastics trend. (See Exhibit 4–9.)

5. Set your stop loss. The initial stop loss point for S&Ps should be 20 points above the most recent high for short positions or 20 points under the recent low for long positions. The stop can be changed after each new peak or valley in the stochastics, with the stop 20 points from the new peak or valley on the S&P chart.

6. Take profits or exit on the close. If the three-minute stochastic gives a signal contrary to your position from a point below 20 or above 80, this is where you should take your profit. Make sure you are out by the close, if not stopped out.

EXHIBIT 4–9

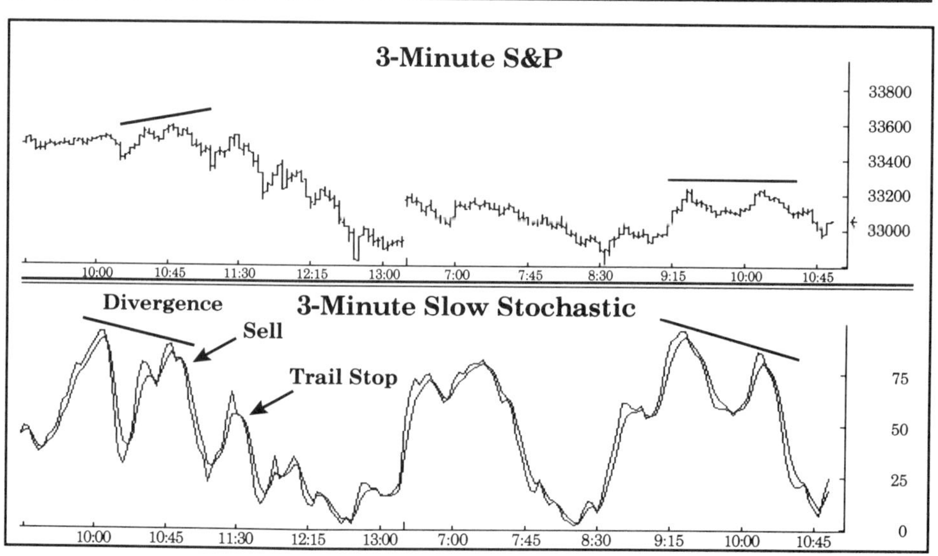

Swing Reversals plus Stochastics

This day-trading idea combines several technical elements: pattern recognition (something we haven't talked much about), stochastics, and divergence. We assume that most of our readers have some understanding of stochastics and stochastic divergence, since we've described them in detail in the previous chapter. However, the pattern recognition portion is a new element and requires a brief explanation.

The goal of pattern recognition is to try to predict market turning points by observing a sequence of price movements that occur regularly and that have some predictive value. The one described here is called a "key reversal" or "swing reversal" (see Exhibit 4–10). This is a three-bar pattern with a swing low that makes a new short-term low followed by a third bar, which does not make a low and whose close is above the swing close. The reverse of this pattern would be used for identifying market tops.

With this pattern in mind, the trading system is as follows:

1. Use 30-minute bars on the S&P futures and a nine-period slow stochastic.

2. Watch for the short-term key reversal or swing reversal patterns we described above.

EXHIBIT 4–10

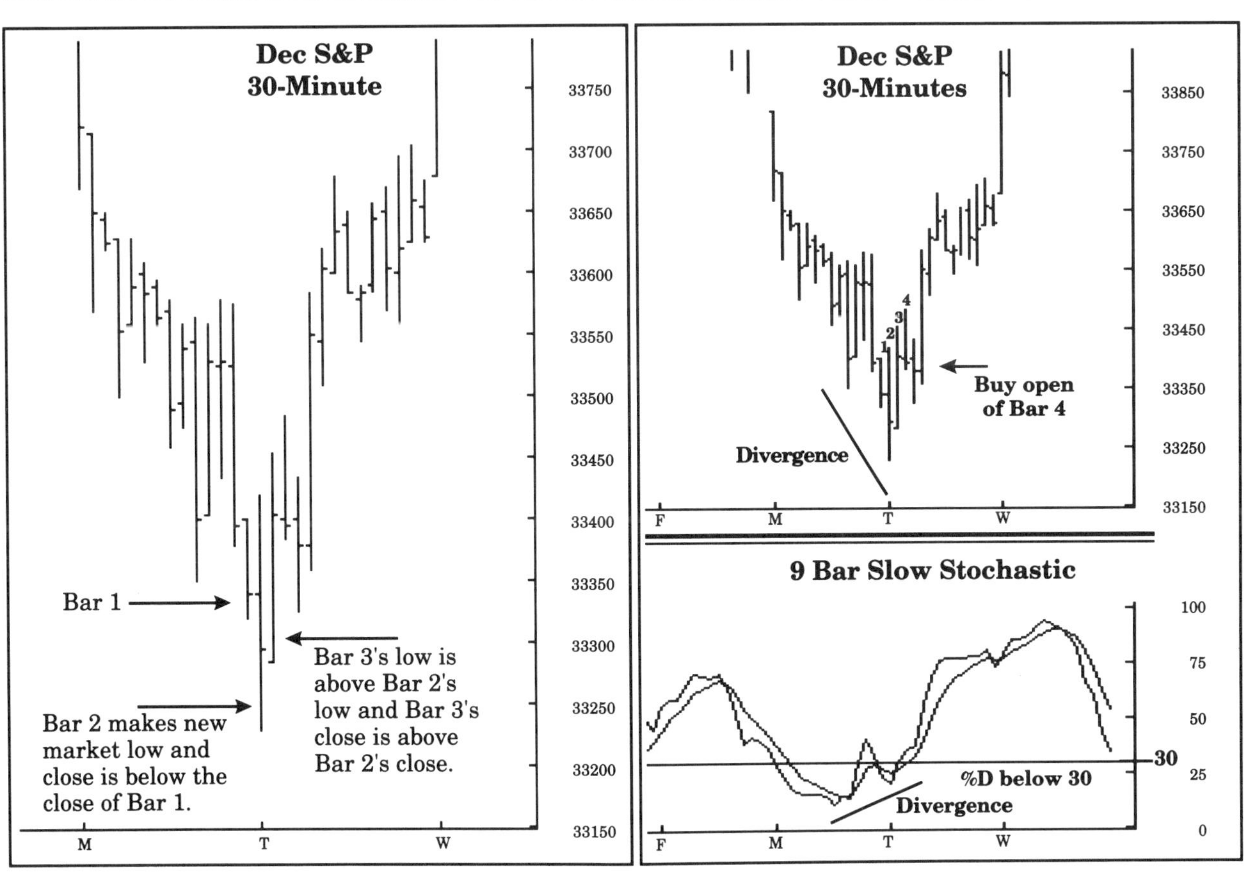

3. Enter the trade when you've observed a key reversal pattern that is accompanied by a stochastic reading (%D) below 30 for a buy pattern, or above 70 if it's a sell pattern.

4. Set a protective stop a tick or two outside the swing high or low. If this stop is too far away to be comfortable, use a tighter dollar stop.

5. Exit on any key reversal patterns in the opposite direction, or at the close. (Again, See Exhibit 4–10.)

Your chances for success will be greater if you wait for a divergence between the stochastic and the underlying futures prices. However, the divergence is not strictly necessary.

Appendix

Technical Studies Formulas

We have discovered that technical study calculations differ from one software vendor to another and from one author or trader to another. Some of the differences may be the result of programmer error or misunderstanding, and some may be honest attempts to improve a formula. It can be disconcerting to have two computer screens side by side displaying an RSI, for example, from two vendors, with different values. Our opinion is that there is no "right" formula. As long as your usage of a study is consistent, your results should be similar to those that come from a slightly different source. If a slight change in an indicator produces wildly different trading results, you should wonder if you have overly curve-fitted the study to the data, rather than blame an errant calculation.

The following formulas represent common usage. They are not intended to be definitive, and should not be treated as such.

2. Compute a moving average of the n most recent average prices:

$$X = 1/n\sum_{i=1}^{n} X_i$$

3. Compute the mean deviation of the n most recent typical prices:

$$MD = 1/n\sum_{i=1}^{n} |X_i - \overline{X}|$$

Commodity Channel Index (CCI)

There are four steps to calculate CCI:

1. Compute today's average price, using high, low and close:

$$X1 = 1/3\,(\text{High} + \text{Low} + \text{Close})$$

4. Compute the Commodity Channel Index:

$$CCI = (X1 - \overline{X}) / (0.015*MD)$$

where
n = number of periods in data base
X_1 = current typical price
X_2 = prior typical price
X_n = oldest typical price in the data base

$\sum_{i=1}^{n}$ stands for the sum of items following the symbol, starting

with 1 and ending with n, e.g. $\sum_{i=1}^{n} X_i = X_1 + X_2 + X_3 \ldots + X_n$

symbol, starting with 1 and ending with n, e.g.
$| \quad |$ signifies "absolute value"; difference should be added as if all were positive numbers.

Directional Movement Indicator (DMI) and Average Directional Movement Index (ADX)

See the appropriate section in the Technical Studies chapter.

Momentum

$$M_t = P_i - P_{i-n}$$

where
M_t = current momentum value
P_i = current price
P_{i-n} = price n periods ago

Moving Averages

Simple

$$MA_t = P_t + P_{t-1} + P_{t-2} + \ldots + P_{t-n} / n$$

where
MA_t = current moving average value
P_t, P_{t-1}, etc. = prices t-n periods ago
n = number of periods in the calculation

Weighted. The most common method of weighting a moving average simply multiplies each day's price by the number of days ago the price occurred. In a 10-day weighted moving average, the price today is given 10 times more weight than the price 10 days ago.

$$WMA_t = W_1P_t + W_2P_{t-1} + W_3P_{t-2} + \ldots W_nP_{t-n} / n$$

where
WMA_t = current moving average value
W = the number of periods ago the price occurred
P_t, P_{t-1}, etc. = prices *t-n* periods ago
n = number of periods in the calculation

Exponential Moving Averages

$$EMA_t = EMA_{t-1} + (SF * (P_t - EMA_{t-1}))$$

where
EMA_t = present EMA value
EMA_{t-1} = prior EMA value
SF = smoothing factor. The most common smoothing factor is SF = $2/n + 1$, where n is the number of periods in the calculation.

Moving Average Convergence Divergence (MACD)

MACD consists of a first line that is the difference between two exponential moving averages, and a second "signal" line which is an exponential moving average of the first line.

The first line is computed as follows:

$$MACD1_t = (EMA1 - EMA2)$$

where
$MACD1_t$ = current MACD
EMA1 = an exponential moving average
EMA2 = an exponential moving average

Normally MACD uses 12 days for EMA1 and 26 days for EMA2. This gives the MACD that Appel recommends for the sell side of the stock market, but which most practioners use for both long and short signals. Appel's buy configuration uses 8-day and 17-day EMAs, respectively.

The signal line is computed as follows:

$$SIG_t = SIG_{t-1} + (SC * (MACD1_t - SIG_{t-1}))$$

where

SIGt = current signal line value

SIGt-1 = previous signal line value

MACD1t = current MACD value

SC = smoothing constant. This is derived from the number of days in the exponential calculation (see Moving Average section of this Appendix).

Parabolic

The first ParabolicSAR (Stop and Reverse) point in a data series is the extreme price of the prior Parabolic trade; thus $SAR_1 = EP_{prior}$. Subsequent SARs are calculated as follows:

$$SAR_t = SAR_{t-1} + (AF * (EP_{prior} - SAR_{t-1}))$$

where

SAR_t = current SAR

SAR_{t-1} = prior SAR

EP = extreme price

AF = acceleration factor. The AF normally starts at 0.02 and steps up in increments of 0.02 to a maximum of 0.20.

Percent R

$$\%R_t = ((High_n - Close_t) / (High_n - Low_n)) * 100$$

where

$\%R_t$ = current %R

$High_n$ = the highest price for the past *n* trading periods

Low_n = the lowest price for the past *n* trading periods

$Close_t$ = current close

n = number of periods in the calculation

Rate of Change

$$ROC_t = (P_{i/Pi-n}) * 100$$

where

ROC_t = current rate of change value

P_i = current price

P_{i-n} = price *n* periods ago

Relative Strength Index (RSI)

The RSI calculation is a two-step process. First, calculate the Close-to-Close price differences as follows:

$$U_t = (UP_1 + UP_2 + . . . + UP_n) / n$$
$$D_t = (DN_1 + DN_2 + . . . + DN_n) / n$$

where

U_t = the Up average for the n period

D_t = the Down average for the n period

UP_1 = the first upward Close-to-Close price difference in the data series, UP_2 the second, etc.

DN_1 = the first downward Close-to-Close price difference in the data series, DN2 the second, etc.

n = the number of periods in the calculation

Then:

$$RSI_t = (U_t / (U_t + D_t)) * 100$$

Slow Stochastics

Slow stochastics are derived from fast stochastics, which in turn are derived from the basic stochastic calculation for raw %K, which is:

$$\%K\ raw_t = ((Close_t - Low_n) / (High_n - Low_n)) * 100$$

where

$\%K\ raw_t$ = current raw %K

$Close_t$ = current close

$High_n$ = the high of the past n periods

Low_n = the low of the past n periods

n = number of periods

Then

$$\%K_t = ((\%K_t - 1 * 2) + \%K\ raw_t) / 3$$

where

$\%K_t$ = current fast %K

$\%K_{t-1}$ = prior fast %K

$\%K\ raw_t$ = current raw %K

2 = a smoothing constant

%D is a three-period moving average of %K. thus:

$$\%D_t = ((\%D_{t-1} * 2) + \%K_t) / 3$$

Slow stochastics are derived as follows:

%K slow = %D fast

%D is again a three-period moving average of %K.

$$\%D\ slow_t = ((\%D\ slow_{t-1} * 2) + \%K\ slow_{t-1}) / 3$$

where
$\%D\ slow_t$ = current slow %D
$\%D\ slow_{t-1}$ = slow %D for the prior period
$\%K\ slow_{t-1}$ = slow %K for the prior period

Index

U

V

W–Y

Also Available from Business One Irwin:

THE HANDBOOK OF ECONOMIC CYCLES
Jake Bernstein's Comprehensive Guide to Repetitive Price Patterns in Stocks, Futures, and Financials
Jake Bernstein
This veritable "catalog of cycles" gives you 150 charts and graphs you can use to forecast, well in advance, the most reliable opportunities in virtually all markets. Bernstein, one of the world's foremost authorities on cyclical/seasonal analysis in the futures market, reveals some of the most consistently reliable and repetitive market patterns uncovered by more than 15 years of research. (304 pages, $8^{1}/_{2}$ x 11)
ISBN: 1-55623-294-2

THE BUSINESS ONE IRWIN GUIDE TO TRADING SYSTEMS
Bruce Babcock
Presents historical tests of various trading system approaches in 10 markets over a five-year period so you can choose the right system for your situation. You'll become a better system developer and a far better system buyer. (316 pages, $8^{1}/_{2}$ x 11)
ISBN: 1-55623-126-1

THE MONEY MARKET
3rd Edition
Marcia Stigum
More than 100,000 copies sold in previous editions! The most comprehensive, authoritative, and respected source on the money market. Completely revised with new chapters on medium term notes, futures, options, and loan participations, plus in-depth coverage of banking, domestic and Euro, and the commercial paper market. (1,250 pages)
ISBN: 1-55623-122-9